Plato argues that a leader at times *must* lie to his people.

Robert S. Bennet illumines the gray area of political contributions and political favoritism in his opening statement in the public hearing of the "Keating Five."

Mario Cuomo discusses how public confidence in government integrity can be restored.

Elder Witt examines whether current corruption is more or less severe than in the past.

Janet Hook writes of the fall and defiant farewell of Speaker of the House Jim Wright.

David H. Rosenbloom looks to the U.S. Constitution as a source for ethical judgments.

These are among the philosophers, politicians, and social thinkers who provide insight into ethical and moral issues facing government and people.

ESSENTIALS OF GOVERNMENT ETHICS

Peter Madsen, Ph.D., is Executive Director of the Center for the Advancement of Applied Ethics, Carnegie Mellon University. His articles on ethics have appeared in many leading journals.

Jay M. Shafritz, Ph.D. is a professor of Public and International Affairs, at the University of Pittsburgh, and is the author of over two dozen reference and textbooks, including six anthologies.

Drs. Madsen and Shafritz are co-editors of *Essentials of Business Ethics,* available in a Meridian edition.

Also edited by Peter Madsen, Ph.D.,
and Jay M. Shafritz, Ph.D.:

ESSENTIALS OF BUSINESS ETHICS

ESSENTIALS OF
GOVERNMENT ETHICS

EDITED AND
WITH INTRODUCTIONS BY

Peter Madsen, Ph.D.
and
Jay M. Shafritz, Ph.D.

A MERIDIAN BOOK

MERIDIAN
Published by the Penguin Group
Penguin Books USA Inc., 375 Hudson Street,
New York, New York 10014, U.S.A.
Penguin Books Ltd, 27 Wrights Lane,
London W8 5TZ, England
Penguin Books Australia Ltd, Ringwood,
Victoria, Australia
Penguin Books Canada Ltd, 10 Alcorn Avenue,
Toronto, Ontario, Canada M4V 3B2
Penguin Books (N.Z.) Ltd, 182–190 Wairau Road,
Auckland 10, New Zealand

Penguin Books Ltd, Registered Offices:
Harmondsworth, Middlesex, England

First published by Meridian, an imprint of New American Library,
a division of Penguin Books USA Inc.

First Printing, March, 1992
10 9 8 7 6 5 4 3 2 1

REGISTERED TRADEMARK—MARCA REGISTRADA

Printed in the United States of America
Set in Times Roman

LIBRARY OF CONGRESS CATALOGING-IN-PUBLICATION DATA
Essentials of government ethics / edited and with introduction by
   Peter Madsen and Jay M. Shafritz.
        p.   cm.
     ISBN 0-452-01091-8
     1. Political ethics.   I. Madsen, Peter, 1946–   II. Shafritz,
Jay M.
   JA79.E77   1992
172—dc20   91-29183
                                                        CIP

CONTENTS

FOREWORD

One doesn't have to get very far beyond the front page of a daily newspaper to realize how important it is to have a clear understanding of public ethics. There are many groups for whom those issues are particularly pertinent—public officials, of course, but also citizen volunteers, the press, everyone who votes or pays taxes—in short, all citizens of a democracy.

The issues were perhaps most dramatically addressed during the Senate hearings on Watergate, where Senator Sam Ervin's relentless pursuit of the wrongdoing in the White House provided a TV spectacle to which millions of Americans became addicted. They sat through endless hours of questioning, much of which was painfully repetitive. Their direct payoff was in the drama of whether a particular witness would find a narrow escape or would reveal an even more shocking act. They saw the profound embarrassment of officials at the highest levels of government for whom thoughtful consideration of ethical dilemmas was driven out by the immediacy of the power they wielded.

The issue of public ethics is perhaps one of the most complex of current times. The press provides very intense scrutiny over all actions—increasingly, the private ones as well as the public ones—of public officials; the glories showered on Woodward and Bernstein represent an extremely tantalizing prize. Thus, an ethical violation is very likely to be extremely costly, and this risk should serve both to make public officials careful in their ethical choices, and also highly risk averse.

This decision environment of elected or other public officials is one that too often poses the complex dilemma of a choice between an action that raises some ethical question and one that may be associated with diminished performance.

Politicians have to solicit campaign contributions, and those who give—especially the large givers—are very likely to have special interests that they will want served. Certainly everyone knows that a quid pro quo arrangement to vote a particular way in exchange for the contribution is bribery, and is widely viewed as totally unacceptable. But people are more sophisticated today. The quid pro quo discussion can be replaced by a wink of an eye or an extra squeeze in the thank-you handshake. In the continuing relationship of mutual dependency and support, neither side is interested in breaking such implicit agreements.

What if the politician is also a practicing lawyer—as many of them are—and can provide related or even unrelated legal services for someone with a special case to plead. What is a fair fee to be charged? When is the ethical line crossed?

America is a nation whose laws have accumulated for over two hundred years. The response of the political system to each identified case of wrongdoing is the passage of a new law attempting to preclude the possibility of that event. The system of such controls reminds one of the cartoonist's image of a teenager's tree house—boards and nails protruding in all directions, with new ones tacked on to cover the holes in the old. Each new law provides one more constraint on honorable public officials trying to get the job done. The build-up of these constraints makes it all the more difficult to be effective in the job, and so many find they have to cut some corners. To what extent has the CIA, with its permission to operate with limited oversight and great secrecy, become the vehicle by which Presidents get around these constraints? As we find ways to constrain the CIA with greater oversight, what is the next means by which a President will pursue what he or she believes to be an important mission of the Presidency.

The ethical problems in contemporary government are compounded by the frequent flow of individuals between the private and the public sectors. The ethical rules differ quite a bit between the two. In nations where the functions of government are all carried out by career civil servants, the two sets of ethical rules can be well established and understood. Where people move back and forth, as they do in the United States, some may not fully appreciate the differences.

The private sector is largely immune to press surveillance; everything in the public sector is subject to aggressive journalism.

Whistle-blowers get fired in the private sector, they become heroes in the public sector. Mutual back-scratching is a very much standard business practice, but it must be much more limited in the public. The giving of gifts to customers at the end of the year is a common if not standard practice; government officials are not supposed to accept gifts, even small ones.

A car and driver assigned to a senior corporate executive are generally viewed as being available for taking them on trips for personal business. The Chief of Staff of the Bush White House made front-page headlines when he used his assigned driver to take him to a stamp auction in New York. Another government official was fired because he had his secretary proofread the galleys of a book he had written previously and was having published. There are much more strict limits on public officials' rights to use resources assigned to them.

The public-private flow is a particular problem for the individuals who leave a senior position in government and then use their contacts and influence to help them represent their private clients before their former colleagues. This problem was dramatized by the number of former Reagan Adminstration people who established lucrative consulting practices that way. In many cases, they represented foreign governments in ways inimical to U.S. national interests. In our kind of citizen government, where most appointed officials stay only a few years, the problems can become severe. We can impose controls, but will that serve as too high a barrier to the recruitment of effective public officials?

Conflict of interest is a standard ethical concern. In the public sector it attains a much greater saliency than elsewhere. Indeed, the appearance of a conflict of interest can be fully as serious as an actual conflict. If a government official who happens to hold 100 shares of IBM stock given to him as a child buys a personal computer for the office, is he precluded from buying an IBM computer? Must he recuse himself from the decision if he buys a large number of them? Clearly, the purchase will have negligible effect on IBM's earnings, but some public officials have been challenged for less. How many shares would be enough to represent a true conflict?

Such ethical dilemmas are a continual and far from trivial concern in the daily decisions of all public officials. They constitute a perpetual confrontation of a mixture of loyalties to the elected officials they serve and who may have appointed them, to the public, to the applicable laws, and to themselves, with respect to their narrow self-interest and their professional and personal integrity.

The book by Drs. Madsen and Shafritz presents some absorbing materials to enable the reader to think harder about these issues, whether as a student preparing for public service, as a public official, or as a citizen. They can get behind some of the more visible scandals that have rocked public officials over the past two decades, from Watergate to Iran-Contra.

In each such scandal, there is, in retrospect, a clear lesson of what should not have been done. Particularly obnoxious were the ones that could be explained only by personal greed. But many of the scandals are clear *only* in retrospect: they highlight the daily dilemma of an elected official who wants to be re-elected and knows just how much of a campaign fund he needs, or a well-meaning public official who has some broader governmental objectives that can be frustrated by long-neglected laws or rules that might come to life in the hands of his enemies. They must develop the judgment to know how to recognize the ethical line that may not be crossed.

To help in developing those perspectives, the book also contains thoughtful essays that address the ethical issues in more fundamental terms. There are principles involved, whether those be associated with issues of inappropriate personal gain, legitimate occasions for using lies and deception, and the role of professional ethics in providing guidelines on practices that are unacceptable.

One would hope that reading the horror stories of the scandals reported here would be sufficient to deter even the most callous exploiter of the public trust. Nevertheless, loopholes always seem to become available when someone tries hard enough to find them. We all need greater understanding of the issues involved in getting both ethical and effective government. This book should contribute to that.

—Alfred Blumstein, Dean
School of Urban and Public Affairs
Carnegie Mellon University

INTRODUCTION

To raise the question of government ethics is like lifting the lid on a Pandora's box of troubles. Usually the phrase, in its negative connotation, refers to illegal and corrupt activities on the part of public officials. Watergate, the Iran-Contra affair, and the "Keating Five" come readily to mind as some of the most glaring instances of the problem of ethics in government. The Housing and Urban Development scandal, bribery at the Food and Drug Administration, and the highly publicized corrupt practices that have characterized the Pentagon procurement process demonstrate that the problem permeates bureaucratic operations as well. With a seemingly constant supply of similar scandals at the state and local levels, many citizens have concluded that America is in the throes of a crisis in government ethics. There appears to be a steady rise in corruption in Statehouses, county agencies, and city halls throughout the nation. Graft, illegal patronage, and kickbacks commonly grab the local headlines. In effect, then, by way of an attempt to describe what "right" behavior is, government ethics can be understood as a term that runs contrary to the propensity of officials at any level of government to misuse their office and engage in criminal, self-serving activities; it becomes the antithesis of public wrongdoing and corruption.

But the significance of the moral principles involved needs to be construed as meaning much more than just a reaction against public wrongdoing, illegalities, or the misuse of office. To say that there is an ethics crisis in government also means that there is a host of hard choices and public policy quandaries having ethical dimensions that serve to make the task of governing that much more difficult. Many social issues and dilemmas are fundamentally questions of ethics—for example, abortion, euthanasia, capital punishment, gun control, war, the poor, and the homeless. We look to those who serve the public's interest for guidance and resolution of these essentially ethical matters. Public officials, be they elected, appointed, or career service employees, must successfully navigate numerous moral mazes in carrying out their responsibilities and must address more human troubles than might ever fit into Pandora's mythological box. "Government ethics," then, is a term that should be understood as denoting both the problem of official mischief *and* the complexities of the many moral intricacies in government.

This collection of pertinent readings deals with both of these aspects of the much-heralded ethics crisis in government, as well as outlining ways on how best to manage it. We have compiled diverse materials from books, scholarly journals, popular magazines, and government reports on the issue. Appropriate classics from the disciplines of philosophy and ethics can be found as well. The authors represented in this volume offer a variety of perspectives: academic, political, legal, and journalistic. As a composite, these materials form what, we believe, are the essentials of government ethics in the sense that they provide a clear picture of the complex crisis of ethics in government, as well as ways to address it.

Mischief-making in Government

One way to grasp the depth of this crisis as it manifests itself in the mischief-making of public officials is to focus upon the well-known depiction of American democracy as a government of law, as opposed to one of men. This concept means that the law provides a framework within which justice can prevail so that tyranny by one or by many is an impossibility. The capricious nature of humans is held in check by the steady rule of law. Both those who govern and those governed, the former being merely the representatives of the latter in the process of government, are equals before the law and must accede to it. Indeed, the American Revolution was fought in large part to implement this rule of law and to upset the traditional "divine right of kings" to rule. Rights are inalienable and shared by all as democracy replaces autocracy; and governance by law displaces governance by the personal whims of a tyrant—be he king or bureaucrat.

Recurrent scandals and instances of official mischief in government, however, pose a genuine threat to the democratic notions of the rule of law, equality, and individual rights. When a public official misuses his or her office for self-gain, then the rule of law no longer seems to apply, and there is, in effect, a return to a form of tyranny. By engaging in self-aggrandizement, corrupt representatives of the people put themselves above the law. Thus, the democratic concept of the rule of law is subverted by their single-minded objective to promote self-interest rather than the public's interest.

Moreover, a public official's act of wrongdoing is destructive of the claim that in a democracy all individuals are equal. Along with the pig in George Orwell's *Animal Farm*, who cannot accept the idea of equal treatment, these self-interested officials are willing to say, "But, some of us are more equal than others." Mischief-making in government is preeminently an act whereby the notion of equal access to public goods is overturned so that public office becomes a kind of privileged access. When left undetected, fraud, bribery, kickbacks, and other abuses in government wrest power from the hands of the people and lift a few to positions of control, which distorts a social process that assumes the equality of all participants.

On closer analysis it also becomes evident that individual rights are subsequently greatly affected by acts of mischief-making in government. First of all, it is obvious that in cases in which money is the issue, corruption undermines economic rights. Consider bribery, which often occurs within the competitive process of governmental purchasing. When contracts are awarded illegally by means of a bribe, the losing competitors can be said to have had their rights to a fair and impartial bidding process abridged. Moreover, the public's right to have purchases made in its name for products or services in the most efficient and least costly fashion is also subverted by bribery. This form of corruption makes a mockery of economic considerations. The few that feed at the public trough deny the rights of others to enter a fair system of economic competition. Democratic rights also suffer when an executive, legislator, or judge accepts a bribe. Vote buying, influence peddling, and favoritism are all examples of the denial of various individual rights.

There is ample evidence in American history to force the

conclusion that the current crisis of government ethics is not merely a contemporary one. During the American Revolution, the Continental Army's clothier general, James Wilkerson, was found to be falsifying his accounts and pocketing the difference. The development of the transcontinental railroad, completed in 1869, was marked by collusion between a construction syndicate and certain members of Congress, who padded the bill to the taxpayers by some $50 million. And, of course, there was the infamous Boss Tweed of New York, who stole $200 million from the city in 1873, and the renowned Teapot Dome Scandal of the 1920's, in which Secretary of the Interior Albert B. Fall took payoffs to lease oil-field rights secretly in Wyoming. In short, American government has a history checkered by official mischief.

Such infamous events raise questions about causes and controls. What are the reasons for official misconduct? How can it be controlled and eliminated? There has been a good deal of speculation on both of these topics. For many, the single most important cause of corruption in government is individual greed. Certain personalities tend to have flawed characters that dispose them to engage in illegal activities. This line of reasoning lays blame, then, upon a kind of psychological disorder, in which the individual is the sole source of the mischief-making.

Others have argued that corruption in government is a much more complex phenomenon. In this view, it is suggested that a mix of variables, such as opportunity, risk, and organizational culture, have a role to play as well. If the opportunity presents itself, and the risk of getting caught is low, and if the organization does not foster an ethical climate, then chances are fairly good that corruption will take place. This organizational explanation of governmental mischief, then, claims that such conduct is less the function of individual disposition and more the result of institutional dysfunction.

And, finally, there are those who carve out a middle ground between these two explanations of causes. They argue that corruption is due to both human failure and institutional influences. Neither one of these two factors can fully account for wrongdoing according to this third hypothesis. Rather, an integrated view needs to be adopted that places official mischief at the intersection where individuals and institutions meet. Thus, this third view holds that mischief-making in government (and elsewhere, for that matter) is a highly complex, systemic phenomenon, requiring that both people and the places where people work be considered and addressed.

With respect to controls, one can find many suggestions that deal with both individual and institutional causes of ethical lapses. From those who see human disposition toward greed as the cause of the unwanted behavior, the suggestion is that more "law and order" legislation be enacted. Increase the penalties for such mischief as fraud, waste, and abuse of power, then people will be deterred from such activities and will keep their deviant dispositions in check. Others will argue that you can't legislate morality, and they will suggest that various new institutional mechanisms be put into place that will regulate such factors as opportunity and risk, thereby injecting ethics into the work environment. Organizations need to be developed along new, more innovative lines, in which ethics is of high concern, if the rate of illicit conduct is to be halted.

Some of the institutional changes that are recommended to address mischief in government include the conducting of internal "ethics audits" that would identify sensitive situations which might tempt an individual to act in a questionable fashion. Once the situation is identified, it can be changed so as to remove the temptation. Another approach is to reinforce an awareness that ethics is an expectation within the governmental unit. This attitude can be fostered by the introduction of such items as a code of conduct or a written statement of the values and beliefs of the unit, or by including ethics in any process of performance appraisal. A steady stream of internal communications that emphasize the high expectation of ethical conduct on the job can reinforce the notion that ethics matter. And, of course, there is no substitute for ethical leadership from the top as a way to encourage a morally principled climate by example.

Perhaps the most useful organizational development strategy that can be used to instill a new ethical awareness is an ethics training program. Such training is a useful tool that can accomplish two interrelated tasks. First, such programs can alert public officials to the kinds of behaviors that should be avoided. It can familiarize them with the ways in which they are required to comply with laws, regulations, and rules. Second, training in ethics can help participants develop skills in moral reasoning on the job. The goal in this case is empowerment rather than compliance; during ethics training one should ideally experience personal growth by acquiring strategies and techniques of moral analysis that will prove helpful in fulfilling one's governmental responsibilities. Increasingly government agencies are providing ethics training for their employees as a means of institutionalizing ethics in government.

These various organizational strategies for instilling ethical behavior are aimed primarily at government bureaus and their career employees who carry out the day-to-day operations of government. But what about those elected and politically appointed officials who are not, strictly speaking, bureaucrats? How can ethics be made to matter to these individuals? One control that has been suggested is to reduce the time an electee has in office. The idea behind term reductions or limitations is that elected officials, and those whom they appoint to policy-making positions, would not be able to accumulate as much power as they do when they are returned to office election after election. If power tends to corrupt, then reducing power through time in office should reduce the attendant corruption.

Others argue that the best form of control over the conduct of elected officials is to have a vigilant electorate. "You get what you vote for" can be taken as the leading thesis of this argument. If the voters do not scrutinize a candidate for office well, then they have only themselves to blame. It is suggested that voters include a consideration of a candidate's moral character in their deliberations, in addition to whatever a candidate's political position might be. Yet for some, this suggestion has escalated to an extreme. We now see moral character becoming a controversial issue in political campaigns, with a good deal of mudslinging about the ethical qualifications and sexual habits of one's opponent. In some districts, this debate over moral character becomes *the* issue, and voters never learn about how the candidates might represent them once in office. Moreover, the media have taken hold of the character issue and, according to a number of its critics, have gone overboard in revealing the private lives of politicians, perhaps abridging their rights to privacy.

Although there are many suggestions on the table, there will be those who will hold that any grand scheme to control and eliminate mischief-making in government is doomed to failure. There is no magic wand available to change the nature of American governance, which is too often characterized by corruption. For those who subscribe to this more cynical view, a piecemeal approach to the problem makes the most sense. It is often suggested that ethics reform focus upon the single most problematic aspects of the ethics crisis, rather than attempt any large-scale remodeling.

While there are a variety of "single most problematic aspects" of government ethics, the one that has generated the greatest amount of debate in recent years is political campaigning and, more specifically, campaign funding. The very large amounts of money necessary today to run a campaign for a major political office create a good deal of opportunity for mischief-making. For example, the role of political action committees, or PACs, has been raised time and again as a questionable form of influence peddling and vote buying. The spending of these political funds has also come under scrutiny, especially the practice of certain Congressional officeholders in keeping unspent campaign funds for personal use.

As this brief overview demonstrates, misconduct in government has wide parameters. The suggested steps for reforming the questionable ethics of those in government have also been wide-ranging. Because the debate over suspect government practices will continue as long as the corruption itself does, the controversy has a long lease on life. Much of the materials found in this volume are designed to further the consideration of the problems of government corruption and the resulting distortion of ethics in government. As a totality, they comprise many of the essential voices that should be heard in the debate over mischief-making in government.

Moral Mazes in Government

Ethical issues, problems, and dilemmas—moral mazes—have become a thematic focus of the rapidly growing field of applied ethics. Applied ethics has gained momentum in the academic discipline of philosophy for the past three decades as all sectors of contemporary life are besieged by concrete, often perplexing, moral questions. Government ethics can be viewed as a branch of the movement of applied ethics alongside such areas as medical ethics, business ethics, professional ethics, and legal ethics. As ethical considerations began to cloud practice in these areas, applied ethics was offered as a way to think through a moral maze and manage it.

What makes applied ethics such an important area is its concern with practical problems. In fact, one definition of applied ethics is that unlike its theoretical counterpart, which is an academic discipline concerned with "pure" questions, such as the definition of the good, the existence of evil, and the design of normative ethical theories and principles, applied ethics is the activity of analyzing an ethical issue, problem, or dilemma that has practical consequences in society. Abortion and euthanasia (medical ethics), "whistleblowing" and corporate social responsibility (business ethics), confidentiality and conflicts of interest (professional ethics), and the attorney-client privilege (legal ethics) are among some of the more pressing practical examples of moral mazes that are of interest to applied ethicists.

When the topic of government ethics is raised, the practical problems of public administration that are most important seem to fall into one of two kinds of moral mazes. First, there are dilemmas of administrative responsibility, in which an official experiences a basic conflict in duties, obligations, and/or loyalties. And, second, there are dilemmas of administrative choice, in which officials are confronted with having to make and reach a decision that can best be called a quandary, because a simple right or wrong answer is elusive. Each of these basic moral mazes in public administration needs to be elaborated to get a clear picture of the essentials of government ethics.

A word on definition about the term "public administration" as used here is needed, however. For some, "public administration" is a term reserved for a specific kind of governing by a specific kind of individual. In this more narrow definition, public administrators are career public managers who engage in a host of activities within the bureaucratic framework of government. In this context public administration usually means managing one of the various public services delivered by governmental units and mandated by law, such as transportation, welfare, or education.

For our purposes, however, public administration will mean

much more than this narrow designation; we use it in its most expansive sense to denote any governmental function, whether be it legislative, executive, or judicial, and at any level of government. All who engage in doing the public's business are public administrators in this wider understanding, whether they make and pass laws, execute those laws, or interpret them in court. The advantage of using this wider definition is its comprehensiveness: no public official or function will be inadvertently excluded. If we keep in mind that all government functionaries are public administrators and that all government functions form part of public administration, then it will be clear that the "ethics of public administration" is a synonymous expression for "government ethics."

Moral Mazes: Conflicts of Responsibilities

The best way to gain an overview of the moral maze wherein conflicts of responsibilities plague public administrators is to employ the analytic strategy found in almost all branches of applied ethics—that of stakeholder analysis. A stakeholder is any individual or group that might be affected by the outcome of a process. Since every decision has its stakeholders, the responsible decision maker seeks to insure that there is the maximum possible stakeholder satisfaction. And this is where the problem lies. How does a decision maker provide the utmost stakeholder satisfaction?

In order to answer the question of stakeholder satisfaction within the context of public administration, one needs first to identify the various stakeholders who will impinge upon the administrative decision making. This identification takes on even more importance in the arena of public administration than in other contexts, such as business management or medicine, because in the administration of the public's business the decision maker is also a representative being entrusted to safeguard several fundamental concepts, not the least of which are those of justice, equality, and the enjoyment of individual rights. In other words, public administration is unique, because the governmental decision-making process is, by definition, "of the people, by the people, and for the people." That's what *public* administration automatically implies. Thus, public officials occupy a special position, because all people have at least an indirect stake in their decision making. It is correct to say, then, that government officials have the general responsibility (or burden) to ensure the satisfaction of a majority of the people with each administrative decision that they make.

Because the public is the first group that needs to be identified as a stakeholder, the first obligation of public administrators is what we call "the general responsibility" of officials to the people. It is this general responsibility that lends to public administration its unique character among the professions. It is the essence of the profession of public administration; it is what stands behind the old adage that "the public service is a public trust." The public trusts that its public administrators, from a small-town bureaucrat right up to and including the President of the United States, will fulfill their general responsibility as best they can. And it is precisely how well they discharge this general responsibility that determines their perceived success or failure as public administrators.

But the "general responsibility" of public administrators is merely one responsibility among many. Consider the role of a public manager in the task of policy making. He who has the job of devising an acceptable policy on any public issue will be confronted by a host of groups, each of which has its own demands that need to be considered before a policy is finally devised. The administrative process in public policy making is often a matter of negotiating with various constituents with varying views, which represent conflicts of responsibilities, and possible interests, for the public manager charged with making the policy.

Which groups might be counted as stakeholders in the policy-making process? Some are obvious; others are not so apparent. The most well-known are probably public interest groups that vocally let their concerns be heard and attempt to influence the final policy. Interest groups are genuine stakeholders; their level of involvement is demonstrated by the fact that they have organized themselves to be major actors in the policy-making process. Interest groups lobby public administrators, spend money to influence public opinion, offer expert testimony at public hearings, collect signatures for referendums, and so on. In these organized attempts to be part of the policy-making process, public interest groups pose a formidable responsibility to public managers—they simply cannot be ignored in policy decisions, regardless of whether or not one agrees with the particular stand they advocate.

Client groups are another obvious stakeholder in the formation of policy to whom public managers are responsible. Usually public policy is made with reference to certain groups within an administrative area. For example, the Veterans Administration makes policy about veterans, welfare agencies about those who are poor, labor departments about employers and their employees, and so on. Since administrative areas have their own particularized client groups who will be affected by future policies, public managers must ensure that the interests of their clients are as protected as any others in the policy process.

Other more obvious stakeholders include the public manager's peers, supervisors, and subordinates. The administrative agency in which a public manager finds himself or herself will be affected by the outcome of the policy-making process, since it is the organization that must implement policy provisions. Of course, the degree to which an agency and its administrators will be affected will vary from policy to policy, but there is no doubt that whatever gets decided will play a role in the professional lives of these individuals. Indeed, a policy might reduce or increase the numbers of agency administrators, creating a work-place crisis in that agency. Thus, the colleagues of a public manager involved in policy decision making have a real claim as stakeholders in his or her decisions.

Among the less obvious stakeholders that nonetheless should be included in this analysis are the media, the court system, legislative bodies, public executives, and various professional associations that represent the interests of public managers. Each of these groups or entities can make a genuine, if indirect, claim on the attention of a public manager who is cast in the role of policy maker.

Stakeholder analysis illustrates the first kind of moral maze that constantly confronts public administrators. Because there are so many bona fide stakeholders, public administrators must pay heed to each of their claims. Thus, by necessity, the administrator is confronted with an inevitable conflict of responsibility. The pressures of competing claims from diverse stakeholders serves to make the job of public administrators that much more difficult. It can even be said that an essential part of the art of public

administration lies in knowing how to balance the various responsibilities and how to reach decisions that can satisfy an assembly
of stakeholders, each with their own legitimate claims. This conflict of responsibility, then, is the moral maze that often functions
as an obstacle to the effective and ethical discharge of the duties
of public administrators.

Another kind of conflict also becomes apparent when the public administrator finds himself adrift in a sea of competing duties
and obligations, each of which has a claim on his attention.
Rather than becoming a matter of to whom the public administrator owes responsibility, as it is in the conflict of stakeholder
ethics, it is necessary to recognize that there are differing kinds of
responsibilities existing on different levels that also can come into
conflict. Applied ethicists argue that the concept of responsibility
is a multifaceted one. Individual actors are presented with situations that contain conflicting duties and obligations as a matter of
course. In public administration, one can detail these competing
pressures according to a hierarchy of levels of ethics, each of
which has its own set of responsibilities.

First, there is personal morality. Under its precepts one's basic
sense of right and wrong is operative, and one's closely held
values—often called "core values" by ethicists, because they form
the core of one's being—come into play. Personal morality is a
function of our past and is dependent upon many factors, including our parental influences, religious beliefs, cultural and social
mores, and our own past personal experiences. Public administrators, like all individuals, have recourse to personal morality and
its dictates whenever they are confronted with ethical issues,
problems, and dilemmas.

Second in the hierarchy is professional ethics. Like others in
their own chosen professions, public administrators recognize a
set of professional norms and rules that obligate them to act in
certain "professional" ways. Professional ethics comprise guidelines on how one properly comports oneself within a profession,
so as not to discredit oneself or one's colleagues who also practice
the profession. More often than not, these guidelines are codified
by professional associations and serve as formal rules of conduct,
which may even be used to judge the behavior of the members of
the association. On rare occasions, members may be publicly
disgraced, fined, or even expelled by the professional group for

violations of the group's code of ethics. Examples of professional norms include requirements to serve the public's interest, avoid conflicts of interest whether real or apparent, and uphold the Constitution of the United States. The American Society for Public Administration and the International City Management Association are two examples of the many professional associations that exist in public administration. There are, however, professional groups for every major function within public administration.

A third level of ethics, with its own set of responsibilities, is organizational ethics. Every organization has an environment or culture that includes both formal and informal rules of ethical conduct. Public organizations typically have many such rules. Public laws, executive orders, and agency rules and regulations—all can be taken as formal organizational norms for ethical behavior. Organizational culture requires that those who constitute the organization act in ways that further its goals and objectives. In this sense, organizational ethics makes its own special kinds of demands upon organizational members and presents them with specific responsibilities that require set behaviors.

Fourth, and finally, there is social ethics. Administrative responsibilities require behavior that abides by such concepts as justice, equality, and the rights of individuals. Social ethics is formal to the extent that it can be found in the laws of a given society; informal, to the extent that it is part of an ethical conscience of society. The requirements of social ethics oblige members of a given society to act in ways that both protect individuals and further the progress of the group as a whole. In public administration, social ethics plays an important role in the defining of public policy and its implementation.

It should be clear by now that responsibility as a concept is not straightforward and simple. Rather, individuals are confronted with an array of responsibilities. Public administrators are no exception. Often, they will be caught in a situation in which different levels of ethics, with their varying obligations, will clash and conflict to produce a dilemma of responsibility. For an example of such a conflict in public administration consider the Iran-Contra Affair in general, and Oliver North in particular.

As we now know, the Iran-Contra Affair involved the violation of a Congressional ban on military aid to the revolutionary forces in Nicaragua known as the Contras. The scheme involved the United States' being covertly engaged in the sale of illegal arms to Iran; the proceeds from those sales shifted to the Contras, who in turn used the money for their continuing revolution against the ruling Sandinista government. As the major operative in the scheme, Marine Lieutenant Colonel Oliver North, assigned to the National Security Council in the White House, serves as an excellent case study in the conflict of responsibility. (See Chapter 2, specifically the selection concerning the Iran-Contra Affair, for a more detailed account of this incident.) North has admitted that he found it necessary to lie to Congress about the Iran-Contra arms deal in order to further what he called national security goals. Thus, by overseeing the illegal sale of arms to Iran and illegally channeling profits to the Contras, North reached a decision that one set of responsibilities was higher than another. He justified his lies to Congress as necessary for national security. North violated the formal rules of organizational ethics and social ethics in illegally supplying military aid to the Contras and in lying to Congress to cover it up. He argued, however, that he upheld his own personal morality and sense of duty to the country by acting as he did. Caught between his own interpretation of what was right and wrong on the personal level and that which his organization and society had deemed to be right and wrong, North chose the former over the latter. For many, he was a hero for doing so. Yet for many others, his actions were criminal and unconstitutional.

As the North case suggests, responsibilities have the propensity to conflict, thanks to the fact that there are various levels of ethics and morality, each with its own set of obligations and duties. Perhaps the most difficult aspect of being a public administrator is managing the clash of responsibilities between the competing claims of stakeholders and the varying levels of ethics. Chapter 4 deals most directly with the confusion that might arise from these incompatibilities. The two broad topics covered there— lying for the public good and the "dirty hands" dilemma— demonstrate just how confounding this moral maze can be.

Moral Mazes: Quandary Decisions

The second general kind of moral maze in public administration has to do with quandary, or hard-choice, decisions. Because there are so many difficult decisions to be made in public policy, public administrators need to be adept at moral reasoning and the analysis of ethical issues to deal better with such quandaries, or hard choices. The discipline of applied ethics has long been concerned with hard choices and quandary ethics. A typical example is "the lesser-of-evils quandary." In this instance an individual is faced with choices none of which can be described as desirable. This kind of moral problem presents an array of alternatives in which the least evil choice must be uncovered and enacted. The lesser-of-evils quandary is all too common in public-policy decision making. Consider policies dealing with the environment. Regulators at all levels of government have to make lesser-of-evil choices in order to conserve natural resources. Cleaning up the air, land, and sea is a very costly proposition. Many critics of the Bush Administration's Clean Air Act have argued that its provisions will increase the cost of products to consumers, bankrupt many businesses, and mean the loss of numerous jobs. Environmental experts, however, counter that taking costly steps now is the wiser choice, if the environment is to be preserved for future generations. In this context, higher costs, bankruptcies, and the loss of jobs are lesser evils than an environment damaged beyond repair.

Another kind of applied ethics quandary deals with the problem of choosing among alternatives each of which embodies a bona fide, but conflicting, ethical principle. This dilemma can be called "the quandary of ethical alternatives." As opposed to choosing among evils, the choice must be made among viable alternatives; a persuasive argument based upon ethical principles could be advanced in favor of any of the alternatives. Perhaps the best example of this quandary is the ever explosive issue of abortion. Once again, legislators across the country are choosing how they will vote on the abortion question, given a recent Supreme Court decision that allows the states the opportunity to institute restrictions upon abortions performed in their jurisdictions. In deciding how to vote, these elected officials will be caught in the moral maze of choosing between two seemingly justifiable positions—the right to life and the right to choose. When examined out of the context of abortion and the rancor of this unending debate, these two rights are beyond objection. Most people would hold that the right to life and the right to choose are fundamental ethical rights, but their juxtaposition in the abortion debate creates a quandary decision for public administrators.

The problems of ethical alternatives and their solutions will confront public administrators often, since the sheer number of such quandaries continues to rise. Euthanasia and the right to die, gun control, art and obscenity, justifiable war, capital punishment, free speech issues, affirmative action, entitlement programs, and so on—all of these and more offer concrete examples of an issue standing in need of a policy that only public administrators can provide.

A third dilemma that receives attention in the literature of applied ethics can be called the "values quandary." A values quandary occurs when an individual is confronted with choosing a course of action among several possible alternatives, each of which is based upon a particular value that most people would agree is a desirable one. In public administration, difficult value choices are common in public policy. For example, municipalities have the power to decide whether to allow private business concerns to start development projects within their boundaries. Often the consideration of development projects will result in zoning wars, in which citizens will protest the project because they perceive it as detrimental to their own interests and values.

In such situations, what municipal-policy decision makers must choose among are competing values such as progress, economic advancement, and public accommodation, on the one hand; and the values of individual self-determination, privacy, and private interests on the other. This particular kind of quandary is even more apparent when the development project is one that deals with the building of a halfway house for prisoners or the start-up of a toxic-waste plant. While both of these projects have desirable values—prisoner reform and a clean environment—many will voice other opinions and will express the NIMBY syndrome: "We should have these projects, but 'Not in My Backyard.' " Deciding whether to go ahead with publicly necessary projects that nonetheless require some public sacrifices is a typical values quandary in public administration.

A final quandary that can be outlined is one that involves some personal consequences to the decision maker. This example can be labeled the "quandary of conviction." It is an appropriate title for decisions that will have some effects on the one who chooses the solution. The prescription that "one should have the courage of one's convictions" suggests that even in the face of adverse personal consequences, one should do the "right" thing. In public administration, the quandary of conviction is no less typical than elsewhere.

The act of "whistleblowing" in government is the best example of this type of dilemma. Even with the passage of various federal and state protection laws, whistleblowers in government risk much in terms of personal consequences. Lower performance appraisals, loss of career opportunities, ostracism by coworkers, demotion, and even firing are all possible outcomes of the act of whistleblowing in government employment. When faced with the choice of halting a specific activity or not, public administrators must weigh the consequences to self and decide if they truly wish to become a "moral hero." Whistleblowing is risky business and requires that a public administrator have the courage of her convictions.

As has been outlined, a useful framework exists that can be used to examine the moral mazes of government. By focusing upon administrative responsibility and choice, it can be seen that public administrators are faced with a host of moral alternatives that require them to be adept at stakeholder analysis, to recognize ethical obligations at various levels, and to be prepared to engage in "quandary" ethics, characterized by hard choices at the policy level. In the chapters that follow, we will have ample opportunity to refer to and employ this framework.

Preview

It has been argued in this Introduction that there is a crisis of ethics in government and that it manifests itself in two ways: in mischief-making and in moral mazes. Chapter 1 begins this book with an extended discussion of the scope of this crisis. It contains survey data from public administration professionals, examines the very possibility of administrative ethics, and the role of ethics from a Constitutional perspective. The chapter concludes on a pessimistic note, with an essay that details how all the attention to ethics at the federal level may be becoming a real obstacle in the governing process.

The remaining chapters treat the twofold crisis in ethics in differing fashion. Chapter 2 recounts perhaps the most dramatic ethics scandals of the last two decades: Watergate, the Iran-Contra Affair, the resignation of the Speaker of the House Jim Wright, and the "Keating Five." It begins, however, with a recollection of the ethics of U.S. Senator Daniel Webster that should serve as a reminder that the loss of ethics is not just a contemporary problem in American government. Chapter 3 continues the theme of mischief-making and takes up the issues of ethics and politics. It covers the problems of campaign financing, along with the use of campaign funds and the place of PACs in the governing process, and the question of what role the private lives of politicians should play in their holding of public office.

The next two chapters shift the focus and examine the issue of moral mazes in government. Lying for the public good, the "dirty hands" dilemma, making hard choices in public administration, and the ethical difficulties of public-policy decision making are raised and discussed. The final two chapters deal with ethics at the state and local government levels and the steps that might be taken to address the ethics crisis at all levels.

By emphasizing the fact that government ethics is confronting a twofold crisis embodying the dimensions of corruption on the one hand, and the solving of complex ethical dilemmas on the other, it is hoped that this collection of essential readings will be useful both to those who practice the art of public administration as well as to those who study it in college in preparation for such practice.

CHAPTER 1

THE SCOPE
OF GOVERNMENT ETHICS

Introduction

As the general Introduction to this book has intimated, there is much more to the topic of "government ethics" than one might anticipate. In fact, there are many more potential issues that can be explored under this heading than even those two major categories—moral mischief and moral mazes—cited at the outset. This first chapter, then, will demonstrate that the realm of government ethics is as rich as it is complex. Thus, the crisis of government ethics will require much more than a quick fix.

This wide scope of government ethics is neatly portrayed by James S. Bowman in the lead essay of the chapter. "Government Ethics: A Survey," provides an instructive overview that reveals the opinions, observations, and attitudes of public administrators about the problems that the pursuit of ethics poses and ways to address them within their organizations. This survey measures items such as the extent to which morality in general society has an effect on ethics in government, the level of integrity in governmental agencies, and the role of standards in organizational conduct. The responses of practitioners in the field to these issues should prompt much reflection about the breadth and depth of the ethical crisis in government.

Another set of important issues is painted by Dennis F. Thompson in "The Possibility of Administrative Ethics." Thompson raises radical and fundamental questions in his provocative analysis, which attempts to answer whether there is such a thing as administrative ethics at all. There are two commonly accepted administrative theories that Thompson says undercut and displace the possibility of ethics in government. The "ethic of neutrality" holds that administrators make their decisions on behalf of others and must remain morally neutral if representative government is to work at all. But if administrators are indeed morally neutral when they make representative decisions, then it is not possible to hold them ethically accountable. Likewise, the "ethic of structure" claims that organizations—and not individuals— are responsible for the design, development, and implementation of public policies, and, hence, we cannot and should not cast moral judgments about government officials, who merely find themselves existing, conforming and unaccountable, somewhere in the organizational structure.

Now, if either of these two theories were to hold sway, then it would seem to follow that administrative accountability is a chimera. Administrators would not be liable for their actions. Administrative ethics that, by its definition, would strive to make moral judgments of those actions would be an impossibility. The only way to clear a path for the reality of administrative ethics would be to demonstrate that these two theories are somehow mistaken. This is the task that Thompson sets for himself in the remainder of his analysis. He argues that the genuine student of government ethics needs to pay attention to several theoretical issues, as well as to the more practical ones.

Another theoretical consideration to be explored is the impact that the U.S. Constitution has on the question of ethics. What does the Constitution have to say concerning this subject? Can interpretations of the Constitution have an effect on our understanding of the ethics crisis in government? These and other thematic questions form the concerns of David H. Rosenbloom in "The Constitution As a Basis for Public Administrative Ethics." His analysis includes an extended discussion of the idea of "constitutionally based ethics," which may at times be in variance with other legal requirements that regulate the behavior of administrators. Rosenbloom charts out this idea and shows how Constitutional law, especially in the areas of substantive rights and due process rights, has done much to change the face of ethics and conduct in the government workplace.

This chapter ends with more practical concerns involving ethics and its place in government. "Who Wants to Work in Washington?" by Robert E. Norton, asks the question of whether the severe ethics laws imposed upon public servants since Watergate have some serious diminishing returns in the form of deterring highly qualified individuals from serving in key administrative posts. Has the so-called "sleaze factor" led to paranoia, so that a new "moral mania" has created undesirable consequences for effective government leadership? Norton effectively outlines the provisions of the various ethics laws and points out that when these laws are coupled with the relatively low salaries of public administrators, a strong disincentive is created. His perspective casts doubt upon the chances for reforming the mischief-making of public officials by introducing increasing legislative controls. At the very least, Norton argues that the implementation and institutionalization of ethics in government is no easy matter.

What, then, is the scope of ethics in government? The proper answer is that it would seem that there are numerous considerations— some theoretical, some practical—that need be included in a thoughtful and thorough analysis of the topic. The scope of government ethics is misconstrued, if the rubric denotes only mischief-making, wrongdoing, or corruption. Rather, government ethics is a patchwork of interrelated questions, each needing its own particular answer. In other words, government ethics is an intricate and tangled web standing in need of unraveling. Let the unraveling begin.

Government Ethics: A Survey
James S. Bowman

How do public officials themselves view the ethics of govern-ment? "Government Ethics: A Survey," by James S. Bowman, charts some specific answers to this question. Bowman's survey gauges the prevailing attitudes and opinions of public officials on the status of ethics in society and within governmental agen-cies. He also reviews mechanisms, such as a code of conduct, ethics training, and executive leadership, that are often useful in addressing the ethics crisis in government.

Bowman found that most public administrators agree with the assertion that "society suffers from a 'moral numbness' "; almost 75 percent of those responding to the survey hold that the issue

James S. Bowman, "Government Ethics: A Survey," adapted from "Ethics in Government: A National Survey of Public Administrators," *Public Administration Review* (May/June, 1990), pp. 345–353. Reprinted with permission of the author.

of criminality distracts from the more subtle and important issue of resolving ethical dilemmas in the government workplace; just over half say that supervisors are under pressure to compromise their personal morality, and 60 percent doubt that the "ethical standards of elected and appointed officials are as high as those held by career civil servants."

Bowman asserts that the data he has collected should be a clear mandate for the American Society for Public Administration (ASPA)—the nation's preeminent professional association of public officials and academics in the field—to place ethics on its agenda and assist public officials in the management of this difficult area.

The 1980s, a time characterized by privatization, materialism, and self-righteousness, spawned fraud on Wall Street, embezzlement at the Department of Housing and Urban Development, influence peddling at the Justice Department, profiteering among defense contractors, tawdry presidential campaign tactics, resignations in Congress, and contempt for the Constitution inside the White House. Duplicity and hypocrisy in major social institutions erode the American spirit—the desire to contribute to the commonweal through commitment, compassion, and conscience. Yet not only has this period seen some of the most ignoble incidents in the country's history, but it has also witnessed a deepening interest in ethics. In the post-Watergate era, the citizenry has come to expect higher standards, as a broad range of activities in both the public and private sectors is now seen as immoral.

Government plays a significant role in creating feelings of mutual obligation and respect in society. Despite the significance of managers in interpreting the public good, few studies have examined their attitudes as they pertain to contemporary ethical problems in public affairs. Perceptual data such as these are clearly important, since ethical public administration implies action, that is, it attempts to answer the question "What should be done?" The purpose of this effort, then, is to explore ethical concerns of administrators about society and government in general, as well as organizational and behavioral standards in particular.

The Research Study

To investigate this subject, a questionnaire (consisting of agree-disagree statements, as well as several multiple choice and open-ended items), plus follow-ups, was mailed in Spring 1989 to a random sample of 750 administrators who are members of the American Society for Public Administration (ASPA); usable replies were received from 59 percent of those contacted. The typical participant parallels the association at large, which is white, male, well-educated, experienced in government, middle or senior level management, relatively high income, moderate to liberal in political philosophy, and holds at least a six-year membership in ASPA.

The survey results examine three topics: perceptions regarding ethics in society and government; the nature of integrity in public agencies, and overall organizational approaches to moral standards.

Ethics in Society

Several questions were asked in order to gauge the respondents' perceptions of ethical concerns in the nation. The data indicate that most respondents do not believe that the contemporary fascination is merely transitory. Nearly 70 percent think that interest in ethics "seems to be steadily growing over time." This outlook, however, is tempered by the lack of a clear consensus about whether this increased attention is just rhetorical in nature. Thus, while a plurality (48 percent) disputes that "ethics is similar to the weather: everyone talks about it, but no one does anything about it," a large minority (39 percent) agree, and another 12 percent are uncertain.

Over 60 percent of the administrators, further, agree that "society suffers from a 'moral numbness' following a decade of scandals involving Wall Street, religious organizations, the Pentagon, and the White House." Indeed, almost three-fourths of the respondents believe that "incidents of outright criminality in government distract attention from more subtle, genuine ethical dilemmas." Survey participants, then, see a growing interest in ethics but are not sure that anything will come of it—perhaps because the public may not have the necessary energy to cope with widespread manifestations of the problem.

The next statement places these results in comparative perspective vis-à-vis industry. Nearly 90 percent reject the claim that "government morality in America is lower than business morality." These individuals plainly do not see private enterprise as a standard for behavior in public life, especially when it does business with government. Most, for instance, were not surprised at charges of corruption among defense contractors in 1988. Over 90 percent of the respondents appear to accept columnist Haynes Johnson's observation that it was a scandal "just waiting to happen." If corporate behavior leaves a good deal to be desired, public administrators do not necessarily see government as a source of inspiration. Over three-fourths of them reject the idea that the "Reagan Administration did a good job in enforcing ethical standards."

In short, although these administrators may not see government behavior as exemplary in the 1980s, they doubt that its morality is lower than that found in business. However self-serving such views may be, ASPA members do endorse a double standard, one for industry and a much higher (and more publicized) one for government, as illustrated by this comment: "The public service *must* be seen as absolutely above reproach, it is just not good enough to follow the examples seen every day in the private sector" (original emphasis; city administrator from the Plains States). Given these data, little basis exists for traditional American optimism, faith in government, free enterprise, and respect for law. Indeed, are nationally publicized scandals only symptoms of more pervasive problems that occur in the conduct of daily management?

Integrity in Agencies

To attempt to answer this question this section explores moral behavior inside public organizations. Respondents were asked to react to this statement: "All people, especially managers, encounter ethical dilemmas at work." Ethical matters clearly "come with the territory" in the workday life of public agencies.

Interestingly, most respondents (67 percent) believe that ethical concern can be empowering in organizations. A similar proportion of managers reject the claim that "expressions of ethical concern . . . evoke cynicism, self-righteousness, paranoia, and/or laughter." Likewise, almost 60 percent dispute the assertion that ethics is "meaningless because organizational cultures encourage a Machiavellian philosophy of power, survival, and expediency." A professional administrator, then, is a professional not simply because of expertise, but because of adherence to high standards.

In short, despite evidence of both ethical paralysis in society and moral problems in public agencies, many of these managers are comfortable raising these issues at work. At the same time, however, just over half of the sample concede that supervisors are under pressure to compromise personal standards. The source of this stress appears to be top levels of the organization. Sixty percent doubt that the "ethical standards of elected and appointed officials are as high as those held by career civil servants," and nearly 75 percent dispute the contention that senior "management has a stronger set of ethical standards than I do."

Many respondents, in fact, identify career/noncareer relations as the most important ethical issue facing the public service today. Written questionnaire comments paint a portrait of politicians as exploitative, opportunistic, self-serving job jumpers, with little regard for the public:

- "The inability of many elected officials to distinguish between the ethical and nonethical . . . forces public servants into daily dilemmas, and casts a pall on everyone." (an assistant to a West Coast city manager)
- ". . . [E]xamples should be set by senior level of management. Unfortunately, that is the *most* unethical level within my organization." (original emphasis; a young local government professional also from the Northwest)

To summarize, it is evident that these practitioners encounter dilemmas, that ethics can be empowering in organizational cultures, and that considerable conflict exists between elected/appointed officials and careerists in the public administration community. What role do organizations serve in building an environment conducive to integrity? To answer this question, three topics are examined next: organizational policies, professional codes, and ethical activities in agencies.

Moral Standards in Organizational Conduct

Organizational Policies

Key factors in ethical behavior include not only one's values but also those of one's peers, subordinates, and superiors as embodied in written policies and unwritten expectations. It is not surprising, then, that over three-fourths of the executives agree that "while each individual is ultimately responsible for his/her behavior, organizations define and control the situations in which decisions are made." Although American individualism encourages an emphasis on personal conscience, the fact remains that organizations are major agencies of social control. Clearly some kind of institutional foundation for professional conduct is desirable, since many decisions in government must supersede personal preferences.

In order to set the stage for more specific responses, survey participants were first asked their overall impressions about organizational approaches toward ethics. Nearly one-fourth of the respondents believe that institutions have a reactive, negative, primitive, "low road" approach to ethics, one that reinforces popular suspicions and focuses on wrongdoing. A "high road," affirmative strategy that encourages ethical behavior and deters, rather than merely detects, problems characterizes less than 7 percent of organizations, according to these respondents.

Almost two-thirds of the sample believes that most agencies employ no consistent approach. A local government manager from the West says the reason for this is that they "accept unethical behavior as an evil that will exist and can't reasonably be eradicated." As a result, "Wild variations [occur]," according to a mid-Atlantic state official, "from one organization to another and from one time period to another." If a key function of management is to create moral consciousness in organizations, imbue them with high purpose, and act as a steward of the system, then this responsibility is not being discharged in a reliable manner.

It appears that typically there is no agreed-upon, usable standard or procedure to assist decision making in most offices. Consequently, many agencies either ignore, shift responsibility, or simply have no strategy whatsoever for dealing with ethics. A Virginia manager reports that "most bureaus I have worked for have tried to overlook ethical issues, deny them, or sweep them under the rug." In short, an incoherent, frequently passive, and/or reactive philosophy found in many departments is not likely to support, nurture, or benefit employees seeking to resolve ethical dilemmas in a responsible manner.

In an organizational age, tools of leadership are primarily institutional in nature. Surprisingly, perhaps, earlier studies found that nearly all business and government executives regard codes of conduct as the single most valuable way to promote ethics, possibly because they are seen as an important indicator of professionalism. Less than 3 percent of the respondents are satisfied that "there is no real need for codes of ethics in work organizations."

While virtually all see a genuine need, the respondents are less certain about the actual effect of such a standard. The sample is divided over whether the performance of agencies with codes differs from those that do not have them. While 40 percent believe that a difference is discernible, 40 percent are unsure, and 20 percent do not think that there is. One reason for this disunity may be that little effort is made to enforce ethical rules in many bureaus. Thus, approximately the same number agree as disagree that "there is an ongoing effort to reinforce an ethics code in my agency."

In light of the existence of codes, these data suggest that they may not be conducive to exemplary moral behavior. Can professional associations, especially those with a broad, interdisciplinary scope, promote effective ethical standards?

A Professional Code: The ASPA Case

If, as suggested at the outset, public management in a democracy needs to be a moral endeavor, then it seems appropriate that an organization such as the ASPA should encourage awareness of the ethical bases of public service. In 1984, after several years of debate and with some reluctance, the society adopted a twelve-point code of ethics for its members.

Such a standard must meet at least two criteria to be productive: acceptability and enforceability; that is, not only must those governed by the code believe in (or at least acquiesce to) its principles, but the policy must also have an enforcement mechanism. Prior to assessing the Society's document against these criteria, respondents' awareness of it must be determined. They were asked, "Are you familiar with the ASPA Code of Ethics?" Among those answering affirmatively (57 percent of the total sample), 34 percent said, "I have heard of it," 56 percent reported that "I have a general familiarity with it," and just 10 percent indicated that "I am quite familiar with it."

Those survey participants who indicated familiarity with the ASPA credo were asked questions pertaining to its acceptability and enforceability. Most of these respondents (70 percent) affirm that the "Code provides an appropriate set of standards" to guide public administrators. One reason why the remaining 26 percent are undecided (the rest disagree) may be a recognition that more tailored policies are needed for different workplaces. A middle manager in the federal government believes that "there is no sense spitting in the wind. Ethical standards must be part of the organizational culture if they are truly to work."

The acid test of acceptability is, of course, whether the ideals embodied in the code are actually practiced. Nearly 70 percent report that they either often or occasionally use the Code or its principles on the job. However, in response to the question, "With what frequency is the ASPA code and/or its principles used by your agency in daily management?" nearly two-thirds indicate that it is "seldom" used.

With respect to enforceability, the second criterion of a meaningful standard, over 95 percent agree that in order for the Code to be given weight, it must first be taken seriously by top management—apparently something that is not now the case. Interestingly, a large plurality would endorse a proposal giving ASPA power to enforce the Code (31 percent are undecided; 29 percent disapprove). Hesitancy on the part of members to do this appears to stem from a lack of genuine familiarity with the credo and the legitimacy of a general professional society to effect sanctions.

To summarize, these practitioners have some acquaintance with the ASPA document, but over 40 percent admitted they have none. Among those indicating familiarity (57 percent), just 10 percent claimed substantial knowledge of the Code, while a majority reported general familiarity and over one-third said that they "had heard of it."

How these data are interpreted depends upon the kind of code one thinks that ASPA developed: aspirational, educational, or regulatory. The results may be seen as a measure of success if the statement is taken as part of an image-building initiative and as a general description of inspirational ideals. As an educational document, one that seeks to explain professional norms, the Code may be somewhat less effective. If a substantial proportion of the membership is either completely unaware of (or has only a modest acquaintance with) the Code, then it is reasonable to assume even less understanding of the explanatory guidelines accompanying the statement. It follows that a regulatory effort, with rules and enforcement mechanisms that assume consensus on the aspirational and educational value of the Code, seems premature at this juncture. Yet the findings from both the acceptability and enforceability measures suggest that a regulatory initiative may be feasible at some time in the future.

Ethical Activities in Organizations

Since professionals have an important function in making public policy, an association of professionals may be well positioned to encourage more meaningful agency codes. In government, neither lawmakers nor professional schools, at least currently, are likely to fulfill this role. To provide a context for this activity on the part of a professional society, survey participants were first asked which techniques seem to work best (and least) in fostering ethics in their own organizations (approximately 50 percent replied). The answers to this free response question focused on three key topics.

Leadership. There is, in the eyes of both these managers and management theorists, no substitute for leadership. The distinguishing characteristic of the executive function, according to organizational analyst Chester Barnard, is that it requires not merely conformance to a complex code of morals but also the creation of a moral code for others. Over one-half of the respondents cited the importance of this task. ASPA members clearly believe that the standard should be set at the top. A local government employee from New England argues that "ethical behavior begins with the chief executive officer who serves as a role model and who does not tolerate unethical behavior." Employees must know what is expected, and managers ought to work to set the example in daily operations by talking about the needs of the public, as well as the agency, and the ethical implications of them.

What works best, then, is "quiet diplomacy," that is, "trusting people and letting them know you trust them. [Do not have] so many approvals and double checks that assume everyone is unethical" (a federal middle manager). Three leadership styles that are not productive are laissez-faire, authoritarian, and rhetorical. The first approach ignores ethical situations until it is too late and then lets "employees hang on their own" (a Florida local government middle manager). The authoritarian style—issuing edicts, mandating compliance, using scare tactics—assumes that people "will act unethically, and the job of management is to punish them when they get caught" (a California administrator). Finally, many managers denounced the hypocrisy inherent in the rhetorical strategy, which relies on platitudes and generalities by devoting lip service (but no substantive policy) to organizational integrity.

Training. A large number of survey participants recommend an organizational training and development strategy to fortify leadership-by-example. Again, a composite, three-part picture can be developed from the written comments to provide substance to this approach. First, and essential, is to define the agency mission and identify activities necessary to pursue it. Several administrators suggest that a values clarification exercise, to determine reasonable and relevant measures of behavior, would be helpful. This could include a survey of staff members to ascertain the existence and nature of ethical dilemmas. Second, and relatedly, managers should seek to achieve a "positive buy-in by involving employees in the goals and process of creating an agency ethics code" (a senior official in a local Northeast government). Last, in the words of a top nonprofit manager from the Midwest, "Practice what you preach." Thus, according to many respondents, a declaration of ideals, while certainly an important starting point, is only a beginning.

All too often, other respondents claim, agencies publish regulations and expect employees to comprehend and apply them automatically. Instead, scheduled training, conducted by line managers with the assistance of outside experts, provides reinforcement of standards. This makes ethics less an application of engraved principles, and more of a relationship with other people who share similar values. Such training encourages leadership throughout the organization irrespective of rank or function; effective modeling can come from the bottom as well as the top when first-line supervisors and middle managers set a clear standard for their units.

Ethics in agencies, in short, means verbal and behavioral management leadership—it is necessary to "walk the talk." Respondents recognize, however, that leadership without training and development can incapacitate an organization by disempowering employees. An authentic effort, one that is neither a public relations exercise nor a wish list, honors democracy.

Administration. A genuine code, then, is a consensus document, one with clear guidelines for, and application to, all employees without exception. Yet principles without processes to help people wrestle with competing claims are never sufficient. Thus, how ethical concerns are defined and reported is crucial in day-to-day business. Not every dilemma will have a "right" solution, but it should be possible to agree on a problem-solving procedure. A number of respondents believe that agency principles should be interpreted by an active ethics board, which would render advisory opinions, reward honorable behavior, and correct questionable activity. Examples of administrative practices that vitiate an agency program include inconsistent application of rules, the use of double standards, punishment of whistleblowers, secrecy, and "cat and mouse procedures that catch the innocent but are useless against those who are unprincipled" (a federal professional/technical employee).

To conclude, most respondents believe that leadership behavior must include and be supported by an organizational training strategy that focuses on a code of ethics. And not surprisingly from a group of professional administrators, they are concerned that fair procedures be designed to make the canons real in daily agency life. Such activities can raise expectations and lively possibilities; as they do, people will find it easier to act with integrity when they are supported by colleagues who themselves act in the same manner.

Conclusion

This study provides empirical evidence on ethical issues in public management. The respondents indicate that ethics is hardly a fad, and that the government has the obligation to set the example in society. They further believe that ethics in the workplace can be empowering, but that most organizations and their leaders do not have a consistent approach to accomplish this goal. There is, however, a belief that properly designed codes of conduct can have a crucial role in fostering integrity in agencies.

Clearly, administrators think that a compelling need exists for guidance to address ethical and unethical conduct in government. The broad, deep consensus among these respondents reveals that the issue has become one of establishing responsive programs, not merely of raising general awareness. The initiatives discussed here can be meaningful if they are institutionalized through ethical leadership and standards of practice. In a professional association like ASPA, practitioners and academicians alike can play significant parts in this vital task. Indeed, as the society enters the final decade of the century, it would be difficult to identify a more essential mission upon which to focus.

The Possibility
of Administrative Ethics
Dennis F. Thompson

Dennis F. Thompson's "The Possibility of Administrative Ethics" deals with the contention that, while morality has a place in private life, it is not a possibility in organizational life. Thompson addresses the two main arguments that purport to show that administrative ethics is an impossibility: (1) the "ethic of neutrality," which argues that administrators are not free to follow the dictates of their own moral principles but must obey those of the organization, and (2) the "ethic of structure," which argues that organizations themselves and not those who administer them should be held accountable for the actions of the group. It is often argued that if either of these positions happens to be correct, then there is no possibility of administrative ethics.

But Thompson goes on to demonstrate that both the ethic of neutrality and the ethic of structure are flawed theories. In his view, public administration requires that individuals not suppress their moral autonomy when accepting public office; that public administrators can and should be held accountable over and above the organizations in which they happen to serve. Thus to Thompson, administrative ethics is not only a possibility but a reality needing greater recognition.

Is administrative ethics possible? The most serious objections to administrative ethics arise from two common conceptions of the role of individuals in organizations—what may be called the ethic of neutrality and the ethic of structure. Both of these views must be rejected if administrative ethics is to be possible.

Administrative ethics involves the application of moral principles to the conduct of officials in organizations.[1] In the form with which we are primarily concerned here (ethics in public organizations), administrative ethics is a species of political ethics, which applies moral principles to political life more generally. Broadly speaking, moral principles specify (a) the rights and duties that individuals should respect when they act in ways that seriously affect the well-being of other individuals and society; and (b) the conditions that collective practices and policies should satisfy when they similarly affect the well-being of individuals and society. Moral principles require a disinterested perspective. Instead of asking how an action or policy serves the interest of some particular individual or group, morality asks whether the action or policy serves everyone's interest, or whether it could be accepted by anyone who did not know his or her particular circumstances, such as race, social class, or nationality. Moral judgments

Dennis F. Thompson, "The Possibility of Administrative Ethics," *Public Administration Review* (September/October 1985), pp. 555–561. Reprinted with permission from *Public Administration Review* © 1985 by the American Society for Public Administration (ASPA), 1120 G Street N.W., Suite 500, Washington, DC 20005. All rights reserved.

presuppose the possibility of a person to make the judgment and a person or group of persons to be judged.

The most general challenge to administrative ethics would be to deny the possibility of ethics at all or the possibility of political ethics. Although a worthy challenge, it should not be the primary concern of defenders of administrative ethics. Theorists (as well as practitioners when they think about ethics at all) have been so preoccupied with general objections to ethics that they have neglected objections that apply specifically to ethics in administration. They have not sufficiently considered that even if we accept the possibility of morality in general and even in politics, we may have doubts about it in organizations.

To isolate more specifically the objections to administrative ethics, we should assume that the moral perspective can be vindicated and that some moral principles and some moral judgments are valid. Despite disagreement about how morality is to be justified and disagreement about its scope and content, we nevertheless share certain attitudes and beliefs to which we can appeal in criticizing or defending public actions and policies from a moral perspective.[2]

The more direct challenge to administrative ethics comes from those who admit that morality is perfectly possible in private life but deny that it is possible in organizational life. The challenge is that by its very nature administration precludes the exercise of moral judgment. It consists of two basic objections—the first calls into question the subject of the judgment (who may judge); the second, the object of judgment (who is judged). The first asserts that administrators ought to act neutrally in the sense that they should follow not their own moral principles but the decisions and policies of the organization. This is the ethic of neutrality. The second asserts that not administrators but the organization (and its formal officers) should be held responsible for its decisions and policies. This is the ethic of structure. Each is called an ethic because it expresses certain norms and prescribes conduct. But neither constitutes an ethic nor a morality because each denies one of the presuppositions of moral judgment—either a person to judge or a person to be judged.

I. The Ethic of Neutrality

The conventional theory and practice of administrative ethics holds that administrators should carry out the orders of their superiors and the policies of the agency and the government they serve.[3] On this view, administrators are ethically neutral in the sense that they do not exercise independent moral judgment. They are not expected to act on any moral principles of their own but are to give effect to whatever principles are reflected in the orders and policies they are charged with implementing. They serve the organization so that the organization may serve society. Officials are morally obliged to serve the organization in this way because their acceptance of office is voluntary: it signifies consent. Officials know in advance what the duties of office will be, and if the duties (or their minds) change, officials can usually leave office.

The ethic of neutrality does not deny that administrators often must use their own judgment in the formulation of policy. But their aim should always be to discover what policy other people (usually elected officials) intend or would intend; or in the case of conflicting directives to interpret legally or constitutionally who has the authority to determine policy. The use of discretion on this view can never be the occasion for applying any moral principles other than those implicit in the orders and policies of the superiors to whom one is responsible in the organization. The ethic of neutrality portrays the ideal administrator as a completely reliable instrument of the goals of the organization, never injecting personal values into the process of furthering these goals. The ethic thus reinforces the great virtue of organization—its capacity to serve any social end irrespective of the ends that individuals within it favor.

A variation of the ethic of neutrality gives some scope for individual moral judgment until the decision or policy is "final." On this view, administrators may put forward their own views, argue with their superiors, and contest proposals in the process of formulating policy. But once the decision or policy is final, all administrators fall into line, and faithfully carry out the policy. Furthermore, the disagreement must take place within the agency and according to the agency's rules of procedure. This variation puts neutrality in abeyance, but "suspended neutrality" is still neutrality, and the choice for the administrator remains to "obey or resign."[4]

Three sets of criticisms may be brought against the ethic of neutrality. First, because the ethic underestimates the discretion that administrators exercise, it impedes the accountability of administrators by citizens. The discretion of administrators goes beyond carrying out the intentions of legislators or the superiors in the organization, not only because often there are no intentions to discover, but also because often administrators can and should take the initiative in proposing policies and mobilizing support for them.[5] The ethic of neutrality provides no guidance for this wide range of substantive moral decision making in which administrators regularly engage. By reinforcing the illusion that administrators do not exercise independent moral judgment, it insulates them from external accountability for the consequences of many of their decisions.

A second set of objections centers on the claim that officeholding implies consent to the duties of office as defined by the organization. While it may be easier to resign from office than from citizenship, it is for many officials so difficult that failure to do so cannot be taken to indicate approval of everything the organization undertakes. For the vast majority of governmental employees, vested rights (such as pensions and seniority) and job skills (often not transferable to the private sector) supply powerful incentives to hold on to their positions. Even if on their own many would be prepared to sacrifice their careers for the sake of principle, they cannot ignore their responsibilities to their families. Higher level officials usually enjoy advantages that make resignation a more feasible option. They can return to (usually more lucrative) positions in business or in a profession. But their ability to do so may depend on their serving loyally while in government, demonstrating that they are the good "team players" on whom any organization, public or private, can rely.

Furthermore, the dynamics of collective decision making discourage even conscientious officials from resigning on principle. Many decisions are incremental, their objectionable character apparent only in their cumulative effect. An official who is involved in the early stages of escalations of this kind (such as aid increases, budget cuts, troop commitments) will find it difficult to object to any subsequent step. The difference between one step and the next is relatively trivial, certainly not a reason to resign on principle. Besides, many decisions and policies represent compromises, and any would-be dissenter can easily be persuaded that because his opponents did not get everything they sought, he should settle for less than what his principles demand. For these and other reasons, an official may stay in office while objecting to the policies of government; a failure to resign therefore does not signify consent.

Proponents of the ethic of neutrality may still insist that officials who cannot fulfill the duties of their office must resign, however difficult it may be to do so. But as citizens we should hesitate before endorsing this as a general principle of administrative ethics. If this view were consistently put into practice, public offices would soon be populated only by those who never had any reason to disagree with anything the government decided to do. Men and women of strong moral conviction would resign rather than continue in office, and we would lose the services of the persons who could contribute most to public life.

Because we do not want to drive persons of principle from office, we should recognize that there may be good moral reasons for staying in office even while disagreeing with the policies of the government. This recognition points to a third set of objections to the ethic of neutrality—that it simplifies the moral circumstances of public office. It tends to portray officials as assessing the fit between their moral principles and the policies of the organization, obeying if the principles and policies match, resigning if they diverge too much. What is important on this view is that in resigning, the individual express "ethical autonomy," which Weisband and Franck, in their otherwise valuable plea for resignations in protest, define as "the willingness to assert one's own principled judgment, even if that entails violating rules, values, or perceptions of the organization, peer group or team."[6] "The social importance of ethical autonomy," they write, "lies not in what is asserted but in the act of asserting." The ethic of neutrality encourages this and similar portrayals of an isolated official affirming his or her own principles against the organization at the moment of resignation. The ethic thereby neglects important considerations that an ethical administrator should take into account in fulfilling the duties while in office.

THE SCOPE OF GOVERNMENT ETHICS

First of all, as an official you have obligations to colleagues, an agency, and the government as a whole. By accepting office and undertaking collective tasks in an organization, you give others reason to rely on your continued cooperation. Your colleagues begin projects, take risks, make commitments in the expectation that you will continue to play your part in the organization. If you resign, you disappoint these expectations, and in effect break your commitments to your colleagues. A resignation may disrupt many organizational activities, some of which may be morally more important than the policy that occasions the resignation. Presidential Assistant Alexander Haig deployed this kind of argument in October 1973 in an effort to persuade Attorney-General Elliot Richardson to fire Special Prosecutor Archibald Cox. Richardson claimed that he would resign rather than dismiss Cox. Haig argued that resignation or disobedience at this time would jeopardize the President's efforts, which were at a critical stage, to reach a peace settlement in the Middle East.[7] The argument understandably did not convince Richardson (his commitment to Congress and Cox were too clear, and the connection between his resignation and the Middle East settlement too tenuous), but the *form* of the argument Haig invoked was sound. An official must consider his commitments to all of his associates in government and the effect of his intended resignation on the conduct of government as a whole. Officials also have more general obligations to the public. Officials should not decide simply whether they can in good conscience continue to associate themselves with the organization. This could be interpreted as merely wanting to keep one's own hands clean—a form of what some have called "moral self-indulgence."[8]

A third way in which the ethic of neutrality distorts the duties of public administrators is by limiting their courses of action to two—obedience or resignation. Many forms of dissent may be compatible with remaining in office, ranging from quiet protest to illegal obstruction. Some of these, of course, may be morally wrong except under extreme circumstances, but the ethic of neutrality provides no guidance at all here because it rules out, in advance, the possibility of morally acceptable internal opposition to decisions of the organization, at least "final decisions."

The problem, however, is how we can grant officials scope for dissent without undermining the capacity of the organization to accomplish its goals. If the organization is pursuing goals set by a democratic public, individual dissent in the organization may subvert the democratic process. We should insist, first of all, that would-be dissenters consider carefully the basis of their disagreement with the policy in question. Is the disagreement moral or merely political? This is a slippery distinction since almost all important political decisions have moral dimensions. But perhaps we could say that the more directly a policy seems to violate an important moral principle (such as, not harming innocent persons), the more justifiable dissent becomes. An official would be warranted in stronger measures of opposition against decisions to bomb civilian targets in a guerrilla war than against decisions to lower trade barriers and import duties.[9] In cases of political disagreement of the latter sort, straightforward resignation seems the most appropriate action (once the decision is final). Dissenters must also consider whether the policy they oppose is a one-time incident or part of a continuing pattern and whether the wrongness of the policy is outweighed by the value of the other policies the organization is pursuing. Furthermore, dissenters must examine the extent of their own involvement and own role: how (formally and informally) responsible are they for the policy? What difference would their opposition make to the policy and to the other policies of the organization? To what extent does the policy violate the ethics of groups to which they are obligated (such as the canons of the legal or medical professions)?

These considerations not only determine whether an official is justified in opposing the organization's policy, but they also help to indicate what methods of dissent the official may be justified in using to express opposition. The more justified an official's opposition, the more justified the official is in using more extreme methods. The methods of dissent may be arrayed on a continuum from the most extreme to the most moderate. Four types of dissent will illustrate the range of this continuum and raise some further issues that any would-be dissenter must consider.

First, there are those forms of dissent in which an official protests within the organization but still helps implement the policy, or (a slightly stronger measure) asks for a different assignment in the organization. In its weakest form, this kind of dissent does not go much beyond the ethic of neutrality. But unlike that ethic, it would permit officials to abstain from active participation in a policy they oppose and to continue their protest as long as they do so in accordance with the accepted procedures of the organization.[10]

One danger of this form of protest is what has been called the "domestication of dissenters."[11] A case in point is George Ball, who as undersecretary of state in the Johnson administration persistently argued against the government's Vietnam policy in private meetings:

> Once Mr. Ball began to express doubts, he was warmly institutionalized: he was encouraged to become the in-house devil's advocate on Vietnam. . . . The process of escalation allowed for periodic requests to Mr. Ball to speak his piece; Ball felt good . . . (he had fought for righteousness); the others felt good (they had given a full hearing to the dovish option); and there was minimal unpleasantness.[12]

In this way dissenters can be "effectively neutralized," and contrary to their intentions, their dissent can even help support the policy they oppose. It is important therefore to consider whether this effect is inevitable, and, if not, to discover the conditions under which it can be avoided.

In a second form of dissent, officials, with the knowledge of, but against the wishes of their superiors, carry their protest outside the organization while otherwise performing their jobs satisfactorily. This is the course of action taken by most of the 65 Justice Department attorneys who protested the decision to permit delays in implementing desegregation decrees in Mississippi in August of 1969.[13] The attorneys signed and publicized a petition denouncing the attorney-general and the president for adopting a policy the attorneys believed violated the law and would require them to act contrary to the ethical canons of the legal profession. They also believed that resignation would not fulfill their obligation to act affirmatively to oppose illegality. Several of the dissenters argued for stronger actions that would directly block the policy, and some gave information to the NAACP Legal Defense Fund, which was opposing the Justice Department in court. Most of the attorneys declined to engage in these stronger actions, however, on the grounds that obstruction would weaken public support for their dissent.

This kind of dissent usually depends, for its efficacy as well as its legitimacy, on the existence of some widely accepted standards to which the dissenters can appeal outside the organization. Professional ethics or even the law may not be sufficient, since people disagree on how to interpret both, but appealing to such standards may at least reassure the public that the dissenters are not using their office to impose the dictates of their private consciences on public policy. When dissenters oppose democratically elected officials, they must find ways to show that they are defending principles that all citizens would endorse.

The third form of dissent is the open obstruction of policy. Officials may, for example, withhold knowledge or expertise that the organization needs to pursue the policy, refuse to step aside so that others can pursue it, or give information and other kinds of assistance to outsiders who are trying to overturn the policy. A few officials may adopt this strategy for a short time, but organizations can usually isolate the dissenters, find other officials to do the job, and mobilize its own external support to counter any opposition that arises outside the organization. In any such event, the dissenters are not likely to retain much influence within the organization. Effective and sustained opposition has to be more circumspect.

We are therefore led to a fourth kind of dissent: covert obstruction. Unauthorized disclosure—the leak—is the most prominent example. Leaks vary greatly in purpose and effect. Some simply provide information to other agencies that are entitled to receive it; others embarrass particular officials within an agency but do not otherwise subvert the agency's policies; others release information to the press or public, ultimately reversing a major government policy; and at the extreme, still others give secrets to enemy agents and count as treason. Short of that extreme, we still may want to say that unauthorized disclosure is sometimes justified even when it breaches government procedures or violates the law, as in the release of classified documents.

An analogy is sometimes drawn between official disobedience and civil disobedience. Many democratic theorists hold that citizens in a democracy are justified in breaking the law with the aim of changing a law or policy, but only in certain ways and under certain conditions. Citizens must (1) act publicly; (2) commit no violence; (3) appeal to principles shared by other citizens; (4)

direct their challenge against a substantial injustice; (5) exhaust all normal channels of protest before breaking a law; and (6) plan their disobedience so that it does not, in conjunction with that of other citizens, disrupt the stability of the democratic process.[14]

Even if one thinks that civil disobedience is justifiable, one may not agree that official disobedience is warranted. Officials cannot claim the same rights as citizens can, and, it may be said, the analogy does not in general hold. But the analogy may not hold for the opposite reason. In extreme cases of governmental wrongdoing, so much is at stake that we should give officials greater scope for disobedience than we allow citizens. In these cases we might be prepared to argue that the standard conditions for civil disobedience are too restrictive for officials. If we insist, for example, that disobedience always be carried out in public, we may in effect suppress much valuable criticism of government. Fearful of the consequences of public action, dissenting officials may decide against providing information that their superiors have declared secret but that citizens ought to know. The point of relaxing the requirement of publicity would be not to protect the rights of dissenters for their own sake but to promote public discussion of questionable actions of government. We may wish to retain some form of the requirement of publicity, perhaps by establishing an authority to whom a dissenter must make his or her identity known. But this requirement, as well as the others, should be formulated with the goal of maximizing the responsibility of governmental officials, not with the aim of matching exactly the traditional criteria of civil disobedience.

The important task, with respect to disobedience as well as the other forms of dissent, is to develop the criteria that could help determine when each is justifiable in various circumstances. The ethic of neutrality makes that task unnecessary by denying that ethics is possible in administration. But, as we have seen, that administrative neutrality itself is neither possible nor desirable.

II. The Ethic of Structure

The second major obstacle to administrative ethics is the view that the object of moral judgment must be the organization or the government as a whole. This ethic of structure asserts that, even if administrators may have some scope for independent moral judgment, they cannot be held morally responsible for most of the decisions and policies of government. Their personal moral responsibility extends only to the specific duties of their own office for which they are legally liable.

Moral judgment presupposes moral agency. To praise or blame someone for an outcome, we must assume that the person is morally responsible for the action. We must assume (1) that the person's actions or omissions were a cause of the outcome; and (2) that the person did not act in excusable ignorance or under compulsion. In everyday life, we sometimes withhold moral criticism because we think a person does not satisfy one or both of these criteria. But since usually so few agents are involved and because the parts they play are obvious enough, we are not normally perplexed about whether anyone can be said to have brought about a particular outcome. The main moral problem is what was the right thing to do, not so much who did it. In public life, especially organizations, the problem of identifying the moral agents, of finding the persons who are morally responsible for a decision or policy, becomes at least as difficult as the problem of assessing the morality of the decision or policy. Even if we have perfect information about all the agents in the organizational process that produced an outcome, we may still be puzzled about how to ascribe responsibility for it. Because many people contribute in many different ways to the decisions and policies of an organization, we may not be able to determine, even in principle, who is morally responsible for those decisions and policies. This has been called "the problem of many hands,"[15] and the assumption that it is not soluble underlies the ethic of structure.

Proponents of the ethic of structure put forward three arguments to deny the possibility of ascribing individual responsibility in organizations and thereby to undermine the possibility of administrative ethics. First, it is argued that no individual is a necessary or sufficient cause of any organizational outcome.[16] The contributions of each official are like the strands in a rope. Together they pull the load: no single strand could do the job alone, but the job could be done without any single strand. Suppose that for many decades the CIA has had a policy of trying to overthrow third-world governments that refuse to cooperate with their operatives, and suppose further that many of these attempts are morally wrong. No one presently in the agency initiated the practice, let us assume, and no one individual plays a very important role in any of the attempts. If any one agent did not do his or her part, the practice would continue, and even particular attempts would still often succeed. How could we say that any individual is the cause of this practice?

A second argument points to the gap between individual intention and collective outcomes. The motives of individual officials are inevitably diverse (to serve the nation, to help citizens, to acquire power, to win a promotion, to ruin a rival). Many praiseworthy policies are promoted for morally dubious reasons, and many pernicious policies are furthered with the best of intentions. In many organizations today, for example, we may well be able to say that no official intends to discriminate against minorities in the hiring and promoting of employees; yet the pattern of appointments and advancements still disadvantages certain minorities. Here we should want to condemn the pattern or policy (so the argument goes), but we could not morally blame any individual official for it.

A third argument stresses the requirements of role. The duties of office and the routines of large organizations require individual actions which, in themselves harmless or even in some sense obligatory, combine to produce harmful decisions and policies by the organization. Although the policy of the organization is morally wrong, each individual has done his or her moral duty according to the requirements of office. The collective sum is worse than its parts. In a review of the policies that led to the financial collapse of New York City in the mid-1970s and endangered the welfare and livelihoods of millions of citizens, one writer concludes that no individuals can be blamed for the misleading budgetary practices that helped bring about the collapse: "The delicately balanced financial superstructure was a kind of evolutionary extrusion that had emerged from hundreds of piecemeal decisions."[17]

If we were to accept these arguments, we would let many guilty officials off the moral hook. Without some sense of personal responsibility, officials may act with less moral care, and citizens may challenge officials with less moral effect. Democratic accountability is likely to erode. How can these arguments be answered so that individual responsibility can be maintained in organizations?

First, we should not assess an official's moral responsibility solely according to the proportionate share he or she contributes to the outcome. "Responsibility is not a bucket in which less remains when some is apportioned out."[18] If a gang of 10 thugs beats an old man to death, we do not punish each thug for only one-tenth of the murder (even if no single thug hit him hard enough to cause his death). Further, in imputing responsibility we should consider not only the acts that individuals committed but also the acts they omitted. Even though in the CIA example no one initiated the wrongful policy, many officials could be blamed for failing to try to halt the practice. Admittedly, there are dangers in adopting a notion of "negative responsibility."[19] One is that such a notion can make individuals culpable for almost anything (since there seems to be no limit to the acts that an individual did not do). But in the context of organizations we can more often point to specific omissions that made a significant difference in the outcome and that are ascribable to specific persons. Patterns of omissions can be predicted and specified in advance.

The force of the second argument, which points to the gap between individual intention and collective outcome, can be blunted if we simply give less weight to intentions than to consequences in assessing moral culpability of officials, at least in two of the senses that "intention" is commonly understood—as motive and as direct goal. It is often hard enough in private life to interpret the motives of persons one knows well; in public life it may be impossible to discover the intentions of officials, especially when the motives of so many of those questioning the motives of officials are themselves questionable. Insofar as we can discover motives, they are relevant in assessing character and may sometimes help in predicting future behavior, but administrative ethics does better to concentrate on actions and results in public life.[20]

What about officials who directly intend only good results but, because of other people's mistakes or other factors they do not foresee, contribute to an unjust or harmful policy? Here the key question is not whether the officials actually foresaw this result, but whether they should have foreseen it.[21] We can legitimately hold public officials to a higher standard than that to which we hold ordinary citizens. We can expect officials to foresee and take into account a wider range of consequences, partly because of the general obligations of public office. Where the welfare of so many is at stake, officials must make exceptional efforts to anticipate consequences of their actions.

Moreover, the nature of organization itself often forestalls officials from plausibly pleading that they did not foresee what their actions would cause. Organizations tend to produce patterned outcomes; they regularly make the same mistakes in the same ways. While officials may once or twice reasonably claim they should not have been expected to foresee a harmful outcome to which their well-intentioned actions contributed, there must be some (low) limit to the number of times they may use this excuse to escape responsibility. In the example of discrimination in employment, we would say that officials should recognize that their organizational procedures (combined with social forces) are still producing unjust results in personnel decisions; they become partly responsible for the injustice if they do not take steps to overcome it as far as they can.

The requirements of a role insulate an official from blame much less than the earlier argument implied.[22] The example of the New York City fiscal crisis actually tells against that argument as much as for it. Mayor Beame was one of the officials who disclaimed responsibility for the allegedly deceptive accounting practices on the grounds that they were part of organizational routines established many years earlier and could not be changed in the midst of a crisis. But Beame had also served as comptroller and in the budget office during the years when those accounting practices were initiated.[23] In ascribing responsibility to public officials, we should keep in mind that it attaches to persons, not offices. It cannot be entirely determined by any one role a person holds, and it follows a person through time. These features of personal responsibility are sometimes ignored. Public officials are blamed for an immoral (or incompetent) performance in one role but then appear to start with a clean slate once they leave the old job and take up a new one. This recycling of discredited public figures is reinforced by the habit of collapsing personal responsibility into role responsibility. Another way that officials may transcend their roles should also be emphasized. Even when a role fully and legitimately constrains what an official may do, personal responsibility need not be completely extinguished. Officials may escape blame for a particular decision, but they do not thereby escape responsibility for seeking to change the constraints of role and structure that helped produce that decision, and they do not escape responsibility for criticizing those constraints. Criticism of one's own past and current performance, and the structures in which that performance takes place, may be the last refuge of moral responsibility in public life.

Administrative ethics is possible—at least, the two major theoretical views that oppose its possibility are not compelling. We are forced to accept neither an ethic of neutrality that would suppress independent moral judgment, nor an ethic of structure that would ignore individual moral agency in organization. To show that administrative ethics is possible is not of course to show how to make it actual. But understanding why administrative ethics is possible is a necessary step not only toward putting it into practice but also toward giving it meaningful content in practice.

NOTES

1. It may be assumed that there is no important philosophical distinction between "ethics" and "morality." Both terms denote the principles of right and wrong in conduct (or the study of such principles). When we refer to the principles of particular professions (e.g., legal ethics or political ethics), "ethics" is the more natural term; and when we refer to personal conduct (e.g., sexual morality), "morality" seems more appropriate. But in their general senses, the terms are fundamentally equivalent. For various definitions of the nature of morality or ethics, see William Frankena, *Ethics,* 2nd ed. (Englewood Cliffs, NJ: Prentice-Hall, 1973), pp. 1–11; Alan Donagan, *The Theory of Morality* (Chicago: University of Chicago Press, 1977), pp. 1–31; G. J. Warnock, *The Object of Morality* (London: Methuen, 1971), pp. 1– 26.

2. Cf. the method of "reflective equilibrium" presented by John Rawls, *A Theory of Justice* (Cambridge, MA: Harvard University Press, 1971), pp. 48–51.

3. For citations and analysis of some writers who adopt part or all of the ethic of neutrality, see Joel L. Fleishman and Bruce L. Payne (eds.), *Ethical Dilemmas and the Education of Policymakers* (Hastings-on-Hudson, NY: The Hastings Center, 1980), pp. 36–38. Cf. John A. Rohr, *Ethics for Bureaucrats* (New York: Dekker, 1978), pp. 15–47.

4. Cf. George Graham, "Ethical Guidelines for Public Administrators," *Public Administration Review*, vol. 34 (January/February 1974), pp. 90–92.

5. Donald Warwick, "The Ethics of Administrative Discretion," in Joel Fleishman *et al.* (eds.), *Public Duties* (Cambridge, MA: Harvard University Press, 1981), pp. 93–127.

6. Edward Weisband and Thomas M. Franck, *Resignation in Protest* (New York: Penguin, 1976), p. 3.

7. J. Anthony Lukas, *Nightmare: The Underside of the Nixon Years* (New York: Bantam, 1977), p. 588.

8. On "complicity," see Thomas E. Hill, "Symbolic Protest and Calculated Silence," *Philosophy & Public Affairs* (Fall 1979), pp. 83–102. For a defense against the charge of moral self-indulgence, see Bernard Williams, *Moral Luck* (Cambridge: Cambridge University Press, 1981), pp. 40–53.

9. For an example of the latter, see Weisband and Franck, p. 46.

10. Cf. Graham, p. 92.

11. James C. Thomson, "How Could Vietnam Happen?" *Atlantic* (April 1968), p. 49. Also see Albert Hirschman, *Exit, Voice and Loyalty* (Cambridge, MA: Harvard University Press, 1970), pp. 115–119.

12. Thomson, p. 49.

13. Gary J. Greenberg, "Revolt at Justice," in Charles Peters and T. J. Adams (eds.), *Inside the System* (New York: Praeger, 1970), pp. 195–209.

14. See Rawls, pp. 363–391.

15. Dennis F. Thompson, "Moral Responsibility of Public Officials: The Problem of Many Hands," *American Political Science Review*, vol. 74 (December 1980), pp. 905–916.

16. John Ladd, "Morality and the Ideal of Rationality in Formal Organizations," *Monist*, vol. 54 (October 1970), pp. 488–516.

17. Charles R. Morris, *The Cost of Good Intentions* (New York: W.W. Norton, 1980), pp. 239–240. For some other examples of structuralist analyses, see Herbert Kaufman, *Red Tape* (Washington, DC: Brookings, 1977), pp. 27–28; and Richard J. Stillman, *Public Administration: Concepts and Cases*, 2nd ed. (Boston: Houghton-Mifflin, 1980), p. 34.

18. Robert Nozick, *Anarchy, State and Utopia* (New York: Basic Books, 1974), p. 130.

19. Cf. Bernard Williams, "A Critique of Utilitarianism," in J. J. C. Smart and Bernard Williams, *Utilitarianism* (Cambridge: Cambridge University Press, 1973), pp. 93–118.

20. But cf. Joel L. Fleishman, "Self-Interest and Political Integrity," in Fleishman *et al.* (eds.), pp. 52–92.

21. But cf. Charles Fried, *Right and Wrong* (Cambridge, MA: Harvard University Press, 1978), esp. pp. 21–22, 26, 28, 202–205. More generally on "intention," see Donagan, pp. 112–142; and J. L. Mackie, *Ethics* (New York: Penguin, 1977), pp. 203–226.

22. On role responsibility, see H. L. A. Hart, *Punishment and Responsibility* (New York: Oxford University Press, 1968), pp. 212–214; and R. S. Downie, *Roles and Values* (London: Methuen, 1971), pp. 121–145.

23. Dennis F. Thompson, "Moral Responsibility and the New York City Fiscal Crisis," in Fleishman *et al.* (eds.), pp. 266–285.

The Constitution As a Basis for Public Administrative Ethics
David H. Rosenbloom

David H. Rosenbloom explores the possibilities of a "constitutionally based ethics" in his "The Constitution As a Basis for Public Administrative Ethics." He argues that since the 1970s various interpretations of the Constitution by the Supreme Court have set some new ethical requirements for governmental administrators. The legal upshot of this constitutionally based set of ethics is to make public officials liable for conduct that violates constitutionally established rights. In other words, many people who can be called stakeholders in the process of government were granted or had extended to them various rights

David H. Rosenbloom, "The Constitution As a Basis for Public Administration Ethics." Previously unpublished article. Printed with permission of the author. Charts by Donad Pettit.

in separate Supreme Court cases dealing with issues such as equal protection, due process, and free speech for public employees. Thus there now exists a Constitutional mandate that public administrators uphold these rights—in effect a new moral guide for administrators.

Moreover, according to Rosenbloom, this constitutionally based ethics has forced a new way of thinking and administering in government. Now public officials must be mindful of the substantive and procedural rights of individuals. They must choose that course of action that achieves the compelling interests of government with the least damage to the individual rights of citizens. Constitutionally based ethics inevitably imposes a set of values upon administrators that cannot help but conflict with the traditional value of efficiency.

Public administrators and government officials are expected to adhere to a variety of ethical codes and approaches. Insofar as these are consistent, can be learned, and are realistic, they present few difficulties for administrative practice. When codes or requirements are vague, however, unrealistic, and in conflict with one another, they complicate the issues involved in acting ethically under all circumstances. For almost all of U.S. administrative history the two prime ethical requirements were: (1) refraining from using public property and/or office for purely private purposes or gain; and (2) avoiding waste of government resources. These requirements were widely violated, especially during the period from 1829 to 1883, when patronage was rife. Public office, however, was still formally and legally viewed as a "public trust" to which many private interests had to be subordinated. A large variety of measures, including conflict-of-interest laws, Executive Orders, and agency regulations have been enacted in addition to various codes of ethics that attempt to restrain self-interest.

Since the 1970s, a new and very important dimension has been added to the codes that public administrators and officials must follow—that of "constitutionally based ethics." Moreover, the ethical requirements that are derived from the Constitution are difficult to apply, sometimes require an elaborate balancing of concerns, and are often at odds with traditional administrative values such as efficiency, and economy, and effectiveness. This article outlines contemporary Constitutional ethics for public administrators.

Development

The argument that the Constitution provides a basis for public administrative ethics was most convincingly advanced by John A. Rohr in a book called *Ethics for Bureaucrats* (1978).[1] Rohr viewed the Constitution and its interpretation by the courts as encompassing "regime values" that are ethically binding on public administrators and officials. He observed that:

> Because students of public administration either already hold or aspire to positions of leadership within the bureaucracy of a particular regime, the values of that regime are the most likely starting point for their ethical reflections. . . . Because the Constitution of the United States is the preeminent symbol of our political values, an oath to uphold the Constitution is a commitment to uphold the values of the regime created by that instrument. Thus the oath of office provides for bureaucrats the basis of a moral community that our pluralism would otherwise prevent. It is the moral foundation of ethics for bureaucrats. [pp. 60–61]

Constitutional ethics is an area in which morality, as viewed by Rohr, coincides with law. During the 1970s, the U.S. Supreme Court handed down a number of decisions that would make public administrators potentially liable, in a legal sense, for conduct that violates "clearly established statutory or constitutional rights of which a reasonable person would have known . . ." (*Harlow* v. *Fitzgerald*, 1982).[2] The "reasonable person" in this context refers to the public administrator because "a reasonably competent public official should know the law governing his conduct."

The Supreme Court's decisions holding that public administrators may be liable for breaches of individuals' Constitutional rights were revolutionary.[3] In the past, most public administrators and public officials could not be sued on this basis. The change was the capstone of a large number of decisions, beginning in the 1950s, that made public administration more responsive to such Constitutional values (and requirements) as equal protection, due process, and a robust interpretation of individual civil rights and liberties. The landmark cases may be well known to many public administrators. *Brown* v. *Board of Education* (1954, equal protection), *Goldberg* v. *Kelly* (1970, due process), and *Pickering* v. *Board of Education* (1968, public employees' free speech) are among the most salient.[4] Put differently, between the beginning of the 1950s and the end of the 1970s, the clients, employees, inmates, and patients of public administrative organizations were afforded a vast new array of Constitutional rights to protect them in their encounters with official administrative action.[5]

There are many real and potential conflicts between America's administrative doctrine and its Constitutional law. For instance, due process is not necessarily the most efficient process; efforts to protect the public fisc by excluding nonresidents from state or local benefits may be contrary to a judicially recognized Constitutional right to travel, as well as to equal protection; and taking adverse action in the name of effectiveness against public employees who engage in whistleblowing is likely to violate their right to freedom of speech. Consequently, public administrators who are well versed in traditional administrative values, *and whose administrative action is correct according to those values,* are nevertheless vulnerable to suits seeking damages from them for violation of individuals' Constitutional rights. Since among those individuals may be their subordinate employees and job applicants, the potential liability of public administrators for violations of Constitutional rights is vast indeed.

Public administrators' knowledge of Constitutional values, reasoning processes, and requirements can be equated with ethics for three reasons. First, as Rohr contends, because public administrators take an oath of allegiance to the Constitution, its values become morally binding upon them. Second, the standard for potential liability is a moral one—knowledge of Constitutional requirements, which a reasonable public official should have. Third, a premise underlying liability in this context is a familiar moral one: public officials should do as little harm to individuals' rights as possible. In the Supreme Court's words, liability for public administrators is a means of influencing "officials who may harbor doubts about the lawfulness of their intended actions to

THE SCOPE OF GOVERNMENT ETHICS

err on the side of protecting citizens' Constitutional rights" (*Owen* v. *City of Independence,* 1980).[6] The point for public administrators is to internalize Constitutional law and use it as a moral (as well as a legal) guide for their official behavior.

Constitutional Values and Reasoning Processes

Like many ethical codes, the Constitution's requirements are sometimes ambiguous, depend on elaborate balancing of competing concerns, and are not necessarily clearly established in their application to novel circumstances. Consequently, the ethical base of the Constitution reaches beyond clearly established case law. It includes values that must be applied in situations that have not previously arisen. In practice, Constitutional ethics requires specific reasoning processes. Constitutional rights have a *structure.* Certain questions or concerns must be weighed in a sequential order. For instance, one cannot think productively about the Constitutional right to equal protection unless one understands how different types of policy classifications of individuals, such as those based on race, sex, or age, are treated by the courts.

The discussion in this section explains the structure of Constitutional substantive, due process, privacy, and equal protection rights in the context of public administration. It makes clear how the Constitution can be used as an ethical base by indicating how contemporary Constitutional law requires public administrators to incorporate Constitutional values into their thinking when exercising discretion and making decisions.

Substantive Constitutional Rights

Constitutional substantive rights include the free exercise of religion and freedom of speech, press, assembly (association), and travel, among others. Substantive rights are fundamental to the American system of government. They are not absolute, however. They can be abridged under certain circumstances, but rarely, if ever, simply for the sake of administrative convenience. The Supreme Court has repeatedly observed that "the Constitution recognizes higher values than speed and efficiency" (*Stanley* v. *Illinois,* 1972),[7] and consequently, "the fact that a given law or procedure is efficient, convenient, and useful in facilitating functions of government, standing alone, will not save it if it is contrary to the Constitution" (*Immigration and Naturalization Service* v. *Chadha*, 1983).[8] Rather, a statute, policy, or administrative action that infringes upon a substantive Constitutional right must serve a demonstrable compelling governmental interest in the fashion that is least restrictive of that right.

More elaborately, the general structure of substantive Constitutional rights is as follows:

Threshold question:
1. Does the governmental action at issue restrict a substantive Constitutional right of an individual or a group?
2. If not, there is no violation of the Constitution.

Setting the Standard:
1. Does the action serve a compelling or paramount governmental interest in a rational way?
2. If not, the action violates the Constitution.

Establishing the Means:
1. Has the government employed the means for achieving its compelling interest that is least restrictive of substantive Constitutional rights?
2. If not, the action violates the Constitution.

Figure 1 (on page 54) presents the structure of substantive rights in the form of a flow chart.

The ethical base of substantive Constitutional rights should be fully evident. Such rights are highly valued as moral goods. They are considered necessary for individual intellectual and moral development. American government is pledged by the Declaration of Independence to protect them and is restrained by the Bill of Rights and the Fourteenth Amendment from violating them. Restricting such rights in the absence of a compelling need, irrationally or gratuitously, or by a means that is more harmful to them than necessary is both unconstitutional and unethical in the American political culture.

In order to meet the ethical requirements of not violating substantive Constitutional rights, public administrators may often

FIGURE 1
STRUCTURE OF SUBSTANTIVE RIGHTS
(freedom of speech, association, exercise of religion)

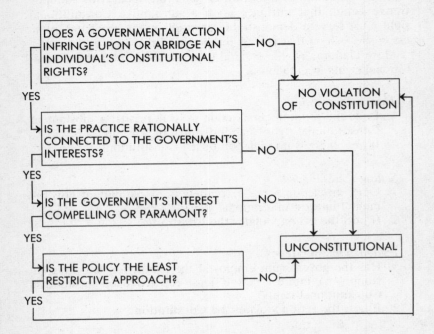

have to give careful consideration to their actions. First, they must be able to identify actions that have implications for such rights. This ability requires general knowledge of Constitutional law and attention to judicial reasoning. Second, they must be able to distinguish between government interests that are compelling and those that are not. In practice, there is no specific test for determining a compelling interest. Presumably, such interests must be vital to the government's ability to function continually and properly. As mentioned earlier, traditional administrative values such as economy, efficiency, and effectiveness are very unlikely to be viewed by the courts as compelling interests. Finally, a great deal of attention must be used in choosing the means to achieve the compelling interest. All plausible alternatives must be evaluated in the light of the extent of their incursion on substantive Constitutional rights. The means that can achieve the compelling interest while doing the least damage to such rights must be selected, almost regardless of cost. Indeed, a federal court once noted that "inadequate resources can never be an adequate justification for the state's depriving any person of his constitutional rights" (*Hamilton* v. *Love*, 1971).[9]

In view of the complexity of the structure of substantive Constitutional rights, public administrators, judges, and others are bound occasionally to reach different conclusions regarding the constitutionality of governmental actions. However, the ethical public administrator will go through the required thought process that has been outlined and will always seek to do the least necessary damage to individuals' substantive Constitutional rights.

Privacy Rights

Privacy rights spring from the Fourth Amendment's protection of "the right of the people to be secure in their persons, houses, papers, and effects, against unreasonable searches and seizures. . . ." Like other Constitutional rights, the concern for privacy has a cognate in ethics. Snooping, eavesdropping, listening in on other people's phone calls, or reading others' mail is generally considered immoral in American society. For administrative actions, other than those involving law enforcement, the key to avoiding breaches of privacy rights lies in the requirement that searches or investigations be *reasonable* in their inception and scope. Reasonability, in turn, depends upon a number of factors, as outlined below:

Threshold question:
1. Does the individual whose privacy is at issue have a reasonable expectation of privacy (that is, one that society is prepared to support) in the specific context involved?
2. If not, there is no violation of privacy rights.

Procedure, rationale, and reasonableness:
1. If there is a proper warrant for the search, it will be Constitutional.

2. If there was probable cause for the search, it will be Constitutional.
3. If a search, other than for purposes of law enforcement, was reasonable in its inception and scope, it will be Constitutional.

The structure of privacy rights is outlined in Figure 2.

FIGURE 2
STRUCTURE OF PRIVACY RIGHTS

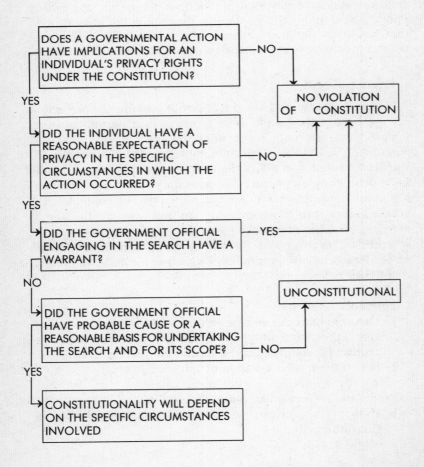

As in the case of substantive Constitutional rights, differences in judgment may arise concerning the appropriateness of governmental action having implications for privacy rights. The threshold question allows for different conclusions. Society is probably not prepared to support a clerk typist's view that her boss should not look inside her filing cabinet for copies of correspondence, whereas it may be prepared to support the same claim of a medical doctor whose files contain information on her patients. Similarly, it is less likely that an employee has a reasonable expectation in his desk drawers than in his briefcase. The case law regarding a reasonable expectation of privacy is exceedingly complex and outcomes often turn on very fine points. Its general thrust, however, is clear: the more likely it is that someone will legitimately regard an area or item as private, the more likely it will be that the threshold of potential invasion of privacy will be crossed by administrative action.

Even if an individual does have a reasonable expectation of privacy, an administrative search will be Constitutional if it meets the test of reasonableness. One of the first requirements is that the public administrator have a clear objective in undertaking the search. Embarking on a "fishing expedition" to see what may turn up is not likely to pass Constitutional muster. Further, the scope of the search must be limited and be closely connected to the administrative function involved. Whereas a search of an employee's files requires only reasonableness, the search of his or her house would require a warrant. When clients of administrative agencies, rather than employees, are involved, similar considerations apply. Midnight searches of welfare recipients' homes without warrants are likely to be unconstitutional, whereas visits by caseworkers, during normal business hours, after notifying the recipient in advance will generally be Constitutional (see *Wyman* v. *James*, 1971; *Parrish* v. *Civil Service Commission*, 1967).[10]

From an ethical perspective, the structure of the Constitutional right to privacy cautions that the public administrator respect individuals' privacy and think carefully about undertaking searches or investigations. Attention must also be paid to information solicited on forms and applications. Depending on the areas it addresses, it may invade an individual's reasonable expectation of privacy and thereby trigger Constitutional concerns.

The Constitutional Right to Procedural Due Process

The Constitutional right to procedural due process, found in the Fifth and Fourteenth amendments, is intended to guarantee that any procedure in which the government deprives an individual of life, liberty, or property will be fundamentally fair. At a minimum, fairness usually requires that the person to be so deprived be given notice of the reasons for the government's action and an opportunity to respond to them. In its most elaborate formulation, procedural due process requires an opportunity for a full-fledged jury trial, with all the technical rules of evidence and procedure it entails, and a right to appeal adverse verdicts.

Procedural due process is important in day-to-day public administration, because it governs the procedures for adverse personnel actions, the termination of welfare benefits and residence in public housing, and the revocation of some types of licenses and permits. Collectively, such benefits or governmental largess are considered a form of "new property" or "property interests" that are treated similarly to traditional property under contemporary Constitutional law (Reich, 1964; *Goldberg* v. *Kelly*, 1970; *Cleveland Board of Education* v. *Loudermill*, 1985).[11]

The extent of process that is due in any given administrative context depends upon a balancing of three considerations:

1. The private interest, such as liberty or property affected by the government's action;
2. The risk that the procedures used will result in an error, and the probable value of additional or other procedures in reducing the error rate;
3. The government's interest in using the procedures afforded, including the administrative and financial burdens that other procedures would entail.

This structure is presented graphically in Figure 3.

Again, the relationship between Constitutional requirements and ethics is readily apparent. Both the ethical duty to be fair to

The Constitution As a Basis for Public Administrative Ethics

FIGURE 3
STRUCTURE OF PROCEDURAL DUE PROCESS RIGHTS

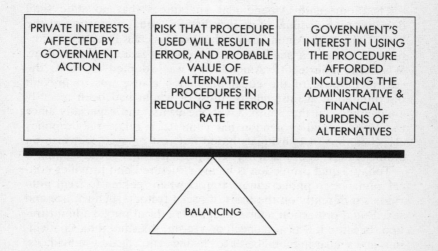

| PRIVATE INTERESTS AFFECTED BY GOVERNMENT ACTION | RISK THAT PROCEDURE USED WILL RESULT IN ERROR, AND PROBABLE VALUE OF ALTERNATIVE PROCEDURES IN REDUCING THE ERROR RATE | GOVERNMENT'S INTEREST IN USING THE PROCEDURE AFFORDED INCLUDING THE ADMINISTRATIVE & FINANCIAL BURDENS OF ALTERNATIVES |

BALANCING

—DUE PROCESS REQUIRES AN APPROPRIATE BALANCE AMONG THESE FACTORS

—THE MORE SUBSTANTIAL THE PRIVATE INTEREST, THE MORE ELABORATE THE PROCEDURES REQUIRED ARE LIKELY TO BE IN ORDER TO AVOID ERRORS

—AT SOME POINT, ADDITIONAL OR SUBSTITUTE PROCEDURAL PROTECTIONS MAY BECOME SO COSTLY THAT THEY WILL NOT BE REQUIRED

others and the Constitution counsel that considerable care be taken to ensure that individuals are not harmed on the basis of arbitrary, capricious, malicious, or just plain erroneous decisions. Of public administrators, who owe a duty to the public, as well as to the specific individuals upon whom they act, both ethics and the Constitution also require a balance that incorporates the public interest in economical and efficient government.

Equal Protection

The Fourteenth Amendment guarantees that no state shall deprive any individual in its jurisdiction "equal protection of the laws." The Fifth Amendment's due process clause has been interpreted to place a similar restraint on the federal government. When the Fourteenth Amendment was adopted in 1868, the central purpose of the equal protection clause was to prevent discrimination against blacks, most of whom had been recently emancipated in the South. Over the years, and especially since the 1950s, equal protection has come to regulate public policy classifications of individuals based not just on race, but also on ethnicity, sex, age, residency, and perhaps other social factors.

Today, equal protection is highly structured and provides ethical guidance to public administrators when seeking to treat individuals differently on the basis of social factors, such as race and sex. Equal protection analysis supports ethical public administration, because it acts as a check on racism, sexism, ethnic chauvinism, and similar immoral bases for taking action against individuals. The general structure of equal protection is as follows:

Threshold question:
1. Does the public policy or practice implicitly or explicitly classify individuals in either an invidious or benign way?
2. If not, there is no violation of equal protection.

"Suspect" classifications:
1. If the classification involves race or ethnicity, its constitutionality is considered suspect.
2. Suspect classifications can be either invidious or benign.

Invidious suspect classifications:
1. Invidious suspect classifications will be Constitutional only if the government can show a compelling interest in using them.
2. The government's claim of compelling interest will be subject to strict judicial scrutiny (that is, probing judicial analysis).
3. If an invidious suspect classification serves a compelling governmental interest and survives strict scrutiny, it may

still be unconstitutional if it is not the least restrictive alternative for achieving the policy objective.

Benign suspect classifications:
1. Benign classifications, such as in affirmative action, are intended to help a group (presumably minorities) who have been discriminated against in the past.
2. Federal policies may be Constitutional if there is a rational basis for them.
3. Nonfederal public policies may be Constitutional if they can meet the strict scrutiny test by demonstrating a compelling governmental interest, such as attempting to remedy past unconstitutional discrimination by the government itself.
4. Benign suspect classifications meeting the above tests will be Constitutional only if they are "narrowly tailored" (that is, limited in scope and duration, realistic, of little or no burden to any group of individuals, and rationally related to a legitimate governmental purpose).

Nonsuspect classifications:
1. Classifications based on factors other than race or ethnicity, such as age, sex, residency, and income, are not suspect.
2. Nonsuspect classifications will be Constitutional if there is a rational basis for them in serving a legitimate governmental function and if they can survive ordinary judicial scrutiny.

Figure 4 (on page 62) maps out the general structure of equal protection rights.

It is important to remember that classification and intention are critical to equal protection rights. If two individuals who are essentially identically situated are treated differently by the government, the appropriate Constitutional concern is due process, not equal protection. Policies that do not explicitly or implicitly create classifications but have a harsher impact on blacks than on whites will not violate equal protection unless the disparate effect is intentional.

FIGURE 4
GENERAL STRUCTURE OF EQUAL PROTECTION RIGHTS
(5th and 14th Amendments)

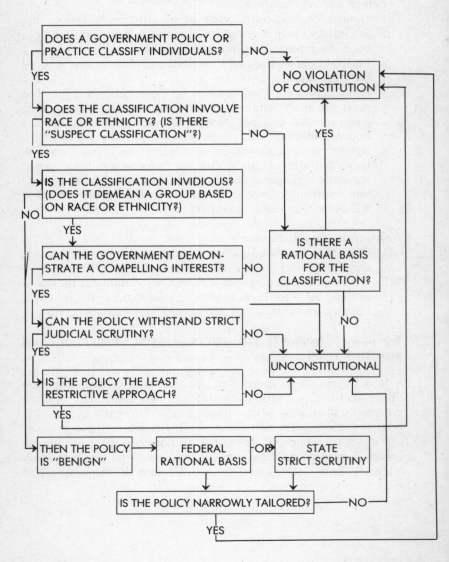

Using the Constitution As a Basis for Public Administrative Ethics

There is a close relationship between many Constitutional rights and appropriate ethical principles for public administrators. The Constitution is both a technical and moral guide for public administrators, who take an oath to support it. Their oath of office obligates public servants to follow the Constitutional law as it affects them in their official capacities. The outlines presented in this article are only guides to the general structure of Constitutional rights at present. Interpretations are often in flux. New cases can result in new law being forged. The application of older frameworks may be modified as judges place greater weight on one factor or another and strike different balances among them.

But following the Constitutional law need not be daunting. Major court decisions are reviewed and discussed in the news media. Most public administrators have access to attorneys employed by their agencies or governmental units. Professional publications, such as the *PA Times* and *IPMA Newsletter* outline relevant cases. Articles in *Public Administration Review* and other professional journals analyze Constitutional trends and decisions. Eventually, agency handbooks and manuals may routinely be adjusted to comply with the broad intent of new developments in Constitutional law.

There are at least two limitations to the Constitution as a basis for public administrative ethics. One can be readily overcome, but the other is inherent. Aggravated noncompliance with Constitutional decisions by a governmental party to a case is not common, though sometimes resources do not exist to implement completely a judicial decision. It is not uncommon, however, for public officials who are not direct parties to a case to refuse to adjust their practices broadly in order to comply with the evolving Constitutional law. For instance, from a technical perspective, the rulings of a federal judicial circuit do not extend beyond that circuit. There is no requirement that public administrators in one circuit adjust their practices so that they comply with the rulings in another circuit. Sometimes this nonalliance is wise, as the circuits disagree or the direction of the law is unclear. In other cases, though, it is unethical, because the same conditions that are known to be unconstitutional are allowed to persist. Prison and public mental health reforms are good examples of the latter. Despite the clear direction of Constitutional law in these areas, many jurisdictions have waited to be sued before bringing their facilities up to Constitutional standards. In fact, a majority of the states have been subject to judicially mandated prison reforms. Such noncompliance can be a useful legal and/or administrative strategy, but it is difficult to view intentionally depriving individuals of their Constitutional rights as ethical administration.

The inherent limitation of the Constitution as a basis for public administrative ethics is that, like law generally, it provides only a minimal floor for acceptable behavior. The Constitution has condoned slavery and legally mandated racial segregation in the past. Today, of course, such practices are considered completely unethical. But contemporary Constitutional interpretation permits capital punishment and fails to treat public policy classifications based on sex as suspect. Perhaps these and other practices that are currently Constitutional will be considered unethical by future generations. Consequently, although it may be appropriate to treat the Constitution as a very important base for public administrative ethics, it should not be considered a complete guide to ethical administrative behavior.

NOTES

1. John A. Rohr, *Ethics for Bureaucrats* (New York: Marcel Dekker, 1978).
2. *Harlow* v. *Fitzgerald*, 457 U.S. 800 (1982).
3. David H. Rosenbloom, *Public Administration and Law* (New York: Marcel Dekker, 1983); David H. Rosenbloom and James D. Carroll, *Toward Constitutional Competence: A Casebook for Public Administrators* (Englewood Cliffs, NJ: Prentice-Hall, 1990).
4. *Brown* v. *Board of Education*, 347 U.S. 483 (1954); *Goldberg* v. *Kelly*, 397 U.S. 254 (1970); *Pickering* v. *Board of Education*, 391 U.S. 563 (1968).
5. Rosenbloom, *Public Administration*.
6. *Owen* v. *City of Independence*, 445 U.S. 622 (1980).
7. 405 U.S. 645 (1972).
8. 462 U.S. 919 (1983).
9. 328 F. Supp. 1182 (1971).
10. *Wyman* v. *James*, 400 U.S. 309 (1971); *Parrish* v. *Civil Service Commission*, 425 P.2d 223 (1967).
11. Charles Reich, "The New Property," *Yale Law Journal*, vol. 73 (1964), pp. 733–787; *Goldberg* v. *Kelly*, 397 U.S. 254 (1970); *Cleveland Board of Education* v. *Loudermill*, 470 U.S. 532 (1985).

Who Wants to Work in Washington?
Robert E. Norton

This final piece in Chapter 1 narrows the scope of government ethics to a pessimistic view. "Who Wants to Work in Washington?" by Robert E. Norton, gives a very realistic account of the consequences of the passage and stringent interpretation of ever more ethics laws at the federal level. Norton suggests that because of these "ethics barriers" many highly qualified individuals from the business world are choosing not to accept high-level appointed positions in government. The results of this "moral mania," coupled with the fact that federal appointees can seldom expect to earn as much in the public sector as they did in private industry, is that good government suffers.

Norton evaluates the Bush Administration's plan to reform federal ethics regulations and again finds reason for gloom and doom. "Who Wants to Work in Washington?" offers a good deal to ponder. If it is indeed the case that ethics laws are having a negative effect upon who will serve in public office and the quality of that service, then there may be a diminishing return to them. And if these laws *are* counterproductive, in which direction does the nation turn to implement ethics in government?

Your secretary sounds a bit flustered. The White House is calling. *The White House!* Brain revving like a sewing machine, you pick up the phone and are told the Administration is looking for a person to fill position X, and your name has surfaced. Would you be at all interested?

Say you would like to think about it, and think hard. The next call may be from a Cabinet Secretary, or if the job is exalted enough—gulp—from the President himself. Your first emotions of pride and patriotism need to be tempered by some more

Robert E. Norton, "Who Wants to Work in Washington?" *Fortune* (August 14, 1989), pp. 77–82. © 1989 The Time Inc. Magazine Company. All Rights Reserved.

practical considerations: Are you prepared to put your life and your finances on public display in fishbowl-on-the-Potomac? Can you afford to take a government job, even for only a few years?

Recently the soiled-laundry list of Washington turpitude and scandal—Michael Deaver, John Tower, Jim Wright. the Department of Housing and Urban Development—has provoked ever tighter interpretations of the federal ethics laws. The current level of persnicketiness has left recent appointees stunned. Says a key aide to a Cabinet Secretary, fresh from the costly and nerve-racking vetting: "I really feel that if average Americans knew what you went through, they would say, 'That's not what we intend.' "

Even as ethical barriers to public service have risen, pay for policy makers and senior civil servants has sunk far below the norms of corporate America. Adjusted for inflation, senior managers' salaries in government, linked historically to Congress's, have plummeted over the past 20 years. Except for a few dozen top jobs, *maximum* pay ranges from about $70,000 to $82,500. Of several hundred people approached for senior jobs in the Bush Administration, fully 40 have refused service on financial grounds alone.

The 51 percent pay raise recommended recently by a presidential commission would have done little more than restore purchasing power lost since 1969. When Congress shot it down, reacting to voter outrage, the salary increases for several thousand senior civil servants died, too. These key managers have themselves been voting, with their feet. Among the very best—those who have won presidential merit awards—the average quit rate in 1986 and 1987 ran at 24 percent annually, with 75 percent of the departees going to industry.

More than five months into the Bush Administration, almost 20 percent of 200 upper-level Cabinet jobs that require presidential appointment [were] still vacant. Though that's about as full up as the Reagan Administration was at the same point, the average period between nomination and confirmation has doubled in the past 20 years, to more than three months.

The incentives for avoiding Washington may well increase. Sleaze has led to paranoia. President Bush has already proposed a new ethics bill, and congressional task forces are busily designing reforms of existing ethics laws. Lawmakers say that the ethics laws are sure to be revised, next year at the latest. The danger is that Congress will weave a bad law that further tangles the existing web of restrictions on public servants. As for pay increases, both President Bush and House Speaker Thomas Foley have recommended them, but politics, rather than sound personnel policy, is likely to shape the final legislation. At peril is one of American government's historical strengths: the cross-pollination brought about by the periodic swapping of roles between bureaucrats and businessmen.

Donald J. Atwood got his phone call just before Christmas, a feeler for the number 2 job at the Defense Department, that of deputy secretary. Vice chairman of General Motors, Atwood, 65, was looking forward to retirement after 29 years at GM. An interview with John Tower followed, well before Tower's own nomination as Secretary of Defense collapsed. After a few more phone calls, the last from President Bush, Atwood said yes. His reasons for coming to Washington, like those of nearly all the past and present public servants interviewed for this article, were laudable. What government and particularly the Defense Department need, says Atwood, are "people who have an understanding of how a business operates and how it is managed."

Atwood knew that his pay would be only $89,500, vs. $625,000 [in 1988] at GM, and that he would probably have to sell his GM stock. (He owned or had options on some 140,000 shares last year.) But he was unprepared for the other sacrifices he was asked to make. All his stocks had to go: AT&T, Exxon, Kodak, even Disney. (Companies that do more than $25,000 a year with the Defense Department are off-limits.) GM cashed out his stock options and other incentives, normally paid over a period of years, at their present value. All these transactions meant capital gains taxes. Atwood declines to put a figure on his losses, but they easily came to $1 million.

That's not all. The ethics enforcers—full-time, federally paid attorneys working with the General Counsel, at the Office of Government Ethics, and in the Defense Department—were uncomfortable because Atwood would be receiving a GM pension and other normal retirement benefits. The theory, Atwood recalls with an edge to his voice, was that if there were a recession GM might be forced to shore up the pension fund, "and that if the recession were deep enough, I would be in a position to give General Motors contracts to prevent it from going bankrupt so it could fund the pension fund and I could receive my pension." The solution: Atwood had to buy an insurance policy, guaranteeing payment of his pension in the event of GM's insolvency. "The ethics team thought that was such a good idea that I then had to take out a second one to cover my life insurance benefits and a third one to cover my health care benefits."

Appointees must sever professional and social as well as financial connections with their past. For John E. Robson, Deputy Secretary of the Treasury and former chief executive at G. D. Searle, one of the more painful steps was resigning from his directorships. He had to give up not just posts on five corporate boards but also several nonprofit positions, including a trusteeship at St. John's College in Annapolis, Maryland, that he had held for 17 years. No laws or rules forbid nonprofit service, but the Administration's ethics counselors, says Robson, "encourage you to become more or less monastic in your approach."

As a potential nominee, you should consider the extent of the financial disclosure you must make. The basic form for executive branch employees requires the listing of any asset valued at more than $1,000, or that generated $100 or more in income during the current year and the last calendar year combined. These include but are "not limited to stocks, bonds, tax shelters, bank accounts, real property, mutual funds, commodities futures, personal businesses, and partnership interests." You can exclude your personal residence, unless you rent it out, but must list precious metals as well as the cash value of your life insurance policies. Once you've added up your assets, you check off one of six boxes, from "$1,001–$5,000," to "over $250,000." In separate sections you must list liabilities of more than $10,000 (not including the mortgage on your home); any agreements or arrangements with employers such as pensions; positions held outside the government, including nonprofit and educational posts; and details of any compensation in excess of $5,000 paid by one source. For ambassadorial appointments, you, your spouse, and your children over 12 must also take an AIDS test.

The Senate confirmation committees have financial disclosure forms of their own, which must also be filled out. These ask for much of the same information, but sometimes in more detail and always in entirely different ways. Robson hired two lawyers and a big accounting firm to do the paperwork. Says he: "I've tried to look at the forms objectively, but it got to be a difficult chore. You find yourself asking, Why is this information going to be important either to public knowledge or to my behavior?"

The basic financial disclosure report, including home address and phone number, is available for review or copying at the Office of Government Ethics in downtown Washington—by anyone, be he Soviet spy, gossip columnist, or brother-in-law. The curious merely attest that they will not use the highly personal and detailed financial information for commercial or criminal purposes or for soliciting money.

America got along without detailed ethics laws until the 1960s. The Kennedy Administration introduced basic rules prohibiting executive branch employees from making policy on matters in which they had a financial interest. Simple disclosure of such information as creditors' names was required in 1965, but only by top officials.

Watergate was the watershed in ethics laws. Congress imposed financial disclosure rules for Senators, Congressmen, and senior staff in 1976 and in 1978 passed the Ethics in Government Act, requiring the financial disclosures that are still in force. The law also set forth rules restricting employment of executive branch officials after they leave government, the broadest of which is a one-year period during which former government employees may not lobby the agency at which they served. Willfully ignoring the disclosure rules is punishable by a fine of up to $5,000. Post-employment violations carry criminal sanctions of up to two years in jail.

Congress wants to go even further. A bill passed [in 1988] would have widened the postemployment restrictions, banning a variety of contacts between former officials and the government. Ronald Reagan vetoed it, noting that it was confusing (it set different standards for three categories of senior Administration officials and different ones for Congress) and that it seemed more likely to punish people for their service to the nation than to prohibit unethical conduct. Another bill, setting forth postemployment restrictions for Defense Department officials involved in procurement, did pass. It carries felony sanctions of up to five years in jail.

A more sweeping bill [has] now [passed] in Congress. It . . . bans . . . Defense Department officials from working for any major defense contractor for two years after leaving government. Accepting compensation of $250 or more during that time could lead to a fine of up to $250,000. Congressman Les AuCoin (D-Oregon), a supporter of the bill, says the aim is to attract managers "who are more interested in the national interest than their own career interest."

Congressman AuCoin, meet Chief Executive Norman R. Augustine, the highly regarded chairman of Martin Marietta, which derived 80 percent of its $5.7 billion in sales last year from government contracts for such products as the Titan space boosters. An aerospace engineer who has spent a third of his 30-year career in government service, Augustine, 54, is said to have turned down positions in both the Reagan and Bush Administrations. He won't talk about that, but he will say this: "I've concluded that there's no way I can serve in government." The conflict-of-interest laws are "sufficiently vague and subject to *ex post facto* interpretation. They've got criminal sanctions. No one wants to be the test case ten years down the road. I certainly don't."

Moral mania creates other kinds of risks for presidential appointees. The test of an action, statement, or behavioral quirk is no longer whether it is right or understandable, excusable or trivial. The test, and it is put exactly this way to potential appointees: how would it look on the front page of the *Washington Post?* Says E. Pendleton James, a chief headhunter in the Reagan White House, now running his own executive search firm: "What worries me is that we're going to wind up with a government of wimps—people who've never done anything controversial, never tried a new idea, never taken risks."

The spotlight can paralyze those who have nothing to hide. Robert Fulton, Oklahoma's secretary of social services, was chosen in February [1989] for the top welfare administration post in the Department of Health and Human Services. Fulton agreed to come to Washington, fired up with plans to "show that Republicans could do something about the welfare crisis." But the right-to-life lobby, already incensed because it felt Bush's HHS secretary,

Louis Sullivan, was soft on abortion, attacked Fulton. Parents of children born at an Oklahoma hospital with spina bifida, a congenital and often fatal birth defect, had sued their doctors in 1985, alleging they had withheld care from the infants. Fulton headed the agency that oversaw the hospital at the time of the suit, but the alleged malpractice happened before he took over. No matter. He was criticized for not punishing the doctors, even though the lawsuit has yet to come to trial. The Bush Administration bowed to pressure from six conservative Senators, and Fulton withdrew his nomination on June 1.

More recently, Drew Altman, New Jersey's commissioner for human services, was forced to pull his name from consideration for head of the Medicare division at HHS, partly because he had endorsed a universal medical insurance plan proposed by Democratic presidential candidate Michael Dukakis. Also, Robert B. Fiske had to withdraw his nomination as deputy attorney general: he was head of the American Bar Association's judicial screening committee when it criticized some of Reagan's choices for the bench.

Low salaries are corroding the government at many levels. Says Chase Untermeyer, director of presidential personnel: "The typical appointee tends to be either an older, well-established individual who's unconcerned about the pay level, or a younger person—some as young as 30—for whom pay is not a consideration." Recruiting for specialized but less visible jobs has become particularly hard. The National Institutes of Health has been unable to hire a single senior biomedical research scientist (salary range: $68,700 to $78,600) from industry or academe in the past ten years.

At the same time, starting salaries for entry-level civil servants are not competitive. Top pay for a beginning engineer at the National Aeronautics and Space Administration is $25,000—that includes a 30 percent premium for hard-to-fill jobs like those in engineering and medicine. Top graduates with a B.S. in engineering can command up to $40,000 in business.

Some senior employees leave government early simply because they cannot afford to stay. H. Robert Heller, 49, quit in June as a Federal Reserve governor. An economist with a background in banking and international monetary policy, Heller considered his

Fed position the ultimate job, and he took more than a 50 percent pay cut when he left BankAmerica in 1986 to accept it. But his $82,500 salary produced biweekly take-home pay of only $1,844.

Being of a statistical turn of mind, Heller calculated that the $15,000 salary paid to a governor when the Fed was created in 1914, adjusted for inflation, would be $180,000 today—or $750,000 if it had kept up with increases in the average manufacturing wage. He also checked to see what retirement benefits he could look forward to if he continued to serve at the Fed to age 65, and found he would qualify for a pension of $1,139 a month—or only $633 for his wife if he died. Had the 51 percent pay raise passed, Heller would have stayed at the Fed. Instead he is taking a job at Visa International, where he reportedly will earn about $250,000 a year.

If the pay had gone up, Noel W. Hinners might still be associate deputy administrator at the National Aeronautics and Space Administration, the No. 3 job. Hinners, 53, came to Washington in 1963 as an AT&T employee on the Apollo project and joined NASA in 1972. He managed to get by on his salary, $80,500 last year, in part because he still lives in the suburban Maryland house he bought in 1965 for $32,500. But with a son nearing college age, Hinners began thinking about leaving government for a job in education or industry when the pay increase fell through. He says, "You find out that a year in school costs $15,000, and you haven't saved that up."

But the new postemployment legislation really made up his mind. Although not officially a procurement official, Hinners was involved in a large number of major NASA contracts, and attorneys warned him that a tough interpretation of the law would bar him from working for any aerospace company for two years after leaving government. Hinners quit on May 13, 1988, three days before the law was supposed to go into effect. He is now vice-president for strategic planning at Martin Marietta. His salary doubled. Eighteen other senior technical people blamed the new rules for their departures from NASA.

Has ethics enthusiasm gone too far? Robert F. Drinan, a Jesuit priest who as a Massachusetts Congressman during the 1970s voted for the Ethics in Government Act, says, "Maybe the day has come for a little deregulation." Drinan, now a law professor at Georgetown, thinks the tough restrictions are steering his students away from government service. But other supporters of the 1988 law, most prominently the self-styled citizens' lobbying group Common Cause, are pushing for even more stringent ethics regulations.

President Bush's reform bill will frame the debate in the months ahead. Many of its proposals are sound. One alone would go a long way toward making government service less burdensome to corporate executives: a deferral of capital gains taxes that result from stock, real estate, or business divestiture required by conflict of interest rules. The idea is to be able to move all the money into a blind trust or mutual fund and pay capital gains only when that investment is cashed out.

Another sensible suggestion would make the ethics laws more uniform across the branches of government by extending them to include members of Congress and their staffs. Administration officials, for instance, have long been prohibited from accepting gifts or free travel. If Congress had been similarly circumscribed, the kind of unseemly conduct that led to the resignations of House Speaker Jim Wright and Democratic whip Tony Coelho would be clearly prohibited. Members of Congress may note that the recent scandals were uncovered under existing rules and that the examples of Wright and Coelho have already had a salubrious effect: More than half the members of the House are now on the record as favoring an outright ban on the $2,000 speaking fees that some members have used as a standard supplement to their income. But bringing Congress under the same rules as the rest of the government would make members more likely to think before enacting even more burdensome ethics laws.

The Bush plan would also bring civil penalties such as fines for conflict of interest violations, reserving criminal sanctions for the most serious cases. This might relieve a potential public servant's worry about being branded a criminal for some technical infraction. It would also make the laws more enforceable. Justice Department prosecutors have been reluctant to unleash the full fury of a criminal indictment in marginal cases.

Some of Bush's recommendations are just plain dumb. The bill would require, for instance, disclosure of the actual dollar value of an appointee's assets rather than the ranges required under

THE SCOPE OF GOVERNMENT ETHICS

present law. A better approach would be to simplify the forms by requiring disclosure of assets only over a given amount, say, $10,000. The Bush plan would require that appointees and civil servants disclose the amount of their home mortgage, which is now exempted. The idea is that public servants could be influenced by the mortgage lender, a risk that seems much too unlikely to justify the invasion of privacy.

At this writing [1989], the Administration is also planning to ask for pay increases of up to 25 percent for senior civil servants and higher raises in a small number of critically skilled positions, for instance, NASA scientists or NIH researchers. A better proposition would be to uncouple executive government compensation permanently from the pay levels of Congress and to construct a more rational, market-based mechanism for adjusting federal salaries.

Like morality, ethics is tough to legislate. Within the year the Administration and Congress will try anyway. The best outcome would be a revision of existing laws and pay standards that would encourage experienced managers to work in Washington—not discourage them.

CHAPTER 2

SCANDAL AND CORRUPTION IN GOVERNMENT

Introduction

In her biography, *So It Goes,* TV journalist Linda Ellerbee relates an episode of White House antics during the first Reagan Administration, which is interesting for its ethical considerations and for the conclusion she draws from it. Her story can be called "Richard Allen and the pizza." Allen was President Reagan's first national security adviser, who was undone (and eventually forced to resign) for allegedly accepting a thousand dollars and a Seiko watch from a Japanese magazine writer to arrange an interview with Reagan's wife, Nancy. The acceptance of gifts is highly regulated in the federal government, and the Allen affair became a scandal. Ellerbee tells how the same week that the Allen story broke, the President was in Cincinnati for a fund-raising dinner speech. After dinner, the President and his entourage were still hungry, so White House aide Ed Rogers ordered forty pizzas with extra cheese from pizza shop owner Mike LaRosa. LaRosa later told reporters that Rogers wanted him to donate the pizza and offered him a pair of Presidential cuff links in return. LaRosa agreed to the donation, figuring it would be good publicity for the cost of the pizza. After all, he liked Reagan.

Comparing these two episodes, Ellerbee muses about the relative nature of values and ethics. "If taking one thousand dollars was wrong, was taking four hundred dollars worth of pizza right?" she asks. But her concluding notes to the story give us a good insight into government ethics: ". . . the government is like a pizza, when it comes to morality, they can always slice it any way they want, and someone else will pay for the cheese." And she also observes: "While it may be true that in a septic tank the really big chunks always rise to the top, it's also true that the smaller pieces clog the system, too."

When it comes to mischief-making in government, any mischief will take its toll on the democratic process, whether it is the act of a President misusing his office or the misdeeds of an unknown clerk in a county agency. This chapter examines scandal and corruption in government. It takes into its purview: (1) Presidential wrongdoing in the Watergate episode; (2) the complex usurpation of policy by Presidential advisers during the Iran-Contra Affair; (3) misconduct on the part of a Speaker of the House; (4) the alleged influence buying of a group of U.S. Senators called the "Keating Five"; and (5) a survey of graft and corruption in state and local governments.

But the lead article of the chapter, "Daniel Webster's Retainer," underscores the crisis in government ethics in two distinct ways. First, it affirms the fact that corruption in government is hardly something new. There are many historical precedents in addition to this account of wrongdoing on the part of Webster. His seeking a retainer in 1833 to work on behalf of the Second Bank of the United States rather than against it and the apparent slush fund established for him by Britain's Lord Ashburton in exchange for his vote on the disputed northeastern boundary of the U.S. are but two items in a long list of infamous doings in American history. This account is an excerpt from *Ethics in Government,* written by Senator Paul H. Douglas of Illinois. Published in 1952, Douglas makes some assertions about the level of ethical standards of Congress at that time. He says that he refers to Daniel Webster's corruption not to tarnish his memory but to point out the "great moral progress which we have made during the last century." Douglas further holds "that there has been an appreciable long-time improvement in the level of political morals." In short, Douglas's book on ethics in government would have us believe that the period of the 1950s was one of high moral standards and ethics in government—at least when compared to that of more than a hundred years earlier.

Many would argue that the conduct of President Richard M. Nixon and his Administration began the current ethics crisis in government. The Watergate scandal, which caused a President to resign from office in disgrace, was marked by political espionage, the use of governmental agencies for partisan purposes, and "dirty tricks"—illegal activities used against those who appeared on Nixon's "enemies list." Thus, the second selection of the chapter assesses the impact of Watergate on all levels of government. "Watergate: Implications for Responsible Government" is part of a report by Frederick C. Mosher and a team of experts from the National Academy of Public Administration.

If Watergate was the preeminent government scandal of the 1970s, the Iran-Contra Affair of Ronald Reagan's Administration was the 1980s' example of how government can be corrupted. The selection concerning the Iran-Contra Affair, reprinted here, consists of an excerpt from the "Executive Summary" of the *Report of the Congressional Committees Investigating the Iran-Contra Affair*. Whereas Watergate involved the misuse of government influence to accumulate personal power, the Iran-Contra episode can be held up as the misuse of government authority to achieve a foreign policy objective that the people, through its representatives in Congress, had specifically rejected. Both episodes, then, count as concrete examples of an ethics crisis, because they both involve a misuse of power that was damaging to the democratic process itself.

The events leading up to and surrounding Speaker Jim Wright's resignation over charges of unethical conduct are portrayed by Janet Hook in "Passion, Defiance, Tears: Jim Wright Bows Out." Wright became the first Speaker of the House of Representatives to resign amid charges of ethical improprieties. He was scrutinized by the House Ethics Committee for a year for violating rules on gifts and income. And in the Senate, the "Keating Five" has become a household phrase, thanks to the alleged influence buying of savings-and-loan magnate Charles Keating, who contributed large sums to the campaigns of five Senators, seemingly in exchange for their assistance in his efforts to gain favorable treatment for his failing enterprises. An overview of the scandal is provided here by reprinting excerpts from Robert S. Bennett's (Special Counsel to the Senate Ethics Committee) "Opening Statement," in effect an informal indictment, when hearings were held by the committee.[1]

"Grass-Roots Graft" closes this chapter, with an in-depth look

---

[1]The Senate Ethics Committee held that four of the "Keating Five" displayed "Poor Judgment" but ordered further investigation of Senator Alan Cranston. Cranston's case is yet to be considered by the whole Senate.

at the ethics crisis in government at the state and local levels. W. John Moore shows that opportunities for corruption and an increased effort on the part of federal prosecutors have led to the uncovering of mischief throughout the nation's Statehouses and city halls. Moore also surveys the attempts of some local governments to implement controls on the rise of corruption.

What the various selections of this chapter have in common is that they sound an alarm; there is no doubt that the nation is in the throes of a crisis. If the trend in American government is one that finds unethical conduct to be commonplace, then the American people need to be alarmed. For as public officials continue to betray the public trust, the erosion of democracy necessarily follows.

Daniel Webster's Retainer
Senator Paul H. Douglas

This brief excerpt from *Ethics in Government* by Senator Paul H. Douglas, originally published in 1952, relates the questionable activities of Daniel Webster, "the great orator of the Senate," in the early and mid-1800s. It is instructive as a reminder that ethics problems have a long history in America and that government ethics is not just a contemporary issue. Douglas recalls Webster's involvement in the debate about whether the Second Bank of the United States should be granted a renewal of its charter. Webster had written the President of the Bank, Nicholas Biddle, and requested that he be paid a retainer not to become an opponent of the charter renewal. Douglas also relates the role that Webster had in the northeastern boundary treaty with Britain, apparently accepting retainers and fees—a kind of "slush fund"—from a British banking house.

The excerpt closes with Douglas's claiming that the 1950s could be held up as a model of high political morality when contrasted to Webster's retainers. He sees "great moral progress" having been made in the last century and continued improvement in political morals. One wonders whether Douglas would reach these same conclusions today.

Senator Paul H. Douglas, "Daniel Webster's Retainer." Reprinted by permission of the publishers from *Ethics in Government* by Paul H. Douglas (Cambridge, MA: Harvard University Press). Copyright © 1952 by the President and Fellows of Harvard College.

. . . [Daniel] Webster was the great orator of the Senate, the revered leader of the Northern Whigs, and Secretary of State in the cabinets of William Henry Harrison and John Tyler. Speaking of the Massachusetts Senator, Carlyle once said that no man could be as great as Daniel Webster seemed to be. Nor in fact was Webster!

Webster was the defender, on the floor of the Senate, of the Second Bank of the United States, which was seeking a renewal of its charter and which was being opposed by President Andrew Jackson. As the bank struggle reached its climax in 1833, Webster kept somewhat aloof from it but on December 21st wrote Nicholas Biddle, the President of the Bank, as follows: "Sir— Since I have arrived here I have had an application to be concerned professionally against the Bank which I have declined of course, although I believe my retainer has not been renewed, or refreshed as usual. If it be wished that my relation to the Bank should be continued it may be well to send me the usual retainers."[1]

This letter, which has seldom been surpassed for its essential blackmail, brought the desired result. The retainer was "refreshed" and Webster girded on the sword of his oratory to do battle for his employer. That others were in a similar position is seen from a memorandum in the Biddle papers in which Nicholas Biddle in 1837 listed the loans which had been made by the Bank "to members of Congress, editors of newspapers and officers of the general Government." Along with Webster there were no less than fifty-four such other men on the list, including both Clay and Calhoun, as well as numerous former cabinet members, three vice-presidents of the United States, and several of the leading editors of the country.[2]

As another sidelight on Webster, one should mention his diplomatic dealings with Great Britain, which have been analyzed by Professor Ralph W. Hidy in his work, *The House of Baring in American Trade and Finance,* and by Professor Samuel F. Bemis in his *John Quincy Adams and the Foundations of American Foreign Policy.* From an examination of the Baring papers, Professor Hidy discovered that Webster was also in receipt of retainers and fees during the 1830s and 1840s from the British banking house of the Barings. This fact assumed sharp significance when

Lord Ashburton came later to this country as British Minister and negotiated with Webster a settlement of the disputed northeastern boundary. Ashburton was himself a member of the Baring family and had been an active partner in the banking firm. Professor Bemis has studied the papers of Lord Aberdeen which are now in the British Museum and has struck a treasure trove in the correspondence between Ashburton (Baring) and Lord Aberdeen, who was the British Foreign Minister. From this correspondence it is clear that Ashburton and Webster were on very close terms. Through Webster, Ashburton discovered that Jared Sparks, Professor of History at Harvard, knew of a map which ostensibly upheld the British claims but which Professor Bemis believes to have been spurious. Webster had previously received appreciable fees from the Barings[3] and there is no doubt that Ashburton (Baring) drew on Lord Aberdeen for approximately $14,000. This was for the ostensible purpose of financing Sparks's trip from Cambridge, Massachusetts, to Augusta, Maine, to convince the Maine legislators that the British claims were correct. Since this trip cost only a relatively few dollars, it is obvious on the basis of internal evidence[4] that "slush" was paid to someone. Professor Bemis believes that Webster was the intermediary. All this may help to explain Webster's acquiescence to a northeastern boundary treaty which was distinctly unfavorable to the United States and his reluctance to push American claims in the Oregon Country.

I do not mention this to besmirch the memory of Daniel Webster for in many ways that gentleman served our country well. But I do so to show the great moral progress which we have made during the last century. . . .

I shall use one further basis for comparison. Our Civil War was fought under the direction of the noblest politician in our history—Abraham Lincoln. And yet, as even that most loving of biographers, Carl Sandburg, relates, there was not only demoralizing graft in virtually every department of government during this period of peril, but Lincoln at times not only put men into positions where he knew they would enrich themselves but also actually used dishonest men to corrupt others in order to obtain what we would consider beneficent ends. Let the skeptic on this point read Sandburg's account of how Lincoln used the corruptionist Simon Cameron, and how Nevada was brought into the

Union and cast the deciding vote to ratify the 13th Amendment, thus freeing the slaves throughout the country. Such tactics would certainly not be countenanced today; nor would the brazen venality of the General Grant era, which Mark Twain satirized in his *Gilded Age*. The railroads of the country then bought legislators as they would cattle in order to obtain land subsidies, and the erstwhile transcendentalist and friend of Emerson, Sam Ward, acted as "king" of the Washington Lobby and corrupted Congress on a wholesale scale.

My own conclusion is, therefore, that there has been an appreciable long-time improvement in the level of political morals. But occasionally there are relapses and these generally come in the wake of great wars. This was true after the Civil War in the period of General Grant to which I have referred and there was another relapse after World War I in the administration of President Harding. The same form of backsliding seems to have occurred in our public life since the end of World War II. Just why moral standards should slip backwards at such times is still something of a mystery. Perhaps war uses up such a large part of the idealism of many men that they tire of living on so unselfish a plane. Perhaps the brutalities of war, which are as real as its idealism, coarsen other men and make them ready to use unworthy means. Possibly this tendency to relapse is heightened by the fact that many war profiteers have made fortunes at a time when others have sacrificed their lives, thus making men feel that the wages of virtue are death and that selfishness ultimately triumphs. These sharp contrasts within society, as well as the fact that the positive idealism of the announced war aims is seldom realized later, disillusion men and make them despair of the life of virtue. In the meantime, the profiteers and speculators who have waxed fat during the war pursue their prosperous course and are ready to practice corruption to achieve their ends. Whatever may be the causes there is no doubt that a backwash of materialism appears at the end of big wars. Nevertheless we should not mistake such temporary setbacks for long-time movements. After each period of moral relapse, the public becomes aroused at the disclosures. Indignation arises, apathy ends, and reforms begin. In the process many who had hitherto drifted with the tide wake up to the realities of right and wrong and, looking at the victims of the disclosures, murmur, if they have compassion in their hearts, "there, but for the grace of God, go I." As they resolve that they will behave better in the future, the level of public morality moves upward.

NOTES

1. See Reginald C. McGrane, *The Correspondence of Nicholas Biddle*, p. 218.

2. Ibid., Appendix I, pp. 357–359. The list with the amounts of the "loans" includes such men as William Appleton of Massachusetts ($10,000), Daniel Webster ($17,782.86), D. D. Tompkins of New York ($10,000), Louis McLane of Pennsylvania ($5,150), S. Smith and Buchanan of Maryland ($1,540,000), James Monroe ($10,596), John C. Calhoun ($4,400), John H. Eaton ($9,000), W. H. Crawford ($1,500), Henry Clay ($7,500), Amos Kendall ($5,375), William C. Rives of Virginia ($5,500), Joel R. Poinsett of South Carolina ($13,100), John Forsythe of Georgia ($20,000), and R. M. Johnson of Kentucky ($10,820). Among the newspaper editors who received large "loans" were James Watson Webb of the New York *Courier and Enquirer* ($18,000), Gale and Seaton, publishers of the *Globe* in Washington ($32,350), Duff Green of the United States *Telegraph* in Washington ($15,600). It is reassuring that the names of John Quincy Adams, Thomas H. Benton, and Francis P. Blair do not appear on Biddle's list.

3. Ralph W. Hidy, *The House of Baring in American Trade and Finance . . . 1763–1861*. The Barings began to pay a retainer to Webster as early as 1831 (p. 100). In 1839, he accepted a special gift of $500 from the Barings and issued an opinion that American state legislatures had possessed the legal and constitutional power to contract loans abroad (p. 284). In the 1840s he fought the repudiation of these foreign loans which had been placed in large part through the House of Baring (p. 316). In 1843, he received a fee from the Barings of $100 and his overdue debt of 482 pounds sterling or about $2,200 was canceled by them (p. 321). Apparently he got $200 more in 1844 (p. 554). He asked for the "profit on the rise of a given quantity of stock within a year" from November 1843, as payment for his services in aiding the resumption of payments in Pennsylvania. This was refused. The American representative of the Barings added: "The only way to do with Mr. Webster is not to give him credit . . . because he has no sense of what is right in money affairs" (pp. 553–554).

4. For the evidence, see Samuel F. Bemis, *John Quincy Adams and the Foundations of American Foreign Policy*, pp. 585–588. Bemis's conclusions are stated earlier in p. 480. "He [Ashburton] paid somebody, presumably Webster, over fourteen thousand dollars—to be exact, two thousand nine hundred ninety-eight pounds sterling and one shilling—to 'compensate' Jared Sparks, . . . and with this 'stimulant' help defeat the 'schemes' of the Democratic Governor of Maine, John Fairfield, and . . . William Pitt Preble, to prevent a radical truncation of their state's territory." As Bemis comments (p. 480), "This large sum was much more than necessary to cover Sparks's traveling expenses from Boston to Augusta and back. A hundred pounds, or four hundred and fifty dollars, would have sufficed for that." For a defense of Webster and Sparks, see Sidney Aronson's unpublished essay, "Samuel Flagg Bemis and the Webster-Ashburton Treaty of 1842," History Department, Harvard University.

Watergate: Implications for Responsible Government
Frederick C. Mosher and Others

This report of the Watergate scandal represents the analysis of a panel from the National Academy of Public Administration to the Senate Select Committee on Presidential Campaign Activities. The opening thesis of the report is that Watergate has had a "shattering impact upon American government at all levels." The questions of what caused Watergate and the changes in government that might prevent future Watergates are then addressed. Among the causes that the panel investigates are: (1) that Watergate was a one-time, aberrant event, the result of "a particular combination of circumstances and of people"; (2) that it grew as an extension of trends begun long ago in American government, which, if unchecked or allowed to flourish without consequence, will continue into the future; and (3) that it was the culmination of a trend, a kind of "cataclysmic shock." It is argued that all three of these interpretations seem plausible and that systemic forces may have shaped the behavior of the Watergate perpetrators.

The panel surveys both the political and administrative climate that immediately preceded the events of Watergate. It points out that one of the sinister aspects of the Nixon Administration was the tendency to blur the distinction between politics and the administration of government, because accumulating Presidential power was the prime motivation of Nixon's men. To prove its point, the panel presents a side-by-side analysis of administrative changes that the Nixon team sought to implement and the many questionable practices that it engaged in. The report concludes with the panel's reviewing the ethical mandates of public office and offering suggestions for changes that might be implemented to enforce those mandates. They suggest that codes of conduct be made

Frederick C. Mosher *et al.*, *Watergate: Implications for Responsible Government* (National Academy of Public Administration, 1974). Reprinted by permission.

more sophisticated, that political appointees be trained in the ethics of public service, that a Federal Service Ethics Board be established, and that each Federal agency appoint an ombudsman to hear complaints of ethics violations within that agency.

Overview

Practitioners and scholars in the field of public administration have an extraordinary interest in the quality of governmental institutions. They share with all citizens a concern that the competence and dependability of governments be achieved and secured. But, beyond this, those who have committed most of their lives to public service—advisers on public policy, practitioners sworn to faithful execution of the laws, and educators of present and future administrators—feel a special obligation to preserve the values that have so long contributed to an effective and progressive social order. They particularly appreciate the absolute necessity of integrity of the leaders in every branch of government—legislative, executive, and judicial. Without such integrity, government cannot gain and retain the confidence of the people it serves.

For these reasons, this Panel of the National Academy of Public Administration is gratified and challenged by the invitation of the leaders of the Senate Select Committee on Presidential Campaign Activities to present its views on issues emerging from the Committee's hearings. The revelations, immediately or remotely associated under the umbrella term "Watergate," have had a shattering impact upon American government at all levels. They have played a major role in causing the citizenry to develop, and to give voice to, growing disillusionment, cynicism, and even contempt for government and politics generally. But there is also a potentially favorable side. The very dimensions of the scandals so far revealed provide an opportunity for reexamination and reform, not of the electoral process alone, but also of other related practices and institutions.

Some of the seeds which grew to Watergate were undoubtedly planted many years and many administrations ago. But the development of these seeds into malpractices seriously injurious to our democratic form of government calls for sober reevaluation of our political and administrative systems and the application of appropriate remedies.

This report is not directed to the identification of individual misdeeds or culprits. Rather it is an effort to identify underlying sources and pitfalls, and to suggest changes in American government and administration which will help make future Watergates less likely, and which will improve the effectiveness and credibility of democratic government over the long range.

Aberration, Extension, or Culmination?

Are the various deviations from proper behavior that are popularly associated with Watergate to be regarded as one-time events, the product of a particular combination of circumstances and of people, mostly at high levels, in a political organization and in the administration? Were they unique in American history and unlikely to recur in the future?

Or was Watergate simply an extension of trends in American politics and government that have been underway for a long time and which could, unless deliberately checked or reversed, be expected to continue, and even worsen, in the future? More profoundly, is it a reflection of developments and deterioration in the very fabric of American society, social, economic, moral, and technological?

Or, finally, was Watergate a cataclysmic shock, a peaking of the trends and forces suggested above, from which society and government may not recover without severe surgery?

It appears to this Panel that Watergate permits all three of these interpretations. Surely it was an aberration in the sense that it resulted from bringing into positions of enormous power a group of people who shared characteristics of personal and ideological loyalty and inexperience in social responsibilities. Surely it will not soon recur—not necessarily because such a collection of people may not again be assembled, but because of the disastrous consequences for many of those involved individually and for the administration generally. Surely it is not the first scandal which sullied American public life. We have had Credit Mobilier, Teapot Dome, political corruption of public relief programs in the

1930s, and Internal Revenue malfeasance in the early 1950s, although none of these had the pervasiveness and shattering impact of Watergate.

On the other hand, one may observe that most of the perpetrators and directors of Watergate misdeeds were reputedly honest and upright persons before they entered the political campaign and/or the administration. Few if any had any record of unethical or dishonest, let alone criminal, activity. This suggests that Watergate was a product of a *system* which shaped and guided the behavior of its participants. (System, as the word is used here, is primarily the product of trends and forces from the past.)

President Nixon, as well as others in his administration, has defended some of his and their actions on the grounds that the same things were done by predecessors in high office. Regardless of the validity of this contention as defensive argument, it is entirely true that many of the actions deplored in this report and elsewhere have precedents in previous administrations of both parties. Indeed, the evidence suggests that most of such practices were growing gradually or sporadically during past decades. They include, for example: (1) use of governmental powers and resources in behalf of friends, against opponents (enemies); (2) politicization of the career services; (3) political espionage on American citizens; (4) excessive secrecy, usually on grounds of national security, whether or not justifiable; (5) use of governmental personnel and resources for partisan purposes, including political campaigns; (6) solicitation of political contributions from private interests with implicit or explicit assurances of support or favor, or of absence of disfavor; and (7) "dirty tricks."

Some have argued that Watergate was a logical, if not inevitable, consequence of trends in the larger systems of our society. Thus one reads and hears that its forebears include, among many other things: the weakening of the family unit and with it the sense of responsibility to and for others; the decline of personal and, therefore, of social morality and of the influence of the churches; the growing interdependence of major elements of the society and of the economy, and of the government with both of these; the increasing power of the national government; the growing interrelationships of the national government with other governments in the world; the increasing prevalence in both public and private spheres of huge bureaucracies, in which the individual is submerged; and the growing dominance of technology.

It would be both inappropriate and impossible for this Panel to address these alleged negative trends in the space and time permitted. The Panel does, however, agree that forces such as these may have contributed to Watergate. But it also believes that government, particularly the national government, has been in the past, and should be in the future, strong, beneficent, and flexible enough to influence these forces toward the benefit of the American people. The ethical and effective conduct of government must provide the model and the leadership for American society.

Watergate is thus both an aberration and an extension of earlier trends. It may also be a culmination of some, if not all, of those trends. As suggested earlier, the revelations in the 12 months of 1973 should themselves deter possible future perpetrators from at least the most blatant of such misdeeds. Certainly, these revelations have alerted the American people and their elected representatives to the danger of future Watergates and initiated a search for legal and other means to thwart or minimize them. Many basic reforms of American government, including the framing of the Constitution itself, have been sparked by conspicuous failings, scandals, tragedies, or disasters.

The Watergate revelations have already stimulated a great deal of concern and discourse about means of political and governmental reform. And there is reason to believe that the Congress and the people whom it represents are more receptive to basic changes than they have been in a long time. The "horrors" which have been, and are still being, exposed have a potentially positive side. They offer an opportunity for corrective actions, many of which should have been taken long ago. If the opportunity is grasped, Watergate will be more than an extension of long-term trends; it will be truly a culmination and watershed.

The Watergate Climate

Some of the witnesses before the Select Committee spoke about the unique and, it would appear, altogether unpleasant "climate" which pervaded the top levels of the administration and the Committee to Reelect the President during and before the Watergate period. In the words of John Dean, Watergate was an "inevitable outgrowth of a climate of excessive concern over the political impact of demonstrations, excessive concern over leaks, and insatiable appetite for political intelligence all coupled with a do-it-yourself White House staff regardless of the law."

The Watergate climate, for convenience, may be treated from two perspectives, the political and the administrative, even though the close interrelationship of the two was one of its central and most sinister features. The prime motivating drive behind both political and administrative activities seems to have been Presidential *power,* its enlargement, its exploitation, and its continuation. Power was perhaps sought by some in the Presidential entourage for its own sake, but it seems fair to conclude that most sought to impose upon the government the ideological views of the President. Paradoxically, a part of that ideology as expounded was to limit the powers of the national government; to return more powers to the people and their elected representatives at state and local levels. The zest for power in the Presidential office is a perfectly expectable, normal, and proper behavior of Presidencies, particularly in the current century—but within limits and constraints, many of which are embedded in the Constitution, and always subject to accountability.

The political climate in the months and, to a lesser extent, for several years before the 1972 election was apparently characterized by an obsessive drive for reelection of the President. It seems to have colored, or sought to color, governmental plans, decisions, and behavior during that period, even in fields of activity intended and believed to be politically neutral—administration of the revenue laws, antitrust prosecutions, allocation of grants and contracts, clearance of career service appointments and promotions, and many others.

Synchronized by the White House and its immediate appendage, the Committee to Reelect the President, the program was directed primarily, if not almost exclusively, to the reelection of the President, not to the victory of his party or of other nominees of the same party in the same general election. It is evident that the imperative to reelect was so driving as to override many other considerations, including the public interest and normal ethical and legal constraints.

The President, in explaining the behavior of his subordinates, described them as "people whose zeal exceed their judgment, and who may have done wrong in a cause they deeply believed in to be right." But some of those whose behavior the President described so mildly readily admitted later that, in their minds and consciences, the demand to reelect was so overwhelming as to justify acts admittedly criminal. John Mitchell, in his testimony before the Select Committee, made it clear that he considered the reelection of President Nixon to be more important than his obligation to tell the President that people around him were involved in perjury and other crimes, even though he could find no Constitutional basis for such a conclusion.

The political environment, both before and following the campaign of 1972, was entirely consonant with that of the campaign itself. The Administration was in a state of siege from its critics, some of whom were seen as threats not only to it alone, but also to the security of the nation itself. Administration proposals were advanced, the potential costs of which so far exceeded their potential benefits, even in strictly political terms, as later to be construed as stupid, even absurd. The White House became a command post for conduct by the President's staff of near warfare against those whom it considered "enemies."

Following the "mandate" of the 1972 election, the Administration moved to cleanse itself of senior officials in many executive agencies who were considered to be hesitant or doubtful followers of the views and ideology of the President. In terms of top-level political appointees, the transition between the first and second Nixon terms was as extreme as most transitions from one party to the other. Many experienced Republicans in key posts were replaced by others, usually younger, in whom the Administration presumably had greater confidence of personal and ideological loyalty, and who were innocent of prior allegiances to the agency of their appointment or its associated clienteles. In this and other ways the Administration undertook to carry out and enforce its electoral "mandate," even before the inauguration in 1973.

The administrative climate was, to some extent, a product of the political climate: aggressive efforts were made to use administrative machinery to carry out political and policy ends, and growing frustration and exasperation developed over alleged bureaucratic impediments. In part, it was a further step in the evolution of a strong Presidency—a movement which had begun generations earlier and which students of American government have generally approved, at least since the report of the President's Committee on Administrative Management (the Brownlow Report) submitted in 1937.

Taken individually, the majority of changes that the Administration instituted or sought were consistent with sound administrative practices; indeed, a good many leaders in public administration had recommended some of them earlier and specifically endorsed them after they were proposed by the President. They included:

- Formation of regions with common headquarters and boundaries to encompass many of the domestic field agencies and activities
- Establishment of regional councils to provide better coordination of federal activities in regions and areas
- Delegation of federal powers from Washington to the field
- Unconditional grants to state and local governments (called general revenue sharing)
- Broader categories of, and fewer strings on, functional grants to state and local governments (called special revenue sharing)
- Formation of a Domestic Council to parallel, in domestic affairs, the National Security Council in foreign affairs
- Strengthening of the managerial role of the Bureau of the Budget (which became the Office of Management and Budget), and vesting of all of its statutory powers in the President
- Consolidation of the activities of most of the domestic departments in four "superdepartments," rationally organized according to subject matter areas
- Formation of a "Federal Executive Service" to encompass all supergrade employees whose qualifications would be approved and whose assignments and salaries would be flexible according to managerial needs
- Encouraging the administrative practices associated with the term "management by objective"
- Placing postal activities in a quasi-governmental corporation and removing the Postmaster General from the Cabinet
- Interposing above the specialized, professionalized, "parochial" bureaucracies generalists with a broader perspective

But these mostly constructive actions and proposals were accompanied by a number of others which students of government, even those with the strongest commitment to Presidential energy and influence, found questionable. These included:

- Usurpation by the White House of powers over both policy and day-to-day operations heretofore carried on in the departments and other established agencies
- Enormous growth of the White House staff, accompanied by the establishment of a tight hierarchy within it
- Bypassing of departments and agencies in areas of their assigned responsibilities, first in international and defense matters through the staff director of the National Security Council, and later through the staff director of the Domestic Council
- Veiling of White House activities on grounds of national security or executive privilege
- Negating of substantial majorities of both houses of the Congress on policy and program matters through accelerating use of the veto power and impoundment of funds
- Interposition of White House aides between the President and the official heads of the executive agencies, such aides having been appointed without confirmation or even public knowledge
- The abortive attempt to interpose Presidential counselors in the White House with substantial control over established departments

Considered singly or separately, few of the actions or proposals in the foregoing lists would be cause for great alarm. However, if all of them had been effectuated, the administrative weather could have become very stormy indeed. The American state then would have approached a monocracy, ruled from the top through a strictly disciplined hierarchical system. It would have become difficult to pin responsibility for decisions or actions upon anyone short of the top man, and he was, for the most part, inaccessible and unaccountable. As some of his appointees have pointed out, the only ultimate means of holding the President answerable following his election or reelection is impeachment.

The administrative and political aspects of the governmental climate were increasingly interlocked, at least until the spring of 1973. Together they constituted a critical threat to many of the values and protections Americans associate with a democratic system of government, including:

- The right to participate or be represented in decisions affecting citizens
- The right to equal treatment
- The right to know
- Free and honest elections
- Assurance of Constitutional protections such as those in the First and Fourth Amendments
- A balance of countervailing powers to prevent usurpation by any single power—as among the branches of government, the political parties or sectors of parties, interest groups, and geographic sections
- Ethical conduct of public officials in pursuit of the public interest

This panel entertains no delusions that these precepts have not been violated or threatened before—well before—the first Nixon administration. It is possible that many of the revelations of the last two years were repetitions of earlier actions never revealed. Indeed, we owe our present knowledge to an obscure and lonely guard in the Watergate Apartments, to the fact that there was an unmarked police car nearby, to a couple of aggressive reporters, to the Senate Select Committee, to the Special Prosecutors, and to some unidentified leaks to the press. The problems we here address are not partisan problems. They are problems for all parties, for all citizens.

Epilogue
Ethics and Public Office

Most of this report has concerned, directly or indirectly, the subject of ethics in the public service. So did most of the hearings before the Senate Select Committee. The investigative power of the Congress may well be a more effective instrument than the criminal procedures of the courts in exposing, and thereby protecting the public from, unethical behavior on the part of its officials.

> The only thing that could and can avail the body politic *in extremis* is the charter of the Select Committee, committing it to the investigation of unethical—not just illegal—conduct in the 1972 campaign. The unethical is not necessarily—not even often—the illegal, as Congress attested in separating the two. It was the unethical not the illegal, activities in 1972 that did this country down. . . .[1]

Many of the actions associated with Watergate, the burglary of offices, the forgery of a letter, the laundering of money through Mexico, and so on, were clearly criminal. But in their relation to the national interest each by itself was less than crucial. What was important were the attitudes of mind, the modes of conspiring, and the narrow goals of those behind them. Many of these kinds of matters lie beyond the range of criminal law.

Public officials are of course bound by the same criminal laws as apply to other citizens. But their obligations to the public as a whole entail an additional and more rigorous set of standards and constraints associated with the concept of public trust. Many practices which are permissible, even normal, in the private sector are, or should be, forbidden in government: acceptance of certain kinds of gifts, discussion of appointments under certain circumstances, promise or threat of governmental action under some circumstances, carrying and secreting of large amounts of cash, withholding of information to which the public should be alerted, and, conversely, leaking or other disclosure of other kinds of information which should be private.

One of the characteristics of many of those implicated in Watergate was their perception of the roles and responsibilities of government, a perception which was at best simplistic, and at worst venal and dangerous. A democratic government is not a family business, dominated by its patriarch; nor is it a military battalion, or a political campaign headquarters. It is a producing organization which belongs to its members, and it is the only such organization whose members include *all* the citizens within its jurisdiction. Those who work for and are paid by the government are ultimately servants of the whole citizenry, which owns and supports the government.

Complementary to the ingenuousness of the appreciation of the sense of the word "public" in these recent developments was the apparent lack of understanding of "service." In a society in which sovereignty presumably rests in the people, it is indispensable that its officials be regarded and regard themselves as servants, not masters, of the people. They must have and exercise powers, but their powers are delegated, usually for temporary periods.

A ten-point Code of Ethics for Government Service was adopted by Congress in a concurrent resolution in 1958, and its provisions were subsequently incorporated in the *Federal Personnel Manual*. In May 1961 President Kennedy issued Executive Order 10939 as a Guide on Ethical Standards to Government Officials; it was specifically pointed to those occupying positions of highest responsibility. Many federal agencies have issued their own minimal standards of conduct, applying to the specific business of the individual agencies, and most of them have some machinery for guidance and enforcement through legal counsel or inspectorates. Yet Watergate happened.

The Panel has considered a number of possible steps the government might take to strengthen ethical standards, particularly of noncareer officials, and suggests them for the consideration of the Select Committee. They include:

- Improving and making more sophisticated the codes and guidances of ethics in public service
- Incorporating in the oath of office, sworn to by all new officers and employees, the Code of Ethics, and requiring each at the time to read it and certify in writing that he or she has done so
- Requiring that new political appointees attend briefing sessions on the ethics of public service; such briefings would cover ethical conduct, accountability, the nature of checks and balances in government, the importance of responsiveness to the public, and the relationships between career and noncareer services
- Creating a Federal Service Ethics Board, comparable to similar boards that have been established in some state and local

governments, to set forth general guidelines for all employees and to investigate particularly important and difficult ethical questions that are brought before it
• Providing a governmentwide ombudsman or one in each major agency to consider complaints of ethical violations in the federal service

The effectiveness of codes and mechanisms for their enforcement depends first upon continuing scrutiny of the decisions and actions of public officials: by their fellows in administration, by the other branches of government, by their professional associates in and out of government, by the media, and by the general public. Such scrutiny in turn hinges on openness and accountability. For those who might be tempted to unethical behavior for want of understanding or conscience, the threat of future revelation and scrutiny can be a considerable deterrent.

But there is no "fail-safe" mechanism whereby appropriate ethics of public officers and the public interest may be assured, and whereby the ethics of public employees may be enforced. Ultimately, the assurance of high standards of ethical behavior depends upon the people who aspire to and gain public office, and more particularly upon the system of values they have internalized. The Panel reiterates its urging that the educational institutions around the nation, especially those professional schools which provide significant numbers of public officials, focus more attention on public service ethics. A guiding rule of such instruction and of subsequent official decisions should be that propounded many years ago by Thomas Jefferson:

Whenever you are to do a thing, though it can never be known but to yourself, ask yourself how you would act were all the world looking at you, and act accordingly.[2]

NOTES

1. Milton Meyer, "From Deliquescence to Survival—Watergate and Beyiond," *Center Report,* Center for the Study of Democratic Institutions (February 1974), p. 27.
2. In a letter to Peter Carr from Paris, France, August 19, 1785.

The Iran-Contra Affair
Executive Summary of the
Report of the Congressional Committees
Investigating the Iran-Contra Affair

The Administration of President Ronald Reagan was shocked by a number of ethics scandals. There were incidents, collectively referred to as the "sleaze factor," involving more than 100 high-level individuals in the Administration who were either indicted or formally investigated for alleged improprieties. But the most devastating scandal to touch the Reagan Administration was given the name "the Iran-Contra Affair." This incident involved a complex web of deception that had the effect of subverting the will of Congress on the issue of continued United States military backing of the revolutionary guerrilla forces in Nicaragua known as the "Contras." The scheme involved the sale of arms to Iran and the transfer of the proceeds from those sales into the hands of the Contras. Clandestinely, additional money from governments and international figures was raised for these "freedom fighters," as Reagan had referred to them on many occasions. Congress had already passed the Boland Amendment, however, which prohibited the United States from actively supporting the Contras' military effort.

The affair catapulted Marine Lieutenant Colonel Oliver North into national prominence. North was a central figure in the affair, having set in motion and overseen many of its transactions. He appeared before Congress and admitted having lied about his surreptitious activities on behalf of the Contras. North was equally proclaimed a national hero (another Reagan attribution) and vilified as a national disgrace. Reprinted here is an excerpt from the "Executive Summary" of the *Report of the Congressional Committees Investigating the Iran-Contra Affair*.

Executive Summary of the Report of the Congressional Committees Investigating the Iran-Contra Affair (Senate Select Committee on Secret Military Assistance to Iran and the Nicaragua Opposition and House Select Committee to Investigate Covert Arms Transactions with Iran) (Washington, DC: U.S. Government Printing Office, 1988).

Findings and Conclusions

The common ingredients of the Iran and Contra policies were secrecy, deception, and disdain for the law. A small group of senior officials believed that they alone knew what was right. They viewed knowledge of their actions by others in the Government as a threat to their objectives. They told neither the Secretary of State, the Congress nor the American people of their actions. When exposure was threatened, they destroyed official documents and lied to Cabinet officials, to the public, and to elected representatives in Congress. They testified that they even withheld key facts from the President [Ronald Reagan].

The United States Constitution specifies the process by which laws and policy are to be made and executed. Constitutional process is the essence of our democracy and our democratic form of Government is the basis of our strength. Time and again we have learned that a flawed process leads to bad results, and that a lawless process leads to worse.

Policy Contradictions and Failures

The Administration's departure from democratic processes created the conditions for policy failure, and led to contradictions which undermined the credibility of the United States.

The United States simultaneously pursued two contradictory foreign policies—a public one and a secret one:

- The public policy was not to make any concessions for the release of hostages lest such concessions encourage more hostage-taking. At the same time, the United States was secretly trading weapons to get the hostages back.
- The public policy was to ban arms shipments to Iran and to exhort other Governments to observe this embargo. At the same time, the United States was secretly selling sophisticated missiles to Iran and promising more.
- The public policy was to improve relations with Iraq. At the same time, the United States secretly shared military intelligence on Iraq with Iran and [Lt. Col. Oliver] North told the Iranians in contradiction to United States policy that the

United States would help promote the overthrow of the Iraqi head of government.

- The public policy was to urge all Governments to punish terrorism and to support, indeed encourage, the refusal of Kuwait to free the Da'wa prisoners who were convicted of terrorist acts. At the same time, senior officials secretly endorsed a Secord-Hakim [Richard V. Secord and Albert Hakim] plan to permit Iran to obtain the release of the Da'wa prisoners.
- The public policy was to observe the "letter and spirit" of the Boland Amendment's proscriptions against military or paramilitary assistance to the Contras. At the same time, the [National Security Council] staff was secretly assuming direction and funding of the Contras' military effort.
- The public policy, embodied in agreements signed by [CIA] Director [William J.] Casey, was for the Administration to consult with the Congressional oversight committees about covert activities in a "new spirit of frankness and cooperation." At the same time, the CIA and the White House were secretly withholding from those Committees all information concerning the Iran initiative and the Contra support network.
- The public policy, embodied in Executive Order 12333, was to conduct covert operations solely through the CIA or other organs of the intelligence community specifically authorized by the President. At the same time, although the NSC was not so authorized, the NSC staff secretly became operational and used private, non-accountable agents to engage in covert activities.

These contradictions in policy inevitably resulted in policy failure:

- The United States armed Iran, including its most radical elements, but attained neither a new relationship with that hostile regime nor a reduction in the number of American hostages.
- The arms sales did not lead to a moderation of Iranian policies. Moderates did not come forward, and Iran to this day sponsors actions directed against the United States in the Persian Gulf and elsewhere.
- The United States opened itself to blackmail by adversaries

who might reveal the secret arms sales and who, according to North, threatened to kill the hostages if the sales stopped.
- The United States undermined its credibility with friends and allies, including moderate Arab states, by its public stance of opposing arms sales to Iran while undertaking such arms sales in secret.
- The United States lost a $10 million contribution to the Contras from the Sultan of Brunei by directing it to the wrong bank account—the result of an improper effort to channel that humanitarian aid contribution into an account used for lethal assistance.
- The United States sought illicit funding for the Contras through profits from the secret arms sales, but a substantial portion of those profits ended up in the personal bank accounts of the private individuals executing the sales—while the exorbitant amounts charged for the weapons inflamed the Iranians with whom the United States was seeking a new relationship.

Flawed Policy Process

The record of the Iran-Contra Affair also shows a seriously flawed policymaking process.

Confusion

There was confusion and disarray at the highest levels of Government.

- [Robert C.] McFarlane embarked on a dangerous trip to Tehran under a complete misapprehension. He thought the Iranians had promised to secure the release of all hostages before he delivered arms, when in fact they had promised only to seek the hostages' release, and then only after one planeload of arms had arrived.
- The President first told the Tower Board [the Tower Board was the panel appointed to review the affair named after its chairman, John Tower] that he had approved the initial Israeli shipments. Then, he told the Tower Board that he had not. Finally, he told the Tower Board that he does not know

whether he approved the initial Israeli arms shipments, and his top advisers disagree on the question.

- The President claims he does not recall signing a Finding approving the November 1985 HAWK shipment to Iran. But [Vice-Adm. John M.] Poindexter testified that the President did sign a Finding on December 5, 1985, approving the shipment retroactively. Poindexter later destroyed the Finding to save the President from embarrassment.

- That Finding was prepared without adequate discussion and stuck in Poindexter's safe for a year; Poindexter claimed he forgot about it; the White House asserts the President never signed it; and when events began to unravel, Poindexter ripped it up.

- The President and the Attorney General [Edwin Meese III] told the public that the President did not know about the November 1985 Israeli HAWK shipment until February 1986—an error the White House Chief of Staff explained by saying that the preparation for the press conference "sort of confused the Presidential mind."

- Poindexter says the President would have approved the diversion, if he had been asked; and the President says he would not have.

- One National Security Adviser understood that the Boland Amendment applied to the NSC; another thought it did not. Neither sought a legal opinion on the question.

- The President incorrectly assured the American people that the NSC staff was adhering to the law and that the Government was not connected to the Hasenfus airplane. His staff was in fact conducting a "full service" covert operation to support the President which they believed he had authorized.

- North says he sent five or six completed memorandums to Poindexter seeking the President's approval for the diversion. Poindexter does not remember receiving any. Only one has been found.

Dishonesty and Secrecy

The Iran-Contra Affair was characterized by pervasive dishonesty and inordinate secrecy.

North admitted that he and other officials lied repeatedly to

Congress and to the American people about the Contra covert action and Iran arms sales, and that he altered and destroyed official documents. North's testimony demonstrates that he also lied to members of the Executive branch, including the Attorney General, and officials of the State Department, CIA and NSC.

Secrecy became an obsession. Congress was never informed of the Iran or the Contra covert actions, notwithstanding the requirement in the law that Congress be notified of all covert actions in a "timely fashion."

Poindexter said that Donald Regan, the President's Chief of Staff, was not told of the NSC staff's fundraising activities because he might reveal it to the press. Secretary [of State George] Shultz objected to third-country solicitation in 1984 shortly before the Boland Amendment was adopted; accordingly, he was not told that, in the same time period, the National Security Adviser had accepted an $8 million contribution from Country 2 even though the State Department had prime responsibility for dealings with that country. Nor was the Secretary of State told by the President in February 1985 that the same country had pledged another $24 million—even though the President briefed the Secretary of State on his meeting with the head of state at which the pledge was made. Poindexter asked North to keep secrets from Casey; Casey, North, and Poindexter agreed to keep secrets from Shultz.

Poindexter and North cited fear of leaks as a justification for these practices. But the need to prevent public disclosure cannot justify the deception practiced upon Members of Congress and Executive branch officials by those who knew of the arms sales to Iran and of the Contra support network. The State and Defense Departments deal each day with the most sensitive matters affecting millions of lives here and abroad. The Congressional Intelligence Committees receive the most highly classified information, including information on covert activities. Yet, according to North and Poindexter, even the senior officials of these bodies could not be entrusted with the NSC staff's secrets because they might leak.

While Congress's record in maintaining the confidentiality of classified information is not unblemished, it is not nearly as poor or perforated as some members of the NSC staff maintained. If the Executive branch has any basis to suspect that any member of the Intelligence Committees breached security, it has the obligation to bring that breach to the attention of the House and Senate Leaders—not to make blanket accusations. Congress has the capability and responsibility of protecting secrets entrusted to it. Congress cannot fulfill its legislative responsibilities if it is denied information because members of the Executive branch, who place their faith in a band of international arms merchants and financiers, unilaterally declare Congress unworthy of trust.

In the case of the "secret" Iran arms-for-hostages deal, although the NSC staff did not inform the Secretary of State, the Chairman of the Joint Chiefs of Staff, or the leadership of the United States Congress, it was content to let the following persons know:

- Manucher Ghorbanifar, who flunked every polygraph test administered by the U.S. Government;
- Iranian officials, who daily denounced the United States but received an inscribed Bible from the President;
- Officials of Iran's Revolutionary Guard, who received the U.S. weapons;
- Secord and Hakim, whose personal interests could conflict with the interests of the United States;
- Israeli officials, international arms merchants, pilots and air crews, whose interests did not always coincide with ours; and
- An unknown number of shadowy intermediaries and financiers who assisted with both the First and Second Iranian Channels.

While sharing the secret with this disparate group, North ordered the intelligence agencies not to disseminate intelligence on the Iran initiative to the Secretaries of State and Defense. Poindexter told the Secretary of State in May 1986 that the Iran initiative was over, at the very time the McFarlane mission to Tehran was being launched. Poindexter also concealed from cabinet officials the remarkable nine-point agreement negotiated by Hakim with the Second Channel. North assured the FBI liaison to the NSC as late as November 1986 that the United States was not bargaining for the release of hostages but seizing terrorists to exchange for hostages—a complete fabrication. The lies, omissions, shredding, attempts to rewrite history—all continued, even after the President authorized the Attorney General to find out the facts.

It was not operational security that motivated such conduct—not when our own Government was the victim. Rather, the NSC staff feared, correctly, that any disclosure to Congress or the cabinet of the arms-for-hostages and arms-for-profit activities would produce a storm of outrage.

As with Iran, Congress was misled about the NSC staff's support for the Contras during the period of the Boland Amendment, although the role of the NSC staff was no secret to others. North testified that his operation was well-known to the press in the Soviet Union, Cuba, and Nicaragua. It was not a secret from Nicaragua's neighbors, with whom the NSC staff communicated throughout the period. It was not a secret from the third countries—including a totalitarian state—from whom the NSC staff sought arms or funds. It was not a secret from the private resupply network which North recruited and supervised. According to North, even Ghorbanifar knew.

The Administration never sought to hide its desire to assist the Contras so long as such aid was authorized by statute. On the contrary, it wanted the Sandinistas to know that the United States supported the Contras. After enactment of the Boland Amendment, the Administration repeatedly and publicly called upon Congress to resume U.S. assistance. Only the NSC staff's Contra support activities were kept under wraps. The Committees believe these actions were concealed in order to prevent Congress from learning that the Boland Amendment was being circumvented.

It was stated on several occasions that the confusion, secrecy, and deception surrounding the aid program for the Nicaraguan freedom fighters was produced in part by Congress' shifting positions on Contra aid.

But Congress' inconsistency mirrored the chameleon-like nature of the rationale offered for granting assistance in the first instance. Initially, Congress was told that our purpose was simply to interdict the flow of weapons from Nicaragua into El Salvador. Then Congress was told that our purpose was to harass the Sandinistas to prevent them from consolidating their power and exporting their revolution. Eventually, Congress was told that our purpose was to eliminate all foreign forces from Nicaragua, to reduce the size of the Sandinista armed forces, and to restore the democratic reforms pledged by the Sandinistas during the overthrow of the Somoza regime.

Congress had cast a skeptical eye upon each rationale proffered by the Administration. It suspected that the Administration's true purpose was identical to that of the Contras—the overthrow of the Sandinista regime itself. Ultimately Congress yielded to domestic political pressure to discontinue assistance to the Contras, but Congress was unwilling to bear responsibility for the loss of Central America to communist military and political forces. So Congress compromised, providing in 1985 humanitarian aid to the Contras; and the NSC staff provided what Congress prohibited: lethal support for the Contras.

Compromise is no excuse for violation of law and deceiving Congress. A law is no less a law because it is passed by a slender majority, or because Congress is open-minded about its reconsideration in the future.

Privatization

The NSC staff turned to private parties and third countries to do the Government's business. Funds denied by Congress were obtained by the Administration from third countries and private citizens. Activities normally conducted by the professional intelligence services—which are accountable to Congress—were turned over to Secord and Hakim.

The solicitation of foreign funds by an Administration to pursue foreign policy goals rejected by Congress is dangerous and improper. Such solicitations, when done secretly and without Congressional authorization, create a risk that the foreign country will expect and demand something in return. McFarlane testified that "any responsible official has an obligation to acknowledge that every country in the world will see benefit to itself by ingratiating itself to the United States." North, in fact, proposed rewarding a Central American country with foreign assistance funds for facilitating arms shipments to the Contras. And Secord, who had once been in charge of the U.S. Air Force's foreign military sales, said "where there is a quid, there is a quo."

Moreover, under the Constitution only Congress can provide funds for the Executive branch. The Framers intended Congress's "power of the purse" to be one of the principal checks on Executive action. It was designed, among other things, to prevent the Executive from involving this country unilaterally in a foreign conflict. The Constitutional plan does not prohibit a President from asking a foreign state, or anyone else, to contribute funds to a third party. But it does prohibit such solicitation where the United States exercises control over their receipt and expenditure. By circumventing Congress' power of the purse through third-country and private contributions to the Contras, the Administration undermined a cardinal principle of the Constitution.

Further, by turning to private citizens, the NSC staff jeopardized its own objectives. Sensitive negotiations were conducted by parties with little experience in diplomacy, and financial interests of their own. The diplomatic aspect of the mission failed—the United States today has no long-term relationship with Iran and no fewer hostages in captivity. But the private financial aspect succeeded—Secord and Hakim took $4.4 million in commissions and used $2.2 million more for their personal benefit: in addition, they set aside reserves of over $4 million in Swiss bank accounts of the Enterprise.

Covert operations of this Government should only be directed and conducted by the trained professional services that are accountable to the President and Congress. Such operations should never be delegated, as they were here, to private citizens in order to evade Governmental restrictions.

Lack of Accountability

The confusion, deception, and privatization which marked the Iran-Contra Affair were the inevitable products of an attempt to avoid accountability. Congress, the Cabinet, and the Joint Chiefs of Staff were denied information and excluded from the decision-making process. Democratic procedures were disregarded.

Officials who make public policy must be accountable to the public. But the public cannot hold officials accountable for policies of which the public is unaware. Policies that are known can be subjected to the test of reason, and mistakes can be corrected after consultation with the Congress and deliberation within the Executive branch itself. Policies that are secret become the private preserve of the few, mistakes are inevitably perpetuated,

SCANDAL AND CORRUPTION IN GOVERNMENT

and the public loses control over Government. That is what happened in the Iran-Contra Affair:

- The President's NSC staff carried out a covert action in furtherance of his policy to sustain the Contras, but the President said he did not know about it.
- The President's NSC staff secretly diverted millions of dollars in profits from the Iran arms sales to the Contras, but the President said he did not know about it and Poindexter claimed he did not tell him.
- The Chairman of the Joint Chiefs of Staff was not informed of the Iran arms sales, nor was he ever consulted regarding the impact of such sales on the Iran-Iraq war or on U.S. military readiness.
- The Secretary of State was not informed of the millions of dollars in Contra contributions solicited by the NSC staff from foreign governments with which the State Department deals each day.
- Congress was told almost nothing—and what it was told was false.

Deniability replaced accountability. Thus, Poindexter justified his decision not to inform the President of the diversion on the ground that he wanted to give the President "deniability." Poindexter said he wanted to shield the President from political embarrassment if the diversion became public.

This kind of thinking is inconsistent with democratic governance. "Plausible denial," an accepted concept in intelligence activities, means structuring an authorized covert operation so that, if discovered by the party against whom it is directed, United States involvement may plausibly be denied. That is a legitimate feature of authorized covert operations. In no circumstance, however, does "plausible denial" mean structuring an operation so that it may be concealed from—or denied to—the highest elected officials of the United States government itself.

The very premise of democracy is that "we the people" are entitled to make our own choices on fundamental policies. But freedom of choice is illusory if policies are kept, not only from the public, but from its elected representatives.

Intelligence Abuses

Covert Operations

As former National Security Adviser Robert McFarlane testified, "It is clearly unwise to rely on covert action as the core of our policy." The Government cannot keep a policy secret and still secure the public support necessary to sustain it. Yet it was precisely because the public would not support the Contra policy, and was unlikely to favor arms deals with Iran, that the NSC staff went underground. This was a perversion of the proper concept of covert operations:

- Covert operations should be conducted in accordance with strict rules of accountability and oversight. In the mid-1970s, in response to disclosures of abuses within the intelligence community, the Government enacted a series of safeguards. Each covert action was to be approved personally by the President, funded by Congressional appropriations, and Congress was to be informed.

  In the Iran-Contra Affair, these rules were violated. The President, according to Poindexter, was never informed of the diversion. The President says he knew nothing of the covert action to support the Contras, or the companies funded by non-appropriated monies set up by North to carry out that support. Congress was not notified of either the Iran or the Contra operations.
- Covert actions should be consistent with publicly defined U.S. foreign policy goals. Because covert operations are secret by definition, they are of course not openly debated or publicly approved. So long as the policies which they further are known, and so long as they are conducted in accordance with law, covert operations are acceptable. Here, however, the Contra covert operation was carried out in violation of the country's public policy as expressed in the Boland Amendment; and the Iran covert operation was carried out in violation of the country's stated policy against selling arms to Iran or making concessions to terrorists. These were not covert actions, they were covert policies; and covert policies are incompatible with democracy.

- Finally, covert operations are intended to be kept from foreign powers, not from the Congress and responsible Executive agencies within the United States Government itself. As Clair George, CIA Director of Operations, testified: "To think that because we deal in lies, and overseas we may lie and we may do other such things, that therefore that gives you some permission, some right or some particular reason to operate that way with your fellow employees, I would not only disagree with that I would say it would be the destruction of a secret service in a democracy." In the Iran-Contra Affair, secrecy was used to justify lies to Congress, the Attorney General, other Cabinet officers, and the CIA. It was used not as a shield against our adversaries, but as a weapon against our own democratic institutions.

The NSC Staff

The NSC staff was created to give the President policy advice on major national security and foreign policy issues. Here, however, it was used to gather intelligence and conduct covert operations. This departure from its proper functions contributed to policy failure.

During the Iran initiative, the NSC staff became the principal body both for gathering and coordinating intelligence on Iran and for recommending policy to the President. The staff relied on Iranians who were interested only in buying arms, including Ghorbanifar, whom CIA officials regarded as a fabricator. Poindexter, in recommending to the President the sale of weapons to Iran, gave as one of his reasons that Iraq was winning the Gulf war. That assessment was contrary to the views of intelligence professionals at the State Department, the Department of Defense, and the CIA, who had concluded as early as 1983 that Iran was winning the war. Casey, who collaborated with North and Poindexter on the Iran and Contra programs, also tailored intelligence reports to the positions he advocated. The record shows that the President believed and acted on these erroneous reports.

Secretary Shultz pointed out that the intelligence and policy functions do not mix, because "it is too tempting to have your analysis on the selection of information that is presented favor the policy that you are advocating." The Committees agree on the need to separate the intelligence and policy functions. Otherwise, there is too great a risk that the interpretation of intelligence will be skewed to fit predetermined policy choices.

In the Iran-Contra Affair, the NSC staff not only combined intelligence and policy functions, but it became operational and conducted covert operations. As the CIA was subjected to greater Congressional scrutiny and regulation, a few Administration officials—including even Director Casey—came to believe that the CIA could no longer be utilized for daring covert operations. So the NSC staff was enlisted to provide assistance in covert operations that the CIA could not or would not furnish.

This was a dangerous misuse of the NSC staff. When covert operations are conducted by those on whom the President relies to present policy options, there is no agency in government to objectively scrutinize, challenge and evaluate plans and activities. Checks and balances are lost. The high policy decisions confronting a President can rarely be resolved by the methods and techniques used by experts in the conduct of covert operations. Problems of public policy must be dealt with through consultation, not Poindexter's "compartmentation"; with honesty and confidentiality, not deceit.

The NSC was created to provide candid and comprehensive advice to the President. It is the judgment of these Committees that the NSC staff should never again engage in covert operations.

Disdain for Law

In the Iran-Contra Affair, officials viewed the law not as setting boundaries for their actions, but raising impediments to their goals. When the goals and the law collided, the law gave way:

- The covert program of support for the Contras evaded the Constitution's most significant check on Executive power: the President can spend funds on a program only if he can convince Congress to appropriate the money.

  When Congress enacted the Boland Amendment, cutting off funds for the war in Nicaragua, Administration officials raised funds for the Contras from other sources—foreign Governments, the Iran arms sales, and private individuals; and the NSC staff controlled the expenditures of these funds through power over the Enterprise. Conducting the covert program in Nicaragua with funding from the sale of U.S. Government property and contributions raised by Government officials was a flagrant violation of the Appropriations Clause of the Constitution.

- In addition, the covert program of support for the Contras was an evasion of the letter and spirit of the Boland Amendment. The President made it clear that while he opposed restrictions on military or paramilitary assistance to the Contras, he recognized that compliance with the law was not optional. "[W]hat I might personally wish or what our Government might wish still would not justify us violating the law of the land," he said in 1983.

A year later, members of the NSC staff were devising ways to continue support and direction of Contra activities during the period of the Boland Amendment. What was previously done by the CIA—and now prohibited by the Boland Amendment—would be done instead by the NSC staff.

The President set the stage by welcoming a huge donation for the Contras from a foreign Government—a contribution clearly intended to keep the Contras in the field while U.S. aid was barred. The NSC staff thereafter solicited other foreign Governments for military aid, facilitated the efforts of U.S. fundraisers to provide lethal assistance to the Contras, and ultimately developed and directed a private network that conducted, in North's words, a "full service covert operation" in support of the Contras.

This could not have been more contrary to the intent of the Boland legislation.

Numerous other laws were disregarded:

- North's full-service covert operation was a "significant anticipated intelligence activity" required to be disclosed to the Intelligence Committees of Congress under Section 501 of the National Security Act. No such disclosure was made.
- By Executive Order, a covert operation requires a personal determination by the President before it can be conducted by an agency other than the CIA. It requires a written Finding before any agency can carry it out. In the case of North's full-service covert operation in support of the Contras, there was no such personal determination and no such Finding. In

fact, the President disclaims any knowledge of this covert action.

- False statements to Congress are felonies if made with knowledge and intent. Several Administration officials gave statements denying NSC staff activities in support of the Contras which North later described in his testimony as "false," and "misleading, evasive, and wrong."
- The application of proceeds from U.S. arms sales for the benefit of the Contra war effort violated the Boland Amendment's ban on U.S. military aid to the Contras, and constituted a misappropriation of Government funds derived from the transfer of U.S. property.
- The U.S. Government's approval of the pre-Finding 1985 sales by Israel of arms to the Government of Iran was inconsistent with the Government's obligations under the Arms Export Control act.
- The testimony to Congress in November 1986 that the U.S. Government had no contemporaneous knowledge of the Israeli shipments, and the shredding of documents relating to the shipments while a Congressional inquiry into those shipments was pending, obstructed Congressional investigations.
- The Administration did not make, and clearly intended never to make, disclosure to the Intelligence Committees of the Finding—later destroyed—approving the November 1985 HAWK shipment, nor did it disclose the covert action to which the Finding related.

The Committees make no determination as to whether any particular individual involved in the Iran-Contra Affair acted with criminal intent or was guilty of any crime. That is a matter for the Independent Counsel and the courts. But the Committees reject any notion that worthy ends justify violations of law by Government officials; and the Committees condemn without reservation the making of false statements to Congress and the withholding, shredding, and alteration of documents relevant to a pending inquiry.

Administration officials have, if anything, an even greater responsibility than private citizens to comply with the law. There is no place in Government for law breakers.

Congress and the President

The Constitution of the United States gives important powers to both the President and the Congress in the making of foreign policy. The President is the principal architect of foreign policy in consultation with the Congress. The policies of the United States cannot succeed unless the President and the Congress work together.

Yet, in the Iran-Contra Affair, Administration officials holding no elected office repeatedly evidenced disrespect for Congress' efforts to perform its Constitutional oversight role in foreign policy:

- Poindexter testified, referring to his efforts to keep the covert action in support of the Contras from Congress: "I simply did not want any outside interference."
- North testified: "I didn't want to tell Congress anything" about this covert action.
- [Assistant Secretary of State Elliott] Abrams acknowledged in his testimony that, unless Members of Congressional Committees asked "exactly the right question, using exactly the right words, they weren't going to get the right answers," regarding solicitation of third countries for Contra support.
- And numerous other officials made false statements to, and misled, the Congress.

Several witnesses at the hearings stated or implied that foreign policy should be left solely to the President to do as he chooses, arguing that shared powers have no place in a dangerous world. But the theory of our Constitution is the opposite: policies formed through consultation and the democratic process are better and wiser than those formed without it. Circumvention of Congress is self-defeating, for no foreign policy can succeed without the bipartisan support of Congress.

In a system of shared powers, decision making requires mutual respect between the branches of government.

The Committees were reminded by Secretary Shultz during the hearings that "trust is the coin of the realm." Democratic government is not possible without trust between the branches of government and between the government and the people. Sometimes that trust is misplaced and the system falters. But for officials to work outside the system because it does not produce the results they seek is a prescription for failure.

Who Was Responsible?

Who was responsible for the Iran-Contra Affair? Part of our mandate was to answer that question, not in a legal sense (which is the responsibility of the Independent Counsel), but in order to reaffirm that those who serve the Government are accountable for their actions. Based on our investigation, we reach the following conclusions.

At the operational level, the central figure in the Iran-Contra Affair was Lt. Col. North, who coordinated all of the activities and was involved in all aspects of the secret operations. North, however, did not act alone.

North's conduct had the express approval of Admiral John Poindexter, first as Deputy National Security Adviser, and then as National Security Adviser. North also had at least the tacit support of Robert McFarlane, who served as National Security Adviser until December 1985.

In addition, for reasons cited earlier, we believe that the late Director of Central Intelligence, William Casey, encouraged North, gave him direction, and promoted the concept of an extra-legal covert organization. Casey, for the most part, insulated CIA career employees from knowledge of what he and the NSC staff were doing. Casey's passion for covert operations—dating back to his World War II intelligence days—was well known. His close relationship with North was attested to by several witnesses. Further, it was Casey who brought Richard Secord into the secret operation, and it was Secord who, with Albert Hakim, organized the Enterprise. These facts provide strong reasons to believe that Casey was involved both with the diversion and with the plans for an "off-the-shelf" covert capacity.

The Committees are mindful, however, of the fact that the evidence concerning Casey's role comes almost solely from North; that this evidence, albeit under oath, was used by North to exculpate himself; and that Casey could not respond. Although

North told the Committees that Casey knew of the diversion from the start, he told a different story to the Attorney General [Edwin Meese III] in November 1986, as did Casey himself. Only one other witness, Lt. Col. Robert Earl, testified that he had been told by North during Casey's lifetime that Casey knew of the diversion.

The Attorney General recognized on November 21, 1986, the need for an inquiry. His staff was responsible for finding the diversion memorandum, which the Attorney General promptly made public. But as described earlier, his fact-finding inquiry departed from standard investigative techniques. The Attorney General saw Director Casey hours after the Attorney General learned of the diversion memorandum, yet he testified that he never asked Casey about the diversion. He waited two days to speak to Poindexter, North's superior, and then did not ask him what the President knew. He waited too long to seal North's offices. These lapses placed a cloud over the Attorney General's investigation.

There is no evidence that the Vice President [George Bush] was aware of the diversion. The Vice President attended several meetings on the Iran initiative, but none of the participants could recall his views.

The Vice President said he did not know of the Contra resupply operation. His National Security Adviser, Donald Gregg, was told in early August 1986 by a former colleague that North was running the Contra resupply operation, and that ex-associates of Edwin Wilson—a well-known ex-CIA official convicted of selling arms to Libya and plotting the murder of his prosecutors—were involved in the operation. Gregg testified that he did not consider these facts worthy of the Vice President's attention and did not report them to him, even after the Hasenfus airplane was shot down and the Administration had denied any connection with it.

The central remaining question is the role of the President in the Iran-Contra Affair. On this critical point, the shredding of documents by Poindexter, North, and others, and the death of Casey, leave the record incomplete.

As it stands, the President has publicly stated that he did not know of the diversion. Poindexter testified that he shielded the President from knowledge of the diversion. North said that he never told the President, but assumed that the President knew.

Poindexter told North on November 21, 1986, that he had not informed the President of the diversion. Secord testified that North told him he had talked with the President about the diversion, but North testified that he had fabricated this story to bolster Secord's morale.

Nevertheless, the ultimate responsibility for the events in the Iran-Contra Affair must rest with the President. If the President did not know what his National Security Advisers were doing, he should have. It is his responsibility to communicate unambiguously to his subordinates that they must keep him advised of important actions they take for the Administration. The Constitution requires the President to "take care that the laws be faithfully executed." This charge encompasses a responsibility to leave the members of his Administration in no doubt that the rule of law governs.

Members of the NSC staff appeared to believe that their actions were consistent with the President's desires. It was the President's policy—not an isolated decision by North or Poindexter—to sell arms secretly to Iran and to maintain the Contras "body and soul," the Boland Amendment notwithstanding. To the NSC staff, implementation of these policies became the overriding concern.

Several of the President's advisers pursued a covert action to support the Contras in disregard of the Boland Amendment and of several statutes and Executive orders requiring Congressional notification. Several of these same advisers lied, shredded documents, and covered up their actions. These facts have been on the public record for months. The actions of those individuals do not comport with the notion of a country guided by the rule of law. But the President has yet to condemn their conduct.

The President himself told the public that the U.S. Government had no connection to the Hasenfus airplane. He told the public that early reports of arms sales for hostages had "no foundation." He told the public that the United States had not traded arms for hostages. He told the public that the United States had not condoned the arms sales by Israel to Iran, when in fact he had approved them and signed a Finding, later destroyed by Poindexter, recording his approval. All of these statements by the President were wrong.

Thus, the question whether the President knew of the diversion is not conclusive on the issue of his responsibility. The President created or at least tolerated an environment where those who did know of the diversion believed with certainty that they were carrying out the President's policies.

This same environment enabled a secretary who shredded, smuggled, and altered documents to tell the Committees that "sometimes you have to go above the written law"; and it enabled Admiral Poindexter to testify that "frankly, we were willing to take some risks with the law." It was in such an environment that former officials of the NSC staff and their private agents could lecture the Committees that a "rightful cause" justifies any means, that lying to Congress and other officials in the executive branch itself is acceptable when the ends are just, and that Congress is to blame for passing laws that run counter to Administration policy. What may aptly be called the "cabal of the zealots" was in charge.

In a Constitutional democracy, it is not true, as one official maintained, that "when you take the King's shilling, you do the King's bidding." The idea of monarchy was rejected here 200 years ago and since then, the law—not any official or ideology—has been paramount. For not instilling this precept in his staff, for failing to take care that the law reigned supreme, the President bears the responsibility.

Fifty years ago Supreme Court Justice Louis Brandeis observed: "Our Government is the potent, the omnipresent teacher. For good or for ill, it teaches the whole people by its example. Crime is contagious. If the Government becomes a law-breaker, it breeds contempt for law, it invites every man to become a law unto himself, it invites anarchy."

The Iran-Contra Affair resulted from a failure to heed this message.

Passion, Defiance, Tears: Jim Wright Bows Out
Janet Hook

On May 31, 1989, Jim Wright, after a thirty-four-year career in Congress, became the first Speaker of the House of Representatives to resign from office in disgrace. Janet Hook relives Wright's emotional one-hour resignation speech to his colleagues in the House, where he had the chance both to defend himself and to attack the "self-appointed vigilantes" whose charges of impropriety had led to his resignation. Hook relates the complex set of events that led to Wright's undoing. Formally, Wright had been charged with breaking House rules about gifts and limits on speaking fees and other outside income. His book, *Reflections of a Public Man*, became the focus of the investigation when it was alleged that Wright would sell it to organizations in bulk in lieu of accepting a speaking fee. There were also questions of his relationship to industrialist George Mallick, who gave gifts to Wright in the amount of $145,000 and hired Wright's wife at an $18,000 annual salary when she allegedly did not perform any work. Wright protested that he was the victim of a "mindless cannibalism," in which an obsession with ethics was steering the House off track from its important business. Yet, rather than seeing the Wright affair as an obsession with ethics on the part of public officials, many would claim that it was just another unfortunate episode of mischief-making that constitutes one of the essential problems of the crisis in government ethics.

The House chamber was packed, the air charged with tension. An extraordinary event was clearly about to unfold.

It was 4 P.M. sharp on May 31 [1989] when Speaker Jim Wright of Texas strode onto the House floor, back straight and head high.

Janet Hook, "Passion, Defiance, Tears: Jim Wright Bows Out," *Congressional Quarterly Weekly Report*, Vol. 47 (June 3, 1989), pp. 1289–1294. Reprinted with permission, Congressional Quarterly, Inc.

An hour later, Wright hung his head as he made history.

"Let me give you back this job you gave me as a propitiation for all of this season of bad will that has grown up among us," Wright said quietly. "Give it back to you."

As he announced that he would resign as Speaker June 6 rather than continue fighting charges that he violated House gift and income rules, evidence of bad will was all around.

Sitting impassively before him, several yards to his left, was Newt Gingrich of Georgia, the Republican who instigated the year-long ethics committee investigation that brought Wright down. Gringrich now is expecting to be the subject of an investigation himself.

Sitting several yards to the Speaker's right was House Majority Whip Tony Coelho of California, who five days earlier announced he would resign from Congress rather than face a protracted ethics investigation of his personal finances.

Near Coelho was another member of the Democratic leadership, William H. Gray III of Pennsylvania, who the day before had held a press conference to challenge reports that he was the subject of a Justice Department investigation.

Against that backdrop, Wright portrayed himself as the victim of an obsession with ethics being enforced by "self-appointed vigilantes." He expressed this hope: "All of us, in both political parties, must resolve to bring this period of mindless cannibalism to an end."

Wright's career as the No. 1 House leader had barely begun in 1987 when people began touting him as one of the strongest Speakers of the postwar House. Now, he is ending a 34-year career in Congress as the first Speaker in history to be forced by scandal to leave the office midterm.

The Farewell Speech

Wright's decision to resign the Speakership had been predicted for some weeks. There had been a barrage of news accounts raising questions about his personal finances. And ever since the ethics committee issued a report April 17 detailing charges that Wright may have broken House rules, speculation on his political demise was rampant.

But for everyone except his closest allies, it was unclear until the last moment exactly when and how the Texas Democrat would relinquish his formidable powers.

Then members were called to the floor on May 31. Anxiously they milled around the House chamber as they awaited the Speaker.

Wright felt relieved as he pushed open the door to the chamber. He later described it as "an enormous sense of lifting of a burden."

His colleagues greeted him with a standing ovation. He shook hands with members seated in the front row—Republicans and Democrats—and then placed the notes for his farewell speech on the podium in the well of the House.

He faced an audience comprised of most of his colleagues, dozens of staff members, and a handful of senators, including fellow Texan Lloyd Bentsen, who sat in the centrally located Democratic leader's chair. The public galleries overhead were filled to capacity and included, to the Speaker's right, his wife, Betty, and a daughter from his first marriage. Behind Wright, presiding over the House, sat Majority Leader Thomas S. Foley of Washington—the man expected to be nominated by the Democratic Caucus and elected by the full House to succeed him as Speaker June 6.

Foley pounded his gavel, bringing the House to order. "The chair recognizes the distinguished Speaker of the House," he said.

For the next hour, the House sat riveted as Wright summoned the oratorical skill that is his hallmark but also marks him as a politician of another era. The rap on Wright is that his speaking style doesn't project well on television, but key elements of this defense of his conduct against ethics charges were surely gripping.

His voice broke in sadness and rose in rage; tears welled in his eyes and his hands shook; sweat poured from his brow as Wright unleashed on the House the emotions he'd kept largely to himself for a year.

"I have ached to tell my side of the story," he said. "But today, silence is no longer tolerable; nor for the good of the House is it even desirable."

He spent most of the hour in a point-by-point rebuttal of the major charges being investigated by the House ethics committee: that he had received $145,000 in improper gifts from Fort Worth

developer George Mallick, including an $18,000 annual salary to
Wright's wife that she did not earn, and that he had violated
House rules limiting speaking fees and other outside income by
selling his book, *Reflections of a Public Man*, in bulk in lieu of
collecting speaking fees.

Wright began with an angry, impassioned defense of his wife,
describing in detail the work she had done and criticizing ethics
investigators for concluding otherwise. And Wright somberly
pointed out the irony that Betty Wright quit a job as a congressional staffer years ago in an effort to avoid causing controversy
for her husband.

Then Wright defended his dealings with Mallick, the developer. He said Mallick provided him benefits because of their
longstanding friendship, not any self-serving interest in legislation.

And Wright, waving a copy of his 117-page paperback, said
book sales were too meager ever to fit the ethics committee's
description of a "scheme" to evade outside-income limits.

His detailed, legalistic arguments about House rules were familiar to many members—particularly Democrats who had been
briefed by Wright's lawyers—and a few appeared to doze off as
his self-defense stretched over 45 minutes.

But the dramatic climax came when Wright began painting in
broader political strokes. He portrayed himself as a casualty of a
partisan war being fought through attacks on the personal ethics
of politicians. He pleaded with his colleagues not to seek revenge
on his behalf.

"When vengeance becomes more desirable than vindication,
harsh personal attacks on one another's motives and one another's
character drown out the quiet logic of serious debate," he said.

Head bowed, Wright offered his resignation as "total payment
for the anger and hostility we feel toward each other."

When he was through, his colleagues gave him another standing ovation. He embraced a few. Shook some hands. Then he
returned to his office.

The Origins

By the time the speech was over, the House ethics committee
had postponed a June 1 meeting to vote on Wright's motions to

dismiss the major charges against him. With Wright's resignation now on the table, Democrats expect the matter to be dropped quietly, without any further committee votes.

That will be the official, if anticlimactic, ending to a drama that began almost exactly one year ago in the House ethics committee's offices in the basement of the Capitol.

The central plot—the ethics investigation—was played out largely behind those closed doors. But the political backdrop against which the ethics panel's work was judged was shaped by an array of forces far removed from the inquiry, as diverse as a congressional pay-raise proposal, President Bush's Pentagon nominee, and the criminal record of Wright's top aide.

The ethics committee voted to open a preliminary inquiry into Wright's financial affairs on June 9, 1988. Gingrich had filed a formal complaint, but the partisan edge on the request was dulled when the government-watchdog group Common Cause joined the call for an investigation of Wright. Wright, who had balked at Gingrich's complaint, then bowed to growing pressure and pledged full cooperation.

The next month, in what eventually proved to be a key development, the committee hired an aggressive Chicago trial lawyer, Richard J. Phelan, to head the inquiry.

So long as Phelan was conducting his work in secret and little news of his findings was leaking out, Wright's ethics troubles seemed to have only a marginal effect on his leadership. As the 100th Congress came to an end, praise was heaped on the legislative accomplishments during Wright's first term as Speaker, which included enactment of major welfare, health, and trade bills, and on-time passage of the 13 annual appropriations bills for the first time in years.

Wright traces the attack on his ethics to his November 1987 involvement in U.S. policy in Central America—including diplomacy to foster a regional peace process through personal efforts that the administration criticized as an unwarranted intrusion into executive branch powers.

"From that moment there was nothing but hostility from the administration," Wright said at a luncheon with reporters the day after his resignation announcement. "There was a determination on the part of certain people in the other party to see to it that I was removed."

Wright's aggressive style may have contributed to his downfall in another respect as well. By driving so purposefully to his legislative goals, he infuriated Republicans with heavy-handed use of power and alienated some Democrats with his solo leadership style. When the going got rough on the ethics charges, Wright had only a shallow reservoir of support to rely on.

1989: Political Support Erodes

As the 101st Congress began in January, hardly anyone believed Wright's hold on the Speaker's office was at risk. Democrats remained confident that the ethics committee would clear him.

But then, a seemingly unrelated matter started the erosion of Wright's political base: a proposal to give members of Congress a 51 percent pay raise. Although many thought the proposal was doomed from the start, Wright was blamed by many for its February 7 demise. The issue unleashed a torrent of public criticism and anti-Congress fury that left members feeling especially vulnerable to political fallout if Wright's ethics troubles didn't go away. Conservative groups taunted Democrats by distributing "Foley for Speaker" buttons.

The next month the political stakes were raised dramatically when the Senate, controlled by Democrats, rejected the nomination of John Tower to be defense secretary. Talk by Republicans of exacting revenge on Wright began immediately.

In that atmosphere, Wright for the first time publicly alluded to the possibility that he might relinquish his Speakership if the ethics inquiry weakened him. At an ad hoc luncheon with reporters March 14, Wright said, "If I were convinced in my mind that most of my colleagues didn't want me to be Speaker, I wouldn't run."

Ethics Committee Bombshell

But the most devastating blow came from the ethics committee. On April 13 word leaked out that two Democrats had defected and voted against Wright on a key issue. Suddenly, the confidence of Wright and his allies was shaken. It was no longer safe to assume that this obscure committee would safely bury the charges.

Through leaks to the media, it became clear that the ethics committee would press charges against Wright in a whole sphere he had not addressed when he testified before the committee in September. The Speaker sought another opportunity to defend himself, but the committee said he needed to wait until their interim findings were released. That, in Wright's mind, was his last chance to keep the matter from unraveling.

Wright went public with his defense for the first time April 13, when he appeared at a news conference tearfully defending his wife and pledging to fight the charges.

On April 17, the committee announced it found reason to believe that Wright violated House rules in 69 instances. The set of allegations was far broader than anyone would have predicted when the inquiry began. And the committee released a torrent of information about its findings, including the investigative report by Phelan, which was even harsher in its assessment of Wright's conduct than the committee's own report. Further, the panel said it was still investigating Wright's involvement in a lucrative oil-well deal.

Wright remained convinced that the allegations would be proven false when the committee conducted a disciplinary hearing.

But procedural and legal delays pushed the beginning of the trial-like hearing into June. In the meantime, Wright was pummeled in the press with new allegations about his conduct: free plane rides, preferential investment opportunities, doing favors for a company employing his wife.

Wright's colleagues came to feel like they, too, were living in a state of siege. Nonetheless, Wright, a boxer in his youth, dug in. On May 8, he announced the hiring of a new team of defense lawyers.

Emotional Turning Point

But the lawyers could do nothing for Wright about a matter that was not even related to his financial dealings: the case of Wright's top aide, John P. Mack. On May 11, Mack resigned in the wake of new publicity about a brutal crime—an unprovoked assault on a young woman—that he'd committed as a teenager 16 years ago.

That human drama provoked a far more emotional reaction—both among members and their constituents—than any of the more arcane questions about Wright's finances.

"We lost this thing the day the [Washington] *Post* ran the John Mack story," said Wright ally Charles Wilson, D-Texas. "It was something everybody could relate to and it gave the idea that we are living in an environment of lawlessness and violence."

From that point on, it was no longer a matter of whether Wright would lose his Speakership but when.

The reality of his deteriorating political situation became harder and harder to ignore. On May 17, a group of respected Democrats who had been generally supportive of Wright met and privately discussed the possibility of Wright resigning. Among them was David R. Obey, Wis., whose pessimism about Wright's political future was especially significant because he was an author of the House ethics code and had supported Wright's contention that the ethics committee had misinterpreted the rules.

That meeting was described the next day on the front page of *The New York Times*—a clear signal to other Democrats that the end was near.

Last-Ditch Hope

Wright figured he had one last hope: On May 23 the ethics committee would hear arguments from Phelan and Wright's lawyers on the Speaker's motion to dismiss key charges against him. But when the day was over, key committee members had made it plain that they were not likely to grant Wright's request.

And Phelan let Wright's allies know that there were not enough votes to drop the charges.

He realized at that point, Wright later said, "it would be unrealistic to expect a complete exoneration" without a bitter fight on the House floor.

The next day, his lawyers met with ethics committee representatives and Phelan to discuss a proposal for Wright to step down as Speaker in exchange for the most serious charges against him being dropped. The talks reportedly snagged on the timing of Wright's resignation.

But the sense of inevitability grew. Democrats hoping to move up the leadership ladder began openly campaigning for positions in the post-Wright regime.

Wright said he remained undecided about what he would do as he headed with his wife into seclusion for a Memorial Day weekend in the country. It was there, away from the telephone calls from supporters urging him to continue fighting, that Wright concluded it was time to quit.

"It just came to me that I did have peace and happiness by doing what is best for the institution," he said.

The Final Week

By the time Wright returned to Washington for the most dramatic week of his political career, the dynamics of the situation had been fundamentally transformed.

The pressure on Wright to resign was intensified by Coelho's stunning May 26 decision to step down as whip and resign from Congress, in the wake of a controversy surrounding a "junk bond" deal.

Wright returned to the Capitol May 30 still unwilling to reveal his plans publicly. But he said, "I think I know what I should do. I think I know what I believe to be in my best interest and in the interest of the institution.

"I want to be fair to myself and my family and my reputation and I want to be fair to this institution that I have served for thirty-four years."

The sense of crisis in the Democratic leadership was fueled May 30 by reports that Rep. Gray's staff was being investigated by the Justice Department.

The next morning, Wright began telling his close friends of his decision to resign. He told his Texas colleagues at their weekly delegation lunch. Word spread throughout the Hill like wildfire.

In his speech, Wright said he would resign his House seat by the end of June. After the speech, he and his wife went to his office and listened to television commentary on his resignation. Mrs. Wright became enraged by one ungracious assessment. Wright responded, "Hey, hey, we're liberated now from all that. We don't have to care about what these guys say. Free at last."

Reform or Retribution?

In the wake of the Speaker's announcement, many Democrats believed they found a bright light at the end of the tunnel that is the Wright affair. The departure of Wright and Coelho clears the way for a new leadership team headed by Foley that Democrats hope will help dispel the ethics cloud lingering over their party.

"Long after the reasons are forgotten [the Wright affair] will result in a totally new generation of leadership in the House," Obey said.

But beyond the certainty of a leadership shake-up, it is unclear whether Wright's resignation will result in bitter partisan retribution or broad reform.

It was retribution not reform on the minds of many members who were skeptical that Wright's call for an end to "mindless cannibalism" would be heeded.

Gingrich showed no sign of letting up on his drive to use congressional ethics in general and the problems of the House Democratic leadership in particular as an issue to help Republicans gain control of the House in the early 1990s.

Gingrich said there were another nine or ten Democrats who could face inquiries in the ethics committee. And the Republican National Congressional Committee sent GOP leaders around the country a statement of "talking points" about how to make political capital out of the Democrats' ethics problems.

The paper challenges the contention by some Democrats that the GOP is engaged in "ethical McCarthyism." It urges the GOP to attribute the fate of Wright and Coelho to "character suicides" resulting from the Democratic Party's arrogance of holding majority power in the House for more than three decades.

"When you can abuse the rights of the minority [party in the House] . . . for as long as they have, there could well be a feeling that you can do what you want, ethics be damned," the campaign committee said.

Many Democrats, while weary of the ethics spotlight, don't want to turn it off until Gingrich has been fully examined. Pending in the ethics committee now is a complaint against the Georgia Republican, raising questions about the propriety of his own book-promotion deal.

"This isn't over," said Ronald D. Coleman, D-Texas. "The call of Jim Wright to drop vengeance will fall on deaf ears."

The day allegations about Gray surfaced, ethics committee Chairman Julian C. Dixon, D-Calif., told reporters, "Things seem to be getting out of hand, and I'm hoping the leadership on both sides will join together to bring some order."

But others don't want Congress to get beyond the crisis by sweeping it under the rug. They want the Wright and Coelho resignations to be the beginning of broader institutional reforms.

"You know, some people are saying we've had enough of these ethics questions in Congress, let's move on to other issues," said Fred Wertheimer, president of Common Cause, leading champion of legislation to overhaul campaign-finance law. "Well, Congress does have to deal with other issues, but they can't run away from this one."

Indeed, many members agree that the time has come for changes in the way Congress conducts itself. Having spent the last year with its practices under a media microscope, the crisis of the Democratic leadership may give new impetus to an array of changes to clarify and strengthen House rules and laws governing the relations between private money and the public interest.

Among the ideas already gaining currency are proposals to bar members from accepting speaking fees and expense-paid trips from private groups, to an overhaul of campaign-finance law and closing a loophole that lets senior members convert campaign cash to personal use when they leave office.

Minority Leader Robert H. Michel of Illinois said that Wright's resignation provides "an unprecedented opportunity for the House to begin a bipartisan, comprehensive reformation of this institution and its rules."

Wright himself, in his resignation speech, suggested that the ethics process in the House be revamped and honoraria be abolished.

But he does not see his own downfall as a symptom of the problematic relations between money and politics as activists such as Wertheimer portray it. Wright was more inclined to view his short-lived Speakership as a casualty of his own ambitious political aims.

"I think I was probably obsessed with the notion that I have a limited period of time in which to make my mark upon the future," he said. "Maybe I was too insistent, too competitive, too ambitious to achieve too much in too short a period of time. I couldn't have been any different than I was."

The "Keating Five": Opening Statement of the Special Counsel
Robert S. Bennett

The "Keating Five" refers to those U.S. Senators who accepted large campaign contributions from savings-and-loan chieftain Charles Keating, seemingly in exchange for their influence with banking regulators that would favor Keating's troubled Lincoln Savings and Loan. Keating was charged with looting Lincoln through fraud and mismanagement and forcing the taxpayers through deposit insurance to pay out an amount estimated to be more than $2 billion. The five Senators involved in the scandal were democrats Alan Cranston of California, Dennis DeConcini of Arizona, John Glenn of Ohio, Donald W. Riegle, Jr., of Michigan, and Republican John McCain of Arizona. Only Cranston was held accountable by the Senate Ethics Committee and his case is still pending.

In November of 1990, the Senate Ethics Committee began public hearings into the matter. Reprinted here are excerpts of the hearing's "Opening Statement" made by the committee's Special Counsel, Robert S. Bennett, that sets out the evidence he accumulated against the five Senators. Bennett also addresses the hard questions that the committee members themselves must make in reaching their decision about the guilt or innocence of their five colleagues. Among the most difficult questions that faced the committee is whether the activities of the

Robert S. Bennett, The "Keating Five": Opening Statement of the Special Counsel, Public Hearing of the Senate Ethics Committee, November 15, 1990.

five Senators were any different from what any Senator does
when he provides constituent services.

Let's understand the case, the conduct, that we are considering
in this proceeding. I want to make it absolutely clear that the
ultimate judgment is yours, but the evidence, as I believe it will
clearly show, that this is simply not a case in all instances of
simple and routine constituent service. Let us look at what the
evidence is as to that very initial question of what is the conduct
we're talking about. . . .

These are undisputed:

One . . . several Senators met with regulators about a pending
enforcement matter involving a single company which had sued
the Bank Board in the Federal courts.

Two, the Senators did not have aides present, and more importantly, the chief regulator, Chairman Gray, was specifically directed not to bring aides with him.

Three, Mr. Keating, on whose behalf the meeting was held,
was a major political contributor to each of the Senators who
attended the meeting.

Four, at the meetings on April 2nd and April 9th, the regulators
were asked to withdraw a duly promulgated regulation at the
request of a single company, and were told that the company
would do certain things in return. Now while there is some
dispute as to whether that occurred on April 2, there is no
dispute in light of the transcript . . . that that request was made
along with other documents.

Five, there can be no reasonable doubt . . . that members of
the United States Senate can and must have the power to pressure regulators. . . . But . . . there can be no doubt, no reasonable doubt based on the evidence, that the purpose of these
meetings, at least as to certain Senators, was to pressure the
regulators to take action consistent with the wishes of Charles
Keating. It will be for you to determine whether or not that was
proper or improper.

Six, at the meeting of April 9, 1987, the Senators were told
that a criminal referral was going to be made and that certain
criminal wrongdoing was described by the regulators. It was not

130

SCANDAL AND CORRUPTION IN GOVERNMENT

simply a criminal referral, but there was discussion of such things
as file stuffing and so forth. . . .

Following the meeting two Senators continued to contact regulators on behalf of Mr. Keating and continued to accept political
contributions from him.

Because there is a great deal of misunderstanding about such
subjects as constituent service and political contributions, it is
essential, absolutely essential, if we are to be fair to these five
Senators and to the Senate as an institution, to articulate the
applicable standards and principles on which you must judge the
evidence. To do otherwise might lead to false and unfair conclusions about the conduct that occurred.

It is my responsibility to identify the issues. And you ask me to
identify the hard issues, to ask the hard questions. You ask me to
identify the existing standards, and most important, you ask me
to present the evidence that we've gathered over the past year. It
is your responsibility to judge. You must be fair to the individual
Senators, as individuals, not as the Keating Five. You must be
fair to the Senate as an institution, and you must, of course, be
fair to the American people.

In determining what is improper conduct, the committee must,
as I will repeatedly emphasize, consider the totality of the circumstances surrounding the conduct under inquiry. . . . Let's list
just some of the difficult questions.

[One,] Is there evidence that any of the Senators received
substantial benefits from Charles Keating in the form of payments to campaign committees or other groups in which they had
an interest with the knowledge that they were made with the
purpose of obtaining or awarding special treatment on behalf of
Lincoln or Mr. Keating? . . .

Two, did any of the Senators take action on behalf of Lincoln
or Mr. Keating which under the circumstances went beyond the
norm of routine and appropriate constituent service? Did any of
the Senators in performing what might otherwise be legitimate
constituent service use methods which undermine the public's
confidence and the integrity of its Government?

What are the standards and the principles in this case that exist
now?

One, a Senator should not take contributions from an individual he knows or should know is attempting to procure his services to intervene in a specific matter pending before a Federal agency. . . .

Two, a Senator should not take unusual or aggressive action with regard to a specific matter before a Federal agency on behalf of a contributor when he knows or has reason to know the contributor has sought to procure his services.

Three, a Senator should not conduct his fund-raising effort or engage in office practices which lead contributors to conclude that they can buy access to him.

Four, . . . there is a well-recognized and established appearance standard. . . . A Senator should not engage in conduct which would appear to be improper to a reasonable, nonpartisan, fully informed person. Such conduct undermines the public's confidence in the integrity of the Government and is an abuse of one's official position. Such conduct is wrong, in addition to appearing to be wrong.

At the same time that constituent service demands on members have increased, the cost of election, the cost of running campaigns has skyrocketed. . . . The problem becomes clear. More and more constituents are requesting the assistance of their Congressmen at the same time that those Congressmen must ask more and more of the same constituents for campaign contributions. I ask you this: How can our system of government maintain the appearance and the reality of integrity as these trends continue?

Now none of this is an excuse for wrongdoing, if wrongdoing occurred. It is, however, I respectfully submit to you, a booming warning that unless these trends are recognized and dealt with, we will have more cases like this and the reputation of this body and its members will be in utter ruin.

Now simply because constituent service is generally a good thing, it does not mean, members of the committee, by merely asserting that "what I did was constituent service" . . . that a Senator can erect an impenetrable shield barring ethical inquiry. While important, constituent service cannot be elevated to the status of a religion. And even if it were, it must be remembered that in the history of the world there have been many examples of where many sins have been committed in the name of religion. So, too, many wrongs have been committed in the name of constituent service, and your job will be to determine whether such a case is present here.

Members of this committee, this case is going to force upon you the obligation of giving guidance on the limits of constituent service because in passing judgment on past actions under the standards which currently exist, you inevitably give guidance for the future.

I know that you will be concerned that drawing lines in this area will have a chilling effect on the performance of constituent service in the future. But you should keep in mind that the abuse of constituent service by a few Senators does as much if not more to damage the effectiveness of constituent service by undermining the credibility of all legislators who deal with Federal regulators on behalf of the constituent or contributor.

While strong intervention is often justified, was there, in this case, unduly aggressive intervention by powerful Senators which created a ripple effect that emasculated the civil servants, contrary to the public good and the public's confidence in government?

Even if a member intervenes with a regulator on behalf of an individual constituent in a just case, has the method . . . undermined the public's confidence that the regulator's decision was fair, was honest and based on merit, rather than because there was, and I quote, a political fix? . . .

I have heard in this case a lot about constituent service, but this question must be asked. Charles Keating was not the only constituent in this case. People who lost their life savings because of what has been described by Judge [Stanley] Sporkin as the looting of Lincoln were also constituents of at least some of these Senators. And the taxpayers will have to pay for Lincoln's failure and are also the Senators' constituents.

This case also presents the issue of the propriety of performing constituent service for someone who is a political contributor. Under our system of government, there is absolutely nothing wrong—and this is where there is a lot of public misperception—

if a Senator provides constituent services for a political contributor. . . . That is part of our system. . . . However, members of the committee, this relationship between action and contributions has its limits.

One, a legislator should not immediately conclude that the constituent is always right and the administrator is always wrong, but as far as possible should try to find out the merits of each case and only make such representations as the situation permits. . . . Two, . . . a legislator should not accept any money for representing constituents or anyone else before Government departments. . . . Moreover, the possibility of such a contribution should never be suggested by the legislator or his staff at the time the favor is done. . . .

This afternoon I will give you many instances—many instances there were acts, and money were discussed at the same time, and that hundreds of thousands of dollars, in the case of Senator Cranston, passed in an office in this building.

Now before we start looking at all the trees, which we'll do this afternoon, let's talk about the forest a little bit.

Charles Keating was the Chairman and controlling shareholder of A.C.C., the American Continental Corporation, an Ohio-chartered company. In February of 1984, A.C.C. acquired Lincoln. Lincoln was a federally insured, California-chartered S.&L. Lincoln operated in California, but its executives and most of its employees were in Arizona. . . . And even though it was state-chartered, it had to comply with certain regulations of the Federal Home Loan Bank Board, or the F.H.L.B.B., in order to enjoy the significant benefit of having its accounts protected by Federal insurance. . . .

In May of 1984, three months after A.C.C. acquired Lincoln, the bank board proposed a regulation to limit severely . . . the kinds and amounts of investments that S.&L.'s could make.

The final rule was promulgated in January of 1985. But direct investments which were made prior to December 10, or which were in the works prior to December 10, '84, were grandfathered. In other words, they were allowed to stand. Now although Mr. Keating controlled Lincoln only for a very short period of time, prior to the implementation of the rule, Lincoln made substantial direct investments. . . .

The day after the rule was promulgated, Lincoln applied for an exemption to permit it to make up to $900 million in direct investments. And this was denied. Now throughout this period of time that I've just been talking about that this rule was pending, Lincoln and Mr. Keating aggressively lobbied members of Congress to oppose implementation of the rule. For our purposes, this included Senators Cranston and DeConcini, Senators Glenn and John McCain, who was at that time a Congressman.

Senator Riegle has no recollection and we have found no evidence to indicate that he was asked to take any action on Mr. Keating or Lincoln regarding the direct investment rule.

Senators Cranston, DeConcini, and Glenn, and Representative McCain wrote letters to Chairman Gray and these letters urged Chairman Gray to postpone implementation of the rule to give Congress time to consider the matter.

An essential key to Mr. Keating's strategy was to put as much political pressure on Chairman Gray and the board as possible, and to do this the paper clearly shows that he sought the assistance of many members of Congress and he also raised substantial sums for political contributions to members of Congress, including the five Senators who sit before you today. . . .

The high-water mark of Mr. Keating's strategy came when he, Mr. Keating, engineered a meeting on April 2, 1987, between Chairman Gray and Senators Cranston, DeConcini, Glenn, and McCain. This meeting led to another one on April 9, 1987, between four officials of the Federal Home Loan Bank Board's San Francisco office and those Senators plus Senator Riegle. But Mr. Keating continued to bring political pressure to bear on the board even after those meetings and even after Mr. Gray was no longer chairman.

Mr. Wall, Mr. M. Danny Wall, who was chairman of the board from 1987 to 1989—Senators DeConcini and Cranston contacted him on behalf of Lincoln, on Mr. Keating's request.

Now based on the evidence gathered by special counsel, it is clear . . . that Senators Cranston and DeConcini were important players in Mr. Keating's strategy. . . . Senators Glenn and McCain were active participants in opposing the direct invest-

ment rule and attended the meetings on April 2nd and 9th; they
were not the organizers of the meeting, nor did they play any
meaningful role on Mr. Keating's behalf following the meetings.

Senator Riegle has advised this committee that he has little
recollection of relevant past events regarding the Keating matter,
but that based on his reconstruction of events he firmly believes
that he did nothing wrong. He has told the committee that based
upon his reconstruction of events he is certain that his role was
minor and largely passive.

However, members of the committee, I must reluctantly state
there is substantial evidence that Senator Riegle played a much
greater role than he now recalls. While Senators Cranston and
DeConcini were by far the most active on Mr. Keating's behalf,
the evidence shows that Senator Riegle played an important role
at the early stages. On the other hand, it is to be said for Senator
Reigle, that like Senators Glenn and McCain, his efforts on
behalf of Lincoln appeared to have ended as of April 9, 1987.

Now all of the Senators deny any wrongdoing, and they contend that what they did was appropriate constituent service. It's
unfortunate, members of the committee, that this case has been
called the Keating Five. There are really five separate cases with
some common threads.

While all of the Senators attended the meeting of April 9, 1987,
and all but Senator Riegle attended the meeting with Mr. Gray
on April 2nd of that year, there are differences in their reasons for
attending those meetings, differences in their participation, significant differences in the relationship between and the timing of
Keating contributions and senatorial action. . . .

I wish to emphasize at this early stage that in this case there is
not one single factor that makes what these Senators did proper
or improper. You members of the committee must look at an
entire set of circumstances. . . . You must look at the entire
context to reach the right result.

Grass-Roots Graft
W. John Moore

"Grass-Roots Graft" by W. John Moore ends this chapter with a demonstration that the crisis in government ethics is not confined to the federal level alone. According to Moore, corruption (or at least its exposure) is on the rise in state and local governments as prosecutions and charges of lesser misconduct made by state ethics commissions have skyrocketed. The article is rife with instances of embezzlement, fraud, bribery, and kickbacks that have plagued the nation's Statehouses, courts, and city halls. Moore details the opportunities for local corruption but also suggests its risks, as federal prosecution of state and local officials has doubled in the past decade.

Moore concludes with a discussion of mechanisms that might be useful in dealing with state and local crooks: pumped up enforcement of current laws, new legislation with stiffer penalties, and public exposure by state and local ethics boards. This selection shows, then, that when it comes to mischief-making in government, federal officials have no corner on the market; they just get most of the publicity.

As scams go, the one plotted by Arlington Heights (Ill.) treasurer Lee L. Poder was notable for its elegant simplicity and extraordinary profit. On April 15, Poder allegedly took $20 million from the village firemen's pension fund, which he used as collateral to buy government bonds. Later that day, Poder sold the bonds, making a personal profit of $68,750 on the interest, which he deposited in his personal bank account. Only an alert bank official foiled his scheme by notifying the authorities of the deposits and withdrawals, according to federal prosecutors.

A financial genius Poder is not. Since January 1, he had lost more than $5 million in embezzled Arlington Heights money on bad investments in the stock market, village officials charged. On the lam, Poder proved himself a bit of a bumbler. After escaping

W. John Moore, "Grass-Roots Graft," *National Journal* (August 1, 1987), pp. 1962–1967. Reprinted by permission.

Arlington Heights on a moped, he was arrested on May 8 in Fort Frances, Ontario, for entering the country with a handgun. After 21 days in a Canadian jail, he was turned over to federal authorities in International Falls, Minnesota. Poder has pleaded guilty to federal fraud charges.

Poder's sad story is but one example of mounting corruption and misconduct by state and local government officials. The magnitude of this phenomenon has gone mostly unnoticed because of the public's and the news media's preoccupation with allegations of impropriety at the federal level, including those involving, over the past six years, more than 100 Reagan Administration officials. But Poder is another grim statistic in a recent wave of corruption among scores of state and local officials.

Federal prosecutions of corrupt state and local officials doubled in the past decade, according to the Justice Department's Public Integrity Section. For lesser forms of misconduct, revived state and local ethics commissions have brought an array of additional charges.

"Things are pretty bad and they seem to be getting even worse," said Edward D. Feigenbaum, formerly the staff director for the Council on Governmental Ethics Laws (COGEL) and now an attorney at the Hudson Institute. The group's newsletter bulges with proof: Begun in 1984 as a 16-page quarterly update on ethics issues and corruption charges, it has grown to a 40-page monthly crammed with the latest indictments, prosecutions and convictions of state and local officials around the country.

"Crisis of Confidence"

The roster of public officials tainted by scandal stretches from obscure civil servants to top elected officials. Gov. William P. Clements, Jr., of Texas is embroiled in a dispute over his role, while a trustee of Southern Methodist University, in covering up a football scandal. A Wisconsin attorney general—bearer of a name, La Follette, synonymous with progressive politics—was defeated in 1986 after allegations of ethics violations. Pennsylvania's treasurer was convicted of bribery; his counterpart in New Mexico resigned following allegations of financial chicanery. Connecticut's revenue director quit under fire.

SCANDAL AND CORRUPTION IN GOVERNMENT

State legislators in California, Maryland, and New York have been charged with corruption or mentioned as possible targets of ongoing government probes. The ex-mayor of Syracuse, New York, was indicted in July on charges that he received $1.5 million in kickbacks from city contractors. New political corruption has erupted in Chicago and New York, where venal officials are as much a tradition as the St. Patrick's Day parade.

Scandal has even reached into the judiciary, staining the reputations of judges on state supreme courts in Ohio and Texas and even in Vermont, long known for its clean government. As a result of Operation Greylord, the FBI's controversial undercover investigation of municipal court judges in Chicago, more than sixty judges and lawyers have been indicted on charges from fixing parking tickets to bribery. Six current or former New York judges have been investigated, indicted, or jailed so far this year.

For sheer brazenness, consider the case of Frank D. Polsinello. In December, 1986, Polsinello, chief enforcement official of the New York Board of Elections, wowed COGEL officials at a conference in Hartford, Connecticut, with a rousing speech on ethics. On July 15, Polsinello was indicted on 30 state counts of theft and was accused of unlawfully using board employees to write part of his master's thesis, "Campaign Finance and Disclosure."

These charges have prompted renewed worries that corruption has insinuated itself into the very fabric of government. "We are at a crisis of confidence in government, a crisis that can only be resolved with the fullest possible disclosure of the inner workings of government," the Commission on Integrity in Government, which investigated corruption in New York City and state government, said in its final report in January.

What explains this seemingly rampant corruption? Whether the morality of government officials is better or worse than it used to be, certainly the temptations they face are much greater.

A river of money now flows to the host of companies and contractors doing business with state and local governments. Some are traditional businesses such as construction firms that have thrived on a steady diet of government work. But corruption has gone upscale: State and local governments increasingly pay big bucks to a new class of consultants and contractors, including bond experts, computer specialists, investment bankers and real estate developers. "They have made corruption more conspicuous," said Donald Haider, a professor at Northwestern University's Kellogg Graduate School of Management who was a Republican candidate for mayor of Chicago.

As government and business intermingle, the opportunity for misconduct increases, some political scientists contend. Unlike old-time corruption, in which political bosses provided jobs for votes, the new misconduct often involves conflicts of interest as government employees steer business to outside firms. This "new patronage" has helped spread corruption to government managers. "Patronage is at a higher level. Many people coming into government or politics are doing so for business reasons," said Annmarie H. Walsh, president of the Institute of Public Administration in New York. "A political organization can no longer find jobs for 20 sanitation men, but it is given jobs for 20 managers."

The rising number of cases also reflects political trends. A flood of private money has inundated state and local political systems: Campaign contributions for state and local offices, including judges, have skyrocketed. "Money is really at the heart of it and has been for a while," said Jane Mentzinger, director of state issue development at Common Cause, the public-interest lobby. "People and special interests are trying to use money to gain access and influence with elected or appointed [state] officials similiar to what we see on the national level."

Another explanation for the fast-growing caseload is the federal government's success in throwing a spotlight on state and local corruption. "There is no more corruption today than 20 years ago," said Chicago criminal lawyer Dan K. Webb, a former U.S. Attorney. "But the federal law enforcement machinery is being used more effectively to expose that which went unexposed in the past."

"The reason for the uncovering of corruption that is now almost an epidemic across our society is the federal presence," said G. Robert Blakey, a professor at Notre Dame University Law School.

Corrupting Influences

Bribery has a long, ignoble history. As John T. Noonan, Jr., now a judge on the U.S. Court of Appeals for the Ninth Circuit, wrote in *Bribes* (Macmillan Publishing Co., 1984): "Bribes—socially disapproved inducements of official action meant to be gratuitously exercised—are ancient, almost as ancient as the invention in Egypt of scales which symbolized and showed social acceptance of the idea of objective judgment." In ancient Rome, Cicero almost lost an attempted murder case when defendant Oppianicus greased the skids with the judge, Gaius Staienus. Epiphanius of Alexandria outlined a complete bribery scheme in a letter to the bishop of Constantinople.

During America's Gilded Age of the late 19th century, bribes from the railroads were routinely routed to legislators on the floors of state capitols. Typically, periods of noteworthy graft and corruption were followed by demands for reform. After the outrageous corruption of New York City's Tammany Hall, the Progressives called for a cleanup.

Periodic reform efforts usually met with limited success. After the glare of publicity and the adoption of good-government measures, another cycle of corruption would begin.

"Like roaches, public corruption keeps coming back," said former Watergate Prosecutor Samuel Dash, now a professor at Georgetown University's Institute of Criminal Justice.

Or as Finley Peter Dunne's literary character Mr. Dooley, a saloonkeeper of the Tammany Hall era, remarked, reform movements eventually lose their appeal and "we raysume our nachral condition iv illagal merrimint."

Political corruption remains resistant to easy cures. Blame the age-old problem of greed, traditionalists say. Boss Willie Stark, the protagonist in Robert Penn Warren's novel *All the King's Men*, put it best when he asked Jack Burden, the narrator, to find something incriminating on a respected judge:

" 'But suppose there isn't anything to find?' And the Boss said, 'There is always something.' And I said, 'Maybe not on the Judge.' And he said, 'Man is conceived in sin and born in corruption and he passeth from the stink of the didie to the stench of the shroud. There is always something.' " And, in the book, there was.

Social analysts today say there is a values vacuum: Political corruption, like insider trading or the Iran-Contra affair, reflects the moral malaise of the 1980s, they say. Combine greed and opportunity, and a volatile mixture is formed.

Campaign contributions are the easiest way to gain influence, and the amount going to state legislators has skyrocketed, up 57 percent in California from 1984–86. In Texas, for example, contributions to state representatives in 1985, a nonelection year, rose 46 percent from 1983. Contributions from political action committees (PACs) increased by 174 percent over the same period, according to Common Cause of Texas. Texas Senate figures revealed similar data, with total contributions up 8 percent and PAC dollars up 64 percent. "If we seriously want to address the root cause of undue influence in Texas political life, we have to address the issue of money," said John Hildreth, executive director of Common Cause of Texas.

Recent revelations that the law firms representing Texaco Inc. and Pennzoil Co. gave a total of more than $400,000 in campaign contributions to the Texas Supreme Court judges likely to hear their billion-dollar lawsuit have drawn attention to the upsurge in campaign spending on judicial races. "What's at stake here is the actual integrity of the judiciary in almost all the states in the union," Roy Schotland, a Georgetown University Law Center professor, told *Common Cause Magazine*.

In Texas, the Commission on Judicial Conduct received 390 complaints about judges in fiscal 1985. The number of complaints in the current year [1987] will likely top 700, according to Robert C. Flowers, the commission's executive director.

Scandal already has arrived at some state high courts. An Ohio Supreme Court judge lost his reelection bid in 1986 (despite spending $1.7 million on the race) after he received a campaign contribution from a union with alleged links to organized crime. The Texas Commission on Judicial Conduct publicly censured two state Supreme Court judges for unethical conduct linked to campaign contributions, and Governor Clements has asked them to resign; they also face impeachment by the state Senate. Leaders of the Texas bar have recommended that the state move to merit selection of judges.

New Opportunities

Expected to do more with less federal aid, states and cities now administer more programs, control bigger budgets and spend more money than they did a decade ago. The operating budget for the New York Legislature has quadrupled in the past decade to $157 million, or approximately $750,000 for each of the 211 state legislators, according to *The New York Times*. And state and local agencies are taken more seriously now that they regulate everything from banking to telephones. This expansion of state and local activity creates opportunities for corruption as public and private functions merge.

Some political scientists worry that the distinction between government and business is lost. "The fact that there really isn't a black line between the private sector and the public sector is important to this issue of corruption," said Guthrie S. Birkhead, dean of Syracuse University's Maxwell School of Citizenship and Public Affairs. "As public and private become more alike," Birkhead mused, "a lot more cases called public corruption by the press are uncovered." But some, such as the Wedtech scandal that has engulfed both politicians and business executives, could just as easily be considered private corruption, he added.

"Contracting out" exacerbates this situation. With federal aid down dramatically during the Reagan era, states and cities confront a budget crunch and in response, have turned to contracting for services as an economy move.

Critics such as the American Federation of State, County and Municipal Employees have long argued that such practices lead to increased corruption. Al Bilik, an executive director of the AFL-CIO's public employee department, said that contracting of services is often conducted outside traditional governmental processes such as competitive bidding. "There is also a lack of accountability once that contract is let," he added.

Many law enforcement experts also worry that in those areas where government and business intersect, conditions are ripe for corruption. "The opportunities for misbehavior have increased tremendously as governments have gone to contracting out as a way to, quote, save money, produce efficiencies," said Joseph E. diGenova, the U.S. Attorney for the District of Columbia.

Many scandals involve public officials receiving kickbacks in return for lucrative contracts. In New York and Chicago, federal investigations continue into the mushrooming scandal involving city officials and companies seeking contracts to track down money owed for parking-ticket violations. In Pennsylvania, allegations surfaced in 1984 that state and local government officials were offered bribes in return for a $5.4 million computer contract. Among those convicted in the case were computer company executives and Pennsylvania treasurer R. Budd Dwyer, who later committed suicide. The computer company allegedly made an illegal $300,000 contribution to Dwyer's reelection campaign.

Some contend that the free-market approach cleanses rather than pollutes government. Corruption flourishes in a closed system in which government decisions are based on political fealty, they say, and as services deteriorate, citizens are forced into petty corruption to accomplish everything from finding an apartment to obtaining a permit.

John Tepper Marlin, president of the Council on Municipal Performance in New York, said the focus on contracting out is unfair. Isolated examples of corruption ignore the savings inherent in privatization and the petty corruption that plagues many municipal governments, he said. "The day-in, day-out normal malfeasance of the public sector is worse than the one-time, one-shot corruption that might occur when you contract privately," he said.

Federal Clout

Federal efforts to deal with corrupt state and local officials once were limited to studies conducted by blue-ribbon panels, such as the 1929 Wickersham Commission report or the Katzenbach study on organized crime and corruption commissioned by President Johnson. Former FBI director J. Edgar Hoover had little interest in federal, state, or local corruption.

In the early 1960s, prompted by Attorney General Robert F. Kennedy, the Justice Department shifted its focus from bank robbery to corruption, labor racketeering, organized crime, and white-collar criminals. "Ever since then, it has been a major focus of the Justice Department's criminal justice activities," Dash noted. And starting in the early 1970s, after Hoover's reign, the FBI helped the Justice Department initiate a successful crackdown on corrupt lawmakers and officials.

The Abscam investigation led to the convictions of several House Members and Senator Harrison A. Williams, Jr., D-N.J.

Other Justice Department investigations led to the downfalls of former Illinois Governor Otto J. Kerner, Maryland Governor Marvin Mandel, Oklahoma Governor David Hall, and Tennessee Governor Ray Blanton.

Aggressive U.S. Attorneys throughout the country also have rooted out more corrupt activity than local officials were able to discover in the past. "There is not a change in amount of corruption but a change in investigative techniques," said Phillip Heymann, a Harvard University Law School professor who approved the controversial Operation Greylord while an assistant attorney general during the Carter Administration.

The Justice Department has relied on federal statutes unavailable to local prosecutors. And only the federal government can easily foot the bill for costly, wide-ranging undercover operations that often lead to major corruption scandals. For example, federal prosecutors have uncovered links between corruption in Chicago and New York. "We get involved when the state or local authorities either won't or can't deal with public corruption," explained Floyd I. Clarke, the assistant director of the FBI's criminal investigative division.

The Justice Department has scored highly publicized victories that criminal law experts believe justify the time, effort, and expense. A continuing investigation by the U.S. Attorney's office into corruption in the District of Columbia government has already resulted in the conviction of deputy mayor Alphonse G. Hill and a guilty plea by Ivanhoe Donaldson, formerly a top aide to [former] Mayor Marion S. Barry. An investigation by Rudolph W. Giuliani, the U.S. Attorney for the Southern District of New York, into New York municipal corruption has resulted in several convictions in a huge kickback scam involving parking-ticket collection contracts. The U.S. Attorney's office in Philadelphia won a major case in July.

Yet there are rumblings of dissatisfaction with the federal prosecutors. Civil liberties experts have opposed some of their undercover techniques. Leaks of ongoing probes have plagued investigations in New York, Tampa, and Washington. Six black political groups, in a brief filed on July 7 [1987] with the U.S. District Court for the District of Columbia, said that as a result of the leaks, Mayor Barry and other District officials were victims of the "white power structure" that was using law enforcement agencies "to discredit black leadership."

Other critics assert that ambitious and overzealous prosecutors can indulge in overkill. Unsuccessful prosecutions have left victorious politicians embittered about their treatment. In Florida, eleven of fifteen local officials tried on corruption charges were acquitted. "The federal prosecutor's zeal increases and his appetite is more avaricious when the bait is a public official," complained Bruce M. Lyons, a Fort Lauderdale (Florida) attorney and president of the National Association of Criminal Defense Lawyers.

In the most significant setback for federal prosecutors, the U.S. Supreme Court recently rejected a broad definition of "mail fraud" under which many corrupt state and local officials were prosecuted. Some prosecutors played down the decision, asserting that the Justice Department could rely on other laws, particularly the Racketeer Influenced and Corrupt Organizations Act (RICO). But Blakey of Notre Dame, a former Senate aide who drafted the RICO statute, said the mail fraud decision "decimated, in the literal sense, one out of 10 federal cases involving state and local corruption."

Coping with Corruption

The level of enforcement by state and local authorities is spottier than that of federal prosecutors, but there are signs of accelerating activity. One indicator is the enactment of new state ethics laws. Five state ethics commissions were created in the past two years. Some cities have also acted. Skeptics doubt that the states and cities have imposed regulations restrictive or punitive enough to do the job, but others contend that the new ethics laws work. "This is prevention and, in this instance, prevention is worth a pound of cure," said David H. Martin, [former] director of the U.S. Office of Government Ethics.

Most statutes give state ethics bodies new powers to deal with campaign financing conflicts of interest, financial disclosure and whistle-blowers. Georgia, New Hampshire, Oklahoma and West Virginia have created ethics agencies.

Most legislatures have expanded on existing ethics statutes that were enacted after the 1972–74 Watergate scandals. An Indiana bill protects whistle-blowers and limits gifts from prospective bidders for contracts. After a lengthy battle between Governor Mario M. Cuomo and the Democratic leadership in the Assembly, the New York Legislature enacted one of the nation's strictest ethics laws. It requires legislators and their aides to file extensive financial disclosure forms. State employees earning more than $30,000 a year and the chairmen of political parties in major counties must do the same. Legislators and aides will no longer be permitted to collect legal fees if they represent clients before state agencies.

Virginia's General Assembly passed a bill barring legislators from voting on issues in which they have a financial interest. Chicago's new ethics code demands that city aldermen and other officials disclose their outside income. New York's city council has endorsed an anticorruption proposal with some teeth. The bill, subject to clearance by the state Legislature, would revoke the pension of any city official convicted of a crime committed while in office.

"We are really seeing a sort of rebirth of ethics legislation," said Stephan W. Stover, COGEL's chairman and administrator of the Ohio Supreme Court. "The existence of ethics laws and ethics commissions to interpret and enforce the laws has served as a major deterrent to public corruption and unethical behavior."

John H. Larson, chairman of the California Fair Political Practices Commission, said that reforms requiring more disclosure by public officials and lobbyists are working. "To the extent that everyone knows that they will be under scrutiny and their finances disclosed," the laws prevent conflicts of interest and other violations, he added. Yet in a key omission, the state's disclosure laws don't apply to legislators. And the U.S. Attorney's office in Los Angeles is investigating alleged corruption in the Legislature.

In some instances, ethics boards merely suggested the possibility of improper behavior, and voters responded by turning suspect officials out of office. Bad publicity stemming from ethics board actions played a role in the electoral defeats of some officials, including Wisconsin's attorney general, the chief justice of Ohio's Supreme Court and a Maryland legislator. "The strongest arrow in our quiver has been the mere reprimand," said R. Roth Judd, executive director of the Wisconsin Ethics Board, "because citizens see the ethics board as an independent, fair-minded body of citizens and its decisions have credibility. Our experience has been [that] when misconduct is publicized, the electors have thrown the rascals out."

But ethics laws and commissions don't impress everyone. U.S. Attorney Giuliani said the new New York State law fails to go far enough. Even COGEL's Feigenbaum conceded that rotten officials can negate good laws.

Haider of Northwestern stressed that the effort must be made. He recalled the words of the late Wallace Sayre, a legendary Columbia University government professor: "Corruption is endemic to state and local government. The job of the mayor or governor is to prevent it from being an epidemic."

CHASING CORRUPT OFFICIALS

Over the decade from 1975 to 1985, federal prosecutors have stepped up their fight against government corruption. The result is a dramatic increase in indictments and convictions, as listed below. The table also shows the number of officials awaiting trial as of December 31 of each year.

	1975	1980	1985
Federal officials			
indicted	53	123	563
convicted	43	131	470
awaiting trial	5	16	90
State officials			
indicted	36	72	79
convicted	18	51	66
awaiting trial	5	28	20
Local officials			
indicted	139	247	248
convicted	94	168	221
awaiting trial	15	82	49

Source: Justice Department

CHAPTER 3

THE ETHICS OF
POLITICAL CAMPAIGNING

Introduction

Many people observe the quality of campaigns that politicians conduct and conclude that ethics has had no role. Questionable financing, vote buying, the power of special interest groups, the manipulation of the media, the attacking of political opponents' character, negative advertising, and invasion of privacy are now typical features of modern political campaigns. It is argued that these and other forms of campaign mischief make America a leader among democratic nations in voter apathy, alienation, and anger.

The main focus of this chapter is the ethics of political campaigning. We will survey the main issues of campaign financing and spending, the power of special interest groups to influence campaigns via political action committees (PACs), the use of negative campaign advertising, and the question of whether there are certain limits as to how much of a politician's private life should be drawn into the public political arena.

The call for the reform of campaign financing is a perennial feature of the political scene. Reforms, proponents argue, are necessary given such problems as the manner in which campaign donations are offered and collected, how those donations are actually spent, and the vast sums of money needed today to run a successful campaign for national office. Political campaigning is thereby tarnished by influence buying, the misuse of campaign funds, and the need to amass ever larger campaign war chests. In short, the financial side of politics, which is specifically involved in conducting a race for office, is another area in which the crisis in government ethics has manifested itself.

The first selection of the chapter, "From *The Money Chase*," by David B. Magleby and Candice J. Nelson, provides an overview of the issues that crop up under the rubric of campaign financing and its reform. Their review is an excellent primer on the role that money plays in politics. Peter Bragdon then examines a specific question about the spending of money from campaign war chests in "Campaign Funds for Legal Fees: It's Legal, but Is It Proper?" Bragdon exposes the sometimes major expenditures by politicians to cover legal fees that are drawn from campaign coffers.

Another bothersome issue in the area of politics, money, and ethics is the role that political action committees should play in the electoral process. Legally established by Congress in 1971, PACs have come under great criticism as an unfair advantage for special interest groups to get their message in front of a candidate. Moreover, PACs have seen tremendous growth. In 1978 there were 1,949 registered PACs, but by 1988 their number had swelled to 4,828. PACs have been formed by a diverse number of organizations, from labor unions, businesses, and trade and professional associations, to ideological groups that form PACs to further their specific concerns, such as the National Conservative Political Action Committee (NCPAC). But the major ethical problem of PACs centers upon whether they represent a vehicle for undue influence over elected officials.

Critics of PACs claim that when they back a successful candidate for public office, there is a tacit obligation on the part of the newly elected official to vote in ways favoring the interests of the PAC. Interestingly enough, though, studies of voting patterns in Congress give a mixed bag of results, in which no obvious relationship between PAC monies and voting records has been clearly established. So, it is difficult to say with certainty that PACs have the impact of "owning" public officials, which their critics charge.

Nonetheless, some will point out that PACs do have a noticeable effect upon the electoral process with respect to the unequal distribution of PAC contributions. For example, in 1988 PACs contributed $82.23 million to incumbents in the House of Representatives, but only $9.48 million to challengers. In the Senate, $28.67 million went to incumbents, $7.67 million to opponents. Thus, it might be concluded that PACs do much to ensure the status quo and with their contributions add to the problem of incumbency that has led many to call for the shortening of the term that officials serve to ensure that they do not accumulate too much power while in office.

THE ETHICS OF POLITICAL CAMPAIGNING

Robert Allan Cooke takes an unconventional look at PACs in his "The PAC Man Cometh: Should We Bar the Door?" while "Back-Pocket PACs" by *Common Cause Magazine*'s Peter Overby suggests that some U.S. Senators and Representatives are skirting the PAC laws by maintaining "nonfederal account" PACs.

The last problem of ethics and politics addressed in the chapter is what might be called the "mudslinging factor." This term denotes the use of campaign tactics that attack one's opponent as a person rather than just attacking her political positions. Character assassination, *ad hominem* references, negative advertising, and revealing past personal matters, such as drinking habits, sexual conduct, and so on, are all recent examples of the mudslinging factor. According to many political analysts, although they are not a new political phenomenon in America, "dirty" campaigns are now more prevalent than ever.

Given the wide use of the media, especially television, by candidates, negative political advertising has had its impact on the public. This aspect of the mudslinging factor is particularly complex. First, while on the one hand, polls indicate that the public is upset by the amount and the frequency of negative political advertising, controlling it runs into free-speech issues. Passing legislation that outlaws it may create more problems than the advertising itself. Second, although public opinion condemns negative advertising in political campaigns, few would argue with the claim that this mudslinging tactic nonetheless works. Because it is effective, political consultants urge candidates to use it more and more. Hence, like violence, negative political advertising only begets more, and the public gets treated to a steady diet of it each campaign season. "The Ethics of Negative Political Advertising," by Richard E. Vatz and Lee S. Weinberg, examines these and other ethical problems surrounding this complex issue.

In addition to the question of negative political advertising, there is also great concern about the privacy rights of candidates that have had mud slung at them. One need only recall the experiences of Democratic Presidential candidate Gary Hart in this regard to see the importance of the privacy issue. Hart had his marital infidelities publicized in the press, in particular a weekend dalliance that the media were able to document with photos and newsreels. As a result, the front-running Democrat was forced to leave the race. But questions that Hart and others raised at the time still remain: Should the private lives of public officials be a basis upon which the electorate makes its choices, and to what extent do politicians have a right to claim privacy in their lives? Dennis F. Thompson tackles these thorny issues in "The Private Lives of Public Officials."

The upshot of the essential issues raised in this chapter on ethics and politics is perhaps best phrased as a series of interrelated questions: Can politicians divorce themselves from the quest for money to run their campaigns? Are major campaign contributions nothing more than the act of influence buying on the part of special interest groups? Are reforms in this area possible? Need politicians engage in mudslinging to win an election? What rights to privacy can politicians claim, if any? These are difficult questions, requiring hard analysis. The materials collected here should help sort out the answers.

From *The Money Chase*
David B. Magleby and Candice J. Nelson

The excerpt presented here, "From *The Money Chase*," by David B. Magleby and Candice J. Nelson, constitutes the Introduction to a book of the same name, published by the Brookings Institution. While the book deals extensively with many specific issues surrounding the way that Congressional politicians raise and spend campaign money, this brief selection from it presents an overview of the ethical problems inherent in campaign financing. Magleby and Nelson underscore the fact that the cost of running a Congressional campaign has spiraled over the years, with longer campaigns and higher spending per voter. Thus, to stay competitive, candidates must engage in a "money chase" that has serious consequences for Congress and the way that it conducts the people's business. Time spent chasing money means less time for completing important legislative tasks.

Reform of the status quo, however, is easier said than done. Magleby and Nelson outline some of the obstacles to reform,

David B. Magleby and Candice J. Nelson, *The Money Chase: Congressional Campaign Finance Reform* (Washington, DC: The Brookings Institution, 1990), pp. 1–10. Reprinted with permission from the Brookings Institution.

not the least of which is the "politics of reform" itself. They conclude their overview with the observation that regardless of the difficulties involved, the public expectation is that something must be done to reform this essential problem of government ethics.

Money is a necessary means to achieve the democratic ends of American politics. Candidates, political parties, and interest groups all raise and spend money for political purposes, including such essential activities as communicating with voters, registering them, and mobilizing them on Election Day. These activities are universally seen as important and laudable. But the way candidates, groups, and parties raise and spend the money needed to finance such activities has been the subject of considerable controversy and ongoing debate. The issues of who should pay for elections, in what way, and with what expectations have again moved to center stage in American politics.

The first session of the 101st Congress was overwhelmed with problems of compensation and the ethical handling of money. Early in 1989 members fought a bruising battle over a congressional pay raise. Speaker Jim Wright was charged with evading House rules on accepting outside income, which led to his unprecedented resignation. Five members of the Senate were accused of being improperly influenced by Charles Keating, executive of the Lincoln Savings and Loan in California, which was in financial trouble. Although the House succeeded in adopting a proposal that raised salaries in return for the elimination of honoraria, concerns remain that money has a suffocating and corrupting influence on Congress.[1] And nowhere have these concerns been more evident than in debates on how to reform the financing of congressional election campaigns.

Because of rising campaign costs, politicians have been forced to follow a never-ending money chase. They spend countless hours and tremendous energy in fundraising, often to the detriment of their legislative duties. Incumbents in both parties and both houses have increasingly been drawn to political action committees and other big contributors to fill campaign war chests, raising questions of whether these special interests are unduly shaping decisions on public policy. Meanwhile, potential challengers have had an even more difficult job of raising enough money to run competitive campaigns. The result is that in the past few elections House incumbents have been reelected about 98 percent of the time, a situation that threatens to create an entrenched and less responsive legislature.

Nevertheless, the forces inhibiting a major overhaul of the campaign finance system are formidable. Self-interest separates incumbents and challengers, Democrats and Republicans, House and Senate. Reform has also been stymied because of deep philosophical differences over the proper role of government in financing and regulating campaigns. Finally, distrust and perceptions of unfair treatment by leaders and members on both sides of the partisan divide have made this a difficult issue at the interpersonal level. And these divisions have been made worse because students of campaign finance cannot agree why these problems have arisen and how they can best be solved. . . .

Overview of the Issues

The American congressional campaign finance system is burdened with rising costs and marked by decreasing competition. Both too much and too little is spent in congressional elections. Hundreds of House challengers are seriously underfinanced and largely invisible. Instead of contests in 435 congressional districts, competitive elections often take place in fewer than 50. In 1988 just 11 percent of House incumbents were elected with less than 60 percent of the vote; on average 24 percent were elected with less than 60 percent of the vote since 1970.[2] Incumbents can and do spend increasing amounts of money on decreasingly competitive seats. As incumbents become safer in their seats, a permanent majority in the House becomes more and more a reality.[3]

The dynamic in Senate elections has been much different. Twice during the 1980s control of the chamber changed hands, with Republicans picking up several close victories in 1980 and then losing several of those same seats in 1986. Incumbent Senators now expect to have competitive challengers, and thus campaign spending per voter has increased dramatically. Rising costs and competitive elections also mean longer campaigns and a much greater commitment of time from challengers, who now

THE ETHICS OF POLITICAL CAMPAIGNING

routinely start fundraising two years before the election. Because this is a full-time job, they must have an independent means of support early in the period, which means wealthy candidates have a tremendous advantage.

Given such expensive campaigns, where does the money come from? For most House incumbents, the largest source is political action committees, or PACs; for Senate incumbents PACs are not yet so important, but the share of campaign funds that comes from them has been growing. Most challengers for seats in either house receive little from such special interests; PACs do not generally want to offend the politicians in power. Candidates also turn to individual donors who can contribute $500 to $1,000. Such relatively wealthy people share with PACs a policy focus and contribute with the expectation that a legislator they have helped win will respond to their concerns. Given congressional incumbents' preoccupation with reelection, campaign contributions are greatly valued, and those who provide the funds are given special treatment.

The consequences of the money chase are also serious for Congress as an institution. Because limits on what individuals and PACs can give do not take account of inflation, members must constantly expand their donor base. This takes more and more time and effort. Although Congress once prohibited fundraising in congressional offices on Capitol Hill, now one or more staff members in each office may be designated to receive campaign contributions. Fundraising also affects the legislative process itself. Leaders of both parties have commented on the difficulty of scheduling floor business in the evenings because of the competition from Washington fundraising events and the need to accommodate members traveling around the country to raise money. In short, fundraising has become a larger part of the job description of House and Senate members and more important to both houses and both parties than it ought to be. . . .

Not everyone agrees on the specific problems attendant to the current system of campaign finance; indeed, there are very different perceptions of what the problems are. However, observers generally agree that the system needs to be changed. Many of the strongest advocates of reform are confident that their favored solutions would have only positive consequences.[4] But an irony of the current system is that the importance of PACs, often listed as one of the major problems, is itself a product of post-Watergate reform legislation. Others conclude that reform is so complicated and so rife with potential problems that change is likely to do more harm than good.[5] Neither position is tenable. Some reforms in and of themselves would only make existing problems worse. For example, enacting spending limits without providing public financing, or more ready access to money, would make it even more difficult for challengers to run competitive campaigns. But some reforms—reducing the costs of communicating with potential voters, for example—would almost certainly improve the current system.

Congressional campaign finance reform has been a seemingly intractable area of public policy, and the rhetoric of the debate has often been inflamed and prone to overgeneralizations. Advocates of limiting PAC influence have charged that "Washington is corrupt to the core."[6] Defenders of the status quo often divert attention from the issues of rising costs, the increased role of PACs, and declining competition by shifting the terms of argument to "the real corruption," namely honoraria, free trips home for legislators, and the conversion of unused campaign funds to personal use when a member retires from the House.[7] . . .

Congressional campaign finance has been frequently written about in the press. It is a subject tailor-made for editorial writers because of its apparent simplicity and its easily espoused solutions that are seemingly without costs. But editorial writers and news reporters are not alone in these tendencies; academics are also prone to overgeneralization, mere description, or an extremely narrow definition of the research question. This is perhaps best illustrated in the literature on PACs. Although careful authors and scholars have written about this problem and have made significant contributions to understanding it, they have focused on the current system rather than on possible reforms and their likely consequences. . . .

[An evaluation is needed of] possible reforms of congressional campaign finance in light of experience, the judgment of key participants in the current system, and political realities. Most research on campaign finance has either scrutinized the current sources of funds—parties, PACs, or individuals—or examined the relationships between the amount of money spent and electoral success.[8] Books that have examined possible reforms have typically done so only in a concluding chapter; reform has not been their main purpose.[9]

Assessing possible changes in the congressional campaign finance system requires anticipating the behavior of individual contributors, PACs, parties, and candidates, although it is true that no one knows for sure how these participants will behave. Changes have and will continue to occur in the way congressional campaigns are financed, whether or not Congress adopts any of the reforms we discuss. Some of the changes that have occurred since the passage of the last set of reforms include dramatic growth in campaign costs, increases in the number of PACs and in their importance to candidates' overall campaign funds, a diminished role for contributors of modest means, and longer campaigns. In sum, recent changes in the system have had important consequences in their own right and need to be evaluated.

[Thus,] there already exists a substantial literature on the present system and past reform proposals as well as the consequences of the present system for competition, political parties, and interest groups.[10] But this literature does not examine information in light of the debate on reform. . . .

One other reason why much of what has been written about the current system is of limited usefulness is that reform would significantly change the campaign finance system itself. For instance, if all candidates in general elections were given public funds sufficient to enable them to achieve significant voter recognition, candidate recruitment would undoubtedly be made easier and at least some election outcomes less one-sided. We know that the presidential nominating rules have affected the pool of candidates and their strategies.[11] There is every reason to believe that this would be true in congressional elections as well. It is less certain what parts of current behavior will carry over into the new world of reformed campaign finance. . . . It is important to note that although studies of current practices may help predict behavior under reform, it is also likely that in some important respects they will not.

Some issues in the debate on campaign finance reform are empirically resolvable, but many of the most important are not. Take, for instance, the question of whether too little or too much is spent on campaigns. The answer will finally be a judgment based on spending patterns, the implications of spending for competition—or, as we will define it, visibility—and how the costs of campaigns affect the pool of candidates. . . . Too much is spent in some campaigns and not nearly enough in others. But our assessment is premised on a belief in the importance of real electoral competition, something readers may or may not agree with as a basic assumption.

A similar problem arises as to whether special interests are unduly influential. These interests will always have the influence that results from a politically active membership, the ability to provide relevant information, and the like.[12] But what effect do PACs have on Congress? One school of thought defines influence narrowly, using only the results of floor roll call votes. These votes, however, are only one step in the legislative process.[13] Focusing only on them overlooks the involvement of PACs and their affiliated organizations in lobbying for committee assignments for favored members, setting the legislative agenda of subcommittees and committees, helping organize hearings, drafting legislation and amendments to legislation, preparing committee reports, and stopping or redirecting the activities of members and committees in their legislative or policy oversight responsibilities. This more inclusive definition raises two questions: how involved are PACs in these activities, and to what extent is their influence the result of their large and growing role in financing congressional campaigns? Unfortunately, very little attention has been paid to PAC activities in parts of the legislative process that occur away from floor votes.

The problem is not that political science cannot determine the answer to these questions, but rather that to do so requires a very different approach from those already taken.[14] It is also not true that one must adopt an all-or-nothing approach to PACs, as the organizations' defenders often assume. If one believes campaign contributions or honoraria payments give special interests influence over Senators and Representatives, that does not mean interest groups per se should have no influence. The question is what additional leverage special interests obtain as a result of their ability to give money directly to members of Congress, to play a large and growing role in financing their campaigns through PACs, and to retire their campaign debts. It also begs the question to argue that PACs are little different from individual donors who

THE ETHICS OF POLITICAL CAMPAIGNING

make large contributions. If giving campaign money changes the relationship [among] individuals, groups, and members of Congress, as common sense suggests it must, then this leads to a definition of undue influence for both individuals and groups who contribute to campaigns.

Given our focus on what we see as problems with the present system of congressional campaign finance and our desire to assess the consequences, intended and unintended, of possible reforms, we cannot avoid discussing values. Much of what is discussed is open to different interpretations. . . .

The proper role for government in financing and regulating campaigns, the effects of the present system or possible alternatives on candidate recruitment and electoral competition, and the extent to which campaigns should be financed by organized interests with legislative agendas all are examples of topics on which there is substantial disagreement. We do not presume to resolve these disagreements. What we seek to do is identify the issues, evaluate the extent to which their importance is supported by experience, and assess their political consequences.

[It is also important] to assess alternative reform proposals as well as the status quo. What are the administrative limitations of the Federal Election Commission? What would be the implications of public financing for candidate recruitment? Do spending limits by their nature help incumbents? If new restrictions or limitations are placed on campaign money, where is it likely to surface next? Will money spent in these new ways have detrimental effects on the political system? What can be learned from the experience of the states or other nations in the financing of elections? This is a partial list, but it illustrates the important questions that reform raises. . . .

. . . The politics of reform itself needs additional analysis. A record eight cloture votes attempting to override a partisan filibuster were taken on a reform bill in the 100th Congress. Support for reform surfaced in the 1988 vice presidential debate and was frequently discussed in the ethics and congressional salary disputes of 1989. President Bush's proposed changes in campaign laws were the first from an administration on the subject in more than a decade. Both houses of Congress revisited congressional campaign finance in the 101st Congress. A bipartisan task force worked for several months in the House and seemed to be

---

making progress before breaking down along the predictable partisan lines. The Senate created a panel of outside experts to "stimulate discussion and perhaps even break the legislative logjam in Congress."[15] While Congress was deliberating, the Supreme Court handed down another in a series of campaign finance reform decisions, this time concerning independent expenditures.[16] The actions by all three branches of government in 1989–90 are evidence that congressional campaign finance and related ethics issues are now part of the agenda of American politics.

Although there is no agreement on the types of reforms that should be made, the public feels that something needs to be done. Democrats and Republicans, House and Senate candidates, incumbents and nonincumbents all perceive problems with the current system of campaign finance. We hope our discussion will provide the relevant data, inform those who may not have considered all sides of the issue, and facilitate the debate to come.

NOTES

1. The Senate enacted a more modest pay raise for itself and reduced the amount of money Senators could accept in honoraria from 40 percent of their salaries to 27 percent. However, it is possible that the Senate will reconsider a ban on honoraria in the 101st Congress, or after the 1990 elections. [The Senate did ban honoraria in the summer of 1991.]

2. Calculated from Norman J. Ornstein, Thomas E. Mann, and Michael J. Malbin, *Vital Statistics on Congress, 1989–1990* (Washington, DC: Congressional Quarterly, 1990), p. 59.

3. The reelection rate in the House will probably decline somewhat following the redistricting that will occur after the 1990 census. Even if districts are drawn to protect incumbents, members in states that are losing seats fear being put in a district with another incumbent.

4. Philip Stern, *The Best Congress Money Can Buy* (New York: Pantheon Books, 1988).

5. Frank Sorauf, *Money in American Elections* (Glenview, IL: Scott, Foresman, 1988).

6. Amitai Etzioni, *Capital Corruption: The New Attack on American Democracy* (New Brunswick, NJ: Transaction Books, 1988), p. xi.

7. Larry Sabato, "Campaign Finance Reform Ideas: The Good, the Bad & the Ugly," Project for Comprehensive Campaign Reform, April 1989.

8. See, for example, Paul S. Herrnson, *Party Campaigning in the 1980s* (Cambridge, Mass.: Harvard University Press, 1988); Theodore J. Eismeier and Philip H. Pollock III, *Business, Money and the Rise of Corporate PACs in American Elections* (Quorum Books, 1988); Richard P. Conlon, "The Declining Role of Individual Contributions in Financing Congressional Elections," *Journal of Law and Politics*, vol, 3 (Winter 1987), pp. 467–507; Gary C. Jacobson, "The Effects of Campaign Spending in Congressional Elections," *American Political Science Review*, vol. 72 (June 1978), pp. 469–491; and Donald Green and Jonathan Krasno, "Salvation for the Spendthrift Incumbent: Reestimating the Effects of Campaign Spending in House Elections," *American Journal of Political Science*, vol. 32 (November 1988), pp. 884–907.

9. See Larry Sabato, *PAC Power: Inside the World of Political Action Committees* (New York: Norton, 1984); Brooks Jackson, *Honest Graft: Big Money and the American Political Process* (New York: Alfred A. Knopf, 1988); Stern, *The Best Congress Money Can Buy;*

Herrnson, *Party Campaigning in the 1980s;* Eismeier and Pollock, *Business, Money and the Rise of Corporate PACs;* and Sorauf, *Money in American Elections.*

10. For past reform proposals, see Herbert E. Alexander, *Financing Politics: Money, Elections and Political Reform* (Washington, DC: Congressional Quarterly Press, 1976); Robert E. Mutch, *Campaigns, Congress and Courts: The Making of Federal Campaign Finance Law* (New York: Praeger, 1988); and Larry J. Sabato, *Paying for Elections: The Campaign Finance Thicket* (New York: Priority Press, 1989). For effects of the current system on competition, see Jacobson, "The Effects of Campaign Spending in Congressional Elections"; and Green and Krasno, "Salvation for the Spendthrift Incumbent." Consequences for political parties are discussed in Herrnson, *Party Campaigning in the 1980s;* and Sorauf, *Money in American Elections.* Eismeier and Pollock, *Business, Money and the Rise of Corporate PACs,* and Sabato, *PAC Power,* treat interest groups.

11. Byron Shafer, *Quiet Revolution: The Struggle for the Democratic Party and the Shaping of Post-Reform Politics* (New York: Russell Sage Foundation, 1983).

12. Raymond Bauer, Ithiel de Sola Pool, and Lewis Anthony Dexter, *American Business and Public Policy: The Politics of Foreign Trade* (Atherton Press, 1963).

13. John Kingdon, *Congressmen's Voting Decisions* (New York: Harper and Row, 1973).

14. In some ways this is analogous to the debate over community power in American cities. See Nelson Polsby, *Community Power and Political Theory* (New Haven: Yale University Press, 1963); and Robert Dahl, *Who Governs? Democracy and Power in an American City* (New Haven: Yale University Press, 1961).

15. Campaign Finance Reform Panel, "Campaign Finance Reform: A Report to the Majority Leader and Minority Leader, United States Senate," March 6, 1990, p. 1.

16. *Austin* v. *Michigan State Chamber of Commerce,* 110 S. Ct. 21 (1990).

Campaign Funds for Legal Fees: It's Legal, but Is It Proper?
Peter Bragdon

Money collected by a politician for his campaign may not actually be spent in campaigning but may wind up being used for other purposes. In this selection, Peter Bragdon raises the ethical question of using campaign funds to cover the legal fees of incumbents who find themselves in trouble with the law for one reason or another. Although the Federal Election Commission has issued advisory opinions that politicians may draw upon their campaign funds to pay lawyers for their services, Bragdon presents questions about the propriety of such payments, which have gone into the hundreds of thousands of dollars. In addition to those who are currently in office, this practice has also been found among retired politicians, who are able to continue to tap their campaign monies thanks to a

---

Peter Bragdon, "Campaign Funds for Legal Fees: It's Legal, but Is It Proper?" *Congressional Quarterly Weekly Report,* Vol. 47 (November 18, 1989), pp. 3190–3192. Reprinted with permission, Congressional Quarterly, Inc.

special "grandfather clause" in the federal election law that permits certain incumbents to convert campaign funds to personal use. While this provision is being reviewed by Congress, many have found it a boost to their retirement savings if they didn't have the need to spend it on legal fees.

Tennessee Representative Harold E. Ford has always been known in Memphis for his top-notch political organization. But the Democrat's campaign committee has spent almost as freely on lawyers as it has on mobilizing voters. Tens of thousands of campaign dollars have gone toward Ford's effort to clear his name after an indictment on bribery charges.

Ford is not alone. For a number of other members of Congress, political expenses have become synonymous with legal expenses. Taken together, these members have spent hundreds of thousands of dollars from their campaign treasuries in the past year to combat career-threatening ethics charges.

The Federal Election Commission (FEC) has issued advisory opinions stating that such expenditures from campaign funds are legal. And the House ethics committee, formally the Committee on Standards of Official Conduct, has generally regarded the practice as acceptable.

"The rules say you can only use campaign funds for campaign or political purposes," says a spokesman for the ethics committee. "Defending your innocence and therefore your ability to remain in Congress does have a political relationship."

But if legal expenditures from campaign committees are generally within the law and House rules, some are questioning whether it is ethical for members to spend campaign money to fend off concerns about their ethics.

"We are certainly concerned about use of campaign funds for other than campaign uses, everything from legal fees to travel expenses . . ." says David Eppler, an attorney with Public Citizen, a public interest group. "Some of the most troubling ones are the corruption cases, guys like [former Democratic Representative Mario] Biaggi and so forth that use it for their legal expenses."

Biaggi, who was convicted of bribery, extortion and conspiracy before resigning from the House in 1988, spent heavily from his campaign funds in an unsuccessful effort to stay out of jail. His fellow New York Representative Robert Garcia, who was convicted October 20 [1989] on charges of conspiracy and extortion, likewise has been able to fall back on political contributors in his time of legal trouble. During the first half of 1989, Garcia's campaign committee listed $130,000 in legal fee expenditures.

Rules: "Crazy" or Proper?

This practice of campaign-fund spending for legal work has begun to provide some fodder for partisan attacks [on] incumbents; critics say, in essence, that certain members battling legal or ethical inquiries are collecting "campaign" money that they never intend to use for election-related expenses.

In Tennessee, the state Republican Party has blasted Ford for his legal expenditures from campaign funds. Ford, who was indicted on bribery charges in 1987 . . . at one time set up a legal defense fund (called "Trust Ford") separate from his campaign treasury, but his legal expenses are paid primarily from his campaign funds. Reports filed with the FEC show at least $130,000 in legal expenditures by Ford's campaign committee in 1988 and the first half of 1989.

Earlier this fall [1989], the Tennessee GOP passed a resolution calling Ford's handling of his money "a misuse of campaign funds" and declaring that the GOP would withhold assistance from any party nominees who made such use of political money.

"The people of Tennessee don't understand why the rules would permit a politician to take several hundred thousand dollars from a handful of interest groups and use it to pay lawyers to defend him against felony charges unrelated to his service as a member of Congress," says Tennessee GOP Chairman Brad Martin. "While the rules may permit it, we think the rules are crazy."

Ford has not responded to the attacks and has continued to raise money with an eye on his legal expenses.

"There have been several rulings by the Federal Election Commission that a member can use campaign expenditures for legal fees," says Ford aide Mike Lawhead, "so that is how he is defraying costs most recently."

A similar explanation is offered by California Representative

Jim Bates, who until recently was under investigation by the ethics committee because of allegations that he had sexually harassed some members of his staff. Two weeks before the media reported complaints of Bates' behavior in 1988, the Democrat's campaign committee issued $6,000 in checks to Brand & Lowell, a Washington law firm that is well known for its expertise in the field of congressional ethics.

"I got an opinion [from the ethics committee] that that was OK, and that is what we are doing," says Bates. He estimates that the sexual harassment inquiry, which resulted in a "letter of reproval" from the committee . . . will take $15,000 from his campaign fund.

Asked if he considered establishing a separate fund for legal expenses, Bates said: "I suppose I could, but it gets so complicated. . . . I haven't done that, don't intend to."

Costs Add Up

Drawn-out judicial entanglements like those faced by Biaggi, Ford and Garcia obviously result in a significant financial drain. But as Bates and others have found, members can also be hit with big legal bills whether or not their cases ever lead to formal court proceedings.

The high-profile inquiry into former Speaker Jim Wright's ethics was an internal House affair; no criminal charges were filed. Yet Wright's legal expenses were so high that his allies held fund-raisers to help pay them. FEC reports for the first half of 1989 show that the "Jim Wright Appreciation Committee" paid $282,000 for "professional services" to the law firm of Manatt, Phelps, Rothenberg and Evans. That is the firm of William Oldaker, head of Wright's legal defense team.

While there has been no official government confirmation that Pennsylvania GOP Representative Joseph M. McDade is under investigation, in the last year he has been buffeted by media reports that the Federal Bureau of Investigation and a federal grand jury are probing his ties to a defense contractor to determine if he violated election or bribery laws by accepting contributions, speaking fees and gifts.

In the past year, McDade has also paid $79,848.68 in campaign

funds to Brand & Lowell, the same law firm that represented
Bates. McDade's office confirmed that the legal expenditures are
related to the reported investigations.

And Democratic Representative Barney Frank of Massachusetts, who has been at the center of an ethics controversy because
of his past association with a male prostitute, has turned to one of
the most prominent attorneys in the Washington area for help in
arguing his case before the ethics committee. To pay Stephen H.
Sachs, the former Maryland attorney general, Frank's aides established a legal defense fund. That fund, although it has its own
bank account and post office box, is actually a part of Frank's
campaign committee and is subject to the same FEC requirements as his other political receipts and expenditures.

Grandfather Clause

A special clause in federal election law allows campaign funds
to serve as a financial buffer for some members under an ethical
cloud even after they leave office and are no longer politically
active.

Election law amendments (Public Law 96-187) passed by Congress in 1979 prohibited incumbents sworn in after January 7,
1980, from converting campaign funds to personal use when they
retire. But those in office before that deadline may do as they
please with the money once out of office; for some retiring senior
members who benefit from this "grandfather" clause, much of
the political money goes straight into lawyers' pockets.

Former Banking Committee Chairman Representative Fernand
J. St. Germain, D-R.I., is one member who left office after the
100th Congress with a sizable campaign treasury, and with sizable
legal expenses. St. Germain, whose final years in the House were
clouded by investigations into his political and financial ties to the
thrift industry, had nearly $250,000 in his campaign fund after
losing his 1988 reelection bid. In March 1989 his committee paid
$67,500 for legal services to the Washington law firm of Arent,
Fox, Kintner, Plotkin & Kahn.

Tennessee Democrat Bill Boner is another former member
who paid for his time in the ethical spotlight after leaving office.
Boner, elected mayor of Nashville in September 1987, spent his

last two years in the House grappling with reports that he had used his office to build his own bank account and made personal use of his campaign funds.

Two months after he was elected mayor, Boner sought an opinion from the ethics committee as to the propriety of using House campaign funds to pay legal fees associated with investigations by the committee and the Justice Department. FEC records show that Boner then used his campaign committee to pay $292,453.44 in legal bills received between early 1986 and mid-1988.

Such expenditures have helped fuel criticism of the grandfather clause. That criticism peaked November 16, when the House approved an ethics package that abolished the clause.

But preventing retiring members from converting their campaign funds to personal use does not address the question of whether sitting members should be allowed to spend their political money on legal fees.

Eppler at Public Citizen, which has pushed for an end to the clause, says that the legal fees issue has so far been a back-burner concern.

"We haven't pointed specifically to this issue because there are so many wide uses of campaign funds it is hard to say this one is worse than any other."

The PAC Man Cometh:
Should We Bar the Door?
Robert Allan Cooke

Political action committees (PACs) have come under great scrutiny and are often criticized as inappropriate ways to finance political campaigns. For example, President George Bush, in his 1991 State of the Union Address, urged that PACs be banned. In "The PAC Man Cometh: Should We Bar the Door?" Robert Allan Cooke makes a libertarian defense of PACs that emphasizes the rights of individuals. Cooke seeks to rebut four objections to PACs: 1) that they tend to increase political cam-

Robert Allan Cooke, "The PAC Man Cometh: Should We Bar the Door?" Previously unpublished article. Printed with permission of the author.

paign costs; 2) that they undercut the two-party system; 3) that the more affluent PACs have too much power to influence the democratic process, especially the decision-making ability of elected officials; and concurrently, 4) that voters' influence might be undermined because of the control that PACs exert. Cooke suggests that each of these objections is groundless; that PACs should be retained as a vehicle for people to express their Constitutional rights of free speech and freedom of association.

The propensity of our contemporaries to demand an authoritarian prohibition as soon as something does not please them, and their readiness to submit to such prohibitions even when what is prohibited is quite agreeable to them shows how deeply ingrained the spirit of servility still remains within them. It will require many long years of self-education until the subject can turn himself into the citizen. A free man must be able to endure it when his fellow men act and live otherwise than he considers proper. He must free himself from the habit, just as soon as something does not please him, of calling for the police.[1]

—Ludwig von Mises

Since the idea of contract presumes the maturity of man, it is naturally resented on occasion by the child that lives on in all of us. (Breathes there a man who is so startlingly mature that he has never denounced a bank for levying an extra charge for delinquent interest, or never cursed his landlord for refusing to let the rent go over a month?) But if the eternal child yearns at times for the protective status of immaturity, or even for reversion to the womb, his need to escape the paternal power is even more compulsive.[2]

—John Chamberlain

Context

In the United States, the decade of the 1980s will be remembered for its significant economic growth, coupled with a renewed optimism by its citizens. The Reagan theme, "It's morning again in America," epitomized this optimism that reflected the average citizen's belief that things were normal again—that the

United States had reasserted its leadership in a hostile world. After a decade of reflection and self-doubt, we were back on the "right track." This public outlook helped to fuel an economic attitude of "bullishness" that expanded and created new markets. As a result, unprecedented numbers of young people enjoyed a standard of living and income that was usually reserved for older individuals who had invested several years in their careers. The emergence of these young, upwardly mobile adults (yuppies), coupled with unprecedented growth in the small business sector, led to a dramatic increase in the number of millionaires in the United States. This new age of the entrepreneur not only changed the business climate, it also had a political impact. After all, many, if not most, of these new entrepreneurs were familiar only with the economic prosperity and conservative public policy that had shaped the decade—a "Camelot"[3] driven by the pursuit of self-interest.

It is not surprising that within this context social critics and moralists began to examine the meaning of this new affluence. Moderates and cynics alike evaluated the ethical and social dimensions of this prosperity to determine if the values and character of people were changing. This scrutiny was especially triggered by various incidents of professional impropriety; e.g., the insider trading scandal and the problems dogging certain television evangelists, to name just two.

As the coverage of these issues increased, many in the media and the public became obsessed with the idea that a serious flaw had emerged in the American character—one that had been exacerbated by the decade of affluence, namely, greed. Thus, the public debated whether Americans had lost their sense of ethical responsibility. Were the current ethics of these new entrepreneurs worse than that of previous generations? If so, who was to blame? Did the economic system itself encourage unethical behavior? What could be done?

This interest was welcomed by professional ethicists like myself, who had labored in relative obscurity for many years. Relegated to the rather cloistered world of the academy, we were now thrust into the role of social critics, as well as that of counsels and sages. This more public role continues even today, for the questions raised during the 1980s are still with us. They are questions that have forced all professions and institutions to reevaluate the values and standards they promote—the hope being that institutional changes, coupled with the force of the law, will curb the type of unethical and illegal behavior that made headlines in the 1980s. At the least, there are positive steps we can take that will create an environment that discourages unethical behavior.

Nature of the Task

During the last decade, the interest in professional ethics has primarily focused on the business and medical communities. Yet, there has also been an increasing concern about the conduct of elected officials, government employees, and lobbyists. The Watergate scandal may serve as a paradigm of government misconduct, but the 1980s also had its share of problems.[4] Whether this decade witnessed corruption as flagrant as Watergate is a matter for historians to debate. In all fairness, the level of public scrutiny today is unparalleled in our history. As such, we may hold government officials to higher standards than was common in the past—even to the extent of examining private behavior that has little, if any, bearing on the elected office. Yet, it can be argued that this loss of privacy is a small sacrifice to pay for the preservation of the "public trust," the cornerstone of our democracy.

This concept of the public trust has concerned many observers who feel that certain developments have undercut this trust relationship. In particular, there seems to be growing alarm over the rising costs of campaigning for political office and legislative referendums. Some claim that the primary culprit in these spiraling costs is the emergence of political action committees (PACs).[5] Left unchecked, such costs allegedly subvert the democratic process by wielding undue influence to those individuals and groups who can pay the higher price tag.

The purpose of this essay is to examine briefly a few of the arguments for and against PACs—to add some common sense to a debate that is often grounded in emotional diatribe and ideological bias. My conclusion is simple, not profound. Political action committees are vehicles that express the feelings, beliefs, and values of individuals and groups. They are an outgrowth of two factors: (1) the Federal Election Campaign Act (FECA) of 1971, which was amended in 1974 and 1976[6]; and (2) the enduring belief in a political and economic system that supports, in principle, freedom of choice and individual initiative.

Just what are political action committees? Simply put, they are the fund-raising branch of any special interest group that attempts to influence public policy through the election of candidates who are sympathetic to its cause. As such, they collect and distribute funds to support individuals and referendum initiatives that they deem worthy of support. Bertozzi and Burgunder note that the formation of PACs was a legal recognition of the informal corporate and labor fund-raising methods that had already been in place for years—in the case of unions, these practices could be traced back to the 1930s.[7] The goal of the FECA legislation was to constrain individual giving in a way that still enabled candidates and causes to secure the necessary funds for campaign costs. In a way, it was designed to limit the influence of very wealthy contributors so that the workingman and woman could also influence those public policy initiatives that had direct impact on their livelihood and quality of life. As such, it was an attempt to redistribute the balance of political influence away from the wealthy. It is not surprising that unions provided the major support for FECA.[8] And it is not surprising that the serious concern over PACs seemed to emerge after neoconservatives began to raise more money through PACs than their liberal counterparts. During the first half of the 1970s, Democrats received more than two-thirds of all PAC money.[9] The decade that followed shifted PAC revenues to the neoconservatives and Republicans—a success marked by increasingly sophisticated techniques that proved effective in contributing to the political demise of incumbents such as Birch Bayh, Frank Church, and George McGovern in one election year. In fact, these defeats initiated a crescendo of criticism aimed at the apparent unfairness of PACs—a self-righteous prattle that was barely audible when more liberal candidates and causes prevailed.[10]

The Case Against PACs: What's the Fuss?

One might ask, what's all the fuss about PACs—especially since they were used for decades without the severe criticism that now threatens their very existence.[11] There are at least four interrelated objections that are used against PACs.

The first objection is that the legal recognition of PACs by FECA in 1971 has led to spiraling campaign costs. This sanction, in turn, makes it impossible for many worthy individuals to campaign for political office. And it becomes increasingly difficult to fund grass-roots referendums that do not have the glamour that political campaigns tend to generate. Now there is no doubt that during the decade of the 1980s an astounding increase in the number of PACs and campaign funds became evident.[12] The emergence of PACs as a political force has contributed to this escalation of costs. Yet, they are not the only culprits. The increasing reliance on direct mailing techniques and the electronic media have had as much of an impact on costs as the proliferation of PACs. We could certainly cut costs by restricting the use of these new technologies in campaigns. But would this short-term benefit offset the loss of information that would ensue from returning to the old campaign technology? These new techniques may be imperfect at times, and they may result in an abundance of candidates who look as if they were groomed on Madison Avenue. Yet, the average voter has a better chance of evaluating candidates than ever before. They can no longer hide away from public view—hoping to win simply on their laurels. Candidates must make themselves available to the media in order to compete effectively. And when they do, they are exposed to public scrutiny—warts and all.

PACs simply provide a mechanism for gathering funds to compete in this new technological arena. Candidates who choose other electioneering strategies are free to do so. And in some cases, such strategies may work; many candidates have found town meetings and whistle stops more effective than media blitzes. Candidates who choose to rely on newer strategies should be able to do so. If PACs enable candidates without vast personal fortunes to compete by using this new technology, then a positive step has been taken.

There are two basic assumptions that underlie this objection that PACs tend to increase campaign costs. First, it is assumed that PAC funds guarantee political success at the ballot box. Yet, there is ample evidence that this is not the case.[13] Second, it is assumed that PAC money makes incumbents unbeatable. There is no doubt that PAC financial aid favors incumbents—people always want to bet on a winner. Yet, the benefits of incumbency that intrinsically come with the elected office play as much a role in reelection as PAC money does; e.g., franking privileges and free media coverage. Moreover, PAC contributions may be used to unseat incumbents.[14]

The second objection to PACs is that they undercut the two-party system. The growing popularity in establishing PACs has resulted in less reliance on the Republican and Democratic parties for campaign funding. Thus, the candidate feels less party loyalty and cannot be counted on always to follow the dictates of the party's platform when campaigning. If elected, he cannot be counted on to vote routinely with his party colleagues. There is no doubt that PAC support may undercut old notions of party loyalty, but is this a threat to our democracy? If I am a party bureaucrat, the answer is yes. As a libertarian, I am pleased with any development that lessens the stranglehold of the two parties on our political process. To those critics who counter that the political party has simply been replaced with another master, the special interest group supporting the PAC, I would argue that voting is part of the public record. If an elected official's voting record is out of touch with his constituents, there is one place to rectify that—the voting booth on Election Day. In a democracy like ours, this recourse is more effective than any other measure I can think of.

The third objection to PACs is that the more affluent ones subvert the political process by selling political influence to the highest bidder.[15] In other words, legislation is passed or rejected on the basis of what the more affluent PACs will accept. Thus, controversial legislation is defeated or tabled if it offends the PAC. Who are the affluent PACs usually cited for this allegedly unethical influence? Cavanagh and McGovern, for example, include "pro-business" PACs, in general. They also point to the National Rifle Association, Jesse Helms, and the National Conservative Political Action Committee (NCPAC), in particular.[16] Explicitly and implicitly, these authors argue that such PACs champion causes that work against the "common good."[17] Yet, these same authors fail to recognize that these so-called "bad" PACs also represent the views of millions of citizens who agree with the positions that they advocate. The National Rifle Association, for example, is usually cited as a group that undercuts our democracy because it opposes limitations on those rights guaranteed by the Second Amendment to the United States Constitution. It is often portrayed as a monolithic group that is callous about the problems of firearm violence. Yet, the NRA represents millions of responsible gun owners who agree that our societal problems of violence will not be solved by stricter gun control laws. This representation involves both lobbying and safety training. In a democracy, it is a legitimate perspective that deserves consideration. Who are the so-called "good" PACs? Not surprisingly, Cavanagh and McGovern cite Common Cause.[18]

Analogously, elected officials are said to be afraid to champion unpopular causes that offend the source of their campaign funding—fearing the withholding of future revenue or actual retribution through PAC support for opponents. This third objection rests on the assumption that wealth and lobbying corrupt the elected official who is unable to withstand the pressures that affluent PACs bring to bear on the political process. Obviously, there are numerous examples of individuals who avoid confrontation at all costs—who will bend in whichever direction the wind blows.[19] And yet, there are numerous elected officials who stand up for what they believe, however unpopular. When an elected official takes a position, he must accept the consequences of that action. To blame constituents, PACs, political parties, or lobbyists for his failure to stand by his own beliefs about what is in the best interest of his constituents and/or country is a simplistic solution. The bottom line is individual accountability, and that must be presented to the voters for their judgment. To single out PACs as the primary cause for vacillation or timidity is unfair. It is equally ludicrous to assume that the values of PACs do not reflect the values of the elected officials who receive their support. Quite the contrary, PACs tend to support candidates who share common values.[20]

Finally, PACs are often accused of eliminating the average citizen from the political process. In other words, the influence that affluent PACs exert tends to minimize the role of the individual voter at the ballot box. This objection is not to be taken seriously, for the same possibility could be said of the domination of the Democratic and Republican parties. Does the average citizen really feel that a two-party system that controls access into the political process is fairer without the involvement of PACs? If anything, PACs often represent the interests of individual citizens in a way that political parties are often unwilling to acknowledge. For example, the emergence of conservative PACs during the 1980s may trouble more liberal Democrats; but they often represent individual values and beliefs that were ignored by the Democrats and Republicans. The fact that the more conservative PACs gained in strength in the 1980s is a more accurate barometer of public opinion than a poll. You can learn a lot about a person's likes and dislikes by watching how they spend their money—even in the political arena. In other words, the shift in popularity from the dominance of liberal union PACs in the 1970s to the more conservative PACs in the 1980s is not some pernicious plot to undercut the democratic process. Rather, it reflects a change in the political mood of the citizenry.

Parting Shots

Up to this point in the essay, I have discussed the historic context in which PACs became a significant part of the political process. And I have evaluated some of the major objections to the role of PACs within this democratic system. In the process, I have attempted to diffuse these objections—thus, hinting at the positive contributions that PACs may make. At the least, I have suggested that PACs are not as deadly as some critics suggest—although I am willing to admit that it is possible to abuse the use of PACs. Yet, this is a trivial observation, since anything can be abused. I see nothing inherently wrong with the formation of PACs—certainly, it is not an issue involving the deleterious effects of affluence. Indeed, PACs afford just an extension of those freedoms that we hold dear in a democratic society, namely, freedom of speech and freedom of association. They reflect a demand for a mechanism by which individuals can pool their capital to influence public policy in ways consistent with their beliefs and values. In other words, PACs may provide the political clout for points of view that the individual citizen feels are underrepresented by traditional political parties.

I'm afraid those critics who object to PACs are either unfairly blaming PACs for the imperfections of our democratic system or

THE ETHICS OF POLITICAL CAMPAIGNING

are promoting a political agenda that views PACs as a danger because neoconservatives have been more effective in using them than have their more liberal counterparts. In any case, in a free and democratic society there is nothing inherently insidious or evil about the use of PACs. After all, they reflect the freedom of choice that separates our noble experiment from all others:

From each as they choose, to each as they are chosen.[21]

—Robert Nozick

NOTES

1. Ludwig von Mises, *Liberalism in the Classical Tradition*, trans. Ralph Raico, 3rd ed. (Irvington-on-Hudson, NY: Foundation for Economic Education, 1985) pp. 54–55.

2. John R. Chamberlain, *The Roots of Capitalism* (Indianapolis: Liberty Press, 1976), p. 93.

3. Certainly this is a different view of Camelot from that which President John F. Kennedy had in mind.

4. Various social critics and commentators have argued that the Reagan Administration was one of the most corrupt in history. This is an assumption that is debatable.

5. Gerald F. Cavanagh and Arthur F. McGovern, *Ethical Dilemmas in the Modern Corporation* (Englewood Cliffs, NJ: Prentice-Hall, 1988), p. 78.

6. Dan Bertozzi, Jr., and Lee Burgunder, *Business, Government, and Public Policy* (Englewood Cliffs, NJ: Prentice-Hall, 1990), p. 25.

7. Ibid., p. 26.

8. Ibid.

9. Cavanagh and McGovern, p. 77.

10. This self-righteous attitude was probably a holdover from President Jimmy Carter's Administration.

11. Even President George Bush has called for the abolition of PACs.

12. Cavanagh and McGovern, p. 77. From 1977 to 1984 the number of corporate PACs increased by 147 percent. During this same time frame, revenues to these same PACs increased 700 percent.

13. "New Congress Relied on PAC Donations, but Much of Spending Had Little Effect on Results," *Wall Street Journal* (September 24, 1986), p. 32.

14. See p. 169.

15. Cavanagh and McGovern, p. 77.

16. Ibid.

17. Ibid., p. 78.

18. Ibid.

19. Some Congressmen have even been known to vote against legislation they've sponsored.

20. It is also erroneous to assume that there is no room for compromise with positions promoted by PACs.

21. Robert Nozick, *Anarchy, State, and Utopia* (New York: Basic Books, 1974), p. 160.

Back-Pocket PACs
Peter Overby

In this article from *Common Cause Magazine*, Peter Overby exposes a more recent feature of the PAC phenomenon. He defines a "back-pocket PAC" as one that eludes federal registration by being maintained in a nonfederal account that is free from normal monitoring or disclosure rules. According to Overby, the back-pocket PAC is a rapidly growing favorite of Congressional incumbents. As a kind of slush fund, the back-pocket PAC allows special interest groups and individuals to contribute the maximum amount of money allowable in above-board PACs and then even more in these nonregistered accounts. The compilation of politicians who, according to Overby, have maintained back-pocket PACs reads like a Who's Who of American politics, and the list of those who he claims have contributed is revealing as well. It will be interesting to see if Congress in its wisdom will take any action against these back-pocket PACs, given that they seem to circumvent readily the intent of the federal campaign election laws.

Savings and loan executive Charles H. Keating, Jr., gave all the money legally allowed to Ohio Senator John Glenn's 1986 reelection campaign committee. Then he did more.

Sidestepping federal laws intended to thwart just this sort of huge donation, Keating's company, American Continental Corporation, in 1985 and 1986 gave two checks totaling $200,000 to the National Council on Public Policy, a political action committee controlled by Glenn. Although the council was registered with the Federal Election Commission (FEC), it also maintained a "nonfederal" account, outside the reach of federal monitoring and disclosure laws, where the Keating donations were deposited.

Glenn is . . . one of the "Keating Five" Senators who questioned regulators' actions against Keating's now-defunct thrift institution after receiving large contributions from him. Glenn

Peter Overby, "Back-Pocket PACs," *Common Cause Magazine* (July/August, 1990), pp. 26–30. Reprinted with permission from *Common Cause Magazine*.

denies that the American Continental money affected his judgment. The National Council on Public Policy, which closed down both accounts in 1988 after collecting a modest $50,000 beyond the American Continental donations, never attained its intended role as the Ohio Democrat's national forum.

Despite its lackluster history, the council is a notable example of a little-known trend in political slush funds. Some members of Congress, like Glenn, have set up federal PACs but placed part of the PACs' assets in these hard-to-track nonfederal accounts, earmarked for expenses not connected to federal campaigns. Other members have formed PACs registered only at the state level. Either way, the accounts escape federal restrictions and disclosure requirements.

These back-pocket PACs enable members of Congress to collect money from donors who, like Keating, have "maxxed out" at the federal level; from corporations and unions, which cannot give campaign contributions to federal candidates; and from anyone else whose appearance on federal records might be unwanted. Some back-pocket PACs, registered at the state level, file reports with state election boards. Some, like Glenn's state account, registered only as corporations, don't file anywhere.

"Anything other than a candidate's [campaign] committee might have a nonfederal account," says William White, treasurer of Glenn's PAC during its waning days. "There is nowhere that I know of where contributions to a nonfederal account are required to be reported."

A search by *Common Cause Magazine* turned up a number of back-pocket PACs scattered across the country. Some do no more than support other candidates. Senator Dennis DeConcini (D-Arizona), for example, registered his awkwardly named Arizona Leadership for America Search Committee at both federal and state levels; depending almost exclusively on in-state money, it has distributed most of its funds to other candidates. The committee did have one problem—the 1989 disappearance of its treasurer along with $39,686 in what the committee now labels "unauthorized expenditures." The Arizona attorney general is investigating the money's disappearance.

Other back-pocket PACs, working under the guise of party building or issue solving, have successfully explored techniques for collecting and spending special interest money. Three New

Jersey politicians who fall into this category are Governor James Florio, a former fifteen-year congressman, and two current House members—Representatives Robert Torricelli and Jim Courter. "Probably the only thing we could stop someone for is personal use of the money. It's a major loophole," says Frederick Herrmann, director of the New Jersey Election Law Enforcement Commission. "It's really totally in limbo."

Representative Dan Rostenkowski of Illinois, Democratic chairman of the House Ways and Means Committee, stands out as a member who offers contributors multiple ways to donate. He maintains four funds: the Rostenkowski for Congress Committee, separate federal and state accounts of the America's Leaders' Fund, and an account that handles his charitable contributions. The PAC arrangement, coupled with the end of the practice of letting special interests pay honoraria to House members for personal use, enabled the Tobacco Institute to channel more than $7,000 to Rostenkowski in 1988 and 1989. The institute's PAC gave $1,000 to the America's Leaders' Fund federal account; meanwhile, the institute gave $2,000 to the state account, paid Rostenkowski $4,000 in honoraria and twice picked up hotel bills for him and his wife.

Former Representative Tony Coelho (D-California) is closing down his back-pocket PAC this year. But Senator Alfonse D'Amato (R-N.Y.) has a PAC that raised $160,000 last year [1989], according to a *Newsday* investigation. The article concluded that just $8,500 could have been legally donated to a federal PAC and a third of the money went to D'Amato's pollster. A spokesman for the PAC said the polling did not benefit D'Amato, and D'Amato's office said the PAC was designed to rebuild his state's dilapidated Republican Party. In June [1990, the Associated Press] reported that a federal grand jury subpoenaed several people linked to the PAC. D'Amato, who did not respond to requests for comment from *Common Cause Magazine*, told AP he knew of "no impropriety."

These committees represent several means to a single end—to exploit loopholes in federal campaign law. Federal law says individuals may give only $1,000 to a congressional candidate's campaign committee per election (primary, runoff or general), and PACs connected to corporations or unions may give only $5,000.

In many states the door for political money stands wide open by comparison. Corporate contributions are allowed in 30 states, union money in 40. In 26 states, individual donors can give as much as they please. Spending restrictions are similarly lax.

These discrepancies are the attractions of a back-pocket PAC.

A Question of Purpose

Was the Committee for a Clean and Safe America created to resolve longstanding environmental problems or to help Jim Florio get elected governor of New Jersey in 1989? Chemical industry lobbyists give one answer. Committee records suggest the other.

The committee's name evokes soothing images of clean skies and waters, as would befit Florio, a strong supporter of environmental legislation while he was in the House and an author of the Superfund toxic waste cleanup law. Incorporated as a nonprofit organization in New Jersey in March 1987, the committee raised $481,674 and spent $420,715 through March 31, 1989, four days before Florio officially announced for governor. Of some 630 contributions, half came from corporations and other businesses; many would be illegal if made to a candidate's campaign committee.

The committee's early contributors included five eyebrow-raisers: chemical companies American Cyanamid, Ciba-Geigy, GAF Chemical Corp., Merck and Co., and Dow Chemical. Florio's record made him an enemy of the chemical industry or, at best, "a fact of life," as one industry lobbyist says. But in 1987 the companies kicked in a total of $6,000 when his back-pocket PAC solicited money.

David A. Luthman, treasurer of the committee, says it was organized "to promote environmental issues that were significant, particularly in terms of then-Congressman Florio's efforts" and was "supportive of his reelection to Congress."

As two industry lobbyists perceived it, Florio formed the committee to help environmental activists and industry leaders find common ground. Clair Tweedie, the Washington government affairs director for American Cyanamid, says, "he organized this group to develop programs which would bring environmental, business and public groups together." Tweedie recalls a technical seminar and other events sponsored by the committee. "There was a kick-off meeting on that at the Democratic Club [on Capitol Hill]," he says. "There must have been 150 people there."

At the time, Florio was chair of a House commerce and consumer protection subcommittee, wielding regulatory power over the chemical industry. Tweedie asks rhetorically of his decision to donate: "How do you ascribe motives?"

Never, the lobbyists protest, did they suspect that their money was supporting a political operation. But expenditures listed by the back-pocket PAC suggest the opposite. In 1987 and 1988 it paid a political and fundraising consultant more than $100,000. It threw a golf outing to raise money, sent five of its employees and consultants to the 1988 Democratic National Convention in Atlanta, paid $3,600 for a reception at the convention and donated $5,000 to two South Jersey Democratic organizations.

Florio strategists eventually decided that convention costs and some other expenses should have been paid by the gubernatorial campaign, according to Luthman. In 1989 the campaign reimbursed the PAC more than $61,000. Pains were taken to separate the PAC from the gubernatorial effort, Luthman says, adding, "I don't think that anyone was misled."

But the PAC's biggest outlay—less than a month after Florio was elected governor—was purely political. It turned over $50,000, most of its treasury, to the state Democratic committee to pay off debts from Florio's 1981 gubernatorial bid.

Ciba-Geigy lobbyist William T. Lyons seemed surprised when told of the PAC's overtly political activities. Company officials willingly supported an attempt to solve environmental problems by consensus, he says, but would have reacted differently had they known the committee was a PAC. "I was under the impression that this was incorporated as a foundation of some sort," Lyons says. Tweedie's final comment: "If we had thought that that was a campaign financing organization, you would not have seen a penny from American Cyanamid in there."

PAC of All Trades

Young and ambitious, Representative Robert G. Torricelli (D-N.J.) has always been a man in a hurry. He chairs a Science, Space and Technology subcommittee, sits on the Foreign Affairs

THE ETHICS OF POLITICAL CAMPAIGNING

Committee and has been campaigning to succeed Beryl Anthony, Jr., of Arkansas as chairman of the Democratic Congressional Campaign Committee. As a four-term congressman in a heavily Democratic district, he explored running for governor in 1988 and faces only token Republican opposition in his reelection races.

His back-pocket PAC helps. It has fed him, kept his car fueled and his car phone working, and even paid a speeding ticket for one of his aides.

Between January 1, 1987, and March 31, 1990, Torricelli PAC, which is registered only at the state level, took in $143,873 and spent $147,972. Of 83 itemized receipts, 49 would have violated federal law had they gone to his campaign committee. About half the donations were made directly by corporations.

Although one quarter of its money went directly to other—mainly state—candidates and the PAC provided indirect support for various campaigns, scores of the PAC's expenditures seem to be for office-related or personal needs.

Spending in these areas is regulated by House rules, which seek to build a "wall" between official and unofficial funds in order to prevent private interests from financing the official activities of members of Congress. No private funds, other than a member's personal funds, can be used for official expenses. Campaign contributions cannot be used for office-related or personal use but must be spent only for bona fide campaign and politically related expenses.

Torricelli PAC expenditures included $345 a year for the congressman's 1987 and 1988 dues at the Harvard Club of New York (he holds a master's degree from Harvard's John F. Kennedy School of Government), $188 for gifts from Bloomingdale's and the Franklin Mint, $1,318 for flowers and $110 for parking violations. The PAC paid more than $4,000 in 1987 alone for meals at the Capitol, around Washington and in New Jersey.

The PAC earlier this year paid an American Express bill of $1,099 to a shop called Facconnable to buy a gift. American Express says the shop is in Buenos Aires. Another American Express charge was for a $339 gift from Ralph Lauren. A third, for $1,249, was at a New York–area electronics store. Adam Crain, an aide in Torricelli's district office, was ticketed on the New Jersey Turnpike last February for going 77 in a 55-mph zone. The PAC paid the $80 fine.

Torricelli declined to be interviewed for this article and instead issued two prepared statements. The first says the PAC helps him "in supporting statewide political duties, party-building activities and in supporting important state issues." In addition to contributions to state campaigns and charities, the statement says, "the remainder of the PAC expenditures have been for travel, state political activities, PAC fundraising, charitable presentations and administrative expenses."

In a second statement, responding to written questions about specific expenses, the congressman says none benefited his campaign or personal life. An aide declined to identify the purpose of any of the gifts, but said of the Facconnable charge, "Bob hasn't been in Buenos Aires in years."

Torricelli's PAC for a while also paid the lease on a car for the congressman and the bills for a cellular phone. His congressional office account later picked up the lease, although the PAC continued to pay for the phone, gasoline and tolls.

Torricelli's taxpayer-subsidized district office in Hackensack, N.J., has close ties to his PAC. From 1987 until [1990] the PAC treasurer was Barry Rubin, district administrator on the congressional payroll. When Rubin resigned in February to join the Florio administration, Timothy Sean Jackson assumed both roles. Another aide, David Parano, works part-time on the congressional staff and as a consultant to the PAC. The PAC regularly wrote expense reimbursement checks to Rubin, Jackson, chief of staff Victoria Durbin, former press secretary Rita Barry and other congressional staffers in Washington and Hackensack.

The second prepared statement from Torricelli's office says official expenses are carefully segregated from campaign expenses. "A merger [of this kind] would be not only improper but unnecessary," the statement says, since Torricelli's campaigns are well funded. It says that reimbursements to his congressional aides were for political work "done on their own time and apart from their official duties."

No matter where the money went, Torricelli PAC contributor lists show some of it clearly came from fat cats. Anthony Dell'Aquila, a publicity-shy New Jersey millionaire, made his fortune in lingerie and clothing and now has plans to develop the Hoboken waterfront opposite Manhattan. He gave the maximum $2,000 to Torricelli's '88 campaign and $5,000 to the PAC. Isadore

Spiegel, owner of a New Jersey trucking firm, has given Torricelli $8,000 since 1987—$1,000 to his reelection campaign, Friends of Bob Torricelli, and $7,000 to his PAC.

Contribution and other records trace Torricelli's relationship with businessman Russell Berrie, Torricelli's neighbor in an elegant section of Englewood, N.J. Berrie, once on the *Forbes* 400 list as president and chairman of Russ Berrie and Co., manufactures toys, dolls, teddy bears and impulse items—novelties like candles, coffee mugs, keyrings and wall plaques. Overseas contractors supply virtually all of the 11,000 catalogue items.

In the 1986 campaign Berrie gave Friends of Bob Torricelli $2,000. The next year, he and his wife, Uni, jointly gave Torricelli PAC $7,500, one of the largest donations it has received. They gave $2,000 in 1988 to Torricelli's campaign. During the current campaign, while Berrie has given nothing, Uni Berrie has maxxed out with a $2,000 contribution.

The Berries gave to Torricelli PAC because "Mr. Torricelli requested the contribution from Mr. Berrie to be used exclusively for local candidates in the state of New Jersey—state Assembly, state Senate and local county offices," says Joel Simon, an international trade lawyer representing the Berrie company.

In the past three years Torricelli introduced three bills that could have helped Berrie's company—at the businessman's request, according to Simon. In early 1987 he proposed suspending tariffs on "transparent acrylic decorative articles containing a cavity formed in one wall"—in plain English, paperweights. The bill went nowhere, and the product flopped.

Torricelli last year proposed two bills to suspend tariffs on molded toys and dolls. Stuffed toys and dolls are almost all imported and already duty-free. Unstuffed dolls are another matter. More costly and sophisticated, many are "collectibles" still produced in the United States. A domestic manufacturer objected to the bill, which killed it.

"When we lost one, we lost interest in the other," Simon says. All three bills had to go through the Ways and Means Committee. Berrie soon realized that Torricelli, who doesn't sit on Ways and Means, lacked the clout to move them forward. Says Simon: "We weren't politically sophisticated."

Torricelli described the Berrie bills as just some of the 15,000 constituent chores that his office performs every year. Says an aide, "We would be happy to provide a list of those who received help from our office but never contributed to the campaign fund."

Torricelli PAC between 1987 and 1990 gave $36,875 to candidates from borough council to U.S. president.

If a PAC gives more than $1,000 in one year to federal candidates, it must register with the FEC and obey federal contribution limits. Torricelli PAC apparently didn't report one 1988 donation until 1989, although the date on the check was 1988 and it was reported by the recipient in 1988.

State records of Torricelli PAC donations and FEC records of the recipients show three 1988 transfers, totaling $905, to federal candidates—$250 to Representative Richard Gephardt's presidential campaign, $155 to New Jersey congressional candidate Lee Monaco and $500 to New Jersey congressional hopeful Frank Pallone, Jr.

The campaign committee of Representative Roy Dyson (D-Md.) reported a fourth donation—$500 from Torricelli PAC, dated October 26, 1988. But the PAC reported the donation in 1989 instead, so total contributions reported for 1988 fell below the $1,000 amount that triggers mandatory registration with the FEC.

Torricelli says his PAC didn't register with the FEC because its check to Dyson bounced. Although Dyson reported receiving the money before New Year's, Torricelli said it wasn't paid from the PAC account until after January 1. "Had the check cleared," Torricelli's statement says, "Torricelli PAC would have registered with the FEC as required."

The PAC That Misfired

New Jersey Republican Representative Jim Courter's back-pocket PAC was there when he needed it, buying his book, bashing his future opponent and boosting his career. The Fund for Responsible Leadership kept accounts at the federal and state levels; but neither prospered, at least by PAC standards. The PAC's budget remained small, and when it tried to make a preemptive strike against Florio in the 1989 gubernatorial battle between the two men, it had to retreat.

Courter, a neo-conservative on the Armed Services Committee, sought to establish himself in the early '80s as a hawkish expert on military and foreign policy. As part of that effort, the right-wing American Studies Center in 1986 published *Defending Democracy*, a paperback collection of Courter speeches and articles. Courter, who didn't respond to interview requests, has said he received no royalties from the book, which is 259 pages long, unindexed, cheaply made and lists for $14.95 a copy.

Courter's federal PAC account bought $6,000 worth of copies in December 1986. Both the book and the state PAC were underwritten in part by Clifford Sobel, a New Jersey businessman and one of Courter's biggest financial backers. In the book's acknowledgments, Courter gave special thanks to Sobel, "whose generosity made publication of this book possible." Sobel and his wife gave heavily to Courter's campaigns: $2,950 to his 1988 House contest, $3,000 to his 1989 race for governor. But Sobel gave even more to the PAC's state account: $5,000 in 1987 and $2,500 in 1988.

Courter's federal PAC account contributed to only one congressional candidate in 1988. With political analysts already foreseeing a Florio-Courter showdown for governor in 1989, the PAC, which is not a multi-candidate PAC and so is limited by federal law to donations of $2,000 instead of $10,000 per election cycle, gave $5,000 to Frank A. Cristaudo, a Republican who faced the hopeless task of trying to upset Florio. The FEC said Cristaudo had to return $3,000, but could keep $2,000.

Unlike Torricelli PAC, the Fund for Responsible Leadership didn't support its patron's daily activities—no car, no gifts, no restaurant tabs. But without it, Courter would have been nearly an invisible presence at the 1988 Republican National Convention in New Orleans, a key event for any Republican interested in running for higher office. His PAC's state account spent somewhere between $7,400 and $11,000 sending Courter, his wife and some staff members to New Orleans. It picked up the $10,266 tab for a reception at Brennan's, one of the city's most famous restaurants. When Courter purchased tickets to a convention fundraising gala organized by New Jersey GOP moneyman Lawrence Bathgate, now Republican national finance chairman, the back-pocket PAC paid the $10,000 bill.

The spending was in vain. Florio beat Cristaudo 70 to 30 percent in 1988. A year later he whipped Courter 62 to 38 percent. Courter is retiring from the House this year [1990].

The Check's in the Fed-Ex Pouch

As chairman of the Ways and Means Committee, which writes tax legislation and oversees Medicare and Medicaid, Representative Dan Rostenkowski (D-Ill.) ranks among the most powerful players on Capitol Hill. He is also one of the most successful fundraisers in the House, though he doesn't need the money. He is entrenched in his district on Chicago's North Side.

America's Leaders' Fund, a PAC registered at both the federal and state levels, compounds his clout. During the 1988 campaign its federal account handed out $203,761 to 113 candidates, mostly House Democrats. The state account gave a total of $8,500 to candidates for 43rd Ward Democratic committee, county assessor, state Senate and attorney general.

Rostenkowski's back-pocket PAC depends on out-of-state donors. Between January 1, 1987, and March 31, 1990, the state account received 48 contributions totaling $92,800. Just five—amounting to $4,200, or 4.5 percent of the gross—came from Illinois.

A few contributors scored triple plays, putting money in the state account, the federal account and Rostenkowski's campaign committee. Phil-PAC, the political committee for Philip Morris Companies, gave $1,000 to the Rostenkowski campaign in 1987 and $3,000 to the federal America's Leaders' Fund account in 1988. The Philip Morris Management Corp. gave $5,000 to the state account in 1989.

Another steady contributor to the Rostenkowski accounts is FEPAC, the political arm of Federal Express. In 1988 FEPAC gave $5,000 to the Rostenkowski campaign and another $5,000 to the federal America's Leaders' Fund account.

Fed Ex delivered again last September—but with so much money floating around, records apparently can get muddled. Federal Express says that FEPAC gave $5,000 to America's Leaders' Fund state account. The congressman's federal PAC account reported getting $5,000 from FEPAC; his state account, $5,000 from Fed Ex itself. Did the Rostenkowski network get $15,000 or $20,000 in . . . two years from the air courier giant? A Rostenkowski staff member concluded, "We couldn't really figure out what happened."

Why would Fed Ex—the Memphis-based company that pioneered nationwide overnight delivery service—give $5,000 to a PAC in Illinois, where Rostenkowski, not the corporation, would redistribute the money to other candidates? "I'm not sure anyone has given it that much thought," says Fed Ex government affairs director Doug Buttrey, but he ventures two explanations.

With a new hub operation at Chicago's O'Hare Airport, Fed Ex wants its PAC to get more involved in Illinois politics. "Even though you want to be involved in the process in the state," Buttrey says, "it's sometimes hard to know which candidates to support."

In addition, Ways and Means oversees the Customs Service, and Congress is changing customs rules, including those for the small items imported by Federal Express and other couriers. Under current rules, importers of such items do all the paperwork and pay no fees. The revenue-hungry Bush administration recently proposed user fees, and Rostenkowski went along. Led by Federal Express, the express-delivery and overseas airline industries started lobbying to block the proposal.

If customs fees hadn't spurred Fed Ex to open its checkbook, says Buttrey, something else would have. "Every company in the country has issues pending before the Ways and Means Committee," he says. The way members of Congress are raising money now, "you just can't sit idly by on the sidelines and think your voice is going to be heard."

The Ethics of Negative Political Advertising
Richard E. Vatz and Lee S. Weinberg

Few would argue that American political campaigns are paradigms of virtue, given the mudslinging factor that characterizes so many elections. Richard E. Vatz and Lee S. Weinberg analyze the most prominent aspect of this tendency to distort public images in political campaigns—negative political advertising. Although they show that this political phenomenon is not new, they do offer evidence that negative advertising is on the rise.

Richard E. Vatz and Lee S. Weinberg, "The Ethics of Negative Political Advertising." Previously unpublished article. Printed with the permission of the authors

With television emerging as the preeminent vehicle for political exposure, many citizens witness this mudslinging spectacle in the comfort of their own homes every electoral season. But the compelling question is, "Does negative advertising win elections?" The authors offer evidence that negative advertising is a successful campaign tactic under conditions in which the candidate using the negativism is already popular, and in which there is no stable support already in place for the candidate who is depicted in a negative ad. Negative political advertising, however, may backfire on its user if these conditions are not present. Vatz and Weinberg go on to argue that negativism in political campaigns may have a legitimate place.

While hardly a new phenomenon in American political campaigns, the use of negative advertisements in political contests became a major political issue itself in the 1980s and received significant attention in the media and among scholars. With respect to the Congressional elections of 1986 and the Presidential race of 1988, nearly every major source of print and electronic journalism had run a piece pronouncing these elections to be unusually, if not uniquely, "negative." There was near-universal denunciation of the many negative political advertisements as unethical, and some in Congress called for new legislation to make it more difficult to get such political advertisements on the air.

Voters interviewed by the media as they left the polls after voting in those 1986 and 1988 elections seemed, dutifully, to pay homage to this national consensus by indicating their concern at the negativism in these campaigns. Syndicated columnist Tom Wicker considered the 1986 Congressional races as "surely the nastiest, least relevant, most fraudulent campaigns—by the statesmen of both parties—in the history of a long-suffering nation,"[1] while George F. Will observed that, "What is new is not just the amount of negativism, it is the niggling tendentiousness of it."[2]

Political communication expert Kathleen Jamieson characterized the 1988 Presidential campaign of the Republicans as the dirtiest campaign in the modern era. The Republican negative campaign ads were typified by the most memorable one: an ad coupling Presidential candidate Michael Dukakis in Massachusetts with a convicted black murderer (Willie Horton), who had raped a white woman and stabbed her husband while on furlough. Republican National Chairman Lee Atwater and others involved with the Republican campaign defended the ad as focusing on the consequences of an irresponsible liberal furlough policy supported by Dukakis; the fact that Horton was black, they said, was incidental, so no racial scare tactic was intended. Democrats scoffed at the claim that the Republicans intended anything other than to trigger white voters' racial fears with the prospect of a Dukakis Presidency.

Negative advertisements are defined simply as those that attack the opponent rather than selling the candidate, and while most observers agree that there may well have been somewhat more widespread and prevalent negativism in the 1986 and 1988 elections than in the years immediately preceding them, negative campaigning is not new to American politics. In 1983, for example, a Harris poll was taken to assess attitudes toward negative campaigning, and it indicated that 82 percent of the American public deplored the prevalence of negative political advertising.

Jamieson noted in her recent work, *Packaging the Presidency*, that "[h]istorical analysis reveals that from the country's first contested election, strategists have offered voters advertising that . . . vilified opponents."[3] Opponents of Andrew Jackson circulated papers that described the "Bloody Deeds of General Jackson," and Grover Cleveland's opponent in 1884, James G. Blaine, made an issue of Cleveland's having allegedly fathered a child out of wedlock, preserved for posterity in Blaine's famous campaign jingle, "Ma, Ma, where's my pa?" Cleveland's supporters' answer, of course, was, "Gone to the White House, ha ha ha!" So, negative campaigns have always been with us—although not perhaps so widely broadcast—but it is the emerging media coverage consensus that to a large extent has made these negative campaigns so salient and so objectionable to voters.

There has been some support for legislative action to make candidates more personally accountable for the political ads in their campaigns. A bipartisan proposal backed by Republican Senator John Danforth and Democratic Senator Ernest Hollings calls for a new law requiring that candidates who want to mention their opponent in one of their own political commercials must appear personally in the ad to make the statement about their opponent. Inasmuch as mentioning one's opponent necessarily involves a negative statement, the proposal would basically prevent candidates from running negative ads like the Willie Horton commercial, in which neither the voice nor the face of the candidate placing the ad even appears. It is unlikely that a candidate would be willing to appear personally in such a political ad and risk being so closely tied to what many would surely view as a thinly veiled racial appeal.

As to negative ads placed by supporters not involved with the candidate's official campaign, the Hollings-Danforth proposal would require radio and television stations choosing to run such paid political ads to provide free time to the other candidate to respond. Together these provisions would require candidates' placing negative ads to do their own "dirty work" and would discourage the media from accepting such ads. George Will, a supporter of this approach, looks longingly at the biting rhetoric found in British political campaigns and in the House of Commons: "We would have better politics if we were more at ease with politicians being a little less polite *in person* . . . Such muscular invective is to be preferred to the mincing sideswipes and synthetic seriousness of America's negative ads."[4]

Yet there are potential First Amendment issues as well as multiple political problems with such an approach, and such legislative schemes have not, as yet, found wide support in Congress. First, since the protection of political speech is at the heart of the First Amendment, any efforts to regulate campaign ad content will face major legal challenges. Second, even apart from the Constitutional question, it is difficult to distinguish legitimate, but traditional, "mudslinging" negative claims from offensive, or "unethical," ones. And third, the proposed regulation would likely further enhance the already excellent reelection chances for incumbents, because incumbents have a well-documented record on which to run, while challengers must inevitably attack that record in order to unseat the incumbent.

Some other novel solutions have been offered, including a form of self-regulation by the American Association of Political Consultants, whose Code of Ethics mandates that political consultants "refrain from personal or scurrilous attacks on candidates or members of his family," and that they "pledge not to disseminate false or misleading information intentionally . . ."[5]

But whether private self-regulation would be effective is highly doubtful. First, any group finding violations of the code primarily in one party would inevitably be accused of bias. Second, there is no clear agreement on what constitutes "untruth," "deception," and "scurrilousness." Finally, there is the even more serious impediment of a widespread belief among politicians, political consultants, the media, and the public in one simple proposition: negative ads win elections.

But what is the evidence? Does negative political advertising really work, and by what standards should we decide if particular examples of negative advertising violate our sense of decorum or political ethics? On the first question, the effectiveness of negative campaigning is largely a function of two criteria; the stability of the support of the candidate against whom it is applied, and the credibility of the attack and the attacker. For example, attacks by a popular Lyndon Johnson in the 1964 Presidential campaign that implied dangerous volatility in Barry Goldwater, a candidate already perceived as unpredictable, may have been effective. The 1986 Maryland Senatorial campaign, however, offers an informative contrast: Attacks implying radicalism and, some claimed, lesbianism—by little-known former Reagan aid Linda Chavez, in her unsuccessful effort to defeat popular Democratic Representative Barbara Mikulski—were doomed to fail because of Mikulski's stable support and home-grown persona.

While not easily deterred by the claim that some negative campaign messages may be unethical, candidates contemplating such tactics would do well to note that the consequences of a negative campaign are not necessarily limited to the election in which it has been used. Linda Chavez began the 1986 campaign with a virtual blank-slate image. If there was any initial image emerging, it was that of a bright, young, traditional, and conservative female politician. Ironically, for a woman who tried to personify a traditional woman, Chavez's main failing seemed to be that she lacked intuition. As early as her acceptance address, she introduced what many perceived to be mean-spirited innuendo. Throughout her campaign, Ms. Chavez continued with her self-defeating approach, despite its manifest failure, through the final day of the campaign, in which the airwaves were still filled with her advertisements focusing on Mikulski's "radical feminist" aide of five years' past. The negativism had no discernible consequence for Ms. Mikulski's popularity, but it did earn Ms. Chavez a strikingly high negative rating in polls of Marylanders. Thus, while few serious political observers gave Ms. Chavez a chance in the 1986 election, the once-bright prospect of her political future—including, say, a serious run against Senator Sarbanes in 1988—dissolved. And as this is written in early 1991, it does not appear that she will be a viable candidate for a major office in Maryland for the foreseeable future.

Whether effective or not, negative political advertising raises serious ethical issues but should not be deplored uniformly. While technically meeting the definition of negative advertising, it is quite legitimate, for example, to apprise voters of an opponent's public statements. Moreover, even a candidate's political associations may well be considered fair game for political attack. Certainly, the recordless candidates who support Lyndon LaRouche, Jr., can be reasonably tarred with the excesses of their spiritual leader, since such information may well predict the positions that they would take on a variety of issues once they assumed office. Citing actual voting records of candidates is certainly fair game. Moreover, actual films or tapes of the individual, whether to ridicule, such as in the case of Dukakis's riding in a tank, or to seriously condemn, such as Louisiana's former KKK member and U.S. Senate candidate David Duke, should also be considered fair game.

The reasonable criteria by which negative campaigning should be judged are roughly the same as those by which "positive" or self-promoting campaigning should be considered. Such criteria include the following: are the claims factually truthful, are they fairly presented, do they avoid gross misrepresentations of context, and are depictions of opponents and their positions in good taste and within accepted boundaries of puffery?

Regarding factual truthfulness and relevance, for example, we cannot expect attacks on voting records necessarily to include recorded votes that make one's opponent look good. Attacks characterizing voting records must be accorded some latitude. It is not, for example, unfair to depict an opponent as hostile to military preparedness even when his voting record might be described by a scrupulously even-handed observer as "mixed."

Good taste requires sensitivity to avoiding issues and language that debase the campaign and the office. It was acceptable negative campaigning, therefore, to criticize Dan Quayle's militancy in view of his status in the Indiana Reserves during the Vietnam War but is not acceptable to depict him—even jokingly—as a target of an assassination attempt by the Secret Service in the event of the assassination of President Bush. Some calls on taste are close ones, but distinctions are not impossible to make. We believe that it is reasonably clear to say that campaign advertisements that make innuendos about an opponent's sexuality may not be fair game, but a satirizing of his sports background may well be.

Inasmuch as legislation to control negative advertising is unlikely and not intended to outlaw it in any event, negative campaigning is here to stay, as a necessity for attacking incumbents, if nothing else. Negative campaigning can be quite acceptable, we believe, and manifestly it can be effective. There are reasonable standards and criteria by which to evaluate both its ethics and its practicality. It even appears that to some extent there is a substantial correlation between these two aspects of negative campaigning. Thus, negative campaigning violating these standards of propriety will also usually fail, especially against a candidate with stable support, and may have long-lasting negative repercussions for the perpetrator as well.

NOTES

1. Tom Wicker, "Big Losers of 1986?" *The New York Times* (November 14, 1986), p. A35.
2. George F. Will, "So Much Cash, So Few Ideas," *Newsweek* (November 10, 1986), p. 96.
3. Kathleen Jamieson, *Packaging the Presidency* (New York: Oxford University Press, 1984), p. viii.
4. George F. Will, "The Pollution of Politics," *Newsweek* (November 6, 1989), p. 92.
5. Leslie A. Tucker and David J. Heller, "Putting Ethics into Practice," *Campaigns and Elections* (March/April 1987), p. 45.

The Private Lives of Public Officials
Dennis F. Thompson

When it comes to mudslinging in a political campaign, how much should the public be told about the private lives of candi-

Dennis F. Thompson, "The Private Lives of Public Officials." Reprinted by permission of the publishers from *Political Ethics an Public Office* by Dennis F. Thompson (Cambridge, MA: Harvard University Press). Copyright © 1987, by the President and Fellows of Harvard College.

dates? Do candidates for public office and office holders themselves have any rights to privacy? How do we draw the line, if
any, between the public and the private in the world of politics? These and other pertinent issues are thoughtfully considered by Dennis F. Thompson in "The Private Lives of Public
Officials." Beginning with what he calls "the principle of uniform privacy," which assumes that privacy is of value to everyone, Thompson asks if this principle can be applied to those in
the public eye without reservation. The leading question for
Thompson is: Are there any good reasons why the principle of
uniform privacy should not apply to public officials? If there
are good reasons, then a "principle of diminished privacy"
needs to be established and defined that will apply to the case
of politicians.

For Thompson, there is a marked difference between public
officials and ordinary citizens, the former having been granted
certain powers over the latter, and as such it would be impossible to apply privacy uniformly among them. Rather, those in
the public eye can enjoy only a diminished right to privacy,
given the need for accountability in a democracy. He argues
that public officials will have diminished privacy to the extent
that what the public knows of their private lives should be
directly relevant to holding an official accountable for the
duties of public office. If Thompson's argument is acceptable,
then the mudslinging factor of revealing an opponent's private
life can be tested on a case by case basis. It could be asked if
the revelation in question serves the cause of accountability
such that what gets revealed is directly relevant to informing
the public as to whether a candidate could perform the duties
of the office being sought. In other words, although candidates
should expect diminished privacy, not each and every aspect of
their private lives deserves to be placed in the public arena,
and when the line of direct relevancy is crossed by an opponent, mudslinging rather than informing occurs, and the public
is ill-served.

The Value of Privacy

The principle of uniform privacy depends on showing that
privacy has value for public officials for the same reasons, or for

reasons just as strong, as it does for ordinary citizens. Privacy has two kinds of value for the individual—instrumental and intrinsic. Instrumentally, privacy contributes to liberty by ensuring that individuals can engage in certain activities free from observation, intrusion, or inhibiting threats.[1] Public officials need such protection, sometimes even more than citizens, because if their privacy is violated, the exposure is likely to be greater. Privacy also supports fairness and equal opportunity by ensuring that private activities that are irrelevant to public duties do not affect an individual's chances for gaining public employment.[2]

The instrumental justification, though important, does not fully capture the distinctive value of privacy, and some philosophers have therefore sought a justification in the nature of the human relations in which privacy plays an intrinsic role. These relations include love, friendship, and trust, which presuppose a certain degree of privacy.[3] More generally, they are relations that take on a different character when other people observe or know about them.[4] Viewed intrinsically, privacy is justified even if none of the usual harmful consequences (such as loss of a job) is likely to ensue. Because many public officials live in the glare of publicity, the moments alone and with their family and friends are precious, and stand in special need of protection. Furthermore, if officials are to sustain a conception of their own character that is at all independent of their public reputation, they need to be able to escape the public eye from time to time. Without such escape, an official may suffer what Erving Goffman calls stigmatization: "The figure the individual cuts in daily life before those with whom he has routine dealings is likely to be dwarfed and spoiled by virtual demands (whether favorable or unfavorable) created by his public image."[5]

Most of the arguments for the value of privacy to the individual may also be reformulated as arguments for the value of privacy to society. If privacy protects the liberty and opportunities of individual officials, it also can increase the pool of available talent for public positions. Without some assurance of privacy, the unorthodox and the sensitive person is less likely to seek and hold public office, and government loses the competence and diversity that such people may bring. Also, by respecting the privacy of public officials, we may also encourage greater respect for the privacy of citizens. Officials who are in the habit of honoring the privacy of other officials may be more likely to respect that of ordinary citizens. By their own example, officials demonstrate the importance of individual privacy in society. Finally, the titillating details of private lives tend to divert our attention from the larger issues of public life. The quality of deliberation in a democracy is debased when sensationalist exposés of private activities displace discussion of substantial questions of public policy.

The principle of uniform privacy affirms the value of the private lives of public officials, but the principle cannot always be sustained. Public officials are not simply ordinary citizens. They have power over us, and they represent us in other ways. From these differences follows the principle of diminished privacy for public officials. That principle takes precedence over the principle of uniform privacy when the needs of democratic accountability cannot otherwise be met. Because officials make decisions that affect our lives, we want to make sure that they are at least physically and mentally competent; that they do not abuse their power for private ends and are not vulnerable to the improper influence of others; and that they are likely to pursue policies of which we would approve.[6] Their public conduct may reveal much of what we need to know, but in many instances, if we are to hold officials accountable for the power they exercise, we need to learn something about their private lives. (Many officials outside of government also exercise power over us, and insofar as they do, the principle of diminished privacy applies to them too.)

It is sometimes suggested that some officials, especially presidents, ambassadors, and congressmen, represent us not only in their public decisions but also in their private conduct.[7] They stand as symbols for personal values that we share. On this view, political leaders are usually expected to observe higher standards of personal morality than expressed in the "least common denominator of society's . . . standards."[8] Leaders represent our aspirations, not necessarily our behavior. Beyond the symbolism, the way officials conduct their private lives can affect for good or ill the way citizens conduct theirs. Public figures who deal gracefully and courageously with personal difficulties—marital problems, an errant offspring, alcoholism, breast cancer, death of a loved one—not only excite admiration but invite imitation. To be sure, these benefits of diminished privacy might be achieved, and no doubt sometimes are, simply through hypocrisy; it is the appearances that are effective. But since for other reasons (those relating to accountability) citizens will already know something about the private lives of officials, the strategy of hypocrisy cannot be prudently recommended either to society or to officials.

Nevertheless, probity in one's personal life is not a sufficient condition for making moral decisions in public office (many of the major Watergate conspirators evidently led impeccable private lives). It is probably not even a necessary condition (some of the most laudable policies have been made by officials whose personal behavior was hardly exemplary). Indeed, in some cultures flouting private morality may enhance the stature of a public leader. In Indonesia, President Sukarno's "massive preoccupation with sex" was said to be "a matter of admiration rather than disapproval—a demonstration, perhaps, of [his] continuing virility and thus of his political potency as well." [9] Preoccupation with the private virtue of officials may lead us to neglect (or even mistakenly excuse) the public vice they perpetrate through the decisions they make in office. Accountability for these decisions thus may sometimes actually require that citizens know less about the private lives of officials, or at least pay less attention to them. An official may choose, for prudential or for superrogatory reasons, to disclose his or her private affairs, but the principle of diminished privacy does not cogently extend beyond what is directly relevant to holding an official accountable for the duties of public office (in ways to be explained [subsequently]).

Although everyone's privacy deserves respect, public officials must sacrifice some of their privacy for the good of society, including the protection of the privacy of ordinary citizens. One form of an argument for the priority of the principle of diminished privacy is largely utilitarian in character—that the interests of the larger number of citizens take precedence over those of the smaller number—and hence does not fully respect the individual rights of officials. If we could assume that officials consent to the limitation of their privacy, we would have a more satisfactory basis for diminished privacy, and indeed many writers have maintained that the act of seeking or holding public office constitutes such consent. [10] Such an act involves more of a real choice than the status of simply being a citizen, which is sometimes (dubiously) counted as proof of consent.

But while some degree of consent to less privacy does seem to follow from holding some kinds of public office, such consent is not sufficient to negate all claims of privacy for officials. In the first place, the vast majority of public officials (postal employees, clerks, schoolteachers) do not, and should not be expected to, consent to relinquishing rights that an ordinary citizen enjoys simply because they hold a state-supported job, which is otherwise like any other job in society. The Supreme Court has generally rejected the "privilege" doctrine that once warranted the government's denying constitutional rights to public employees.[11] In the second place, even for those officials at higher levels who might be presumed to accept some diminished privacy, the argument from consent does not by itself suggest *what* these officials should consent to. The appeal to consent does not eliminate the need to specify the scope of diminished privacy.

The rationale for diminished privacy provides reasons that any citizen, including a public official, should be able to accept insofar as he or she accepts general principles of democracy. They invoke the necessity of accountability. But the rationale does not justify an unrestrained or general exposure of the private lives of anyone. It implies the private lives should become public only to the extent necessary for certain limited purposes, specifically to ensure democratic accountability. This implication yields two kinds of criteria that should govern any potential intrusion into the private life of an official: substantive criteria, which refer to types of positions and activities; and procedural criteria, which refer to methods of inquiry. The substantive criteria indicate (more or less determinate) boundaries of private life, while the procedural criteria proscribe certain ways of investigating private life, whatever its boundaries may be.

The Scope of Privacy: Substantive Criteria

It is commonly said that the private life of a public official should not be disclosed unless it is relevant to his or her official duties.[12] This view is, at best, a shorthand statement of the substantive criteria for diminished privacy. The ways in which private lives may be relevant are complex. How much privacy a public official should sacrifice depends not only on the nature of the position he or she holds, and the nature of the (presumed) private activities, but also on the relationship between them. For example, the more influential the position, the less are more intimate activities protected. Moreover, the nature of the position and the nature of the activity are themselves complex terms, and each needs to be analyzed separately.

The most important feature of the nature of the position is the level of authority or influence that the official exercises. Consistent with the aim of accountability, we assume that we need to know more about officials who wield more authority over us. The authority need be neither formal nor direct. Typically, top White House aides, as much because of their close association with the president as because of their actual authority, invite more inspection than other officials of similar rank in other offices. It is doubtful that someone less close to President Carter than Hamilton Jordan should have had to endure such public scrutiny of conduct at Sarsfield's Bar, or comments about the wife of an ambassador at a private party.[13]

We should consider not only the level of the position but also the kind of issues with which an official deals. Griffin Bell's confirmation as attorney general ran into opposition when it was revealed that he belonged to several private clubs that excluded women and blacks. Although Bell should have disclosed this information himself, he did resign his memberships, conceding that they were incompatible with the office of attorney general, which he saw as a "symbol of equality before the law."[14] Secretary of State Cyrus Vance and Defense Secretary Harold Brown also belonged to discriminatory private clubs, but no similar objections were raised against them. This suggests that most people regard the close connection between the issues with which the attorney general deals and his club memberships as a significantly distinct factor in such cases. It would be better of course if no cabinet members belonged to discriminatory clubs (and still better if no such clubs existed). But the reasons for denying privacy in these matters to the attorney general are even more compelling than the reasons for denying it to other officials at roughly the same level.

When the connection between memberships and the issues dealt with on the job is more tenuous (and the job is at lower levels of government), we encounter claims of "associational privacy" that would protect the privacy of the memberships. Courts have held, for example, that a policeman's membership in a nudist society is his "private life," and not "his employer's concern." Nudism, the court solemnly observed, is not the only recreational activity for which policemen must remove their weapons.[15] The connection between nudism and law enforcement seems remote enough, but some kinds of political activity may raise problems. In several cities, policemen have won the right to belong to the John Birch Society, secretly if they wish.[16] Such a right should not prevail if we have reason to believe that membership in organizations of this kind adversely affect the fair enforcement of the law.

Another aspect of the nature of the position is the form of the appointment—whether, for example, the official is an elected representative, a political appointee, or a career civil servant. This aspect makes much less difference than is usually thought. Once we take into account the level of the position and the kinds of issues dealt with, most of the differences between the various forms of appointment disappear. We are entitled to know more about a congressman than an analyst in the Office of Management and Budget because the congressman usually has more influence and deals with a more general range of issues. How much we should know about congressmen depends partly on our theory of representation (whether we assess, for example, their character or only their public positions on issues),[17] and more specifically on our theory of legislative ethics (whether we examine their role in the legislative process or only their financial affairs).[18]

But whatever theories we adopt, the privacy of legislators should be determined by much the same criteria that we use for political appointees. The press and the public generally ignored the excessive drinking of Hugh Johnson, the head of Roosevelt's National Recovery Administration, just as they later overlooked the drinking habits of many senators and congressmen.[19] We should want to object to the tacit protection from public comment that these men enjoyed since their drinking evidently had a significant effect on the performance of their public duties. But we would not distinguish the cases on the ground that one is a political appointee and the others are elected representatives.

The traditional distinction between political appointees and career civil servants, prominent in Max Weber's theory of bureaucracy, justified granting more of a "private life" to administrators (who were seen as politically neutral) than to politicians (who were politically committed).[20] But the distinction has now lost most of its significance in the higher levels of the American federal bureaucracy. For most of the top executives, the line between political appointment and career service no longer clearly divides politicians and generalists who make policy, from administrators and specialists who implement it.[21] How much of the private life of high-level executives should be known, therefore, ought to depend more on their influence and the kinds of decisions they make than on the form of their appointments.

The form of appointment, however, affects privacy in one important respect—not what is known but who should know it. Without completely accepting Weber's theory of bureaucracy, we can assume that civil servants are at least initially responsible to their superiors and the norms of the professional service. If so, the circle of persons who know about the private lives of civil servants should be smaller and more specific than the wider public who should know about political appointees and representatives. It is essential for some officials to know perhaps even more about the private life of an intelligence agent or a Strategic Air Command employee than about the private life of a congressman or an assistant secretary, but it is not necessary for so many people to know.

How much an official's privacy should be diminished also depends on the nature of the activity in question—its character and its effects. Although the content of what should be private is largely conventional, a general feature of many private activities is intimacy. We usually expect privacy for our physical condition and our personal relations with family, friends, and certain associates (those with whom we have "privileged" relationships), and for activities carried on "in private" at home. The boundaries of what is intimate are neither precise nor absolute, and even facts are highly relevant to the performance of their duties. But we should be inclined to say that the more intimate the activity, the more compelling must be the connection with the official's position; and, conversely, the less intimate, the less compelling the connection has to be. Consider the legal requirements for financial disclosure that now apply to legislators and high officials in the executive and judiciary.[22] The chief purpose of the requirements is to expose potential conflicts of interest—a purpose obviously related to holding officials accountable. But the relevance would not be strong enough to overcome privacy objections if private financial affairs were not at the edge of intimacy. Our attitude would be very different toward a requirement, for example, that officials list all their friends and the frequency of meetings with them. . . .

A public official can properly claim that much of his or her family life is private. At stake is not only the official's privacy but that of other people. An example of a practice that violates such privacy is what has been called the "transfer technique."[23] This typically involved an investigation into an official's family circumstances to see if he could be persuaded to resign by reassigning him to a location his family would resist. This kind of investigation would be no more acceptable if its aim were to reward the official with an assignment his family liked.

Some facts about family life (such as marriage and divorce) are of course a matter of public record.[24] It is surely proper that these facts be considered when assessing a public official if they are relevant to the office, according to the other criteria we have been using. But the official has no obligation to other parties not to do so. New York Governor Nelson Rockefeller quite properly resisted pleas to explain the reasons for his divorce and remarriage in 1963. Some family members of public officials become, formally or informally, officials themselves (such as the first lady, or the spouse of an ambassador), and they should expect no more privacy than other officials with similar influence and similar functions. In other cases, facts about a family member of an official—a spouse's health, a son's delinquency, or marital problems—might bear on the capacity of the official to do his or her job. But even here, it would seem better to publicize the effects (if and when they occur), rather than the causes.

However, when a candidate for public office makes his family life a campaign issue (for example, by portraying himself as a "good family man"), he opens to public inspection what might otherwise be private. The candidate can hardly complain if the press looks into his family life to verify his boasts. For similar reasons, we may "want to know if there is a big split in someone's life—if he is a professed feminist and at the same time a womanizer."[25] But again there are limits. Because Spiro Agnew was piously lecturing America on parenthood at the time, Jack Anderson and Brit Hume reported that his son had left his wife and was living with a male hairdresser. Anderson and Hume now say they regret the story because it was "going after the son to expose the father."[26] But the real objection is not that Agnew's statements could not legitimately be said to invite scrutiny of his family (arguably, they could). Rather, the objection should be that the effect of the story depended on exploiting readers' prejudices against unconventional styles of life.

We should distinguish two different ways in which an otherwise private activity may affect an official's capacity to perform the duties of public office: the direct effects that come from the official's own attitudes or actions in private life; and the indirect effects that result from other people's attitudes or actions toward the official's private life. In general, it would be better if neither kind of effect was publicized until it showed up in official performance. To probe possible causes before they have produced public consequences usually is to risk exposing affairs that are legitimately private. But often we cannot follow this principle, especially when we are evaluating a candidate for high office.

The direct effects constitute the stronger basis for diminished privacy. When the evidence is compelling, they may override even claims based on intimacy. Although a person's physical condition is conventionally regarded as particularly private in our society, some writers have argued that candidates for public office should have physical examinations, the results of which should be publicly announced.[27] Publicity about serious health problems of high-ranking officials, whether elected or appointed, is now more generally expected. Difficulties still arise when officials and their doctors, believing that a health problem is not serious, decline to disclose the information, and the public and the press become suspicious. Justice Rehnquist's doctors refused to identify the drug that caused an adverse reaction for which he was hospitalized in 1981, saying only that it was one of several used to treat his chronic low back pain.[28] Since the justice had been repeatedly slurring his speech and stumbling over words in court, some observers (including physicians) suspected that he was suffering from delirium tremens as a withdrawal effect of alcohol. A more complete disclosure could have avoided this conclusion. . . .

The most difficult cases concern conduct that should properly be regarded as immoral but that does not directly affect an official's performance on the job. Wife abuse, now treated more seriously than it used to be, is a case in point. The chief of the Securities and Exchange Commission's enforcement division resigned in 1985 within a week of a newspaper report that he had repeatedly beaten his wife. Although his wife's charges had appeared in the public record at the start of the divorce proceedings nearly a year and a half earlier, virtually no one had taken notice until the *Wall Street Journal* reported them in the front-page story that prompted his resignation.[29] By all accounts, the official's performance on the job had been exemplary. But White House officials immediately decided that once he became publicly known as a wife abuser he could not remain in office.

The managing editor of the *Journal* set aside the paper's "general rule" protecting the private life of public officials because of the whole set of facts surrounding the case: that the official "admitted in public the charges of wife-beating . . . that he is one of the most important law enforcement officials in the country . . . that the White House was aware of the issue of family violence and seemed to be concerned about it . . . that he had indicated that he would resign his position at the SEC if that would get his wife to take him back . . . and the questions raised about his indebtedness and . . . the issues in the Southland case [in which not he but a former law client had been charged with a cover-up of a bribery scheme]."[30] Although this editor's justification may seem too much like a laundry list of factors, it comes closer to recognizing the complexity of the case than the responses that other journalists gave. Some seemed to assume that the fact that the conduct appeared in the court record was sufficient reason to print it, or the fact that the official had to spend some time in court was enough to show that the conduct was affecting his job performance.[31]

The official's own admission on the court record is probably a necessary condition for justifying the publicity because without it (or some independent proceeding to establish guilt) we cannot have a reasonable basis for believing the charges. Although not explicitly mentioned by any of the journalists, the most important necessary condition is that the official's conduct is a serious moral wrong. None of the other factors the *Journal* editor cited seems to qualify as a necessary condition. But combined with the admission of guilt and the seriousness of the moral wrong, any one of several of these other factors probably would be sufficient to justify the publicity.

Among the other factors, those connected with the nature of the office are the most significant. Citizens should know if an official responsible for supervising the enforcement of laws repeatedly commits wrongful acts of violence. Such conduct may reveal a disregard for important moral principles underlying the legal system, including those laws that the official is charged with enforcing. The conduct may raise reasonable doubts about future performance on the job even if the official's past performance has been faultless. More specifically, citizens may reasonably expect to know about domestic violence if it provides evidence about the seriousness of the personal financial difficulties of an official whose job involves investigating the finances of other people. In this case, according to the court record, the violence was occasioned by anxieties and arguments about the worsening financial condition of the family.

But whatever factors may be sufficient to justify publicity about what would otherwise be the private life of an official, they do not include the indirect effects from the reaction of the public. It is not enough (even when it is relevant) to point to the public scandal that an official's conduct may cause. The question must always be asked: *should* the public be scandalized?

The Scope of Privacy: Procedural Criteria

Some procedural criteria protect private activities not because the activities are private but because the method of intrusion would be wrong even if the activity were public. These criteria follow from prohibitions against force and fraud, and often, but not always, involve violation of the law. The break-in at the office of Dr. Henry Fielding to collect psychiatric information to discredit Daniel Ellsberg or the planting of a spy on McGovern's campaign staff to look for "dirty stuff . . . who was sleeping with whom . . . who was smoking pot,"[32] a newspaper reporter's posing as a friend to extract confidences from a newly elected politician[33]—all of these may be challenged as improperly forceful or fraudulent, quite apart from whatever invasion of privacy may have occurred. Other criteria, however, derive more specifically from the value of privacy, and it is these on which this article concentrates.

It is often not possible to tell in advance what private activities may be relevant to our assessment of official performance, but this fact should not warrant unlimited inquiry into private lives in the hope that something relevant may turn up. This is not to say that an investigation, prompted by independent evidence and seeking further specific evidence relevant to official performance, should be proscribed merely because it is likely to uncover some purely private information in the process. But even if the boundaries of private life cannot be precisely delineated, we presume that *some* beliefs and activities are protected (as the principle of uniform privacy stressed). We should therefore object to methods that intrude into potentially private conduct in a way that by their nature cannot discriminate among activities that are legitimately a matter of public concern and those that are not. We should seek, among available alternatives, the method that is likely to intrude to the minimum degree necessary; and we should prefer methods that give officials some control over what personal information about themselves is disclosed. A brief analysis of cases in three different areas will illustrate what these procedural criteria imply.

Surveillance of an official at home generally runs afoul of the procedural criteria. Some surveillance of this sort may be illegal, such as the wiretaps that in 1969 were placed on the phones of Morton Halperin and other aides of Henry Kissinger, evidently for the purposes of discovering the source of leaks that supposedly had damaged national security.[34] But whether legal or not, such surveillance should provoke ethical qualms. When a reporter asked Kissinger in 1974 if he had any doubts about the "ethicality" of these wiretaps, he replied that if any of his subordinates had been found guilty of security leaks, it would have "reflected badly on [his] own judgment." The implication is that because the taps involved risks to his own reputation, they were not morally objectionable.[35] Showing that a practice is not in

THE ETHICS OF POLITICAL CAMPAIGNING

your self-interest, however, does not dispose of other, often more important, ethical objections, including those based on privacy. . . .

The private lives of public officials deserve protection because the privacy of all citizens has value. However, because officials must be held accountable in a democracy (in part to safeguard the privacy of others), officials should not expect to enjoy the same protection as ordinary citizens do. What the scope of the private life of officials should be depends on a manifold set of criteria that do not by themselves yield precise boundaries. The criteria are best conceived as a framework of factors about which citizens and officials should deliberate when questions of privacy arise, and to which citizens and officials should refer, to decide when such questions ought to arise.

In democracies, especially the imperfect ones we know, it is important to seek justifiable boundaries between public and private life. The purpose of such boundaries is not only to secure the privacy of officials and citizens; it is also to ensure the publicity of affairs of public import. Spurious claims of privacy shield officials from needful scrutiny by a democratic public, and thereby subvert the democratic processes of deliberation and accountability. The private lives of public officials are as important for what they exclude as for what they include.

NOTES

1. Here it is less important what those activities are than that some significant zone of privacy should be generally respected. Our broader interest in privacy, as Thomas Scanlon points out, is in "having a zone of privacy in which we can carry out our activities without . . . being continually alert for possible observers, listeners, etc." ("Thomson on Privacy," *Philosophy and Public Affairs*, 4 [Summer 1975], pp. 317–318).

2. It is important, however, to distinguish the instrumental value of privacy from the value of liberty or fairness, since they do not always coincide. If an activity is private, an official may claim not only that the activity should not be disclosed (a privacy claim), but also that if the activity is somehow disclosed, the official should not be harmed or disadvantaged because of it (a liberty or fairness claim). Generally, if an activity is protected by privacy, it would also be protected by a principle of liberty or fairness, but some activities that are not private (for example, political speech) may still enjoy protection under a principle of liberty or of fairness.

3. Charles Fried, *An Anatomy of Values* (Cambridge, MA: Harvard University Press, 1970), pp. 140–147; James Rachels, "Why Privacy Is Important," *Philosophy and Public Affairs*, 4 (Summer 1975), pp. 323–332; and Jeffrey H. Reiman, "Privacy, Intimacy and Personhood," *Philosophy and Public Affairs*, 6 (Fall 1976), pp. 26–44.

4. Stanley I. Benn, "Privacy, Freedom, and Respect for Persons," in *Privacy,* Nomos XIII, ed. Roland Pennock and John W. Chapman (New York: Atherton Press, 1971) pp. 3–13.

5. Erving Goffman, *Stigma* (Englewood Cliffs, NJ: Prentice-Hall, 1963), p. 71.

6. See Michael Walzer, "Political Action: The Problem of Dirty Hands," *Philosophy and Public Affairs*, 2 (Winter 1973), pp. 160–180.

7. On the forms and difficulties of symbolic representation, see Hanna Pitkin, *The Concept of Representation* (Berkeley: University of California Press, 1967), pp. 92–111.

8. Edward N. Stirewalt, "Yardsticks for Rulers," *Washington Post*, Aug. 1, 1976, p. C1.

9. J. D. Legge, *Sukarno: A Political Biography* (New York: Praeger, 1972), p. 336.

10. Paul A. Freund, "Privacy: One Concept or Many," in Pennock and Chapman, p. 187; and Westin, p. 375. Cf. *Gertz* v. *Robert Welch, Inc.,* 418 U.S. at 344–345 (1974): "Public officials . . . have voluntarily exposed themselves to increased risk of injury from defamatory falsehoods concerning them."

11. William W. Van Alstyne, "The Demise of the Right-Privilege Distinction in Constitutional Law," *Harvard Law Review*, 81 (May 1968), pp. 1439–1464. Although more recently the Court has revived the distinction, it has still not used it to deny federal employees constitutional rights. See Rodney A. Smolla, "The Re-emergence of the Right-Privilege Distinction in Constitutional Law: The Price of Protesting Too Much," *Stanford Law Review*, 35 (November 1982), pp. 69–120.

12. For example, William L. Rivers and Wilbur Schramm, *Responsibility in Mass Communications*, rev. ed. (New York: Harper and Row, 1969), p. 164.

13. By issuing a thirty-three page statement on the Sarsfield's incident, the White House may have generated more publicity than would otherwise have occurred. Press Secretary Jody Powell claims, however, that the report was an "in-house memo," given only to reporters on request (letter to author, May 12, 1978).

14. *Washington Post*, Dec. 22, 1976, pp. A1, A5; Dec. 23, 1976, pp. A1, A17; and Dec. 24, 1976, pp. A2, A15. Compare the controversy over the relevance of Senator Robert Byrd's earlier association with the Ku Klux Klan to his possible nomination to the Supreme Court: see John L. Hulteng, *The Messenger's Motives* (Englewood Cliffs, NJ: Prentice-Hall, 1976), p. 68.

15. *Bruns* v. *Pomeyleau*, 319 F. Supp. 58 (D. Md. 1970).

16. Benjamin R. Epstein and Arnold Forster, *The Radical Right* (New York: Random House, 1967), pp. 180–181.

17. See Pitkin, pp. 144–167.

18. Ibid., pp. 96–105.

19. See Arthur M. Schlesinger, Jr., *The Coming of the New Deal* (Boston: Houghton Mifflin, 1959), pp. 105–110; and Brit Hume, "Now It Can Be Told . . . or Can It," *More* (April 1975), p. 6.

20. Max Weber, "Bureaucracy," in *From Max Weber*, ed. H. H. Gerth and C. Wright Mills (New York: Oxford University Press, 1958), pp. 197, 199.

21. Hugh Heclo, *A Government of Strangers: Executive Politics in Washington* (Wasington, DC: Brookings, 1977), pp. 34–83, 154–155.

22. *Congressional Quarterly, Congressional Ethics*, 2nd ed. (Washington, DC: Congressional Quarterly, Inc., 1980), pp. 75–88, 182–188. Also see pp. 97–99, 114–116.

23. U.S. House Committee on Post Office and Civil Service, Subcommittee on Manpower and Civil Service, *Final Report: Violations and Abuses of Merit Principles in Federal Employment* (Washington, DC: Government Printing Office, 1976), p. 163.

24. Marriages not on the public record may also be fair game. If President Kennedy had been previously married and the record suppressed, as was widely rumored, the press should have reported these facts. (See Tom Wicker, *On Press* [New York: Viking Press, 1978], p. 111.) Bigamous marriages are also properly a matter of public concern, not merely because they are illegal, but because they may demonstrate an official's attitude toward a major social question. See "Newspaper Wins Bigamist Case," *The News Media and the Law* 2 (April 1978), p. 25.

25. Susan Brownmiller, quoted in Deirdre Carmody, "Campaigns Raising Debates on Privacy," *The New York Times*, Nov. 18, 1979, p. 31.

26. Hume, p. 8. Also see Rivers and Schram, pp. 164, 169.

27. Alan L. Otten, "No More Tiptoeing," *Wall Street Journal*, Sept. 4, 1975, p. 10. The Judicial Council of the American Medical Association has held that a "physician may not discuss the patient's health condition with the press or the public without the patient's consent" (American Medical Association, *Opinions and Reports of the Judicial Council*

THE ETHICS OF POLITICAL CAMPAIGNING

[Chicago, 1977], sec. 6.09). Presumably, proposals for publicizing the results of physical exams would include a requirement that the candidate give his or her consent.

28. Lawrence K. Altman, "A Justice's Health: What Is Private?" *The New York Times,* Jan. 4, 1986, p. A20.

29. Brooks Jackson, "John Fedders of SEC Is Pummeled by Legal and Personal Problems," *Wall Street Journal,* Feb. 25, 1985, p.1.

30. Stuart Taylor, Jr., "Life in the Spotlight: Agony of Getting Burned," *The New York Times,* Feb. 27, 1985, p. 24.

31. See the comments by editors of *The New York Times* (ibid.) and the *Washington Post,* Feb. 27, 1985.

32. J. Anthony Lukas, *Nightmare: The Underside of the Nixon Years* (New York: Viking, 1976), pp. 126–138, 218–219.

33. Rivers and Schramm, p. 166.

34. Lukas, pp. 66–84.

35. "Kissinger's Threat to Resign—June 11, 1974," in *Historic Documents of 1974* (Washington, DC: Congressional Quarterly, Inc., 1975), p. 495.

CHAPTER 4

LYING AND THE "DIRTY HANDS" DILEMMA IN GOVERNMENT

Introduction

Among the most difficult moral mazes that confront government officials is deciding whether it is proper to commit improprieties for the public good. These kinds of quandaries, which include telling a lie for a perceived public good and the "dirty hands" dilemma (explained subsequently), can emerge at any level of government and for any public official, regardless of rank. Moreover, they have been a subject of discussion and analysis by students of government since ancient times. This chapter examines in detail these two moral mazes by bringing together selections from both classic and contemporary sources that inquire into the ethics of doing evil to produce a greater political good.

A "dirty hands" dilemma is a graphic phrase that straightforwardly depicts the problem under consideration. Should public officials engage in acts of wrongdoing that will "dirty their hands" and give the impression that they are corrupt, believing that such an act will nonetheless have good consequences for the public? For example, should public officials lie in order to protect the public? The latter is a classic example of the "dirty hands" dilemma. This problem is the focus of so much discussion that it is a topic worthy of special attention in a book on government ethics and it is treated in this chapter in articles by Peter A. French and Michael Walzer. Thus, after reviewing the general nature of it in great detail, we will go on to examine the specific instance of whether lying is acceptable government procedure.

Public officials dirty their hands when they commit an act generally considered to be a wrong to further the common good. The question concerns the dilemma involved when committing the wrong seems to lead to a good. Thus public officials must decide if they are willing to engage in wrongdoing for the sake of a perceived good, all the while keeping in mind that generally they are prohibited from engaging in wrongdoing. The source of such dilemmas lies in the professional role of a public official that conflicts with the standards of everyday morality. What a public official is required to do at times may clash directly with any number of moral rules. Thus, the "dirty hands" dilemma is the product of a tension between professional roles and moral rules that are the standards of everyday life.

A classic analyst of this dilemma, Niccolò Machiavelli (1469–1527), the Italian political philosopher, saw no such tension. He held that the rules of morality in everyday life should not be applied to the acts of public officials when they are carrying out their professional roles and responsibilities to further the common good. As Machiavelli has put it in the *Discourses:* "When the act accuses, the result excuses." (See the selection of the chapter excerpted from Machiavelli's *The Prince.*) Here it is held that we cannot divorce the person from the role of "public official"; if any moral judgment is to be made, it must be made about the office or the governmental unit in which the official is housed. In other words, we should not apply the ordinary standards of right and wrong to the extraordinary situation of a person who is acting only as a functionary and fulfilling the obligations of a designated role.

To apply moral rules to the role of public official would be tantamount to misunderstanding what it is that public officials do, namely, represent others and further the interests of others. Since public officials are not acting on their own behalf, they surely cannot be held accountable for engaging in activities that normally would be considered wrong in other contexts. For those in this camp, then, there really is no dilemma, and it is permissible, if not a *requirement* of their role, for public officials to do wrong to achieve good.

Of course, another viewpoint clashes with this proposition. It contends that it is a mistake to confuse the role of public official with the person who holds that role; moral rules are still applicable to the acts of the person who commits wrongs, whether that person is a public official or not. An officeholder should be considered separately from the office held. One's role cannot be used as an excuse for an exemption from the rules. Wrongdoing is just that, no matter what the context. This view, then, would hold public officials accountable for their unethical acts, even if those acts were done in the name of the common good and performed by one claiming to be a professional or a mere functionary.

Separate and apart from these questions of accountability and blame, there is little doubt that the most common form of the "dirty hands" dilemma in public administration is that of lying. Before we can adequately discuss this problem, several preliminary distinctions about the phenomenon of lying need to be drawn. Lying can take many forms. Direct falsehoods, exaggerations, omissions, evasions, deceptions of several stripes, and other kinds of duplicity can easily be cited as examples of what could count as an act of lying. There are few who would be so naïve as to claim that the art of politics and the practice of governance are free from any of these moral shortcomings.

Another distinction focuses upon the question of whether public officials have a special obligation to tell the truth or whether their office permits them special excuses to depart from it. On the one hand, it can be argued that knowledge is the cornerstone of democracy—an informed public is a prerequisite for a truly democratic government. Hence, citizens have an inherent right to know the truth of issues facing the government, so that they can make intelligent decisions as voters and constituents. When public officials decide to dirty their hands and not engage in truth-telling whether by direct falsehood, omission, or evasion, then they are abridging the public's right to know. There is, on this account, then, a special obligation for public officials to tell the truth, based upon this inherent need of democracy.

On the other hand, however, it can be argued that public officials in a democracy may be excused at times from the general obligation of truth-telling and from fulfilling their duty not to lie to the public. There may be dire situations or times of crises that threaten the government and its people; under such conditions it may be permissible for a public official to deceive the public for its own good. In other words, when public officials take their oaths of office, they are sworn to do everything in their power to ensure the survival of the government and the safety of the public. It is the very nature of public office, then, that excuses the public official who lies for the public good, because the public good is essentially what the official is required to protect and save from harm. If such protection in times of crises entails that an official engage in deception, then so be it. He is only fulfilling his responsibilities of his office and as such may be excused for his deception. The argument for excusing lies by officials has a long history, the first instance of it appearing in Plato's *Republic*, in which the concept of the "noble" lie—referring to lies for the public good—was first introduced (see the excerpts from *The Republic* included in this chapter).

This line of reasoning about excusing public officials who lie leads directly to the core question about lying in public administration, namely: are such lies justifiable? Again, there is no doubt that lying in government is an activity that appears widespread. (See "Who's Lying Now?" by Deborah Baldwin, for evidence backing this proposition.) But the underlying question remains: are these instances of duplicity allowable, and if so, what are the conditions under which they are justifiable? If we can identify these conditions, then we may be in a better position to decide if the public's right to know has been abridged or if an official's act of lying might be excused. These are among the kinds of issues that Sissela Bok has examined at length in her bestselling book, *Lying: Moral Choice in Public and Private Life*. The selection in this chapter presents an excerpt from the book, detailing her analysis of the conditions under which lies for the public good might be told with justification.

As can be seen, public officials are confronted with a host of issues, problems, and dilemmas of an ethical nature, all of which require sharp skills of critical thinking. Put another way, it seems as if a new job requirement for public administration is the ability to solve a moral problem. Hence, there may have been some truth in Plato's famous dictum found in his *Republic* that holds: "Unless kings become philosophers or philosophers become kings, there is no hope for humanity." We might say that at a bare minimum, what *is* necessary is that public administrators become proficient at moral reasoning. This book has been designed to assist in that task.

The Noble Lie
from The Republic
by Plato

Scholars have long pointed to Plato's (427–347 B.C.) dialogue, *The Republic* (c.370 B.C.), as one of the first extended treatments of the problems of government and its workings. In it, Plato depicts Socrates, the first Western philosopher and Plato's teacher, taking up the question of justice and its nature. This requires Socrates and his young followers in the dialogue to "build" a city-state in their discourse. They explore how justice will function within the perfect city-state. They ask, "What is justice?" and "What is the just government?" In the course of answering these questions, Socrates and his interlocutors pause to consider whether it is proper for a ruler to lie to those who are ruled. What Plato calls the "noble lie" (or the "royal lie" in some translations) is established in *The Republic* as a just course of action for rulers. The argument is that while in general it is wrong for rulers or anyone to lie, sometimes the citizens may be deceived for their own good. With his argument, Plato set in motion a debate that still flourishes today. The central questions consider whether leaders should mislead their citizenry through lies and deception for the public good, or whether the citizenry's right to know the truth should always be upheld? The role of Plato's *Republic,* with its introduction of the concept of the "noble lie," is interesting not only for his arguments supporting this position, but also for the historical import of being the first treatment in Western culture of the topic. The following section of the dialogue occurs between Socrates (the narrator) and Glaucon, with Socrates opening the discussion.

Must we not ask who are to be rulers and who subjects?
Certainly.
There can be no doubt that the elder must rule the younger.
Clearly.
And that the best of these must rule.

Plato, *The Republic* (c.370 B.C.), B. Jowett, trans. (various editions).

That is also clear.

Now, are not the best husbandmen those who are most devoted to husbandry?

Yes.

And as we are to have the best of guardians for our city, must they not be those who have most the character of guardians?

Yes.

And to this end they ought to be wise and efficient, and to have a special care of the State?

True.

And a man will be most likely to care about that which he loves?

To be sure.

And he will be most likely to love that which he regards as having the same interests with himself, and that of which the good or evil fortune is supposed by him at any time most to affect his own?

Very true, he replied.

Then there must be a selection. Let us note among the guardians those who in their whole life show the greatest eagerness to do what is for the good of their country, and the greatest repugnance to do what is against her interests.

Those are the right men.

And they will have to be watched at every age, in order that we may see whether they preserve their resolution, and never, under the influence either of force or enchantment, forget or cast off their sense of duty to the State.

How cast off? he said.

I will explain to you, I replied. A resolution may go out of a man's mind either with his will or against his will; with his will when he gets rid of a falsehood and learns better, against his will whenever he is deprived of a truth.

I understand, he said, the willing loss of a resolution; the meaning of the unwilling I have yet to learn.

Why, I said, do you not see that men are unwillingly deprived of good, and willingly of evil? Is not to have lost the truth an evil, and to possess the truth a good? And you would agree that to conceive things as they are is to possess the truth?

Yes, he replied; I agree with you in thinking that mankind are deprived of truth against their will.

And is not this involuntary deprivation caused either by theft, or force, or enchantment?

Still, he replied, I do not understand you.

I fear that I must have been talking darkly, like the tragedians. I only mean that some men are changed by persuasion and that others forget; argument steals away the hearts of one class, and time of the other; and this I call theft. Now you understand me?

Yes.

Those again who are forced are those whom the violence of some pain or grief compels to change their opinion.

I understand, he said, and you are quite right.

And you would also acknowledge that the enchanted are those who change their minds either under the softer influence of pleasure, or the sterner influence of fear?

Yes, he said; everything that deceives may be said to enchant.

Therefore, as I was just now saying, we must enquire who are the best guardians of their own conviction that what they think the interest of the State is to be the rule of their lives. We must watch them from their youth upwards, and make them perform actions in which they are most likely to forget or to be deceived, and he who remembers and is not deceived is to be selected, and he who fails in the trial is to be rejected. That will be the way?

Yes.

And there should also be toils and pains and conflicts prescribed for them, in which they will be made to give further proof of the same qualities.

Very right, he replied.

And then, I said, we must try them with enchantments—that is the third sort of test—and see what will be their behaviour: like those who take colts amid noise and tumult to see if they are of a timid nature, so must we take our youth amid terrors of some kind, and again pass them into pleasures, and prove them more thoroughly than gold is proved in the furnace, that we may discover whether they are armed against all enchantments, and of a noble bearing always, good guardians of themselves and of the music which they have learned, and retaining under all circumstances a rhythmical and harmonious nature, such as will be most serviceable to the individual and to the State. And he who at every age, as boy and youth and in mature life, has come out of the trial victorious and pure, shall be appointed a ruler and guardian of the State; he shall be honoured in life and death, and shall receive sepulture and other memorials of honour, the greatest that we have to give. But him who fails, we must reject. I am inclined to think that this is the sort of way in which our rulers and guardians should be chosen and appointed. I speak generally, and not with any pretension to exactness.

And, speaking generally, I agree with you, he said.

And perhaps the word "guardian" in the fullest sense ought to be applied to this higher class only who preserve us against foreign enemies and maintain peace among our citizens at home, that the one may not have the will, or the others the power, to harm us. The young men whom we before called guardians may be more properly designated auxiliaries and supporters of the principles of the rulers.

I agree with you, he said.

How then may we devise one of those needful falsehoods of which we lately spoke—just one royal lie [noble lie] which may deceive the rulers, if that be possible, and at any rate the rest of the city?

What sort of lie? he said.

Nothing new, I replied; only an old Phoenician[1] tale of what has often occurred before now in other places (as the poets say, and have made the world believe) though not in our time, and I do not know whether such an event could ever happen again, or could now even be made probable, if it did.

How your words seem to hesitate on your lips!

You will not wonder, I replied, at my hesitation when you have heard.

Speak, he said, and fear not.

Well then, I will speak, although I really know not how to look you in the face, or in what words to utter the audacious fiction, which I propose to communicate gradually, first to the rulers, then to the soldiers, and lastly to the people. They are to be told that their youth was a dream, and the education and training which they received from us, an appearance only; in reality during all that time they were being formed and fed in the womb of the earth, where they themselves and their arms and appurtenances were manufactured; when they were completed, the earth, their mother, sent them up; and so, their country being their mother and also their nurse, they are bound to advise for her good, and to defend her against attacks, and her citizens they are to regard as children of the earth and their own brothers.

You had good reason, he said, to be ashamed of the lie which you were going to tell.

True, I replied, but there is more coming; I have only told you half. Citizens, we shall say to them in our tale, you are brothers, yet God has framed you differently. Some of you have the power of command, and in the composition of these he has mingled gold, wherefore also they have the greatest honour; others he has made of silver, to be auxiliaries; others again who are to be husbandmen and craftsmen he has composed of brass and iron; and the species will generally be preserved in the children. But as all are of the same original stock, a golden parent will sometimes have a silver son, or a silver parent a golden son. And God proclaims as first principle to the rulers, and above all else, that there is nothing which they should so anxiously guard, or of which they are to be such good guardians, as of the purity of the race. They should observe what elements mingle in their offspring; for if the son of a golden or silver parent has an admixture of brass and iron, then nature orders a transposition of ranks, and the eye of the ruler must not be pitiful towards the child because he has to descend in the scale and become a husbandman or artisan, just as there may be sons of artisans who having an admixture of gold or silver in them are raised to honour, and become guardians or auxiliaries. For an oracle says that when a man of brass or iron guards the State, it will be destroyed. Such is the tale; is there any possibility of making our citizens believe in it?

Not in the present generation, he replied; there is no way of accomplishing this; but their sons may be made to believe in the tale, and their sons' sons, and posterity after them.

I see the difficulty, I replied; yet the fostering of such a belief will make them care more for the city and for one another. Enough, however, of the fiction, which may now fly abroad upon the wings of rumour, while we arm our earth-born heroes, and lead them forth under the command of their rulers.

Lies for the Public Good
Sissela Bok

In the history of the literature of ethics, there is very little treatment of lying in any serious or extended fashion. In 1978, ethicist Sissela Bok changed that with her book *Lying: Moral Choice in Public and Private Life*. The selection at hand is taken from Chapter XII of her now classic book. In earlier chapters Bok developed a method for approaching the topic of lying that she now applies to the situation of public officials. Beginning with a review of Plato's position on the rightness of a ruler's telling "noble lies," Bok observes that lying in government is commonplace. Those who reserve the right to lie, she says, do so because they believe that some things in government are best left hidden from public view; those who think otherwise are just not aware of the practicalities and realities of government. Bok, however, does hold otherwise and suggests that lying in government is essentially a symptom of "unwarranted power," in which those who lie to the public do so without the public's consent. She then goes on to raise and answer the question as to whether there are any conditions under which such deceptions are morally justifiable. Her position is that even if there are justifiable lies in government—as in a crisis situation or for national security—engaging in them has its own risks, and hence they should be avoided.

"How then," said I, "might we contrive one of those opportune falsehoods of which we were just now speaking, so as by one noble lie to persuade if possible the rulers themselves, but failing that the rest of the city?"

. . . "While all of you are brothers," we will say, "yet God in fashioning those of you who are fitted to hold rule mingled gold in their generation, for which reason they are most precious—but in their helpers silver and iron and brass in the farmers and other craftsmen."

. . . "Do you see any way of getting them to believe this tale?" "No, not these themselves," he said, "but I do, their sons and successors and the rest of mankind who come after." "Well," said I, "even that would have a good effect in making them more inclined to care for the state and one another."

—Plato, *The Republic*

HUGO: And do you think the living will agree to your schemes?
HOEDERER: We'll get them to swallow them little by little.
HUGO: By lying to them?
HOEDERER: By lying to them sometimes.

. . . .

HOEDERER: I'll lie when I must, and I have contempt for no one. I wasn't the one who invented lying. It grew out of a society divided into classes, and each one of us has inherited it from birth. We shall not abolish lying by refusing to tell lies, but by using every means at hand to abolish classes.

—Jean-Paul Sartre, *Dirty Hands*

The Noble Lie

In earlier chapters three circumstances have seemed to liars to provide the strongest excuse for their behavior—a crisis where overwhelming harm can be averted only through deceit; complete harmlessness and triviality to the point where it seems absurd to quibble about whether a lie has been told; and the duty to particular individuals to protect their secrets. I have shown how lies in times of crisis can expand into vast practices where the harm to be averted is less obvious and the crisis less and less immediate; how white lies can shade into equally vast practices no longer so harmless, with immense cumulative costs; and how lies to protect individuals and to cover up their secrets can be told for increasingly dubious purposes to the detriment of all.

When these three expanding streams flow together and mingle with yet another—a desire to advance the public good—they form the most dangerous body of deceit of all. These lies may not be justified by an immediate crisis nor by complete triviality nor by duty to any one person; rather, liars tend to consider them as right and unavoidable because of the altruism that motivates them. I want, in this chapter and the next, to turn to this far-flung category.

Naturally, there will be large areas of overlap between these lies and those considered earlier. But the most characteristic defense for these lies is a separate one, based on the benefits they may confer and the long-range harm they can avoid. The intention may be broadly paternalistic, as when citizens are deceived "for their own good," or only a few may be lied to for the benefit of the community at large. Error and self-deception mingle with these altruistic purposes and blur them; the filters through which we must try to peer at lying are thicker and more distorting than ever in these practices. But I shall try to single out, among these lies, the elements that are consciously and purposely intended to benefit society.

A long tradition in political philosophy endorses some lies for the sake of the public. Plato, in the passage quoted at the head of this chapter, first used the expression "noble lie" for the fanciful story that might be told to people in order to persuade them to accept class distinctions and thereby safeguard social harmony. According to this story, God Himself mingled gold, silver, iron, and brass in fashioning rulers, auxiliaries, farmers, and craftsmen, intending these groups for separate tasks in a harmonious hierarchy.

The Greek adjective which Plato used to characterize this falsehood expresses a most important fact about lies by those in power: this adjective is *"gennaion,"* which means "noble" in the sense of both "high-minded" and "well-bred."[1] The same assumption of nobility, good breeding, and superiority to those deceived is also present in Disraeli's statement that a gentleman is one who knows when to tell the truth and when not to. In other words, lying is excusable when undertaken for "noble" ends by those trained to discern these purposes.

Rulers, both temporal and spiritual, have seen their deceits in the benign light of such social purposes. They have propagated and maintained myths played on the gullibility of the ignorant, and sought stability in shared beliefs. They have seen themselves as high-minded and well-bred—whether by birth or by training—and as superior to those they deceive. Some have gone so far as to claim that those who govern have a *right* to lie.[2] The powerful tell lies believing that they have greater than ordinary understanding of what is at stake; very often, they regard their dupes as having inadequate judgment, or as likely to respond in the wrong way to truthful information.

At times, those who govern also regard particular circumstances as too uncomfortable, too painful, for most people to be able to cope with rationally. They may believe, for instance, that their country must prepare for long-term challenges of great importance, such as a war, an epidemic, or a belt-tightening in the face of future shortages. Yet they may fear that citizens will be able to respond only to short-range dangers. Deception at such times may seem to the government leaders as the only means of attaining the necessary results.

The perspective of the liar is paramount in all such decisions to tell "noble" lies. If the liar considers the responses of the deceived at all, he assumes that they will, once the deceit comes to light and its benefits are understood, be uncomplaining if not positively grateful. The lies are often seen as necessary merely at one *stage* in the education of the public. Thus Erasmus, in commenting on Plato's views, wrote:

> . . . he sets forth deceitful fictions for the rabble, so that the people might not set fire to the magistracy, and similar falsifications by which the crass multitude is deceived in its own interests, in the same way that parents deceive children and doctors the sick.
>
> . . . Thus for the crass multitude there is need of temporary promises, figures, allegories, parables . . . so that little by little they might advance to loftier things.[3]

Some experienced public officials are impatient with any effort to question the ethics of such deceptive practices (except actions obviously taken for private ends). They argue that vital objectives in the national interest require a measure of deception to succeed in the face of powerful obstacles. Negotiations must be carried on that are best left hidden from public view; bargains must be struck that simply cannot be comprehended by a politically unsophisticated electorate. A certain amount of illusion is needed in order for public servants to be effective. Every government, therefore, has to deceive people to some extent in order to lead them.

These officials view the public's concern for ethics as understandable but hardly realistic. Such "moralistic" concerns, put forth without any understanding of practical exigencies, may lead to the setting of impossible standards; these could seriously hamper work without actually changing the underlying practices. Government officials could then feel so beleaguered that some of them might quit their jobs; inefficiency and incompetence would then increasingly afflict the work of the rest.

If we assume the perspective of the deceived—those who experience the consequences of government deception—such arguments are not persuasive. We cannot take for granted either the altruism or the good judgment of those who lie to us, no matter how much they intend to benefit us. We have learned that much deceit for private gain masquerades as being in the public interest. We know how deception, even for the most unselfish motive, corrupts and spreads. And we have lived through the consequences of lies told for what were believed to be noble purposes.

Equally unpersuasive is the argument that there always has been government deception, and always will be, and that efforts to draw lines and set standards are therefore useless annoyances. It is certainly true that deception can never be completely absent from most human practices. But there are great differences among societies in the kinds of deceit that exist and the extent to which they are practiced, differences also among individuals in the same government and among successive governments within the same society. This strongly suggests that it is worthwhile trying to discover why such differences exist and to seek ways of raising the standards of truthfulness.

The argument that those who raise moral concerns are ignorant of political realities, finally, ought to lead, not to a dismissal of such inquiries, but to a more articulate description of what these realities are, so that a more careful and informed debate could begin. We have every reason to regard government as more profoundly injured by a dismissal of criticism and a failure to consider standards than by efforts to discuss them openly. If duplicity is to be allowed in exceptional cases, the criteria for these exceptions should themselves be openly debated and publicly chosen. Otherwise government leaders will have free rein to manipulate and distort the facts and thus escape accountability to the public.

The effort to question political deception cannot be ruled out so summarily. The disparagement of inquiries into such practices has to be seen as the defense of unwarranted power—power bypassing the consent of the governed. In the pages to come I shall take up just a few cases to illustrate both the clear breaches of trust that no group of citizens could desire, and circumstances where it is more difficult to render a judgment.

Examples of Political Deception

In September 1964, a State Department official, reflecting a growing administration consensus, wrote a memorandum advocating a momentous deceit of the American public.[4] He outlined possible courses of action to cope with the deteriorating military situation in South Vietnam. These included a stepping up of American participation in the "pacification" in South Vietnam and a "crescendo" of military action against North Vietnam, involving heavy bombing by the United States. But an election campaign was going on; the President's Republican opponent, Senator Goldwater, was suspected by the electorate of favoring escalation of the war in Vietnam and of brandishing nuclear threats to the communist world. In keeping with President Johnson's efforts to portray Senator Goldwater as an irresponsible war hawk, the memorandum ended with a paragraph entitled "Special considerations during the next two months," holding that:

> During the next two months, because of the lack of "rebuttal time" before election to justify particular actions which may be distorted to the U.S. public, we must act with special care— signaling to . . . [the South Vietnamese] that we are behaving energetically despite the restraints of our political season, and to the U.S. public that we are behaving with good purpose and restraint.

As the campaign wore on, President Johnson increasingly professed to be the candidate of peace. He gave no indication of the growing pressure for escalation from high administrative officials who would remain in office should he win; no hint of the hard choice he knew he would face if elected.[5] Rather he repeated over and over again that:

> [T]he first responsibility, the only real issue in this campaign, the only thing you ought to be concerned about at all, is: Who can best keep the peace?[6]

The stratagem succeeded; the election was won; the war escalated. Under the name of Operation Rolling Thunder, the United States launched massive bombing raids over North Vietnam early in 1965. In suppressing genuine debate about these plans during the election campaign and masquerading as the party of peace, government members privy to the maneuver believed that they knew what was best for the country and that history would vindicate them. They meant to benefit the nation and the world by keeping the danger of a communist victory at bay. If a sense of *crisis* was needed for added justification, the Domino Theory strained for it: one regime after another was seen as toppling should the first domino be pushed over.

But why the deceit, if the purposes were so altruistic? Why not espouse these purposes openly before the election? The reason must have been that the government could not count on popular support for the scheme. In the first place, the sense of crisis and threat from North Vietnam would have been far from universally shared. To be forthright about the likelihood of escalation might lose many votes; it certainly could not fit with the campaign to portray President Johnson as the candidate most likely to keep the peace. Second, the government feared that its explanations might be "distorted" in the election campaign, so that the voters would not have the correct information before them. Third, time was lacking for the government to make an effort at educating the people about all that was at issue. Finally, the plans were not definitive; changes were possible, and the Vietnamese situation itself very unstable. For all these reasons, it seemed best to campaign for negotiation and restraint and let the Republican opponent be the target for the fear of United States belligerence.

President Johnson thus denied the electorate any chance to give or to refuse consent to the escalation of the war in Vietnam. Believing they had voted for the candidate of peace, American citizens were, within months, deeply embroiled in one of the cruelest wars in their history. Deception of this kind strikes at the very essence of democratic government. It allows those in power to override or nullify the right vested in the people to cast an informed vote in critical elections. Deceiving the people for the sake of the people is a self-contradictory notion in a democracy, unless it can be shown that there has been genuine consent to deceit. The actions of President Johnson were therefore inconsistent with the most basic principle of our political system.

What if all government officials felt similarly free to deceive provided they believed the deception genuinely necessary to achieve some important public end? The trouble is that those who make such calculations are always susceptible to bias. They overestimate the likelihood that the benefit will occur and that the harm will be averted; they underestimate the chances that the deceit will be discovered and ignore the effects of such a discovery on trust; they underrate the comprehension of the deceived citizens, as well as their ability and their right to make a reasoned choice. And, most important, such a benevolent self-righteousness disguises the many motives for political lying which could *not* serve as moral excuses: the need to cover up past mistakes; the vindictiveness; the desire to stay in power. These self-serving ends provide the impetus for countless lies that are rationalized as "necessary" for the public good.

As political leaders become accustomed to making such excuses, they grow insensitive to fairness and to veracity. Some come to believe that any lie can be told so long as they can convince themselves that people will be better off in the long run. From there, it is a short step to the conclusion that, even if people will not be better off from a particular lie, they will benefit by all maneuvers to keep the right people in office. Once public servants lose their bearings in this way, all the shabby deceits of Watergate—the fake telegrams, the erased tapes, the elaborate cover-ups, the bribing of witnesses to make them lie, the televised pleas for trust—become possible.

While Watergate may be unusual in its scope, most observers would agree that deception is part and parcel of many everyday decisions in government. Statistics may be presented in such a way as to diminish the gravity of embarrassing problems. Civil servants may lie to members of Congress in order to protect programs they judge important, or to guard secrets they have been ordered not to divulge. If asked, members of Congress who make deals with one another to vote for measures they would otherwise oppose deny having made such deals. False rumors may be leaked by subordinates who believe that unwise executive action is about to be taken. Or the leak may be correct, but falsely attributed in order to protect the source.

Consider the following situation and imagine all the variations on this theme being played in campaigns all over the United States, at the local, state, or federal level:

A big-city mayor is running for reelection. He has read a report recommending that he remove rent controls after his reelection. He intends to do so, but believes he will lose the election if his intention is known. When asked, at a news conference two days before his election, about the existence of such a report, he denies knowledge of it and reaffirms his strong support of rent control.

In the mayor's view, his reelection is very much in the public interest, and the lie concerns questions which he believes the voters are unable to evaluate properly, especially on such short notice. In all similar situations, the sizable bias resulting from the self-serving element (the desire to be elected, to stay in office, to exercise power) is often clearer to onlookers than to the liars themselves. This bias inflates the alleged justifications for the lie—the worthiness, superiority, altruism of the liar, the rightness of his cause, and the inability of those deceived to respond "appropriately" to hearing the truth.

These common lies are now so widely suspected that voters are at a loss to know when they can and cannot believe what a candidate says in campaigning. The damage to trust has been immense. I have already referred to the poll which found 69 percent of Americans agreeing, both in 1975 and 1976, that the country's leaders had consistently lied to the American people over the past ten years. Over 40 percent of the respondents also agreed that:

> Most politicians are so similar that it doesn't really make much difference who gets elected.[7]

Many refuse to vote under such circumstances. Others look to appearance or to personality factors for clues as to which candidate might be more honest than the others. Voters and candidates alike are the losers when a political system has reached such a low level of trust. Once elected, officials find that their warnings and their calls to common sacrifice meet with disbelief and apathy, even when cooperation is most urgently needed. Law suits and investigations multiply. And the fact that candidates, should they win, are not expected to have meant what they said while campaigning, nor held accountable for discrepancies, only reinforces the incentives for them to bend the truth the next time, thus adding further to the distrust of the voters.

Political lies, so often assumed to be trivial by those who tell them, rarely are. They cannot be trivial when they affect so many people and when they are so peculiarly likely to be imitated, used to retaliate, and spread from a few to many. When political representatives or entire governments arrogate to themselves the right to lie, they take power from the public that would not have been given up voluntarily.

Deception and Consent

Can there be exceptions to the well-founded distrust of deception in public life? Are there times when the public itself might truly not care about possible lies, or might even prefer to be deceived? Are some white lies so trivial or so transparent that they can be ignored? And can we envisage public discussion of more seriously misleading government statements such that reasonable persons could consent to them in advance?

White lies, first of all, are as common to political and diplomatic affairs as they are to the private lives of most people. Feigning enjoyment of an embassy gathering or a political rally, toasting the longevity of a dubious regime or an unimpressive candidate for office—these are forms of politeness that mislead few. It is difficult to regard them as threats to either individuals or communities. As with all white lies, however, the problem is that they spread so easily, and that lines are very hard to draw. Is it still a white lie for a secretary of state to announce that he is going to one country when in reality he travels to another? Or for a president to issue a "cover story" to the effect that a cold is forcing him to return to the White House, when in reality an international crisis made him cancel the rest of his campaign trip? Is it a white lie to issue a letter of praise for a public servant one has just fired? Given the vulnerability of public trust, it is never more important than in public life to keep the deceptive element of white lies to an absolute minimum, and to hold down the danger of their turning into more widespread deceitful practices.

A great deal of deception believed not only innocent but highly justified by public figures concerns their private lives. Information about their marriages, their children, their opinions about others—information about their personal plans and about their motives for personal decisions—all are theirs to keep private if they wish to do so. Refusing to give information under these circumstances is justifiable—but the right to withhold information is not the right to lie about it. Lying under such circumstances bodes ill for conduct in other matters.[8]

Certain additional forms of deception may be debated and authorized in advance by elected representatives of the public. The use of unmarked police cars to discourage speeding by drivers is an example of such a practice. Various forms of unannounced, sometimes covert, auditing of business and government operations are others. Whenever these practices are publicly regulated, they can be limited so that abuses are avoided. But they must be *openly* debated and agreed to in advance, with every precaution against abuses of privacy and the rights of individuals, and against the spread of such covert activities. It is not enough that a public official assumes that consent would be given to such practices.

Another type of deceit has no such consent in advance: the temporizing or the lie when truthful information at a particular *time* might do great damage. Say that a government is making careful plans for announcing the devaluation of its currency. If the news leaks out to some before it can be announced to all, unfair profits for speculators might result. Or take the decision to make sharp increases in taxes on imported goods in order to rescue a tottering economy. To announce the decision beforehand would lead to hoarding and to exactly the results that the taxes are meant to combat. Thus, government officials will typically seek to avoid any premature announcement and will refuse to comment if asked whether devaluation or higher taxes are imminent. At times, however, official spokesmen will go further and falsely deny that the actions in question will in fact take place.

Such lies may well be uttered in good faith in an effort to avoid harmful speculation and hoarding. Nevertheless, if false statements are made to the public only to be exposed as soon as the devaluation or the new tax is announced, great damage to trust will result. It is like telling a patient that an operation will be painless—the swifter the disproof, the more likely the loss of trust. In addition, these lies are subject to all the dangers of spread and mistake and deterioration of standards that accompany all deception.

For these reasons, it is far better to refuse comment than to lie in such situations. The objection may be made, however, that a refusal to comment will be interpreted by the press as tantamount to an admission that devaluation or higher taxes are very near. Such an objection has force only if a government has not already established credibility by letting it be known earlier that it would never comment on such matters, and by strictly adhering to this policy at all times. Since lies in these cases are so egregious, it is worth taking care to establish such credibility in advance, so that a refusal to comment is not taken as an invitation to monetary speculation.

Another form of deception takes place when the government regards the public as frightened, or hostile, and highly volatile. In order not to create a panic, information about early signs of an epidemic may be suppressed or distorted. And the lie to a mob seeking its victim is like lying to the murderer asking where the person he is pursuing has gone. It can be acknowledged and defended as soon as the threat is over. In such cases, one may at times be justified in withholding information; perhaps, on rare occasions, even in lying. But such cases are so rare that they hardly exist for practical purposes.

The fact that rare circumstances exist where the justification for government lying seems powerful creates a difficulty—these same excuses will often be made to serve a great many more purposes. For some governments or public officials, the information they wish to conceal is almost never of the requisite certainty, the time never the right one, and the public never sufficiently dispassionate. For these reasons, it is hard to see how a practice of lying to the public about devaluation or changes in taxation or epidemics could be consented to in advance, and therefore justified.

Are there any exceptionally dangerous circumstances where the state of crisis is such as to justify lies to the public for its own protection? We have already discussed lying to enemies in an acute crisis. Sometimes the domestic public is then also deceived, at least temporarily, as in the case of the U-2 incident. Wherever there is a threat—from a future enemy, as before World War II, or from a shortage of energy—the temptation to draw upon the excuses for deceiving citizens is very strong. The government may sincerely doubt that the electorate is capable of making the immediate sacrifices needed to confront the growing danger. (Or one branch of the government may lack confidence in another, for similar reasons, as when the administration mistrusts Congress.) The public may seem too emotional, the time not yet ripe for disclosure. Are there crises so exceptional that deceptive strategies are justifiable?

Compare, for instance, what was said and left unsaid by two United States presidents confronted by a popular unwillingness to enter a war: President Lyndon Johnson, in escalating the war in Vietnam, and President Franklin D. Roosevelt, in moving the country closer to participating in World War II, while making statements such as the following in his 1940 campaign to be reelected:

> I have said this before, but I shall say it again and again and again: Your boys are not going to be sent into any foreign wars.[9]

By the standards set forth in this chapter, President Johnson's covert escalation and his failure to consult the electorate concerning the undeclared war in Vietnam was clearly unjustifiable. Consent was bypassed; there was no immediate danger to the nation which could even begin to excuse deceiving the public in a national election on grounds of an acute crisis.

The crisis looming before World War II, on the other hand, was doubtless much greater. Certainly this case is a difficult one, and one on which reasonable persons might not be able to agree. The threat was unprecedented; the need for preparations and for support of allies great; yet the difficulties of alerting the American public seemed insuperable. Would this crisis, then, justify proceeding through deceit?

To consent even to such deception would, I believe, be to take a frightening step. Do we want to live in a society where public officials can resort to deceit and manipulation whenever they decide that an exceptional crisis has arisen? Would we not, on balance, prefer to run the risk of failing to rise to a crisis honestly explained to us, from which the government might have saved us through manipulation? And what protection from abuse do we foresee should we surrender this choice?

In considering answers to these questions, we must take into account more than the short-run effects of government manipulation. President Roosevelt's manner of bringing the American people to accept first the possibility, then the likelihood, of war was used as an example by those who wanted to justify President Johnson's acts of dissimulation. And these acts in turn were pointed to by those who resorted to so many forms of duplicity in the Nixon administration. Secrecy and deceit grew at least in part because of existing precedents.[10]

The consequences of spreading deception, alienation, and lack of trust could not have been documented for us more concretely than they have in the past decades. We have had a very vivid illustration of how lies undermine our political system. While deception under the circumstances confronting President Roosevelt may in hindsight be more excusable than much that followed, we could no more consent to it in advance than to all that came later.

Wherever lies to the public have become routine, then, very special safeguards should be required. The test of public justification of deceptive practices is more needed than ever. It will be a hard test to satisfy, the more so the more trust is invested in those who lie and the more power they wield. Those in government and other positions of trust should be held to the highest standards. Their lies are not ennobled by their positions; quite the contrary. Some lies—notably minor white lies and emergency lies rapidly acknowledged—may be more *excusable* than others, but only those deceptive practices which can be openly debated and consented to in advance are *justifiable* in a democracy.[11]

NOTES

1. The *gennaion pseudos* has generated much controversy. Some have translated it as "pious fraud" and debated whether such fraud can be perpetrated. Thus Hastings Rashdall, in *The Theory of Good and Evil*, 2nd ed. (New York and London: Oxford University Press, 1924), bk. 1, p. 195, argued that such frauds would be justifiable "if (when *all* their consequences are considered) they were socially beneficial." Other translations are: "royal lie" (Jowett), and "bold flight of the imagination" (Cornford). The latter represents an effort to see Plato as advocating not lies by the government but stories, and possible errors; an interpretation that is difficult to uphold in view of the other contexts in *The Republic* where lying is discussed, such as 389b: "The rulers of the city may, if anbody, fitly lie on account of enemies or citizens for the benefit of the state." For Plato has endorsed lying by the state is very significant, as truth for him was opposed, not just to falsehood, but to unreality.

2. Arthur Sylvester, "The Government Has the Right to Lie," *Saturday Evening Post*, 18 November 1967, p. 10.

3. Erasmus, *Responsio ad Albertum Pium, Opera Omnia*, vol. 9 (Leiden, 1706; reprinted Hildesheim, 1962).

4. The Senator Gravel Edition, *The Pentagon Papers* (Boston: Beacon Press, 1971), 3:556–559.

5. As early as March 1964, Lyndon Johnson knew that such a hard choice might have to be made. See telephone transcript cited by Doris Kearns in *Lyndon Johnson and the American Dream* (New York: Harper & Row, 1976), p. 197.

6. Theodore H. White, *The Making of the President 1964* (New York: Atheneum, 1965), p. 373.

7. *Cambridge Survey Research*, 1975, 1976.

8. A lie by an experienced adult in a position of authority about private matters that can be protected by a refusal to speak is therefore much less excusable than a lie by the school child: . . . too frightened by the bullying teacher to be able to stand up to him or think of a non-deceptive "way out" on the spur of the moment.

9. *The Public Papers and Addresses of Franklin D. Roosevelt*, 1940, vol. 8, p. 517 (October 30, 1940).

10. See Arthur M. Schlesinger, Jr., *The Imperial Presidency* (Boston: Houghton Mifflin, 1973), p. 356: "The power to withhold and the power to leak led on inexorably to the power to lie . . . uncontrolled secrecy made it easy for lying to become routine." See also David Wise, *The Politics of Lying* (New York: Random House, 1973).

11. For dicussions of lying and moral choice in politics, see Plato, *The Republic;* Machiavelli, *The Prince;* Grotius, *On the Law of War and Peace;* Werner Krauss, ed., *Est-il utile de tromper le peuple?* a fascinating compilation of answers by Condorcet and others in a contest sponsored by Frederick II in 1780 (Berlin: Akademie-Verlag, 1966); Max Weber, "Politics as a Vocation," in *Essays in Sociology*, trans., H. H. Gerth and C. Wright Mills (New York: Oxford University Press, 1946), pp. 77–128; and Michael Walzer, "Political Action: The Problem of Dirty Hands," *Philosophy and Public Affairs* 2 (Winter 1973): 160–180.

==========

Who's Lying Now?
Deborah Baldwin

While philosophical discussions about lying in government are necessary to determine justifiability and the extent of culpabil-

Deborah Baldwin, "Who's Lying Now?" *Common Cause Magazine* (May/June 1989), pp. 32–36. Reprinted with permission of *Common Cause Magazine*.

ity and blame, a more practical question also arises: just how prevalent is lying in government? How much of a real problem is it? Should the public have any concerns over the extent to which they are lied to by those who supposedly represent them? Deborah Baldwin, editor of *Common Cause Magazine*, addresses these concerns in "Who's Lying Now?" She surveys the political scene, in which lying by candidates for public office appears commonplace; she examines several scandals in government in which lying was a central feature; and she provides an overall view of the extent to which lying has become an ingrained feature of government operations. Baldwin's article is also instructive for its illuminating interview with ethicist Sissela Bok, whose 1978 book on lying has become the definitive philosophical treatment of the subject. (An excerpt from Bok's *Lying* precedes this article.)

Former Assistant Secretary of State Elliott Abrams attempted to excuse himself on a technicality. When he told Congress the United States "had not received a dime from a foreign government" to support the Contras, he was *technically* correct because a $10 million donation he'd helped solicit from Brunei never got deposited in the right account.

George Bush and Michael Dukakis got away with it because political ads aren't subject to the same standards as commercial advertising. A Bush ad claimed Dukakis "opposed virtually every defense system we developed." A Dukakis ad claimed Bush had "personally cast the tie-breaking vote to cut $20 billion in [Social Security] benefits." Neither claim was true.

Then there was the consortium of oil companies that assured federal and state officials it would stand ready to clean up oil spills in Prince William Sound in the unlikely event one did occur. . . .

Is lying more common than ever, or does it just seem that way?

Certainly more individuals and institutions are getting caught. Thanks largely to the Iran-Contra affair, 1987 was The Year of the Big Lie, inspiring nominations for the "Academy Awards of Untruth" (*The Washington Post Magazine*), "A Catalog of Whoppers" (*The New Republic*) and a Pinocchio index that ranked lies from little white ones to whoppers (*Spy*). Last year did not seem to be an improvement. By Election Day voters had been deluged with so many half-truths and misstatements that Joe Isuzu—a fictional TV-ad salesman who makes ridiculous claims about Isuzu cars—was invoked during a presidential debate.

Not only are more Joe Isuzus appearing on the political landscape, but they're beginning to wear down public resistance.

As Kathleen Hall Jamieson, a University of Texas professor who has made extensive study of political advertising, observed in the wake of last year's campaign, "Never before in a presidential campaign have televised ads sponsored by a major party candidate lied so blatantly." In the good old days—1968—public outrage forced a particularly misleading campaign ad off the airwaves, but in 1988, she noted, "No such protests greeted either the Boston Harbor or furlough spots. An electorate numbed by the negative campaigns of 1986—and a press corps preoccupied more with ad strategy than content—simply took the visual demagoguery in stride."

Lying is hardly special to Washington or to politics. Where would lying be if it weren't for Madison Avenue, or Wall Street for that matter? It's also true that "everyone lies" to some extent. There are lies told from kindness ("Your speech was great") and from convenience ("Can't make it, conflicting appointment"). People lie to build egos ("Like I was telling the chief . . ."), to avoid embarrassment ("I'm sure I never saw that memo"), to save marriages ("I love you, too, darling") and to save face ("I was going to quit anyway").

Neither is lying new to government. Historian Barbara Tuchman once pieced together a turn-of-the-century case of intrigue and government deception involving President Theodore Roosevelt paying off a Moroccan kidnapper to release a wealthy American hostage. From this saga it appears the U.S. has misrepresented its stance on dealing with terrorists—and duped the press—more than once.

For many Americans the fall from innocence can be traced to the time President Dwight Eisenhower lied about pilot Gary Powers, saying he wasn't a spy even though he was shot down over Russia on a reconnaissance mission. Harvard philosopher Sissela Bok, author of books titled *Lying* and *Secrets,* says Eisenhower meant to make a routine lie for enemy consumption, but it washed back to America and eroded public trust. "I heard many people say that shook them," she recalls.

Watergate and Vietnam certainly rivaled Iran-Contra in terms of government deception and public mistrust. So what made the Reagan years such a watershed?

Many lied, but few were remorseful. Things got so bad during Congress's 1987 investigation of Iran-Contra that Senator Daniel Inouye (D-Hawaii) began to see the Watergate investigation in a new light. "In this case," he yearned, "I've yet to come across one witness who said, 'I'm sorry.' "

Washington's drop in the shame index, epitomized by the incessant lying to Congress about Iran-Contra by Reagan administration officials, is contributing to widening cynicism and shrinking accountability, Bok and others believe.

Bok says she's not convinced the level of lying is increasing so much as people's awareness. "People feel lied to more because they find out about more lying," she says. "They can see politicians on their television screens looking them straight in the eye and saying things they later find out are false." Partly as a result of all the half-baked claims and distortions of last year's presidential campaign, a Gallup poll taken shortly after the elections revealed that 15 percent of those who voted had no confidence in either candidate. "When you add the large number of people who didn't vote, I would say for a democracy that is a disastrous state of affairs," Bok observes.

When people get an exaggerated sense that "everyone lies," she adds, "they become so cynical they protect themselves from believing almost anything."

In the wake of revelations made during the trial of Oliver North, the public can hardly be blamed for having an exaggerated sense of amorality in the nation's capital. With President Reagan's apparent blessings, North and other administration officials fed lines to virtually anyone who would listen.

To some extent their activities reflected longtime practices in politics and government, magnified to a grotesque degree. No one really expects everyone in government to tell the whole truth all the time. If the State Department is negotiating a peace pact in the Mideast, it's not likely to blab about strategy to the foreign desk of *The Washington Post*. Elected officials, too, tend to choose their words carefully depending on their audience; some members of Congress go so far as to prepare different responses to constituent mail when it pours in on a controversial issue like abortion. And it's not unheard of for a member to say one thing and vote the opposite—depending on who's watching.

Holding back information is also a tradition in Washington, where guarding the palace secrets is a way of garnering power. What astounded ethicists during the Iran-Contra affair was the casual way in which government officials refused to give information to Congress and lied outright about what was going on.

Throughout the recent North trial, witnesses suggested that withholding information from Congress was no more venal then pretending not to hear a stranger on the street ask the time. During Congress's Iran-Contra investigation, former national security adviser John Poindexter similarly expressed no apology for advising North, at the time a National Security Council (NSC) aide, to withhold information or provide "evasive" answers. "Adm. Poindexter said his main regret was that he did not have a better damage control plan in the event that Congress and the press discovered what the National Security Council was doing," wrote one observer at the time.

North himself, at least initially, boasted about having lied to Congress—all in the service of a higher cause. When he finally got to trial he said the real problem was that no one told him lying might be illegal.

North is unusual in his willingness to use the word "lie," which retains enough potency, even in these days of moral equanimity, to discourage most people from applying it to themselves. Bok says when she wrote *Lying* in 1978 there was no one like North to quote. In fact, North's and Poindexter's testimony before Congress was such a challenge to ethics traditions in the military that *The New York Times* submitted the following questions to the Joint Chiefs of Staff: "Is it permissible for a military officer to lie? If so under what circumstances, to whom and about what? If not, why not?" (The nation's top military officers declined to reply.)

Throughout the Iran-Contra investigation and subsequent North trial, witnesses have groped for polite ways to say the L word. They have confessed to having told half-truths (as opposed to half-lies), or having told the literal truth instead of the real truth;

many claimed they "forgot" what happened. One observer described former CIA Director William Casey as "not having fully related the nature of events as they had occurred"; others were said to have misrepresented the truth or to have misled; or they misspoke or misstated the truth, or deliberately distorted it. In the latest vernacular they put a "spin" on it, as if truth were a colorful top glancing off in an arbitrary direction. In an apparent drive for precision at one point during the North trial, prosecutor John Keker used the term "a 100 percent, no-getting-around-it lie," as if to clear up the confusion.

Words like "misspoke" are popular, Bok points out, because they imply an inadvertent error and not the intent that is implicit in actual lying. In the process of turning lies into misstatements, of course, personal responsibility vanishes.

Throughout the various proceedings, former national security adviser Robert McFarlane and his attorney Leonard Garment (known in some circles as "the spin doctor" because he handles media relations for his clients so well) insisted that McFarlane might have withheld information or "put a gloss" on the truth, but that he did not lie to Congress. In what was surely a characteristic moment in the North trial, McFarlane suggested that it is customary for national security officials to be less than forthcoming in their dealings with Congress. An obviously frustrated Judge Gerhard Gesell broke in, demanding to know what *that* meant. "Do you tell the truth? Do you not tell the truth? Or do you put a gloss on it?"

His store of vocabulary words not yet exhausted, McFarlane translated: "You don't lie. You put your own interpretation on what the truth is. . . ."

To give but one example of many, McFarlane maintained in a September 12, 1985, letter to Congress that no one on the NSC staff had solicited funds or in any other way assisted the Contras. But in fact the very day before, North had flown to Texas to tell billionaire Nelson Bunker Hunt over dinner that the Contras needed his help financing their war.

When North got on the witness stand he explained why he believed the letter was factually correct: During his fund-raising efforts, he "would not say to a single person, 'Would you give me money?' " He would simply make a pitch about the Contras' needs and later, after he'd left the room, wealthy donors would spontaneously pull out their checkbooks.

To many people this distinction might sound a little hokey— sort of like saying the Indians got their meat not by *killing* scores of buffalo but by driving each one up to the edge of a cliff and then letting it decide for itself whether to jump. But in the highly nuanced business of turning the truth on its head, North *et al.* kept challenging the limits of the English language to come up with new ways to describe the land where fact ends and fiction begins.

People's thinking becomes especially fanciful when there's a bunker mentality that pits insiders against the rest of the world, Bok believes. From the participants' point of view, "No one seemed to understand how important it was to conduct the Contra war in Nicaragua," she says. "If people in Congress didn't understand it, and if citizens didn't understand it, then it had to go on in secret.

Questions of national security often seem to create a compelling rationale for deception, she believes, leading government officials to think they can violate ordinary moral standards for the sake of what's good for their country. They don't realize that the subsequent loss of credibility, as with the Iran-Contra affair, ultimately undermines national interests.

Because the press tends to be adversarial, government officials can easily perceive it as a kind of domestic enemy. In extreme cases otherwise rational individuals seem to lose their moral sense. While interviewing Bok for television, journalist Bill Moyers volunteered that, in effect, as White House press secretary for Lyndon Johnson, he lied to the press and his boss aspired to control the media. Moyers suggested that lying got easier with practice. "I thought often of the line 'I am not a professional liar, and I'm surprised at the extent to which in my infirmity I'm an amateur one.' I kept being surprised at the extent to which I could be an amateur liar."

Bok blames the us-them syndrome for a lot of the deception that has emanated from Washington over the years. "When people are trying to do the best they can and there's pressure from the outside, the attitude becomes self-protective. Certainly, when you're involved in something like the war in Vietnam, when you're being deceptive about things that in fact citizens should know about and you're that defensive, it becomes very tempting to try to be overly secretive," she says. After a while, especially in a sharply partisan atmosphere, the true believers begin to see enemies everywhere and the rationale for secrecy and deception runs deep.

Even when passion is absent, the government plays games with the press, withholding information or distributing it arbitrarily. Both sides recognize the dangers and proceed accordingly, says Robert Kagan, former deputy for policy for the Bureau of Inter-American Affairs during the Reagan administration. As he puts it: "We know from our own personal lives that complete candor is not very easy. Do you tell your parents everything? Of course not. And that pertains to political life as well."

He offers an example from the realm of foreign affairs. "Let's say the current policy is to shunt the PLO aside and build up Israeli moderates' support. If asked, is it U.S. policy to shunt the PLO aside, what are you going to say? You'll say the policy is to bring the two sides together. . . .

"Reporters deal with lies like that every day," he says. "That's a level of, if you want to call it lying, that journalists do not consider egregious. Then there's the other level, the actual-act realm—as in, 'did you guys do this?' If the person says 'no,' and they did, that's called a lie. The more typical answer would be, 'I can't go into that,' or 'you can't use this.' "

Denying everything can be a strategic mistake. When *Time* magazine discovered that Nancy Reagan was borrowing designer dresses—despite her earlier vow not to—she at first denied the charges. After *Time* documented the allegations in print, the first lady was forced to announce she would be returning some of the dresses that a week earlier she said she didn't have.

As Kagan observes, "The blanket denial is a big mistake, and there was a certain amount of that during Iran-Contra."

Some of the same people who brought us the Iran-Contra affair apparently also orchestrated a disinformation campaign designed to rattle Col. Muamar Quaddafi. In August 1986 *The Wall Street Journal* published a front-page story saying that in the wake of the U.S. air raid, Libya was plotting new terrorist attacks and the United States was planning further retaliation. The two nations were described as being "on a collision course."

The article might have gone the way of all forgettable over-statement if two months later *The Washington Post* hadn't front-paged a piece by investigative reporter Bob Woodward charging that the administration had master-minded a "secret and unusual campaign of deception." Based on a memo reportedly written by Poindexter, the *Post* article clearly suggested *Journal* reporters John Walcott and Gerald F. Seib had been used in the kind of coordinated disinformation campaign one associates less with the White House than with CIA propaganda efforts in the Third World. (Walcott strongly contests this version of events.)

Appalled by the revelations in the *Post,* top State Department spokesman Bernard Kalb immediately resigned, delivering a sear-ing commentary on the importance of government and personal credibility. Kalb, who had been a reporter for many years before joining the government, is still angry. "My concern about all this is whether to some degree there is a culture of sleaze that is being accepted," he says. "It brings me back to the Pentagon Papers. If the best we can do is tut-tut and move on, that's a horror."

Kalb was not the first government spokesman to quit because he'd been put in the awkward position of serving as a spokesper-son for an administration that cut him out of the information loop. Jerald terHorst resigned as spokesman for President Gerald Ford because he had been misled about Ford's intention to par-don Nixon. (On the other hand, Elaine Crispin, Nancy Reagan's spokeswoman during the designer dress flap, was unperturbed by having to take reporters' calls when, as she explained delicately in a recent interview, "maybe I didn't have all my answers as I would have liked." Asked if she considered resigning, Crispin was amazed. "Of course there are days when you consider resign-ing," she said, "but never because of the principle—because of the press.")

In their recent book *Best Laid Plans: The Inside Story of America's War Against Terrorism,* Walcott and David C. Martin, a CBS News Pentagon correspondent, offer dizzying, blow-by-blow descriptions of multilayered deception in connection with Reagan-era foreign adventures. Portraying North as almost patho-logically driven to plant erroneous stories both here and abroad, they say when he wasn't telling tales to unsuspecting reporters, he was hoodwinking some of the very foreign nationals he sought to do business with. "To North the truth was raw material to be shaped in the service of a good cause," the authors write in something of an understatement.

"North was a very special person," concedes Walcott, now with *U.S. News & World Report.* "But [North and the others] weren't doing anything to the media they weren't doing to Congress and to one another." As for government attempts at deception, he says, "It's naive to think it's brand new. . . . Attempts to manipulate public opinion are as old as democratic government."

As long as the public perceives the level of manipulation as increasing, however, public confidence is bound to decline, eroding chances for the kind of mutual trust that is necessary in today's world, Bok suggests. While a measure of caution and distrust is indispensable, she argues in her new book, *A Strategy for Peace,* "if distrust becomes too overpowering, societies can no longer function, any more than families or communities, much less plan for longer-term survival."

What Deserves Praise or Blame in Men and Above All in Princes
Niccolò Machiavelli

The term "Machiavellian" has been used to depict leaders whose governing tactics are ruthless and heavy-handed. Its source is Niccolò Machiavelli and his politcal philosophy of "might makes right." The following selection is an excerpt from his best-known book, *The Prince* (1513), in which he counsels leaders to realize that vice, as well as virtue, can bring about desired results. Machiavelli enthusiastically urges that leaders dirty their hands for the successes that it might bring. For Machiavelli, the "dirty hands" dilemma is no quandary at all. In fact, he readily counsels leaders to engage in vice that will bring about both personal and public benefits. Not to dabble in unethical procedures is tantamount to accepting failure and committing an act of cowardice. Given his notorious position, political analysts have for centuries been examining his claims and making attempts to rebut him. But his

Niccolò Machiavelli, *The Prince* (1513), James C. Brogan and others, trans. National Alumni ed., 1907.

advice to those in power on how to keep theirs still holds strong attraction for many as a prime example of political realism.

It now remains to show in what manner a prince should behave to his subjects and friends. This matter having been already discussed by others, it may seem arrogant in me to pursue it farther, especially if I should differ in opinion from them; but as I write only for those who possess sound judgment, I thought it better to treat this subject as it really is, in fact, than to amuse the imagination with visionary models of republics and governments that never have existed. For the manner in which men now live is so different from the manner in which they ought to live, that he who deviates from the common course of practice, and endeavors to act as duty dictates, necessarily ensures his own destruction. Thus, a good man, and one that wishes to prove himself so in all respects, must be undone in a contest with so many that are evilly disposed. A prince that wishes to maintain his power ought to learn that he should not be always good.

Laying aside, then, the false ideas that have been formed as to princes, and adhering only to those that are true, I say that all men, and especially princes, are marked and distinguished by some quality or other that entails either reputation or dishonor. For instance, men are liberal or parsimonious, honorable or dishonorable, effeminate and cowardly or courageous and enterprising, humane or cruel, affable or haughty, wise or debauched, honest or dishonest, good tempered or surly, sedate or inconsiderate, religious or impious, and so forth.

It would, doubtless, be happy for a prince to unite in himself every species of good quality; but as our nature does not allow so great a perfection, a prince should have prudence enough to avoid those defects and vices that may occasion his ruin; and he ought, if possible, to guard against those who can only compromise his safety and the possession of his dominions; but if he cannot succeed in this, he need not embarrass himself in escaping the scandal of those vices, but should devote his whole energies to avoid those that may cause his ruin. He should not shrink from encountering some blame on account of vices that are important to the support of his states; for, everything well considered, there are some things, having the appearance of virtues, that would prove the ruin of a prince should he put them in practice, and others upon which, though they are seemingly bad and vicious, his actual welfare and security depend.

Dirty Hands
Peter A. French

In his *Ethics in Government*, Peter A. French defines the "dirty hands" dilemma: in order to be successful, a public official must do something that would be acceptable from the perspective of private life. For French, the "dirty hands" dilemma is a function of the tension between public and private morality. French examines the Machiavellian position, as well as that of those in the opposing camp. Then he offers a fresh approach to the problem. He suggests that leaders inevitably will commit acts that, from the perspective of everyday morality, are wrong; such acts, while possibly excusable, are nonetheless not necessarily morally exonerated. That is, while most people would not condemn those who engage in such acts, they would still find the act unacceptable from a moral point of view. French intimates that, perhaps, formal penalties for various acts of unethical conduct should be instituted, or those who engage in them should impose self-penalties, such as resignation from office.

Public officials have freely accepted a special obligation to carry out the affairs of their offices in morally acceptable ways. Sometimes, however, a genuine conflict arises between what seems to be required by one's governmental role—for example, action required to protect the national interest—and the moral principles that are generally applied to private citizens. That is, on some occasions a public official may find that the only way he can do his job successfully, meet his official obligations, is to do something that, from the perspective of private life, would be

Peter A. French, "Dirty Hands," *Ethics in Government*, © 1983, pp. 15–24. Reprinted by permission of Prentice Hall, Englewood Cliffs, New Jersey.

morally unacceptable. The problem can easily be focused on acts or threats of acts of violence that may, and often do, present themselves to members of the federal executive branch. Clearly, the President of the United States has accepted the responsibilty for the protection, security, and well-being of the citizens within the borders of the country. His choices of action, or at least some of them, have consequences that are farther reaching and more enduring, and that affect the lives of many more persons than do most of the choices of the rest of us. Enormous acts of violence— for example, acts of war—are in his province and are among the traditional ways he has of maintaining the security of the state. Such far-reaching acts of violence are not even options of behavior for private citizens. Ordinary citizens cannot decide upon and execute an invasion of Cambodia or the dropping of a hydrogen bomb on Moscow. Also, it is a characteristic of such decisions that their intended consequences often play out in the lives of a large number of people who had nothing to do with the making of the choice and were probably unknown to the makers of such choices. Although private citizens can affect the lives of people somewhat remote from them, the frequency of their being able to do so is much lower than that of public citizens.

Former Secretary of State Cyrus Vance's actions of lying to our allies can also be described in terms of a conflict between the requirements of his office and the principles of private-citizen morality. Personal prudence may play no role at all. In Vance's case the acts in question were not violent ones, but that does not affect the issue. Enter Machiavelli. He writes:

> He [the prince] must not mind incurring the scandal of those vices (the practice of vices that nonetheless preserve the state), without which it would be difficult to save the state, for if one considers well, it will be found that some things which seem virtues would, if followed, lead to one's [or the state's], ruin, and some others which appear vices result in one's or the state's greater security and well-being.[1]

In effect, Machiavelli argues that responsible government demands the willingness to dirty one's hands in matters that could mark one as morally reprehensible. In other words, if political executives were to allow the moral guidelines for the behavior of private individuals to direct their governmental actions, they would in a number of instances be failing to properly administer the trust of leadership they assumed by taking office. If, for example, on private moral grounds a president categorically refused to consider the use of nuclear power against an enemy and his views became widely known, he might be seriously weakening the national security to the point of rendering him and the country ineffectual in the community of states and a "mark" for any other country prepared to use nuclear weapons. Ruthlessness, deceit, and other personal vices, quite often, may be seen as virtues in pursuit of the objectives of government, especially national security. To categorically refuse to avail oneself of them seems to violate the obligations of office. But, on the other hand, to be willing to use them, and, indeed, to use them, surely soils one's hands from the perspective of ordinary moral evaluation.

The "dirty hands dilemma" has many aspects. Most people probably believe that a governmental official should not put his personal moral "cleanliness" above the well-being of those whom he has been elected or appointed to protect. Such a view could certainly account for Vance's willingness to lie while also submitting a resignation that took effect after the mission. On the other hand, when Americans learned of the willingness of their government officials to execute violent tactics in pursuit of "national interest" during the Vietnam era, as revealed in the *Pentagon Papers,* many were incensed. It is worth mentioning, however, that many of those same officials when they left public life were offered and assumed highly prestigious positions in the private sector. Former Secretary of State Henry Kissinger remains a highly admired individual despite the fact that he counseled in favor of the infamous Christmas bombing raids of 1972, the Cambodian incursion, and the defoliation and anti-personnel bombings of Vietnam. Former Secretary of Defense Robert McNamara, who engineered the escalation of the Vietnam War, left government to head the World Bank.

There seems to be two popular camps with respect to how "dirty hands" are to be treated. Some people are relatively comfortable, in agreement with Machiavelli, with a divorce between the evaluation of public policy decisions and moral evaluations of the acts and the character of the policy makers. Others assume that "public morality" or "governmental morality" must be derivative, in some way, from personal morality. Those who hold the former position usually argue that government service is too important to be constrained by personal moral evaluation standards. What a person does in office, for moral purposes, should be viewed as the actions of the office. This may account for the popularity of identifying governmental decisions with buildings, for example, "The White House released . . ." "The Pentagon launched . . ." or titles, "The President called . . ." "The Secretary ordered . . ." and sometimes cities, "Washington planned . . ." "Moscow regards. . . ." The latter position, on the other hand, presents the view that offices cannot hide or magically transform personal moral misbehavior. If you sully yourself when you do what is regarded to be required by your governmental office, you are nonetheless "dirty" for having done so. In this view, if doing something is wrong or bad or wicked if it were done by a private citizen, then doing it in office is just as wrong, bad, or wicked.

A number of points must be made before we can evaluate these competitive positions. The Machiavellian or divorce-ability thesis seems to ignore, as Thomas Nagel has pointed out, that "the exercise of power, in whatever role, is one of the most personal forms of individual self-expression, and a rich source of purely personal pleasure."[2] Not only do politicians seek office to serve the needs of the people, they often receive an enormous ego boost from the exercise of political power. A reading of the memoirs of political leaders or of the transcripts of the Watergate tapes establishes that for some politicians the exercise of power is the only way their lives are made meaningful to themselves. If, however, the exercise of political power were a form of personal expression, it would, one would think, fall under the moral scrutiny of accepted individual moral standards, and the prudence/morality problem discussed earlier would again be relevant.

We ought not ignore the fact that government offices place heavy demands upon the officeholder. Those demands might well be different in kind, from the moral point of view, from those placed on private citizens. The assumption of governmental office carries with it, as earlier discussed, the acceptance of a general moral duty, a non-optional requirement to be moral. With that in mind the dirty hands problem may be put in the form of the following question: "Can it be moral, in certain circumstances and because of anticipated consequences, to do things in office that would generally be regarded as morally unacceptable in private life?" Another way of putting the question might be to ask whether [the statement] "it was in the national interest" is, against a negative personal moral evaluation of the action in question, a justification for an official performance of the action.

In the camp of those who regard public morality as derivative of individual morality (private-sector morality), other matters need clarification. Most importantly, the idea of derivability is unclear in this context. Derivability would entail that, by and large, the morality of government office is contained in the principles and concepts of private-sector morality. The principles of morality need be applied only to governmental situations to extract "governmental morality." Nothing in the derivability thesis, however, seems to exclude the possibility that the functions of a governmental office render inapplicable some of the standard principles of morality because the conditions for their application are altered when one changes from a private citizen to a public person. It might be argued that the ordinary principles of private-sector morality apply to ordinary people and to governmental officials except in those instances when the circumstances demand specific kinds of usually proscribed actions in order for the officeholder to meet his official duties. Although standard moral principles are still recognized as applicable to the behavior of government officials, they are, in certain restricted cases, weakened or overridden by the demands of office.

This position is likely to be open to the fate of death by a thousand exceptions. The alternative pole of nonderivability, however, seems to embody the idea, though it was not Machiavelli's view, that the assumption of public office is tantamount to a receipt of a safe passage under the guns of morality. If, for example, Richard Nixon is President, then President Nixon is permitted and even required to do certain things that Citizen Nixon ought never to do. All is not freedom, of course. Richard Nixon, President, in certain instances is held accountable for meeting higher moral standards than would be expected of Richard Nixon, citizen. For example, the presidential office seems to bear a special obligation to attend to the welfare of all members of the society if (debatably) not an obligation to always tell them the truth.

The derivability thesis incorporates the idea that there are not two standards of morality. It grasps the popular intuition that there ought to be a unity to morality. The nonderivability thesis, while arguing for the independence of private citizen and public official morality, recognizes that the offices of government include responsibilities for the general welfare that go well beyond the normal duties of a citizen. Richard Nixon before and after the administration of the oath of office is, in that view, a very different person when considered morally. There seems to be something correct about both theses, yet they both easily become too exclusive to suit our usual evaluations of the conduct of persons in government. The derivability theorists ignore the peculiar responsibilities of governmental offices and demand adherence to the principles of morality or, if they recognize the office's demands, they start down a slippery slope of exceptions that devastates their position. The nonderivability theorists, like Machiavelli, tend to place all of the emphasis on office obligations and so are able to justify the foulest of deeds. Vietnam Era governmental officials, we may be told, did not lack personal morality; rather they saw themselves, while in office, as exempt from the principles of that morality, serving the masters of political expedience and national security that justify virtually anything.

Can we avoid the dirty hands dilemma if we incorporate what seems correct in both theses into a view of the relationship between morality and governmental office? The fact that so many of our moral concepts seem to focus on the person as a private citizen is not to be ignored, but that is not necessarily a constitutive fact of morality. The bias toward private individuals may be only an historical accident or it may be due to an unnecessary, indeed misleading, identification of morality with law. (Hobbes may be responsible for some of our failure to examine the province of morality in government, because his account of the social compact leaves the sovereign outside of the law and in a state of nature [state of war] with all other sovereigns in which, of course, there is no civil justice. Hobbes recognized that constraining the sovereign to the demands of law could hamstring him in the world of national conflict, rendering him unable to carry out his part of the civil arrangement.) It is not inconceivable that morality's *raison d'être* might provoke different kinds of judgments under radically different conditions and hence that, although private-citizen morality is not the source of public-office morality, both may be derived from that general purpose. Although generally speaking, moral principles from the private sector will be applicable to the holders of government offices, that will not be because the public morality is derived from the private, but because those principles are independently applicable to both types of human endeavor. Nagel captures this synthesis very well when he writes:

> Neither private morality nor public morality is ultimate. Both result when the general constraints of morality are applied to certain types of action . . . public and private morality may share a common basis without one being derived from the other.[3]

But how does this solve the problem of "dirty hands"? The position being suggested entails the view that private-citizen moral judgments are sometimes inappropriately made of public figures, and that is tantamount to putting forth what sounds like a dangerous moral excludability thesis that would provide a blanket of moral exoneration for the Johnsons, Kissingers, Bundys, McNamaras, Westmorelands, Richardsons, and Nixons of the Vietnam Era who acted from a conception of national interest rather than self-interest. Exclusion indeed is involved, but not necessarily moral exoneration. To be excluded from one moral judgment is not to be excluded from all.

Let us examine the role aspect of government service. The underlying assumption in the dirty hands dilemma is that there is a difference of a morally significant sort between, for example, Richard Nixon, President, and Richard Nixon, private citizen, or between Cyrus Vance, Secretary of State, and Cyrus Vance, private citizen. It is not uncommon to identify an institutional role with or by the kinds of special obligations anyone in the role must assume. A father, for example, by virtue of assuming the parental role, takes on special obligations to his children; he assumes responsibilities for them that go well beyond those he has to the general public. But parental obligations go only so far, for example, as against the general welfare: A parent ought not to continue to protect a son who is known to be responsible for the great suffering of someone. One may think along similar lines of the responsibilities of soldiers in time of war. By joining the armed services a person assumes certain special obligations to obey the orders of one's commanders, etc. One agrees to try to kill the enemy if so ordered and, indeed, to do a number of things for which one might, if they were done in private life, be punished severely. Here again, however, there are clear limits on the obligations or, more exactly, on the scope of the actions a commander can order. A soldier does not assume an obligation to obey *all* orders of his commander. The "Uniform Code of Military Justice" makes explicit that he must obey only *legal* orders (a point somehow overlooked by the attorneys defending Lt. William Calley for the massacre at My Lai).

Even though there are going to be restrictions (whether set by law, morals, or custom), some social roles deemed important to the furtherance of society often are directly associated with duties that can be met only by doing things that would otherwise negatively affect the moral evaluation of the character or actions of the officeholder. That is one of the reasons why personal prudence cannot be an acceptable basis for governmental action. Actions that are required by the rules that govern role behavior can be, by and large, impersonally associated with the role rather than fully identified with the person who occupies the role. Hence, the usual condemnation that may be associated with the performance of such actions is absent and we concentrate personal evaluations upon role behavior. It is common practice to praise persons who perform their unpleasant governmental role duties well, though if they were not serving in the role we would chastise them (or fear them). Harry Truman, for example, is praised for ordering the bombing of Hiroshima and hastening the end of World War II. Soldiers are awarded medals for killing enemy soldiers under orders. John Kennedy is praised for bluffing the Russians in a deadly game of nuclear poker.

The temptation to overstate the case either on the side of individuals (forcing all types of obligations into a single type) or on the side of institutional (governmental) offices, however, remains. To adopt one view is to ignore real differences between private and public life, and to adopt the other view is to think primarily in terms of roles and ignore important aspects of the choices made by the role players. Would Truman have been a better or a worse president if he had decided not to order the bombing of Hiroshima because he thought that there was no moral justification for inflicting such suffering, despite the national interest? Would we blame Kennedy if he had chosen not to try to bluff the Russians to the brink of nuclear war and instead had decided that national security, with respect to missiles in Cuba, could be compromised in favor of peaceful relations? Suppose the Russians had launched those missiles against American cities. We are reminded of Neville Chamberlain's Munich compromise in the name of preventing a war. Few people would praise Chamberlain's statesmanship, knowing its outcome. These examples suggest that the behavior of persons holding public offices is properly evaluated against moral standards that diverge at important points from and join at others with those commonly applied to private individuals. Sometimes they are more rigorous, sometimes more relaxed. But how does one know when they diverge?

One rather obvious difference between public and private obligations is that the primary emphasis in the public institutions is on *the accomplishment* of certain recognized ends, whereas many private-sector obligations concern the *way* things are done and what particular things are done, and less with outcomes. . . . As suggested earlier, government may profitably be thought of as a device designed to secure and preserve a population. It is concerned with what could or will happen if, . . . with outcomes far more than with means. If morality is to affect or have province over governmental action, it must address the consequentialistic direction of government, and its way of doing so is, primarily, to provide guidelines for evaluating means.

The legitimate ends of government do not always morally justify the means that will bring them about. The massacre of millions of residents of another country might ensure domestic tranquillity and national security, but it is not morally justified. The bald-faced lying of a president to his countrymen might (conceivably) further the national interest, but it is not usually morally justifiable. The conducting of a war in a small Asian country because there is believed to be huge untapped oil deposits there, even if it would improve the national standard of living, is not morally justified. When do the means defeat the ends?

LYING AND THE "DIRTY HANDS" DILEMMA IN GOVERNMENT

When do the hands of a government official become so filthy as to destroy any moral worth his official actions might have had?

Let us further explore the consequentialist justification for public morality. As suggested [previously], there are moral limits on the means justified by ends that most people will agree upon, but other constraints also will be pertinent. . . . [W]hen someone assumes a public office, he is expected to eschew certain personal interests that might otherwise enter into his evaluation of courses of action (for example, the Platonic divestiture of personal interest adopted in many Civil Service codes). One constraint on means then will be that courses of official action chosen solely because they promote personal gain or personal interest are not morally justified. A legislator voting on tax law should not develop a tax rate system that works to his personal advantage. A bureaucrat ought not to assign contracts for government projects to companies in which he is a stockholder. There remains, however, quite a number of other means, including ruthless and violent means, that are arguably necessary to accomplish the genuine purposes for which government itself was founded and in which the official has no personal interest to be satisfied. We must be careful to distinguish cases in which an official's motives are bad when he sets out to achieve the ends of government from those in which he uses the wrong means to bring about otherwise justifiable ends. . . . Here our concern is with the moral control of means.

Bernard Williams[4] has offered an important analysis of the kind of argument that is often put forth to condemn political figures for taking actions in office that involve or amount to violence against people. Even allowing for a distinction between "structured" and "unstructured" violence (the former including judicial executions and police actions, etc.; the latter, war against another state, etc.), most everyone will readily agree that there are violent acts that the state is justified in performing (although no private citizen would be morally justified in doing so). Of course, "anything the state is justified in doing, some official . . . is justified in ordering to be done." That also is unexceptionable. The argument often then proceeds to a third premise to the effect that a person is not justified in ordering something to be done that he would not be prepared to do himself. The conclusion is that preparedness to do those deeds is evidence of a criminal (or highly immoral) character. In concrete terms, one might imagine the argument worked against former President Richard Nixon. Nixon, according to the third premise, would have been justified in ordering the incursion into Cambodia only if he were prepared to, himself, slug it out in the rice paddies with the Cambodian and North Vietnamese soldiers. He was justified in ordering the saturation bombing of Hanoi only if he was willing, if able, to fly a bomber and drop its payload over that city without concern for specific types of targets. Of course, it is argued, if Nixon was of such a character that he was personally prepared to undertake such acts of violence, then he was a morally unfit human being regardless of whether or not he occupied a high political office.

This argument, however, is not very convincing. In the first place we must realize that structured violence is often associated with the tasks of government. It would be wildly absurd if we should have to conclude that only criminally disposed individuals were fit to govern. Even unstructured violence is often associated with the proper exercise of the powers of office. (Threats to national security are not always imaginary—for example, the attack on Pearl Harbor.) The conclusion of the argument must be set aside, and hence this argument cannot be used to relieve government officials of the obligation to, occasionally, order violence. There does, however, seem to be something true in the conclusion when it is worked in regard to certain cases, even though it may not hold true generally.

Suppose that the violent act in question is the assassination of Fidel Castro. Let us say that evidence has been provided by the CIA that Castro is planning an invasion of Florida or providing bases for Russian missiles. Evidence of Castro's plans might justify a violent act by our state against him, and hence a president might be justified in ordering an assassination. But, it might well be said, anyone prepared to coldbloodedly kill someone would have to have some relatively strong criminal tendencies. Hence if the third premise of the argument holds, the President in this case could not be justified in ordering the assassination without destroying his own moral standing.

The problem is not so much with the conclusion as with that third premise. What is the moral force of the position (taken in the third premise) that a person is morally justified only in ordering something he is prepared to do himself? That idea is a part of the popular mythology of heroism. ("I never ask my boys to do something I wouldn't do myself.") But it is not a basic moral principle. Rather, I think that it is best understood as capturing another check on means that is wanted to counteract an extreme consequentialism in public morality.

The situation is something like this: If we demand that governmental officials be prepared to do what they order we might either have to live (or die) with (1) very timid or gentle souls who find it difficult to order any kind of violence or counterviolence, leaving us less than well protected, indeed vulnerable, *or* (2) trigger-happy gangsters who have no compunctions about committing violent acts in response to the slightest provocation. Rather, it seems to me, we want to say that sometimes ordering violence one would never think of doing oneself (violence that one could not conceive of performing oneself) is justified because one occupies a rather special position in the life and structure of the community and has thereby accepted a number of obligations, especially those for its general welfare, that individual citizens need not meet. The fact that one would not normally be willing to do such an act oneself serves as a constraining condition that should make one less likely to rashly order such acts.

Even this constraint may, in certain circumstances, need to be overridden. Events and the immorality of other governments and governmental officials may well delimit the options of office. But, by and large, what may be called "the constraint of personal morality" should check wanton use of the power of violence that resides in many government offices. The ethics of government will thereby arise from a marriage of office obligations and personal morality.

No hands are dirtier than those of the official who orders acts of violence that are unjustified by the circumstances because he was prepared to commit those acts himself.

There remain, however, other ways to view the problem of dirty hands. Coincidentally, some political observers have characterized Cyrus Vance's resignation after the Iranian raid in one of these ways. It will be important to remember that Machiavelli did not try to morally justify the doing of bad deeds by government officials. Machiavelli did not seem to regard political ends, as worthy as they might be, as determinants of the moral status of different types of acts. Even though the end justifies the means for him, it does not *morally* justify it. Otherwise, "the prince" would not have to learn how not to be good. Obviously Machiavelli regarded moral and political (and prudential) judgments to be rather independent of each other. As Michael Walzer has put it:

> If they (political actions) were justified . . . it would only be necessary to learn how to be good in a new, more difficult, perhaps roundabout way. That is not Machiavelli's argument. His political judgments are indeed consequentialist in character, but not his moral judgments. We know whether cruelty is used well or badly by its effects over time. But that it is bad to use cruelty we know in some other way.[5]

Machiavelli clearly recognized that his prince would sometimes need to "do bad," and that the primary justification for doing so is the retention of personal power and its attendant glory. Machiavelli's prince knowingly violates moral constraints and if there were some final moral court that would judge him, we may imagine that he would be found wanting, despite his power and glory. One may see "the prince" as joyously accepting that fate, trading present glory for future punishment.

Max Weber offers a rather different view of the sullied government official. He sees him as a "suffering servant" or even as a tragic hero. The official does bad in order to do good and in doing so he "lets himself in for the diabolic forces lurking in all violence."[6] The office, Weber seems to believe, forces on the officeholder the requirement of moral self-destruction. Assuming office is tantamount to casting oneself into the deepest circles of Hell for a good cause. Weber's view, however, appears to be so cosmic as to lose significance in aiding our understanding of political action, and it implies, as Walzer has suggested, that we must be resigned to living under the rule of officials who have "lost their souls."[7]

Alternatively, and this may have been Vance's position, we may wish to view the dirty hands deeds of governmental officials as discrete actions, as isolatable moral crimes, done for a worthy end. Such crimes ought to be punished even if the end is achieved. It may be believed that when a specific determinate penalty has been paid, expiation is accomplished, purgation completed, the moral slate of the official wiped clean. Albert Camus seems to have held such a view in *The Just Assassins*.[8] In that book he gives the impression that assassins are justified in committing acts of killing if they are prepared to be executed and are executed. Camus' view, in a much less exaggerated form, is defended by Walzer, who writes:

> Just assassination . . . is like civil disobedience. In both men violate a set of rules, go beyond a moral . . . limit, in order to do what they believe they should do. At the same time, they acknowledge their responsibility for the violation by accepting punishment or doing penance.[9]

Walzer goes on to point out that the analogy between law and morality is not a perfect one. Morality provides the reasons for breaking laws in the case of civil disobedience. The law punishes the offender. In the case of dirty hands, it is political reasons that provide the grounds for immoral action, but there is no instrument of punishment. If moral rules were enforced by punishment, as Walzer says, "dirty hands would be no problem. We would simply honor the man who did bad in order to do good, and at the same time we would punish him."[10]

Insofar as we have no such system, individual governmental officials may self-inflict their punishments, and perhaps that is what Cyrus Vance understood himself to be doing when he resigned after having lied to our allies. William Safire reports that after the Vance resignation he interviewed Dr. Arthur Burns, former chairman of the Federal Reserve. Safire asked Burns if a much-needed devaluation were in prospect and if the news of the devaluation would damage the national interest, would Burns lie if he were "put on the spot"? Burns responded, "If the moment came when I saw an overwhelming need to lie in the nation's interest, I would lie. . . . Of course, I would resign immediately afterward."[11]

Although there exists a grand tradition in Western religion of self-initiated confession and expiation, if resignation were the primary way of cleansing dirty hands, government by the more morally sensitive people would be unachievable. Resignation would soon diminish the ranks. Resignation, however, need not be the only penalty that an officeholder may exact upon himself. A

radical though intriguing approach to the problem might be to
catalogue the types of penalties that are appropriate for specific
sorts of immoral actions taken in the proper service of one's
country, state, community, or society. The difficulty with pursuing such a program is that many official actions have so many
significant special features as to make each novel. The catalogue
would be depressingly voluminous. Nonetheless, should one wish
to pursue the idea of moral penalty despite political or public
praise, it could be edifying to compose even a short list.

NOTES

1. Niccolò Machiavelli, *The Prince,* 1532 (New York: New American Library, 1952), p.
93.
2. Thomas Nagel, "Ruthlessness in Public Life," in *Public and Private Morality,* Stuart
Hampshire, ed. (Cambridge: Cambridge University Press, 1978), p. 77.
3. Ibid., p. 79.
4. Bernard Williams, "Politics and Moral Character," in *Public and Private Morality,* pp.
55–73.
5. Michael Walzer, "Political Action: The Problem of Dirty Hands," in *Philosophy and
Public Affairs* (1973–74), pp. 160–180, p. 175.
6. Max Weber, "Politics as a Vocation," in *From Max Weber: Essays in Sociology,* trans.
and ed. by Hans H. Gerth and C. Wright Mills (New York, 1946), pp. 125–126.
7. Walzer, p. 176.
8. Albert Camus, *Caligula and Three Other Plays* (New York, 1958). I am indebted to
Michael Walzer for this reference.
9. Walzer, pp. 178–179.
10. Ibid., p. 179.
11. William Safire, "Vance Quit Because He Lied to Allies" (political commentary), *The
New York Times Service,* May, 1980.

Political Action:
The Problem of Dirty Hands
Michael Walzer

Michael Walzer's point of departure for his analysis of the
"dirty hands" dilemma is the "conventional wisdom" that politicians on the whole are morally worse than others in society.
They act like other morally bereft individuals when they lie,
evade, and act as villains. In other words, for Walzer the "dirty
hands" dilemma is a central feature of political life and not an

Michael Walzer, "Political Action: The Problem of Dirty Hands," *Philosophy & Public
Affairs,* vol. 2, no. 2., pp. 160–180. Copyright © 1973 by Princeton University Press.
Reprinted by permission of Princeton University Press.

LYING AND THE "DIRTY HANDS" DILEMMA IN GOVERNMENT

occasional crisis. Politicians may *systematically* do wrong to achieve good. Politicians, however, are not just like other morally contemptible people because, among other reasons, they do their immoral acts in *our* name. Walzer drives home the point that the wrongdoing of politicians is unique. He then considers three views of the "dirty hands" dilemma offered by Machiavelli, by the German sociologist Max Weber, and the French philosopher and writer Albert Camus. Of the three, he is attracted to Camus, especially his play *The Just Assassins*, for its treatment of the dilemma and the way Camus deals with guilt and punishment.

In an earlier[1] issue of *Philosophy & Public Affairs* there appeared a symposium on the rules of war which was actually (or at least more importantly) a symposium on another topic.[2] The actual topic was whether or not a man can ever face, or ever has to face, a moral dilemma, a situation where he must choose between two courses of action both of which it would be wrong for him to undertake. Thomas Nagel worriedly suggested that this could happen and that it did happen whenever someone was forced to choose between upholding an important moral principle and avoiding some looming disaster.[3] R. B. Brandt argued that it could not possibly happen, for there were guidelines we might follow and calculations we might go through which would necessarily yield the conclusion that one or the other course of action was the right one to undertake in the circumstances (or that it did not matter which we undertook). R. M. Hare explained how it was that someone might wrongly suppose that he was faced with a moral dilemma: sometimes, he suggested, the precepts and principles of an ordinary man, the products of his moral education, come into conflict with injunctions developed at a higher level of moral discourse. But this conflict is, or ought to be, resolved at the higher level; there is no real dilemma.

I am not sure that Hare's explanation is at all comforting, but the question is important even if no such explanation is possible, perhaps especially so if this is the case. The argument relates not only to the coherence and harmony of the moral universe, but also to the relative ease or difficulty—or impossibility—of living a moral life. It is not, therefore, merely a philosopher's question. If such a dilemma can arise, whether frequently or very rarely, any of us might one day face it. Indeed, many men have faced it, or think they have, especially men involved in political activity or war. The dilemma, exactly as Nagel describes it, is frequently discussed in the literature of political action—in novels and plays dealing with politics and in the work of theorists too.

In modern times the dilemma appears most often as the problem of "dirty hands," and it is typically stated by the Communist leader Hoerderer in Sartre's play of that name: "I have dirty hands right up to the elbows. I've plunged them in filth and blood. Do you think you can govern innocently?"[4] My own answer is no, I don't think I could govern innocently; nor do most of us believe that those who govern us are innocent—as I shall argue below—even the best of them. But this does not mean that it isn't possible to do the right thing while governing. It means that a particular act of government (in a political party or in the state) may be exactly the right thing to do in utilitarian terms and yet leave the man who does it guilty of a moral wrong. The innocent man, afterwards, is no longer innocent. If on the other hand he remains innocent, chooses, that is, the "absolutist" side of Nagel's dilemma, he not only fails to do the right thing (in utilitarian terms), he may also fail to measure up to the duties of his office (which imposes on him a considerable responsibility for consequences and outcomes). Most often, of course, political leaders accept the utilitarian calculation; they try to measure up. One might offer a number of sardonic comments on this fact, the most obvious being that by the calculations they usually make they demonstrate the great virtues of the "absolutist" position. Nevertheless, we would not want to be governed by men who consistently adopted that position.

The notion of dirty hands derives from an effort to refuse "absolutism" without denying the reality of the moral dilemma. Though this may appear to utilitarian philosophers to pile confusion upon confusion, I propose to take it very seriously. For the literature I shall examine is the work of serious and often wise men, and it reflects, though it may also have helped to shape, popular thinking about politics. It is important to pay attention to that too. I shall do so without assuming, as Hare suggests one might, that everyday moral and political discourse constitutes a distinct level of argument, where content is largely a matter of pedagogic expediency.[5] If popular views are resistant (as they are) to utilitarianism, there may be something to learn from that and not merely something to explain about it.

I.

Let me begin, then, with a piece of conventional wisdom to the effect that politicians are a good deal worse, morally worse, than the rest of us (it is the wisdom of the rest of us). Without either endorsing it or pretending to disbelieve it, I am going to expound this convention. For it suggests that the dilemma of dirty hands is a central feature of political life, that it arises not merely as an occasional crisis in the career of this or that unlucky politician but systematically and frequently.

Why is the politician singled out? Isn't he like the other entrepreneurs in an open society, who hustle, lie, intrigue, wear masks, smile and are villains? He is not, no doubt for many reasons, three of which I need to consider. First of all, the politician claims to play a different part than other entrepreneurs. He doesn't merely cater to our interests; he acts on our behalf, even in our name. He has purposes in mind, causes and projects that require the support and redound to the benefit, not of each of us individually, but of all of us together. He hustles, lies, and intrigues *for us*—or so he claims. Perhaps he is right, or at least sincere, but we suspect that he acts for himself also. Indeed, he cannot serve us without serving himself, for success brings him power and glory, the greatest rewards that men can win from their fellows. The competition for these two is fierce; the risks are often great, but the temptations are greater. We imagine ourselves succumbing. Why should our representatives act differently? Even if they would like to act differently, they probably cannot: for other men are all too ready to hustle and lie for power and glory, and it is the others who set the terms of the competition. Hustling and lying are necessary because power and glory are so desirable—that is, so widely desired. And so the men who act for us and in our name are necessarily hustlers and liars.

Politicians are also thought to be worse than the rest of us because they rule over us, and the pleasures of ruling are much greater than the pleasures of being ruled. The successful politician becomes the visible architect of our restraint. He taxes us, licenses us, forbids and permits us, directs us to this or that distant goal—all for our greater good. Moreover, he takes chances for our greater good that put us, or some of us, in danger. Sometimes he puts himself in danger too, but politics, after all, is his adventure. It is not always ours. There are undoubtedly times when it is good or necessary to direct the affairs of other people and to put them in danger. But we are a little frightened of the man who seeks, ordinarily and every day, the power to do so. And the fear is reasonable enough. The politician has, or pretends to have, a kind of confidence in his own judgment that the rest of us know to be presumptuous in any man.

The presumption is especially great because the victorious politician uses violence and the threat of violence—not only against foreign nations in our defense but also against us, and again ostensibly for our greater good. This is a point emphasized and perhaps overemphasized by Max Weber in his essay "Politics as a Vocation."[6] It has not, so far as I can tell, played an overt or obvious part in the development of the convention I am examining. The stock figure is the lying, not the murderous, politician— though the murderer lurks in the background, appearing most often in the form of the revolutionary or terrorist, very rarely as an ordinary magistrate or official. Nevertheless, the sheer weight of official violence in human history does suggest the kind of power to which politicians aspire, the kind of power they want to wield, and it may point to the roots of our half-conscious dislike and unease. The men who act for us and in our name are often killers, or seem to become killers too quickly and too easily.

Knowing all this or most of it, good and decent people still enter political life, aiming at some specific reform or seeking a general reformation. They are then required to learn the lesson Machiavelli first set out to teach: "how not to be good."[7] Some of them are incapable of learning; many more profess to be incapable. But they will not succeed unless they learn, for they have joined the terrible competition for power and glory; they have chosen to work and struggle as Machiavelli says, among "so many who are not good." They can do no good themselves unless they win the struggle, which they are unlikely to do unless they are willing and able to use the necessary means. So we are suspicious even of the best of winners. It is not a sign of our perversity if we think them only more clever than the rest. They have not won, after all, because they were good, or not only because of that, but also because they were not good. No one succeeds in politics without getting his hands dirty. This is conventional wisdom again, and again I don't mean to insist that it is true without qualification. I repeat it only to disclose the moral dilemma inherent in the convention. For sometimes it is right to try to succeed, and then it must also be right to get one's hands dirty. But one's hands get dirty from doing what it is wrong to do. And how can it be wrong to do what is right? Or, how can we get our hands dirty by doing what we ought to do?

II.

It will be best to turn quickly to some examples. I have chosen two, one relating to the struggle for power and one to its exercise. I should stress that in both these cases the men who face the dilemma of dirty hands have in an important sense chosen to do so; the cases tell us nothing about what it would be like, so to speak, to fall into the dilemma; nor shall I say anything about that here. Politicians often argue that they have no right to keep their hands clean, and that may well be true of them, but it is not so clearly true of the rest of us. Probably we do have a right to avoid, if we possibly can, those positions in which we might be forced to do terrible things. This might be regarded as the moral equivalent of our legal right not to incriminate ourselves. Good men will be in no hurry to surrender it, though there are reasons for doing so sometimes, and among these are or might be the reasons good men have for entering politics. But let us imagine a politician who does not agree to that: he wants to do good only by doing good, or at least he is certain that he can stop short of the most corrupting and brutal uses of political power. Very quickly that certainty is tested. What do we think of him then?

He wants to win the election, someone says, but he doesn't want to get his hands dirty. This is meant as a disparagement, even though it also means that the man being criticized is the sort of man who will not lie, cheat, bargain behind the backs of his supporters, shout absurdities at public meetings, or manipulate other men and women. Assuming that this particular election ought to be won, it is clear, I think, that the disparagement is justified. If the candidate didn't want to get his hands dirty, he should have stayed at home; if he can't stand the heat, he should get out of the kitchen, and so on. His decision to run was a commitment (to all of us who think the election important) to try to win, that is, to do within rational limits whatever is necessary to win. But the candidate is a moral man. He has principles and a history of adherence to those principles. That is why we are supporting him. Perhaps when he refuses to dirty his hands, he is simply insisting on being the sort of man he is. And isn't that the sort of man we want?

Let us look more closely at this case. In order to win the election the candidate must make a deal with a dishonest ward boss, involving the granting of contracts for school construction over the next four years. Should he make the deal? Well, at least he shouldn't be surprised by the offer, most of us would probably say (a conventional piece of sarcasm). And he should accept it or not, depending on exactly what is at stake in the election. But that is not the candidate's view. He is extremely reluctant even to consider the deal, puts off his aides when they remind him of it, refuses to calculate its possible effects upon the campaign. Now, if he is acting this way because the very thought of bargaining with that particular ward boss makes him feel unclean, his reluctance isn't very interesting. His feelings by themselves are not important. But he may also have reasons for his reluctance. He may know, for example, that some of his supporters support him precisely because they believe he is a good man, and this means to them a man who won't make such deals. Or he may doubt his own motives for considering the deal, wondering whether it is the political campaign or his own candidacy that makes the bargain at all tempting. Or he may believe that if he makes deals of this sort now he may not be able later on to achieve those ends that make the campaign worthwhile, and he may not feel entitled to take such risks with a future that is not only his own future. Or he may simply think that the deal is dishonest and therefore wrong, corrupting not only himself but all those human relations in which he is involved.

Because he has scruples of this sort, we know him to be a good man. But we view the campaign in a certain light, estimate its importance in a certain way, and hope that he will overcome his scruples and make the deal. It is important to stress that we don't want just *anyone* to make the deal; we want *him* to make it, precisely because he has scruples about it. We know he is doing right when he makes the deal because he knows he is doing wrong. I don't mean merely that he will feel badly or even very badly after he makes the deal. If he is the good man I am imagining him to be, he will feel guilty, that is, he will believe himself to be guilty. That is what it means to have dirty hands.

All this may become clearer if we look at a more dramatic example, for we are, perhaps, a little blasé about political deals and disinclined to worry much about the man who makes one. So consider a politician who has seized upon a national crisis—a prolonged colonial war—to reach for power. He and his friends win office pledged to decolonization and peace; they are honestly committed to both, though not without some sense of the advantages of the commitment. In any case, they have no responsibility for the war; they have steadfastly opposed it. Immediately, the politician goes off to the colonial capital to open negotiations with the rebels. But the capital is in the grip of a terrorist campaign, and the first decision the new leader faces is this: he is asked to authorize the torture of a captured rebel leader who knows or probably knows the location of a number of bombs hidden in apartment buildings around the city, set to go off within the next twenty-four hours. He orders the man tortured, convinced that he must do so for the sake of the people who might otherwise die in the explosions—even though he believes that torture is wrong, indeed abominable, not just sometimes, but always.[8] He had expressed this belief often and angrily during his own campaign; the rest of us took it as a sign of his goodness. How should we regard him now? (How should he regard himself?)

Once again, it does not seem enough to say that he should feel very badly. But why not? Why shouldn't he have feelings like those of St. Augustine's melancholy soldier, who understood both that his war was just and that killing, even in a just war, is a terrible thing to do?[9] The difference is that Augustine did not believe that it was wrong to kill in a just war; it was just sad, or the sort of thing a good man would be saddened by. But he might have thought it wrong to torture in a just war, and later Catholic theorists have certainly thought it wrong. Moreover, the politician I am imagining thinks it wrong, as do many of us who supported him. Surely we have a right to expect more than melancholy from him now. When he ordered the prisoner tortured, he committed a moral crime and he accepted a moral burden. Now he is a guilty man. His willingness to acknowledge and bear (and perhaps to repent and do penance for) his guilt is evidence, and it is the only evidence he can offer us, both that he is not too good for politics and that he is good enough. Here is the moral politician: it is by his dirty hands that we know him. If he were a moral man and nothing else, his hands would not be dirty; if he were a politician and nothing else, he would pretend that they were clean.

III.

Machiavelli's argument about the need to learn how not to be good clearly implies that there are acts known to be bad quite apart from the immediate circumstances in which they are performed or not performed. He points to a distinct set of political methods and stratagems which good men must study (by reading his books), not only because their use does not come naturally, but also because they are explicitly condemned by the moral teachings good men accept—and whose acceptance serves in turn to mark men as good. These methods may be condemned because they are thought contrary to divine law or to the order of nature or to our moral sense, or because in prescribing the law to ourselves we have individually or collectively prohibited them. Machiavelli does not commit himself on such issues, and I shall not do so either if I can avoid it. The effects of these different views are, at least in one crucial sense, the same. They take out of our hands the constant business of attaching moral labels to such Machiavellian methods as deceit and betrayal. Such methods are simply bad. They are the sort of thing that good men avoid, at least until they have learned how not to be good.

Now, if there is no such class of actions, there is no dilemma of dirty hands, and the Machiavellian teaching loses what Machiavelli surely intended it to have, its disturbing and paradoxical character. He can then be understood to be saying that political actors must sometimes overcome their moral inhibitions, but not that they must sometimes commit crimes. I take it that utilitarian philosophers also want to make the first of these statements and to deny the second. From their point of view, the candidate who makes a corrupt deal and the official who authorizes the torture of a prisoner must be described as good men (given the cases as I have specified them), who ought, perhaps, to be honored for making the right decision when it was a hard decision to make. There are three ways of developing this argument. First, it might be said that every political choice ought to be made solely in terms of its particular and immediate circumstances—in terms, that is, of the reasonable alternatives, available knowledge, likely consequences, and so on. Then the good man will face difficult choices (when his knowledge of options and outcomes is radically uncertain), but it cannot happen that he will face a moral dilemma. Indeed, if he always makes decisions in this way, and has been taught from childhood to do so, he will never have to overcome his inhibitions, whatever he does, for how could he have acquired inhibitions? Assuming further that he weighs the alternatives and calculates the consequences seriously and in good faith, he cannot commit a crime, though he can certainly make a mistake, even a very serious mistake. Even when he lies and tortures, his hands will be clean, for he has done what he should do as best he can, standing alone in a moment of time, forced to choose.

This is in some ways an attractive description of moral decision-making, but it is also a very improbable one. For while any one of us may stand alone, and so on, when we make this or that decision, we are not isolated or solitary in our moral lives. Moral life is a social phenomenon, and it is constituted at least in part by rules, the knowing of which (and perhaps the making of which) we share with our fellows. The experience of coming up against these rules, challenging their prohibitions, and explaining ourselves to other men and women is so common and so obviously important that no account of moral decision-making can possibly fail to come to grips with it. Hence the second utilitarian argument: such rules do indeed exist, but they are not really prohibitions of wrongful actions (though they do, perhaps for pedagogic reasons, have that form). They are moral guidelines, summaries of previous calculations. They ease our choices in ordinary cases, for we can simply follow their injunctions and do what has been found useful in the past; in exceptional cases they serve as signals warning us against doing too quickly or without the most careful calculations what has not been found useful in the past. But they do no more than that; they have no other purpose, and so it cannot be the case that it is or even might be a crime to override them.[10] Nor is it necessary to feel guilty when one does so. Once again, if it is right to break the rule in some hard case, after conscientiously worrying about it, the man who acts (especially if he knows that many of his fellows would simply worry rather than act) may properly feel pride in his achievement.

But this view, it seems to me, captures the reality of our moral life no better than the last. It may well be right to say that moral rules ought to have the character of guidelines, but it seems that in fact they do not. Or at least, we defend ourselves when we break the rules as if they had some status entirely independent of their previous utility (and we rarely feel proud of ourselves). The defenses we normally offer are not simply justifications; they are also excuses. Now, as Austin says, these two can *seem* to come very close together—indeed, I shall suggest that they can appear side by side in the same sentence—but they are conceptually distinct, differentiated in this crucial respect: an excuse is typically an admission of fault; a justification is typically a denial of fault and an assertion of innocence.[11] Consider a well-known defense from Shakespeare's *Hamlet* that has often reappeared in political literature: "I must be cruel only to be kind."[12] The words are spoken on an occasion when Hamlet is actually being cruel to his mother. I will leave aside the possibility that she deserves to hear (to be forced to listen to) every harsh word he utters, for Hamlet himself makes no such claim—and if she did indeed deserve that, his words might not be cruel or he might not be cruel for speaking them. "I must be cruel" contains the excuse, since it both admits a fault and suggests that Hamlet has no choice but to commit it. He is doing what he has to do; he can't help himself (given the ghost's command, the rotten state of Denmark, and so on). The rest of the sentence is a justification, for it suggests that Hamlet intends and expects kindness to be the outcome of his actions—we must assume that he means greater kindness, kindness to the right persons, or some such. It is not, however, so complete a justification that Hamlet is able to say that he is not *really* being cruel. "Cruel" and "kind" have exactly the same status; they both follow the verb "to be," and so they perfectly reveal the moral dilemma.[13]

When rules are overridden, we do not talk or act as if they had been set aside, canceled, or annulled. They still stand and have this much effect at least: that we know we have done something wrong even if what we have done was also the best thing to do on the whole in the circumstances.[14] Or at least we feel that way, and this feeling is itself a crucial feature of our moral life. Hence the third utilitarian argument, which recognizes the usefulness of guilt and seeks to explain it. There are, it appears, good reasons for "overvaluing" as well as for overriding the rules. For the consequences might be very bad indeed if the rules were overridden every time the moral calculation seemed to go against them. It is probably best if most men do not calculate too nicely, but simply follow the rules; they are less likely to make mistakes that way, all in all. And so a good man (or at least an ordinary good man) will respect the rules rather more than he would if he thought them merely guidelines, and he will feel guilty when he overrides them. Indeed, if he did not feel guilty, "he would not be such a good man."[15] It is by his feelings that we know him. Because of those feelings he will never be in a hurry to override the rules, but will wait until there is no choice, acting only to avoid consequences that are both imminent and almost certainly disastrous.

The obvious difficulty with this argument is that the feeling whose usefulness is being explained is most unlikely to be felt by someone who is convinced only of its usefulness. He breaks a utilitarian rule (guideline), let us say, for good utilitarian reasons: but can he then feel guilty, also for good utilitarian reasons, when he has no reason for believing that he *is* guilty? Imagine a moral philosopher expounding the third argument to a man who actually does feel guilty or to the sort of man who is likely to feel guilty. Either the man won't accept the utilitarian explanation as an account of his feeling about the rules (probably the best outcome from a utilitarian point of view) or he will accept it and then cease to feel that (useful) feeling. But I do not want to exclude the possibility of a kind of superstitious anxiety, the possibility, that is, that some men will continue to feel guilty even after they have been taught, and have agreed, that they cannot possibly *be* guilty. It is best to say only that the more fully they accept the utilitarian account, the less likely they are to feel that (useful) feeling. The utilitarian account is not at all useful, then, if political actors accept it, and that may help us to understand why it plays, as Hare has pointed out, so small a part in our moral education.[16]

IV.

One further comment on the third argument: it is worth stressing that to feel guilty is to suffer, and that the men whose guilt feelings are here called useful are themselves innocent according to the utilitarian account. So we seem to have come upon another case where the suffering of the innocent is permitted and even encouraged by utilitarian calculation.[17] But surely an innocent man who has done something painful or hard (but justified) should be helped to avoid or escape the sense of guilt; he might reasonably expect the assistance of his fellow men, even of moral philosophers, at such a time. On the other hand, if we intuitively think it true of some other man that he *should* feel guilty, then we ought to be able to specify the nature of his guilt (and if he is a good man, win his agreement). I think I can construct a case which, with only small variation, highlights what is different in these two situations.

Consider the common practice of distributing rifles loaded with blanks to some of the members of a firing squad. The individual men are not told whether their own weapons are lethal, and so though all of them look like executioners to the victim in front of them, none of them know whether they are really executioners or not. The purpose of this stratagem is to relieve each man of the sense that he is a killer. It can hardly relieve him of whatever moral responsibility he incurs by serving on a firing squad, and that is not its purpose, for the execution is not thought to be (and let us grant this to be the case) an immoral or wrongful act. But the inhibition against killing another human being is so strong that even if the men believe that what they are doing is right, they will still feel guilty. Uncertainty as to their actual role apparently reduces the intensity of these feelings. If this is so, the stratagem is perfectly justifiable, and one can only rejoice in every case where it succeeds—for every success subtracts one from the number of innocent men who suffer.

But we would feel differently, I think, if we imagine a man who believes (and let us assume here that we believe also) either that capital punishment is wrong or that this particular victim is innocent, but who nevertheless agrees to participate in the firing squad for some overriding political or moral reason—I won't try to suggest what that reason might be. If he is confronted by the trick with the rifles, then we can be reasonably certain that his opposition to capital punishment or his belief in the victim's innocence is not morally serious. And if it is serious, he will not merely feel guilty, he will know that he is guilty (and we will know it too), though he may also believe (and we may agree) that he has good reasons for incurring the guilt. Our guilt feelings can be tricked away when they are isolated from our moral beliefs, as in the first case, but not when they are allied with them, as in the second. The beliefs themselves and the rules which are believed in can only be *overridden,* a painful process which forces a man to weigh the wrong he is willing to do in order to do right, and which leaves pain behind, and should do so, even after the decision has been made.

V.

That is the dilemma of dirty hands as it has been experienced by political actors and written about in the literature of political action. I don't want to argue that it is only a political dilemma. No doubt we can get our hands dirty in private life also, and sometimes, no doubt, we should. But the issue is posed most dramatically in politics for the three reasons that make political life the kind of life it is, because we claim to act for others but also serve ourselves, rule over others, and use violence against them. It is easy to get one's hands dirty in politics and it is often right to do so. But it is not easy to teach a good man how not to be good, nor is it easy to explain such a man to himself once he has committed whatever crimes are required of him. At least, it is not easy once we have agreed to use the word "crimes" and to live with (because we have no choice) the dilemma of dirty hands. Still, the agreement is common enough, and on its basis there have developed three broad traditions of explanation, three ways of thinking about dirty hands, which derive in some very general fashion from neoclassical, Protestant, and Catholic perspectives on politics and morality. I want to try to say something very briefly about each of them, or rather about a representative example of each of them, for each seems to me partly right. But I don't think I can put together the compound view that might be wholly right.

The first tradition is best represented by Machiavelli, the first man, so far as I know, to state the paradox that I am examining. The good man who aims to found or reform a republic must, Machiavelli tells us, do terrible things to reach his goal. Like Romulus, he must murder his brother; like Numa, he must lie to the people. Sometimes, however, "when the act accuses, the result excuses."[18] This sentence from *The Discourses* is often taken to mean that the politician's deceit and cruelty are justified by the good results he brings about. But if they were justified, it wouldn't be necessary to learn what Machiavelli claims to teach: how not to be good. It would only be necessary to learn how to be good in a new, more difficult, perhaps roundabout way. That is not Machiavelli's argument. His political judgments are indeed consequentialist in character, but not his moral judgments. We know whether cruelty is used well or badly by its effects over time. But that it is bad to use cruelty we know in some other way. The deceitful and cruel politician is excused (if he succeeds) only in the sense that the rest of us come to agree that the results were "worth it" or, more likely, that we simply forget his crimes when we praise his success.

It is important to stress Machiavelli's own commitment to the existence of moral standards. His paradox depends upon that commitment as it depends upon the general stability of the standards—which he upholds in his consistent use of words like good and bad.[19] If he wants the standards to be disregarded by good men more often than they are, he has nothing with which to replace them and no other way of recognizing the good men except by their allegiance to those same standards. It is exceedingly rare, he writes, that a good man is willing to employ bad means to become prince.[20] Machiavelli's purpose is to persuade such a person to make the attempt, and he holds out the supreme political rewards, power and glory, to the man who does so and succeeds. The good man is not rewarded (or excused), however, merely for his willingness to get his hands dirty. He must do bad things well. There is no reward for doing bad things badly, though they are done with the best of intentions. And so political action necessarily involves taking a risk. But it should be clear that what is risked is not personal goodness—*that is thrown away*—but power and glory. If the politician succeeds, he is a hero; eternal praise is the supreme reward for not being good.

What the penalties are for not being good, Machiavelli doesn't say, and it is probably for this reason above all that his moral sensitivity has so often been questioned. He is suspect not because he tells political actors they must get their hands dirty, but because he does not specify the state of mind appropriate to a man with dirty hands. A Machiavellian hero has no inwardness. What he thinks of himself we don't know. I would guess, along with most other readers of Machiavelli, that he basks in his glory. But then it is difficult to account for the strength of his original reluctance to learn how not to be good. In any case, he is the sort of man who is unlikely to keep a diary and so we cannot find out what he thinks. Yet we do want to know; above all, we want a record of his anguish. That is a sign of our own conscientiousness and of the impact on us of the second tradition of thought that I want to examine, in which personal anguish sometimes seems the only acceptable excuse for political crimes.

The second tradition is best represented, I think, by Max Weber, who outlines its essential features with great power at the very end of his essay "Politics as a Vocation." For Weber, the good man with dirty hands is a hero still, but he is a tragic hero. In part, his tragedy is that though politics is his vocation, he has not been called by God and so cannot be justified by Him. Weber's hero is alone in a world that seems to belong to Satan, and his vocation is entirely his own choice. He still wants what Christian magistrates have always wanted, both to do good in the world and to save his soul, but now these two ends have come into sharp contradiction. They are contradictory because of the necessity for violence in a world where God has not instituted the sword. The politician takes the sword himself, and only by doing so does he measure up to his vocation. With full consciousness of what he is doing, he does bad in order to do good, and surrenders his soul. He "lets himself in," Weber says, "for the diabolic forces lurking in all violence." Perhaps Machiavelli also meant to suggest that his hero surrenders salvation in exchange for glory, but he does not explicitly say so. Weber is absolutely clear: "the genius or demon of politics lives in an inner tension with the god of love . . . [which] can at any time lead to an irreconcilable conflict."[21] His politician views this conflict when it comes with a tough realism, never pretends that it might be solved by compromise, chooses politics once again, and turns decisively away from love. Weber writes about this choice with a passionate high-mindedness that makes a concern for one's soul seem no more elevated than a concern for one's flesh. Yet the reader never doubts that his mature, superbly trained, relentless, objective, responsible, and disciplined political leader is also a suffering servant. His choices are hard and painful, and he pays the price not only while making them but forever after. A man doesn't lose his soul one day and find it the next.

The difficulties with this view will be clear to anyone who has ever met a suffering servant. Here is a man who lies, intrigues, sends other men to their death—and suffers. He does what he must do with a heavy heart. None of us can know, he tells us, how much it cost him to do his duty. Indeed, we cannot, for he himself fixes the price he pays. And that is the trouble with this view of political crime. We suspect the suffering servant of either masochism or hypocrisy or both, and while we are often wrong, we are not always wrong. Weber attempts to resolve the problem of dirty hands entirely within the confines of the individual conscience, but I am inclined to think that this is neither possible nor desirable. The self-awareness of the tragic hero is obviously of great value. We want the politician to have an inner life at least something like that which Weber describes. But sometimes the hero's suffering needs to be socially expressed (for like punishment, it confirms and reinforces our sense that certain acts are wrong). And equally important, it sometimes needs to be socially limited. We don't want to be ruled by men who have lost their souls. A politician with dirty hands needs a soul, and it is best for us all if he has some hope of personal salvation, however that is conceived. It is not the case that when he does bad in order to do good he surrenders himself forever to the demon of politics. He commits a determinate crime, and he must pay a determinate penalty. When he has done so, his hands will be clean again, or as clean as human hands can ever be. So the Catholic Church has always taught, and this teaching is central to the third tradition that I want to examine.

Once again I will take a latter-day and a lapsed representative of the tradition and consider Albert Camus' *The Just Assassins*. The heroes of this play are terrorists at work in nineteenth-century Russia. The dirt on their hands is human blood. And yet Camus' admiration for them, he tells us, is complete. We consent to being criminals, one of them says, but there is nothing with which anyone can reproach us. Here is the dilemma of dirty hands in a new form. The heroes are innocent criminals, just assassins, because, having killed, they are prepared to die—*and will die.* Only their execution, by the same despotic authorities they are attacking, will complete the action in which they are engaged: dying, they need make no excuses. That is the end of their guilt and pain. The execution is not so much punishment as self-punishment and expiation. On the scaffold they wash their hands clean and, unlike the suffering servant, they die happy.

Now the argument of the play when presented in so radically simplified a form may seem a little bizarre, and perhaps it is marred by the moral extremism of Camus' politics. "Political action has limits," he says in a preface to the volume containing *The Just Assassins,* "and there is no good and just action but what recognizes those limits and if it must go beyond them, at least accepts death."[22] I am less interested here in the violence of that "at least"—what else does he have in mind?—than in the sensible doctrine that it exaggerates. That doctrine might best be described by an analogy: just assassination, I want to suggest, is like civil disobedience. In both men violate a set of rules, go beyond a moral or legal limit, in order to do what they believe they should do. At the same time, they acknowledge their responsibility for the violation by accepting punishment or doing penance. But there is also a difference between the two, which has to do with the difference between law and morality. In most cases of civil disobedience the laws of the state are broken for moral reasons, and the state provides the punishments. In most cases of dirty hands moral rules are broken for reasons of state, and no one provides the punishment. There is rarely a Czarist executioner waiting in the wings for politicians with dirty hands, even the most deserving among them. Moral rules are not usually enforced against the sort of actor I am considering, largely because he acts in an official capacity. If they were enforced, dirty hands would be no problem. We would simply honor the man who did bad in order to do good, and at the same time we would punish him. We would honor him for the good he has done, and we would punish him for the bad he has done. We would punish him, that is, for the same reasons we punish anyone else; it is not my purpose here to defend any particular view of punishment. In any case, there seems no way to establish or enforce the punishment. Short of the priest and the confessional, there are no authorities to whom we might entrust the task.

I am nevertheless inclined to think Camus' view the most attractive of the three, if only because it requires us at least to imagine a punishment or a penance that fits the crime and so to examine closely the nature of the crime. The others do not require that. Once he has launched his career, the crimes of Machiavelli's prince seem subject only to prudential control. And the crimes of Weber's tragic hero are limited only by *his* capacity for suffering and not, as they should be, by *our* capacity for suffering. In neither case is there any explicit reference back to the moral code, once it has, at great personal cost to be sure, been set aside. The question posed by Sartre's Hoerderer (whom I suspect of being a suffering servant) is rhetorical, and the answer is obvious (I have already given it), but the characteristic sweep of both is disturbing. Since it is concerned only with those crimes that ought to be committed, the dilemma of dirty hands seems to exclude questions of degree. Wanton or excessive cruelty is not at issue, any more than is cruelty directed at bad ends. But political action is so uncertain that politicians necessarily take moral as well as political risks, committing crimes that they only think ought to be committed. They override the rules without ever being certain that they have found the best way to the results they hope to achieve, and we don't want them to do that too quickly or too often. So it is important that the moral stakes be very high—which is to say, that the rules be rightly valued. That, I suppose, is the reason for Camus' extremism. Without the executioner, however, there is no one to set the stakes or maintain the values except ourselves, and probably no way to do either except through philosophic reiteration and political activity.

"We shall not abolish lying by refusing to tell lies," says Hoerderer, "but by using every means at hand to abolish social classes."[23] I suspect we shall not abolish lying at all, but we might see to it that fewer lies were told if we contrived to deny power and glory to the greatest liars—except, of course, in the case of those lucky few whose extraordinary achievements make us forget the lies they told. If Hoerderer succeeds in abolishing social

LYING AND THE "DIRTY HANDS" DILEMMA IN GOVERNMENT

classes, perhaps he will join the lucky few. Meanwhile, he lies, manipulates, and kills, and we must make sure he pays the price. We won't be able to do that, however, without getting our own hands dirty, and then we must find some way of paying the price ourselves.

NOTES

1. An earlier version of this paper was read at the annual meeting of the Conference for the Study of Political Thought in New York, April 1971. I am indebted to Charles Taylor, who served as commentator at that time and encouraged me to think that its arguments might be right.

2. *Philosophy & Public Affairs* I, no. 2 (Winter 1971–72): Thomas Nagel, "War and Massacre," pp. 123–144; R. B. Brandt, "Utilitarianism and the Rules of War," pp. 145–165; and R. M. Hare, "Rules of War and Moral Reasoning," pp. 166–181.

3. For Nagel's description of a possible "moral blind alley," see "War and Massacre," pp. 142–144. Bernard Williams has made a similar suggestion, though without quite acknowledging it as his own: "many people can recognize the thought that a certain course of action is, indeed, the best thing to do on the whole in the circumstances, but that doing it involves doing something wrong" (*Morality: An Introduction to Ethics* [New York, 1972], p. 93).

4. Jean-Paul Sartre, *Dirty Hands*, in *No Exit and Three Other Plays*, trans. Lionel Abel (New York, n.d.), p. 224.

5. Hare, "Rules of War and Moral Reasoning," pp. 173–178, esp. p. 174: "the simple principles of the deontologist . . . have their place at the level of character-formation (moral education and self-education)."

6. In *From Max Weber: Essays in Sociology*, trans. and ed. Hans H. Gerth and C. Wright Mills (New York, 1946), pp. 77–128.

7. See *The Prince*, chap. XV; cf. *The Discourses*, bk. I, chaps IX and XVIII. I quote from the Modern Library edition of the two works (New York, 1950), p. 57.

8. I leave aside the question of whether the prisoner is himself responsible for the terrorist campaign. Perhaps he opposed it in meetings of the rebel organization. In any case, whether he deserves to be punished or not, he does not deserve to be tortured.

9. Other writers argued that Christians must never kill, even in a just war; and there was also an intermediate position which suggests the origins of the idea of dirty hands. Thus Basil the Great (Bishop of Caesarea in the fourth century A.D.): "Killing in war was differentiated by our fathers from murder . . . nevertheless, perhaps it would be well that those whose hands are unclean abstain from communion for three years." Here dirty hands are a kind of impurity or unworthiness, which is not the same as guilt, though closely related to it. For a general survey of these and other Christian views, see Roland H. Bainton, *Christian Attitudes Toward War and Peace* (New York, 1960), esp. chaps. 5–7.

10. Brandt's rules do not appear to be of the sort that can be overridden—except perhaps by a soldier who decides that he just *won't* kill any more civilians, no matter what cause is served—since all they require is careful calculation. But I take it that rules of a different sort, which have the form of ordinary injunctions and prohibitions, can and often do figure in what is called "rule-utilitarianism."

11. J. L. Austin, "A Plea for Excuses," in *Philosophical Papers*, ed. J. O. Urmson and G. J. Warnock (Oxford, 1961), pp. 123–152.

12. *Hamlet* III, 4, 178.

13. Compare the following lines from Bertolt Brecht's poem "To Posterity": "Alas, we/ Who wished to lay the foundations of kindness/ Could not ourselves be kind . . ." (*Selected Poems*, trans. H. R. Hays [New York, 1969], p. 177). This is more of an excuse, less of a justification (the poem is an *apologia*).

14. Robert Nozick discusses some of the possible effects of overriding a rule in his "Moral Complications and Moral Structures," *Natural Law Forum* 13 (1968), pp. 34–35 and notes. Nozick suggests that what may remain after one has broken a rule (for good reasons) is a

"duty to make reparations." He does not call this "guilt," though the two notions are closely connected.

15. Hare, "Rules of War and Moral Reasoning," p. 179.

16. There is another possible utilitarian position, suggested in Maurice Merleau-Ponty's *Humanism and Terror*, trans. John O'Neill (Boston, 1970). According to this view, the agony and the guilt feelings experienced by the man who makes a "dirty hands" decision derive from his radical uncertainty about the actual outcome. Perhaps the awful thing he is doing will be done in vain; the results he hopes for won't occur; the only outcome will be the pain he has caused or the deceit he has fostered. Then (and only then) he will indeed have committed a crime. On the other hand, if the expected good does come, then (and only then) he can abandon his guilt feelings; he can say, and the rest of us must agree, that he is justified. This is a kind of delayed utilitarianism, where justification is a matter of actual and not at all of predicted outcomes. It is not implausible to imagine a political actor anxiously awaiting the "verdict of history." But suppose the verdict is in his favor (assuming that there is a *final* verdict or a statute of limitations on possible verdicts): he will surely feel relieved—more so, no doubt, than the rest of us. I can see no reason, however, why he should think himself justified, if he is a good man and knows that what he did was wrong. Perhaps the victims of his crime, seeing the happy result, will absolve him, but history has no powers of absolution. Indeed, history is more likely to play tricks on our moral judgment. Predicted outcomes are at least thought to follow from our own acts (this is the prediction), but actual outcomes almost certainly have a multitude of causes, the combination of which may well be fortuitous. Merleau-Ponty stresses the risks of political decision-making so heavily that he turns politics into a gamble with time and circumstance. But the anxiety of the gambler is of no great moral interest. Nor is it much of a barrier, as Merleau-Ponty's book makes all too clear, to the commission of the most terrible crimes.

17. Cf. the cases suggested by David Ross, *The Right and the Good* (Oxford, 1930), pp. 56–57, and E. F. Carritt, *Ethical and Political Thinking* (Oxford, 1947), p. 65.

18. *The Discourses*, bk. I, chap. IX (p. 139).

19. For a very different view of Machiavelli, see Isaiah Berlin, "The Question of Machiavelli," *The New York Review of Books*, November 4, 1971.

20. *The Discourses*, bk. I, chap. XVIII (p. 171).

21. Weber, *Essays*, "Politics as a Vocation," pp. 125–126. But sometimes a political leader does choose the "absolutist" side of the conflict, and Weber writes (p. 127) that it is "immensely moving when a *mature* man . . . aware of a responsibility for the consequences of his conduct . . . reaches a point where he says: 'Here I stand; I can do no other.' " Unfortunately, he does not suggest just where that point is or even where it might be.

22. *Caligula and Three Other Plays* (New York, 1958), p. x. (The preface is translated by Justin O'Brian, the plays by Stuart Gilbert.)

23. *Dirty Hands*, p. 223.

CHAPTER 5

ETHICS, HARD CHOICES, AND PUBLIC POLICY

Introduction

The "dirty hands" dilemma, dissected in the last chapter, is an example of the kinds of moral mazes that public officials must wrestle with in their public lives. But it represents merely one such example. Moral mazes of all stripes and varieties plague the professional lives of public administrators. There are hard policy choices facing public administrators in areas such as war, foreign policy, taxation, welfare, health and education policy, transportation issues, zoning issues, law and order, and so on. Public officials must constantly address the most difficult issues that confront a society. The problem is that these public policy issues usually have an ethical quandary at their core, so that they present themselves as hard choices for the public official.

This chapter is devoted to the questions that arise in conjunction with two interrelated topics. A general discussion about ethics and making hard choices in government will be offered as a lead-in to the more specific problem of the role that ethics should play in public policy formulation. These two topics—making hard choices in government and deciding ethical public policy—are interrelated in a very fundamental way. It could easily be argued that formulating public policy is the practice of making hard choices in government or, at least, one general kind of hard choice that confronts public administrators. While connections between the topics of hard choices and public policy may be obvious, less evident is the ability to make recommendations about how public administrators can effectively deal with them.

It is unfortunate that most individuals who enter public service are either unprepared or underprepared for the hard ethical choices that their profession will burden them with, and as a result, poor choices are often made, and the public suffers. Elected officials are not elected for their ethical problem-solving abilities, but rather for their political posturings, charisma, and other extraneous factors. Those appointed to government posts are not usually chosen for their dexterity with ethical matters. Nor are those who make public administration their career as professional public managers normally trained in the complexities of moral maze resolution and the making of hard choices. In short, most pubic officials—elected, appointed, or career—lack the kinds of skills necessary to make hard choices and resolve the ethical problems inherent in public policy formulation. Instead, the hard choice is made through a process marked by politics, favoritism, and the interests of special groups.

One way to overcome this lack of skill in the area of ethical analysis on the part of public officials is to provide occasions for these officials to build and develop the necessary tools of analysis through training and education. In addition, organizational development mechanisms could be implemented that would likewise provide an environment in which hard choices would be recognized as part of the territory of public service. Institutionalizing ethics in government can be achieved in these and other ways. This topic is so important that it forms the focus of the last chapter of this book. For our purposes here, however, it is sufficient only to lay out the problems of making hard choices in government and the difficulties of performing ethical analysis in public policy formulation.

Public administration is automatically adverse to treating ethical issues, problems, and dilemmas. The popular conception is that one of the values of public administration is the freedom from having to make hard choices. This approach can readily be seen in the ways that public offices are organizationally construed and the way that those who operate in those organizations behave. A general term used to depict this organizational structure that frees officials from having to make hard choices is "bureaucracy." The parceling up of offices into layers upon layers of administrative structures fosters, organizationally and behaviorally, an attitude that encourages the evading of important issues like moral mazes. A "pass the buck" mentality arises in the modern bureaucratic practice of public administration, in which officials can shrug off hard choices and moral mazes on the assumption that they will be made at the next higher level in the organization. Thus, rather than being involved in a productive dialogue about which decisions to make, most public officials feel obliged to discount them and wait for the next layer of administration to issue the proper directives that they will then follow. In short, when it comes to moral quandaries and their ethical solutions, the bureaucratic response is evasion. The common practice of public administrators in areas needing ethical analysis, then, is no practice at all.

For many this bureaucratic approach to issues is not an accurate picture of government but only a popular misconception and caricature of its internal workings. While it may be the case that bureaucracy creates needless layers of decision making, decisions still do get made, and many of them are hard choices of an ethical nature, resulting in the formulation of solid public policy. The buck does stop somewhere in government, and officials are accountable for their individual decision making. Hence, the practice of public administration does not employ evasion; rather, it requires that individuals be prepared to tackle issues and make hard choices.

The literature on public administration reflects this emphasis upon the individual as decision maker in a governmental context. In this chapter, Terry L. Cooper sets the tone for the discussion by examining the virtues of public administration in his "Hierarchy, Virtue, and the Practice of Public Administration: A Perspective for Normative Ethics." It is Cooper's thesis that certain virtues can be identified in public administration that public officials need to develop as individuals, so that they might be better disposed to make the right choice when confronted with the hard alternatives that make up the practice of public administration. He cites various "goods" as desirable ends that should guide public decision making, such as the public interest, accountability, social order, equality, and the like. According to Cooper, if these goods that are internal to the practice of public administration are achieved in the policy-making process, and if virtues that are also peculiar to the practice are developed, then a normative ethic emerges that can be highly useful in guiding administrators toward correct choices in government.

The second selection of the chapter, "Hard Choices: Justifying Bureaucratic Decisions," by Douglas T. Yates, Jr., takes a different approach to the same issue. Yates shows how the individual decision maker is central to the practice of public administration. He argues that democracy is inherently a debate about values; that in contemporary American government a new democratic process has emerged that views the bureaucrat as having a central role. The public policy formulation process for Yates is one in which public officials choose values, make trade-offs among competing values that exist in conflict, and assume responsibility for the implementation of these value-laden decisions. Yates calls this "bureaucratic democracy." The problem with this process is that if public policy is a matter of dealing with values, bureaucrats are not equipped to resolve value conflicts in public policy on a philosophical level. There is, therefore, the need for a new public philosophy that emphasizes the moral obligation of bureaucrats to discuss more openly and cogently the values and the competition among values that constitute the public policy process.

The article by Douglas J. Amy, "Why Policy Analysis and Ethics Are Incompatible," investigates the reasons why scholars and practitioners of public policy analysis have not included ethical analysis or value analysis into their primary task of evaluating policy. Amy runs through the "standard explanations" for the lack of ethical considerations in policy formulation but concludes that there are other, more subtle, reasons why ethics is neglected by public officials and practitioners of public policy analysis. For Amy, the formidable challenges of a moral evaluation of public policy run counter to the professional and political interests of both analysts and policy makers, and as a result, the question of ethics in public policy is largely ignored.

While it can easily be observed that the hard choices of public policy are heavily laden with value considerations and ethical import, the overriding tendency in American government is to ignore these facts as much as possible. This disregard is the first obstacle that needs to be overcome if the hard choices of public policy are to be adequately dealt with. In addition is the need to insure that the bureaucratic decision-making process and bureaucrats themselves are part of the solution in ethical policy formulation and not part of the problem. Public officials should be equipped with the skills of ethical analysis and value clarification if they are to excel in policy formulation, given the interlocking nature of ethics and policy. Hence, the questions posed by the interface of ethics, hard choices, and public policy count as another essential issue in government ethics.

Hierarchy, Virtue, and the Practice of Public Administration: A Perspective for Normative Ethics
Terry L. Cooper

One of the most difficult dilemmas that public officials must contend with arises in situations in which a superior demands absolute loyalty and makes requests of the official that run counter to his own sense of right and wrong. This common tendency of hierarchical organizations is the point of departure for Terry L. Cooper in his analysis of how "virtue ethics" may be a guide for normative decision making in bureaucracies. Cooper borrows the approach of philosopher Alasdair MacIntyre, whose work in ethics emphasizes the idea that professional practices have their virtues and that it is the responsibility of professionals to develop themselves according to the various goods that define virtuous practice in their profession. In the profession of public administration, Cooper underscores such "internal goods" that may serve as normative guides, such as the public interest, social justice, liberty, and accountability. These are internal goods in the sense that they are indigenous to the practice of public administration and can be set apart from "external goods," which can be obtained outside the practice of public administration, such as money, prestige, status, and power. Thus, virtue in a practice means maintaining a focus on one's professional obligations to achieve internal goods.

A military police officer is instructed by a commander not to issue citations to senior officers for driving while intoxicated.

Terry L. Cooper, "Hierarchy, Virtue, and the Practice of Public Administration: A Perspective for Normative Ethics," *Public Administration Review* (July/August 1987), pp. 320–328. Reprinted with permission from *Public Administration Review* (c) 1987 by the American Society for Public Administration (ASPA), 1120 G Street N.W., Suite 500, Washington, DC 20005. All rights reserved.

Also, certain specified junior officers and noncommissioned officers whose services and support are needed are to be similarly
exempted. However, citations are to be issued strictly to all
other personnel and maximum punishment is to be sought. When
the officer objects to this order on the grounds of its illegality
and unfairness, he is threatened with a poor proficiency rating
and removal from his position.

The design supervisor for a state water project is told by one of
her engineers that the initial specifications for one section of
water main must be changed. It has recently been discovered that
the soil in that area contains toxic wastes which corrode steel
pipes and will eventually enter the water supply. Consequently,
only concrete-jacketed pipe is safe for this area. The supervisor
agrees that the initial design represents a public health hazard
and must be changed. Both go to inform the project chief of this
necessary change. Upon hearing them out, the chief says that it is
too late to incorporate these changes due to the significantly
higher costs and time delays which would be required to complete the design phase. After leaving the chief's office, the supervisor tells the engineer that they have no other choice but to
proceed with the initial specifications.

The tendency of hierarchical organizations to demand absolute
loyalty to superiors and thereby displace other important values,
even those associated with the formal goals of the organization, is
a well documented phenomenon.[1] Furthermore, it is clearly and
overwhelmingly the most frequent occurring problem among the
cases written by the more than 200 participants in administrative
ethics workshops which I have conducted during the last four
years.

An Ethic of Virtue for the
Practice of Public Administration

Examination and analysis of this serious problem are not for the
purpose of arriving at a set of specific recommendations about
what one should do in such risky and painful situations. Nor is
the intention to provide a decision-making model for the analysis

and evaluation of the various alternatives for action in any particular case. Frameworks exist for those purposes.[2]

Rather, this essay considers the general approach to the development of normative administrative ethics which would be most appropriate for public administration and, more specifically, the code of ethics of the American Society for Public Administration (ASPA). The concern is to develop a moral identity for the public administrative role which provides a general orientation for action. The specific purpose is to explore an ethic of virtue for public administration which complements and supports ethical analysis of principles and alternatives for conduct by identifying certain desirable predispositions to act.

Lilla has argued that the analytical approach to administrative ethics amounts to equipping public officials with the means to create self-justifying rationalizations for their questionable conduct.[3] He argues instead for the inculcation of a set of virtues derived from a democratic ethos. My position is that the problem of normative ethics should not be approached with the assumption that these are mutually exclusive options. Rather I find myself more in agreement with Frankena's judgment that an ethic of virtue is necessary to identify the predispositions to act which support courses of conduct which one has identified through some analytical process.[4]

Thus a complete normative ethic for public administration must include: (1) an understanding of appropriate ethical principles, (2) an identification of virtues which are supportive of those principles, and (3) analytical techniques which may be employed in specific situations to interpret the principles. The second item concerning "predispositions" or "inclinations," traditionally called virtues, which move an administrator to act upon principle, even in the face of anticipated resistance or punishment, deserves more consideration than it has received recently in the full development of normative administrative ethics.

In both of the case summaries presented above, subordinates confront organizational superiors with concerns which appear to be rooted in general principles derived from a professional ethic. In the first situation the officer is concerned both about obeying the law and maintaining justice in the enforcement of policy. In the second, the obligation of public servants to act in ways which are beneficent for the public and at least to follow the principle of nonmaleficence (do no harm) seem to be the motivating principles.

In neither of these instances is ethical understanding lacking; both individuals perceive a legitimate ethical issue. Also, both are able to identify what needs to be done to act responsibly. Furthermore, both demonstrate inclinations to act on their perceived obligations. However, in both cases, these would-be ethical public officials find their good intentions thwarted by higher executive authority.

Information is insufficient in the case summaries to make possible more than conjecture about reasons why the superiors resist attempts of their subordinates to conduct themselves ethically. However, it is plausible to infer from the information available that, as is often the case, interorganizational politics is a powerful deterrent to ethical conduct in the first case, and costs in time and money are an overriding concern in the second. Managers responsible for the well being of the organizations seem to allow goods associated with organizational status, position, and power to prevail over the professional ethics of subordinates.

If this problem occurs as frequently as both literature and experience suggest, why might this be so? What virtues support the action needed to maintain one's professional principles, even in the face of resistance and retribution if one is in a subordinate position or, in spite of the pressures to think first of the organization, if one is in an executive role?

Characteristics of a Practice

A useful perspective for analyzing the ethical difficulties inherent in the hierarchical relationships of modern organizations is suggested by the concept of *"practices"* and their *virtues* developed by Alasdair MacIntyre.[5] Although his conceptualization needs revision and development, this general perspective is useful as a beginning point for scholars and practitioners involved in the development of normative administrative ethics. Professional associations such as ASPA may also find it helpful in clarifying the broader ethical dimensions of the public administrative role. To consider the usefulness of this theoretical framework, the following concepts are briefly defined: practice, internal goods, external goods, and virtue.

MacIntyre focuses on "practices" rather than "professions" in dealing with the ethics of groups of people involved in common activities. Practices are forms of activity which possess the following characteristics:

1. They exhibit coherence and complexity.
2. They are socially established.
3. They are carried out through human cooperation.
4. They involve technical skills which are exercised within evolving traditions of value and principles.
5. They are organized to achieve certain standards of excellence.
6. Certain internal goods are produced in the pursuit of excellence.
7. Engaging in the activity increases human power to achieve the standards of excellence and internal goods.
8. Engaging in the activity systematically extends human conceptions of its internal goods.

MacIntyre explains that the skillful throwing of a football is not a practice, but "the game of football is, and so is chess. Bricklaying is not a practice; architecture is. Planting turnips is not a practice; farming is. So are the enquiries of physics, chemistry and biology, and so is the work of the historian, and so are painting and music." He concludes that "the range of practices is wide," including "arts, sciences, games, politics in the Aristotelian sense" and "the making and sustaining of family life."

The concept of practice is more appealing and constructive than that of profession; it is a larger framework within which to develop a normative perspective for public administration. Profession, unfortunately, may connote self-protection and self-aggrandizement and produce images of paternalistic expertise which are not appropriate for public administration in a democratic society. In addition, practice provides a broader concept which permits escape from often petty and generally class-conscious debate over which occupations are properly understood as professions. Practice includes professions and many other human activities.

This notion of practices is particularly appropriate as a conceptual perspective for understanding ethical problems inherent in organizational hierarchies. It suggests that the work of public administration needs to be understood in terms that transcend employment in a particular public organization. Organizations are unequivocally the *setting* for administrative practice, but the practice must have norms of its own. That is the reason for adopting the ASPA code of ethics.

But more broadly, the eight characteristics of practices represent a normative framework that might be used profitably to guide reflection about the ethical development of the public administrative role. They suggest a working agenda and establish some tentative boundaries for inquiry. This concept calls attention to normative dimensions of public administrative activity which need greater clarity, particularly concerning the fourth, fifth, and sixth characteristics.

Internal Goods of a Practice

The concept of internal goods is essential to understanding the nature of practices. These are goods which can be realized only through participating in a particular practice or one very similar. For example, only through pursuing the practice of painting is one able to cultivate the finest sense of color, tone, texture, perspective, line, and proportion, as well as the skill to employ the relationships among these artistic elements in the pursuit of aesthetic excellence which can enrich the lives of others.

These goods which are internal to practices cannot be purchased, stolen, or acquired through persuasion. They must be gained by engaging in a practice and submitting to its standards of excellence until one is able to go beyond them. It is in the nature of internal goods that although they are produced out of competition to excel, "their achievement is a good for the whole community."[6] The ethical norms for a practice of public administration, therefore, must grow out of an understanding of its internal goods.

Can public administration be understood as a practice? As we consider the viability of conceiving of public administration in this way, *internal good* is clearly one of the central concepts upon which normative thinking needs to focus. Although the field has achieved neither precision nor clarity about its internal goods, public administration practitioners are aware of these in a general way. For example, administrators refer to such normative concepts as the public interest, popular sovereignty, accountability, social order, social justice, citizenship development, political equality, efficiency, and liberty as goods which they are attempting to achieve.

What appears to be needed is further discussion, debate, and concensus building about the meaning of these concepts and priorities among them. There is a need to consider *how* certain of these values should be understood as supportive of public administration practice and *how* they may subvert it. For example, the practice may require maintaining a certain balance between social order and social justice, while organizational goals may well favor social order for the sake of organizational stability, predictability, survival, and control. Without some considered consensus about these goods which are internal to the practice of public administration in a democratic society, public administration practitioners remain vulnerable to organizational definitions of what is good and at the mercy of arbitrary organizational authority.

Furthermore, no intelligible way exists to distinguish the work of *public* administration from that of *business* administration without identifying the internal goods which are the unique ends of each. Without clarity concerning the goods toward which the practice is directed, it is impossible to identify the virtues which public administration practitioners should be expected to embody.

External Goods of a Practice

External goods are those which can be achieved in many ways other than engaging in a particular practice. They are genuine goods in that they are necessary to some extent for the support of members of the practice, but they do not contribute directly to the development of a practice. Typical of these external goods, such as money, prestige, status, position, and power, is that they always become the property of some individual, and, furthermore, the more one person has in a fixed-sum situation, the less there is for others. Consequently, external goods are often objects of competition in which there are winners and losers. This is essentially different from the value accrued through the achievement of internal goods, where the value is shared by the community of practice and the larger community as well.

External goods may become the dominant concerns of either organizations or individual practitioners.[7] It is important at this juncture to remember that organizations should not be confused with practices but that they do coexist in an interdependent relationship. Practices typically require support by organizations, and organizations are, in turn, often dependent upon practices for their very reason for existence. However, considerable evidence shows that organizations do *tend* to corrupt the practices which they support as a result of their focus on external goods.[8] In the competitive struggle for the scarce resources necessary for survival, organizations "are involved in acquiring money and other material goods; they are structured in terms of power and status, and they distribute money, power and status as rewards." Organizations have goals oriented around achieving and maintaining these external goods; practices should not allow these to have priority over internal goods.

Practices should be primarily oriented toward their internal goods, the tradition which has evolved from the quest for those goods, and a relationship among those currently seeking such goods.[9] However, most practices are dependent upon organizations for resources and work settings. Consequently, the internal goods of a practice are at risk in an organizational environment dominated by the external goods inherent in organizational survival and growth. Thus, a precarious relationship exists. The practice of organizational management can support or corrupt the integrity of practices which function under their purview.[10]

Virtues and Practices

Finally, the concept of virtue is to be considered. Virtue, along with the internal goods of public administrative practice, is one of the two points upon which fundamental normative thinking most needs to be focused. Virtue has been an important word in ethical thought throughout most of Western philosophical history.[11] It is rooted in Aristotelian thought. However, when the language of moral philosophy in recent decades is considered, a substantial break is evident in the long and lively intellectual history of the concept of virtue.[12] Nevertheless, a revival of interest in virtue has occurred during the last 15 years.[13]

During this recent period the works of four scholars, in addition to MacIntyre, exemplify the revival of interest in virtue as a significant concept in moral philosophy: Stuart Hampshire, James

D. Wallace, R. E. Ewin, and William Frankena.[14] All five reflect a generally Aristotelian perspective, at least in some basic respects. For example, all understand virtues as inclinations or dispositions to act, not just to think or feel in a certain way. They are traits of character, more or less reliable tendencies to conduct oneself in a generally consistent fashion under similar conditions. Furthermore, virtues are not innate and, therefore, must be cultivated. In the work of all four scholars, virtues appear to involve cognitive activity. Virtuous conduct does not amount to merely conditioned reflex behavior; it is not just unthinking habitual response to stimuli, even though the term "habit" is sometimes used to characterize virtues, even by Aristotle. One might say that reason is employed in addressing particular situations, but with a certain preestablished attitude and a conditioned will.

MacIntyre contributes an additional dimension of meaning to the concept of virtue. He understands virtues as the character traits which make it possible for one to engage effectively in a practice by seeking to excel in achieving its internal goods while keeping the external goods of its organizational setting in a position of lesser importance. For example, if beneficence for the citizenry is one of the internal goods of public administration, benevolence on the part of public administrators is an essential virtue. If justice is also an important internal good for public administration practice, then fairmindedness is a necessary attribute for administrators.

Public administrators need to determine which human attributes are most likely to advance the internal goods which are defined as essential to the practice and protect them from organizational pressures, to the extent possible. For example, attributes associated with effective administration and management in the business world, such as competitiveness and profit orientation, may be unsuited to or less appropriate to the interests of a democratic political society. Similarly, virtues such as concern for efficiency which advance organizational goals may not create openness to popular sovereignty if given more than secondary importance. The virtues of the public administrator must be consistent with agreed-upon internal goods of the practice of public administration.

Hierarchy, Virtue, and Normative Ethics

Through the concept of practices, with their standards of excellence, internal goods, and virtues on the one hand, and the analysis of institutions, with their external goods on the other, it is now possible to explore more profoundly the specifically ethical problems of hierarchy and loyalty, as well as the larger question concerning an appropriate perspective for the development of normative ethics for public administration.

Maintaining the Internal Goods and Virtues of a Practice

The most visible ethical, as distinct from tactical, problem which subordinates confront in dealing with superiors can be defined as one of maintaining the internal goods and virtues of their practice in the face of demands for personal or organizational loyalty rooted in external goods. Similarly, executives face the difficulty of maintaining these in order to support the practice(s) under their organizational authority in spite of pressures to place the organization's needs for survival and growth first.

For example, in the first case presented at the beginning of this paper, the problem for the subordinate is to maintain the practice of law enforcement by upholding one of its internal goods—the just treatment of all violators of the law against driving while intoxicated. In all probability this will require a measure of courage on the part of the subordinate, one of the generic virtues of all practices, according to MacIntyre.[15] Indeed, extraordinary courage may be necessary since the commander's orders reflect a primary commitment, not to justice in the practice of law enforcement, but to the external goods of the organizational unit. Those he intends to exempt from the law are perceived as having the ability to provide resources and support for the unit. No doubt the commander's justification, if challenged by his subordinate, will be that he is looking at "the big picture" and acting in such a way that the police unit will be in a stronger position to carry out its mission. He may even convince the subordinate that this is the case; that he is acting ethically in terms of the larger organizational view.

However, it is clear that if the commander is successful in either persuading or forcing the subordinate to obey the order, the organization may be strengthened, but the practice of law enforcement will be weakened. No order which subverts the practice which the organization is established to support can be assumed to be a legitimate order, even in a strict chain of command such as a military unit. It may be legal and/or consistent with organizational politics, but it is illegitimate in terms of the internal goods of law enforcement practice. One must acknowledge, however, that in the "real world" of public administration circumstances may occur in which such an order may be deemed a necessary compromise between the purity of the practice and the survival of its organizational host. The essential point here is that the justification for each such compromise should receive serious and careful reflection. One instance must not become a precedent for future action.

With the second case the engineer and the design supervisor were apparently attempting to uphold safety, one of the paramount internal goods of engineering practice, and we might reasonably infer that the design supervisor was trying to maintain beneficence for the public which would seem to be one of the central internal goods of public administration practice. The internal goods of engineering and public administration then appear to be congruent in this situation. However, the project chief seems more committed to the economical and efficient completion of the project than to safety and the public good that it represents. Economy and efficiency are goods, to be sure, but in this case they appear to be more associated with the external goods of the organization than the fundamental goods of either public administration or engineering. At most they are secondary internal goods.

Reflecting on the conduct of the engineer and the design supervisor, it seems reasonable to view their acts as motivated by a commitment to the internal goods of their practices and supported by the virtues of courage, honesty, benevolence, and prudence. However, in the face of resistance from the project chief, the design supervisor appears to lack sufficient administrative courage to uphold the internal good of her own practice and that of her engineer subordinate. Both practices may be eroded as a result.

Of course, this case might have unfolded differently. The project chief might have reflected a commitment to public beneficence by engaging in ethical analysis of the situation through which he or she seriously weighed safety over against cost factors without simply dismissing the former for the sake of the latter. However, for the chief to have done so might have required rescheduling of the project and a request for budget augmentation. These actions might have made the project chief vulnerable to criticism from superiors and might have required a greater measure of courage and benevolence, both obvious candidates for a list of essential public administrative virtues.

The NASA Tragedy: A Recent Case in Point

A recent tragic example of the seriousness of this problem of preserving the internal goods of a practice was provided by the events leading to the explosion of the U.S. National Aeronautics and Space Administration (NASA) space shuttle on January 28, 1986.[16] It now appears that four vice presidents of Morton Thiokol overruled 12 of its own engineering experts in their strenuous objections to the safety of the launch. This fateful management decision was made, according to Seymour Melman, professor of engineering at Columbia University, using "criteria unique to management—having to do with profitability, security of contracts, *positions of the managers in the hierarchy . . . but not the strengths of materials or design*" (emphasis added).[17]

Morton Thiokol's decision to ignore engineering standards of excellence through the imposition of management authority seems clearly to have been a response to expectations generated by NASA. During the decade before the shuttle tragedy, NASA had begun to orient itself increasingly to pressures for short turnaround time and frequent and reliable launch schedules.[18] Safety, an internal good for manned spaced flight engineering, was sacrificed or at the very least devalued. Redundancy, a standard of excellence for achieving safety in this kind of engineering, was set aside. Prudence, one of the virtues of aerospace engineers involved in maintaining safety for human crew members, was rejected. The external goods of contract security, maintenance of schedules, profit, and marketability appear to have ruled the day.[19]

The most significant factor in the dominance of these external goods is alleged to have been the Reagan Administration's decision to "have as many commercial customers as possible use the shuttle to help defray the astronomical cost of operations."[20] On July 4, 1982, President Reagan stated that the first priority of the United States Space Transportation System is "to make the system fully operational and cost-effective in providing routine access to space."[21] George Will has recently noted this pressure for commercialization of the space program by the President in his promotion of the construction of a space station. Will laments President Reagan's promise that such a space station will produce "jobs, technologies and medical breakthroughs beyond anything we ever dreamed possible." He argues to the contrary that such "commercial bonanzas" from space research are not likely to justify their cost, but more importantly, that such expectations are inconsistent with the goals of science and tend to pervert it. In MacIntyre's terms, they are goods which are external to space research. In words which are remarkable for their clear focus on the internal goods of space science, Will asserts:

> The dignity of our species derives from the fact that we value knowing. We value it not merely for utilitarian reasons, but for its own sake. We will have a space program that is both reasonable and inspiriting only when we are sufficiently inspired by the noble quest to know.[22]

Beneath this most visible ethical problem of protecting the internal goods of a practice from displacement by the external goods of an organization lies a deeper generic problem. This is the prior problem of achieving and maintaining clarity among practitioners about the standards of excellence and internal goods of their practice, as well as the virtues they must cultivate to preserve the practice in institutional settings. Without this kind of clarity, external goods are more likely to prevail.

The Practice of Public Administration

To deal with the specific problem of subversion by public organizations of the practices they were created to support, it is first necessary to clarify the nature of that potential practice or set of practices known as public administration. An attempt is required, at least, to identify and understand its internal goods and virtues. That is the prior task which must be engaged before particular issues can be addressed adequately or general rules of conduct can be prescribed.

At the outset of this discussion, it is important to address the instrumental orientation of the field. Public administration is an instrumental practice, but only in a particular sense. Its reason for being is to create and sustain institutional and other frameworks within which other practices such as public health, planning, accounting, law enforcement, and education may flourish. The justification for supporting other practices is that they provide goods which a democratic citizenry has determined either directly, or through its representatives, to be in its collective interest. Therefore, public administration should not be understood as instrumental in the sense of the "classical paradigm" with its assumptions about the separation of politics from administration. The practice of public administration involves more than the simple subordination of the administrative role to that of the politician and the dominance of functional rationality as the only legitimate style of thought for the administrator. Rather, the role of the public administrator as a fiduciary for the citizenry gives rise to certain internal goods and virtues associated with carrying out the trust inherent in that role.

The table (on page 296) represents an outline of some of the plausible internal goods and virtues associated with three realms of obligation and virtue of government officials identified by Mark Moore.[23] For each of these realms, some of the kinds of internal goods and virtues which seem to be appropriate are indicated.[24] *This table is only illustrative and suggestive in nature; it is intended to be neither a definitive statement nor a decision-making tool.* However, it may help to suggest the kinds of norms, or more importantly at this point, the kind of *normative discussion* that may be needed for the full development of a practice of public administration.

*   *   *

TABLE
The Practice of Public Administration

Realms of Obligation and Virtue	Internal Goods	Virtues
1. Obligation to pursue the public interest	Beneficence for citizenry Justice	Benevolence Courage Rationality Fairmindedness Prudence
2. Obligation to authorizing processes and procedures	Popular sovereignty Accountability Due process	Respect for law Rationality Prudence Honesty Self-discipline Civility
3. Obligation to colleagues	Enhancement of standards of excellence Contribution to achievement of internal goods	Fairmindedness Trustworthiness Respect for colleagues Responsibility for the practices Civility Honesty Prudence Rationality Independence

Obligation to Pursue the Public Interest

For example, one may reasonably argue that beneficence is the central internal good related to the first of the three realms, the obligation to pursue the public interest. The most fundamental test of conduct and policy then would be the extent to which good is accomplished for the citizenry. Achieving good for the organization or the practitioners of public administration would have to be secondary considerations; no act could be deemed acceptable on the grounds that it strengthened the organization or furthered the interests of practitioners unless it first produced significant public good. Benevolence would be the essential virtue for the achievement of this internal good.

Justice would then seem to be the central internal good which follows from public beneficence. Justice defines the most essential political good; it is the fundamental ordering principle of democratic society from which such goods as political equality, representation of the citizenry, and citizenship development are derived. If that is the case, then fairmindedness,[25] rationality, prudence,[26] and courage are essential virtues for the practice of public administration. To achieve just decisions, rules, policies, and distribution of resources, it is essential that the inescapable exercise of discretion by administrators be guided by the inclination to search for and uphold what is fair or just.

However, this fairminded orientation to decisions and conduct needs to be buttressed by the propensity to deal rationally and prudently with problems, rather than simply determining what is fair according to the way one feels or what seems to be advantageous in the short term. And, of course, administrative courage is required if one is to resist the pressures and temptations to decide and act in response to goods which are external to this aspect of the practice of public administration, such as interest group offers of political support, threats of retribution, or organizational advantage.

Obligation to Authorizing Processes and Procedures

When considering the second realm—a public administrator's obligation to authorizing processes and procedures—popular sovereignty, accountability, and due process are critical internal goods around which a public administration practice should be formed. In that case one might reasonably argue that honesty, respect for law, prudence, self-discipline, and civility are essential administrative virtues. If law, including its constitutional foundation, is a reflection of public will, then we might agree that those who implement its provisions should cultivate and maintain respect for the letter and the intent of statutes, while being attentive to their constitutional authority. It may plausibly be maintained also that practitioners should develop their knowledge and appreciation of the role of law and the constitutional tradition in a self-governing society. This implies an avoidance of that cynical attitude which simply sees the law as an opportunity for administrative intervention, reinterpretation, and imposition of one's own views.

Taking the law and legal processes seriously as instruments of popular sovereignty appears to require rational analysis and honesty in seeking to understand the intent of the law where it is vague, ambiguous, or even self-contradictory. Prudent judgment is necessary in its execution. Furthermore, the ability to discipline one's own impulses, impatience, and preconceived convictions in order to serve the will of the people rather than one's own will would seem to be another requisite virtue. It may be argued that upholding popular sovereignty and accountability requires, whenever possible, in both the formation and implementation of public policy, effective provision for citizen participation. Civility, then, would predispose practitioners toward solicitation of open, serious, respectful, and rational exchange of views among the citizenry and between the citizenry and themselves.

Obligation to Colleagues

As concerns the third realm, the obligation of public administration practitioners to colleagues, the essential internal good appears to be the continual enhancement of the standards of excellence with which the practice is carried out. Practitioners have a right to expect their colleagues to strive to achieve clearer and more profound insight into the meaning of beneficence, justice, popular sovereignty, and accountability, as well as more effective ways of realizing those goods in public administrative practice. Both of these require the inclination to approach the practice in a responsible manner, bringing reason and honesty to bear to establish relevant factual material as well as the formation of normative judgments about the nature of the practice. Trustworthiness is an essential virtue for colleagues engaged in such tasks.

The sine qua non for the fulfillment of this obligation to colleagues would seem to be resistance to the dominance of external goods. The ability to keep the external goods of organizations in proper perspective calls for certain dispositions to act. Qualities of character such as independence, respect for colleagues, prudent judgment, and a sense of responsibility for the practice of public administration, as well as other practices which function within an organization, might be identified as crucial. One might also maintain that colleagues ought to be able to expect each other to exercise sufficient independence of mind to discern the difference between the internal goods of public administrative practice and the externally imposed goods of the organization in which they are employed. Practitioners should also be able to assume enough independence of conduct on the part of their colleagues to be assured that they will not give in to organizational demands which are subversive of the practice.

Furthermore, one might insist that colleagues should feel obligated to treat each other with civility, receiving each other's ideas in an open, rational, and fairminded manner. It may be logically argued that the members of a practice should assume that they are bound to respect each other's views about the development of the practice and the threat of external goods. Honest expression of differences is an expression of this respect. Similarly, it may be suggested that a sense of responsibility for the practice(s) commonly assumed and held in trust among colleagues is an essential character trait for establishing the ground of that bond. It is neither friendship nor propinquity that obligates colleagues to each other as practitioners, but their shared responsibility for preserving and enhancing the practice of public administration. This sense of responsibility for the practice should encourage the redefinition of situations in which the commitment of superiors to external goods threatens the internal goods of the practice of public administration. Resistance to illegitimate organizational demands is not necessarily just a conflict between one individual's personal conscience and the goals of the organization, as is often thought. Rather, it may well represent a threat to certain internal goods of the practice which the entire community of practitioners as colleagues are obligated to confront.

Conclusion

These comments suggest the texture of normative ethical reflection and discussion which flow from the perspective which is advocated here. The specific substantive proposals concerning internal goods and virtues are intended to be suggestive and provocative of a focus for normative deliberation, not as a final prescription. The development of such prescriptions is not the work of individuals but of colleagues devoted to a practice—or in *search* of a practice. For example, such a framework might provide a helpful orientation for deliberations about the *American Society for Public Administration Code of Ethics and Implementation Guidelines.*[27] It would encourage rooting an ethical code in a combination of experience and moral philosophy rather than relying too heavily on the politics of the committee process within ASPA.[28]

In its present form the ASPA code of ethics is a conglomeration of prescribed virtues and modes of conduct, with some mention of specific goods, most of which have value and relevance when taken individually. However, what is lacking is a coherent ethical identity for public administration. ASPA's code contains no clear and systematic statement of the internal goods from which the particulars are derived and around which practice ought to be formed. The framework discussed here, on the other hand, would ground prescriptions in some understanding of the underlying internal goods of public administration. On the other, it would focus attention on dispositions to act, on character traits which should be mutually cultivated, and qualities of people being recruited into the field.

The development of prescriptions without some understanding of the internal goods which are fundamental leaves public administrative ethics disconnected from the core of the practice; the promulgation of such prescriptions without a collegial commitment to the cultivation of the virtues which support those internal goods is likely to be an exercise in confusion, futility, and collective self-deception.

NOTES

1. Illustrative examples are: David Ewing, *Freedom Inside the Organization: Bringing Civil Liberties to the Workplace* (New York: E. P. Dutton, 1977); Stanley Milgram, *Obedience to Authority: An Experimental View* (New York: Harper & Row, 1974); Alberto G. Ramos, *The New Science of Organizations* (Toronto: Toronto University Press, 1981); William G. Scott and David K. Hart, *Organizational America* (Boston: Houghton Mifflin, 1979); William H. Whyte, *The Organization Man* (New York: Simon & Schuster, 1956).

2. John Rohr, *Ethics for Bureaucrats: An Essay on Law and Values* (New York: Marcel Dekker, 1978); Terry L. Cooper, *The Responsible Administrator: An Approach to Ethics for the Administrative Role,* 2nd ed. (New York: Associated Faculty Press, 1986).

3. Mark Lilla, "Ethos, 'Ethics,' and Public Service," *Public Interest,* vol. 63 (Spring 1981), pp. 3–17.

4. William K. Frankena, *Ethics* (Englewood Cliffs, NJ: Prentice-Hall, 1973).

5. Alasdair MacIntyre, *After Virtue,* 2nd ed. (Notre Dame, IN: Notre Dame University Press, 1984), pp. 181–225.

6. Ibid., pp. 188–190.

7. With respect to their attraction to external goods, MacIntyre's distinction between practices and organizations is too simplistic. See footnote eight.

8. This tendency is true also of organizations specifically established to support and develop practices such as professional associations. A practice may be corrupted by the external goods sought by its own professional association. Thus the practice may begin to orient itself more toward the pursuit of money, political power, social status, and protection from its clients than the whole-hearted development of the practice.

9. Ibid., pp. 193–194.

10. Ibid., pp. 194–196.

11. Philippa Foot, one of the leaders in regenerating philosophical treatment of virtue, argues in *Virtues and Vices and Other Essays in Moral Philosophy* (Berkeley: University of California Press, 1978) that in developing contemporary thinking on the subject it is best to go back to Aristotle. For Aristotle, moral virtues were understood as habits which constitute our "states of character" specifically concerned with choice. They are the inner, although not innate, dispositions which make it possible for people to resist the pleasures that divert conduct from the good ends of human existence and keep them from being intimidated by the pain which may be required for noble acts. They help people to maintain a "mean" in their conduct between extremes and excesses. Virtues drawn from the political community of which one is a member were seen by Aristotle as essential for the fulfillment of citizenship. Far from being irrelevant to the rough and tumble world of government, Aristotle indicated in *Nicomachean Ethics,* Book II, that the cultivation of these habits of conduct was considered one of the central responsibilities of legislators because without them democratic government would be impossible. According to Richard McKeon in *The Basic Works of Aristotle,* it seems clear that *Politics and Nicomachean Ethics* "treat a common field" (New York: Random House, 1941). Politics without attention to the cultivation of virtue was simply thought to reflect a defective understanding of the ends and purposes of political activity.

12. For examples of this tradition more directly related to American thought, see: Adam Smith, *The Theory of Moral Sentiments,* D. D. Raphael and A. L. Mackie, eds. (Oxford: Clarendon Press, 1976), pp. 216, 231; John R. Howe, *The Changing Political Thought of John Adams* (Princeton: Princeton University Press, 1966), pp. 30–32, 87–88.

13. Peter Geach, discussing the resurgence of interest in ethics of virtue in *The Virtues* (Cambridge: Cambridge University Press, 1977), observed that for some time philosophers had neglected virtue as a subject of serious interest and development, but he offered no insight into the reason for this lapse (Geach, 1977: 1). Foot attributed the neglect of the concept of virtue to the dominance of the analytic school of philosophy, but she indicated also that the situation had begun to change during the previous 10 to 15 years.

14. Stuart Hampshire, *Morality and Conflict* (Cambridge, MA: Harvard University Press, 1983); James D. Wallace, *Virtues and Vices* (Ithaca, NY: Cornell University Press, 1978); R. E. Ewin, *Cooperation and Human Values: A Study of Moral Reasoning* (New York: St. Martin's Press, 1981); William K. Frankena, *Ethics* (Englewood Cliffs, NJ: Prentice-Hall, 1973).

15. MacIntyre, pp. 191–192.

16. *Report of the Presidential Commission on the Space Shuttle Challenger Accident* (Washington, DC: U.S. Government Printing Office, 1986). See especially chapters V, VI, and VII.

17. William C. Rempel, "Shuttle Puts Spotlight on Engineers," *Los Angeles Times* (March 5, 1986), p. 1; J. Michael Kennedy, "Shuttle Veteran Charges Earlier Safety Lapses," *Los Angeles Times* (March 9, 1986), p. 1.

18. William D. Marbach with Mary Hager, John Barry, and William Burger, "1986: A Space Odyssey," *Newsweek* (March 24, 1986), p. 18.

19. Kathy Sawyer, "NASA Has Fewer People Minding the Store Now," *The Washington Post Weekly Edition* (May 19, 1986), p. 31.

20. William Marbach with Ron Moreau, Richard Sandza, and Daniel Pedersen, "No Cheers for NASA," *Newsweek* (March 24, 1986), p. 18.

21. *Report of the Presidential Commission,* pp. 164–165. See the remainder of chapter VIII for the details of these pressures on the space shuttle program. See also an institutional analysis of the problems of multiple expectations and competing accountability systems within NASA in Barbara S. Romzek and Melvin J. Dubnick, "Accountability in the Public Sector:

Lessons from the Challenger Tragedy," *Public Administration Review,* vol. 47 (May/June 1987).

22. George Will, "Who Will Lead the Noble Quest?" *Newsweek* (June 23, 1986), p. 84.

23. Mark H. Moore, "Realms of Obligation and Virtue," in Joel L. Fleishman, Lance Liebman, and Mark Moore, eds., *Public Duties: The Moral Obligations of Government Officials* (Cambridge, MA: Harvard University Press, 1981), pp. 3–31. I have modified Moore's teminology here from "obligation to friends and colleagues" to "obligation to colleagues." When we are identifying the norms of the practice of public administration, "friends" do not represent a legitimate obligation within that role. Rather they represent the obligations of a competing role.

24. The virtues listed here are not intended to be understood as strictly parallel to the internal goods listed in the previous column since some virtues are consistent with more than one internal good and some internal goods require the support of more than one virtue.

25. "Fairmindedness" is used to indicate the virtue which is directly supportive of achieving and maintaining justice although in the philosophical literature "justice" is typically used both for the principle and the virtue. I find this much too confusing.

26. Since "prudence" seems to have acquired negative connotations of preoccupation with self-interest in contemporary discourse, both popular and philosophical, it seems important at least to indicate that this is a relatively recent phenomenon. Through most of the Western philosophical tradition, prudence has been understood quite differently and regarded with greater esteem. For Aristotle, prudence (phronesis) was an essential human quality for moral conduct, as was true also in the thought of St. Thomas Aquinas as he appropriated and incorporated Aristotelian concepts into his Christian theology. In both of these cases prudence meant "practical wisdom," the ability to achieve good ends through the use of good means. Prudence was understood as the deliberative skills necessary to move from principle to specific action in a concrete situation. For treatments of prudence which are generally consistent with this older tradition, see Smith; Ewin; and Josef Pieper, *Prudence* (New York: Pantheon Books, 1959). For one recent view which takes a more negative view of the concept see Frankena. See also David K. Hart's argument for prudence as one of the essential virtues of public administrators in "The Virtuous Citizen, the Honorable Bureaucrat, and Public Administration," *Public Administration Review,* vol. 44, special issue (March 1984), pp. 116–117.

27. Both documents are obtainable from the American Society for Public Administration, 1120 G Street, NW, Suite 500, Washington, DC 20005.

28. See Ralph Chandler's treatment of this problem in "The Problem of Moral Reasoning in American Public Administration: The Case for a Code of Ethics," *Public Administration Review,* vol. 43 (January/February 1983), pp. 32–39.

Hard Choices:
Justifying Bureaucratic Decisions
Douglas T. Yates, Jr.

In "Hard Choices: Justifying Bureaucratic Decisions," Douglas T. Yates, Jr., introduces the idea that the role of the bureaucrat in American government has become preeminent in the public policy formulation process. He claims that American government has developed into a kind of "bureaucratic democracy," in which public administrators choose public policy values and make hard choices when values conflict. The problem with this process is that there is little attention paid to the justification of the bureaucrats' value choices. According to Yates, what is lacking is an open and clear expression from public administrators as to why certain values have been selected. Yates issues a call for a substantive discussion about values and what is involved in choosing them in our "bureaucratic democracy," in order that citizens may have the knowledge that they need to make more intelligent judgments about the governing process.

Questions of value and ethics hang over most public policy discussions like a cloud—or perhaps a thin vapor. We know the questions are critical and ubiquitous, but we typically have trouble setting our hands on them. In this essay, I wish to accomplish two things in considering value conflicts in public policy. The first is to bound the value problem so as to make the scope of discussion more manageable. The second is to suggest an analytical approach to value dilemmas that speaks to the value conflicts public officials face in their daily experience.

Before establishing my arbitrary boundaries and setting out my approach to value conflict, let me say a word or two more about the fundamental value problem as I see it. Unless we specify what kinds of officials, policies, and value problems we are interested in, we might include virtually every imaginable aspect of political life and behavior. The democratic process itself is a source of profound debate about values. So is any discussion of the role of representatives—be they Burkean or pluralist in their role definitions. So is any contemplation of individual interests or the public interest. So is any personalized account of morality—including canons of truth-telling, justifications of means (in relation to ends), and what is called, in old-fashioned terms, obligation and duty.

My strategy is to leave these tantalizing issues to others, in part because I have nothing fresh to say about them, in part, because other contributors to [*Public Duties*] seem to be grappling with these questions in a useful way. Rather, I want to pick out one corner of the map of officials, policies, and value conflicts that has been given much attention in an older literature but not recently. The area I have in mind concerns the role of appointive officials and bureaucrats as makers of public policy in a democratic society. I assume that they have some discretion both in designing the policy and in choosing the process by which the decision will be made. Moreover, I think significant values are at stake in both kinds of choices. I pick the value-choosing role of bureaucrats for three reasons: (1) it is commonly agreed that public policy is increasingly made by administrators, at the stages of both policy formulation and implementation; (2) emphasis on bureaucrats permits me to duck the debate about what constitutes proper representative behavior (when this depends on the choice of one or another broader democratic theory); and (3) in almost any democratic theory you choose, the choicemaking, "valuemaking" aspect of bureaucratic behavior is highly problematic. Whether policy and administration are separable or connected, it does seem odd in a democratic regime to give appointive officials a major role in value choices. It is not merely a matter of who guards the guardians—certainly a time-honored question—but more precisely, who regulates or controls the bureaucratic policy-makers' values and how. I believe bureaucrats also play a further *critical* role in the realm of values to the extent that they set and administer the process by which policy disputes are raised, argued out, heard, and disposed of in the decisionmaking process.

To avoid another long-standing empirical debate about the extent of bureaucratic independence and discretion (from statute or whatever), let me simply assert that bureaucrats are in the business of choosing and balancing values routinely—at least whenever they propose policy or interpret statutes. I can imagine someone replying that there are real constraints on the bureaucrat's ability to choose freely among different values. I cannot imagine anyone saying that the bureaucrat's role in value choice and balancing is a trivial feature of American government.

My first premise then, which is of particular interest and concern in a democracy, is that bureaucrats have a major role in making value choices and establishing processes by which competing values are dealt with in public decisions. Of course, if most public policy decisions turned out to contain only minor value trade-offs for the bureaucrat to worry about, my first premise might be correct but also quite uninteresting. In fact, in certain writings on bureaucracy and administration, the doctrine is advanced that decisions rest (or should rest) on criteria of efficiency and effectiveness (which criteria most reasonable people could agree upon and about which there is arguably only an interesting problem in terms of adequate measurement). Woodrow Wilson argued such a position and Robert McNamara may be understood, if slightly caricatured, to seek the same kind of value neutrality in dispassionate systems analysis, cost-benefit analysis, and the like. In this respect, it would be difficult to argue as a matter of principle that the government should receive less bang for the buck. As I will indicate [subsequently], I believe that there are some policy issues for which this kind of value neutrality, given the name of efficiency, probably obtains or is nearly approximated. But I believe that such policy issues are rare, a minority of public decisions.

Consider the current inventory of pressing public policy issues. These issues include affirmative action, busing, environmental protection, welfare reform, abortion, health insurance, energy policy, and energy "taxes," to name just a few. Now the heroic systems analyst might want to say that, analyzed carefully enough, these are really questions of benefit and cost and that different policies can be settled on efficiency or effectiveness grounds. However, on careful inspection, it turns out that this analytical heroism is at least incomplete and perhaps misguided. Taking any of the issues listed above, it seems plain that the public debate is, in the final analysis, concerned with the application of major public values, however understood, such as liberty, equality, justice, community. To take one example, busing can be construed as a strategy for increasing educational performance on average. But it is hard to avoid the conclusion that in a fundamental way, blacks are making equality claims and whites are making liberty claims (that is, freedom to maintain their neighborhoods); and the government may be seeking to alter existing notions of community.

So the first point is that the daily life of bureaucrats involves the identification and balancing of major public values. If these values were reasonably defined, it might be relatively easy for a bureaucrat to construct—implicitly or explicitly—a value impact analysis for a given policy and to specify relevant trade-offs.

Indeed, I think the first obligation of the appointive official or bureaucrat is to be *explicit* about the value premises and implications of public decisions. The reason for this goes back to the difference between legislators and bureaucrats mentioned above. We might exempt legislators from this value-accounting on the pluralist grounds that they are responding to constituent interests and that this response is considered a legitimate, indeed essential, way to justify value positions in a democratic society. Bureaucrats lack this justification of their policy decisions, and this is why their attention to providing a value analysis is of particular significance. If bureaucrats are going to make value choices, they should inform the rest of us value-laden voters and consumers of policies what the operative values behind public decisions are and how they conflict (when they do).

This value clarification is especially important where policy decision involves policy conflicts and trade-offs. It is there, most especially, that we citizens might want to know why the government is doing X rather than Y. (Obviously too, I believe that many interesting policy decisions will elicit and sustain a subtle analysis of value conflicts as they exist in different policy options.) Thus, if the first question of public policy is "What should government do?" any adequate answer should include a self-conscious assessment of the implications of policy for major public values such as liberty, equality, community, or the public interest.

This much may seem entirely unobjectionable. And we might suspect that given more time, bureaucrats could easily do value impact statements along with their myriad other analyses. In this halcyon world of philosopher-kings—Washington style—a new cover memo would emerge from officials which would comment on equality-efficiency trade-offs, liberty-equality trade-offs, and the like.

We might be happy to achieve this much if we believed the resulting discourse on values would offer clearer choices, illuminate policy dilemmas, and otherwise inform. Unhappily, we know all too well that the language of values is at present insufficiently precise to support impact statements that compare with those of economists, scientists, and other such experts.

I do not wish to delve into the substantive meaning of those timeless public values. I would offer instead a more modest approach to value clarification which will, I hope, add some additional criteria of assessment to debates about the ideas of liberty and equality themselves. . . .

. . . I believe the public official's fundamental moral obligation in a democracy is to pay increased attention to the definition and treatment of values the more these values are in conflict in a decision and the more difficulty there is in doing the accounting of who gets what. In the simple case where, for example, there is a clear and dominant equality principle at stake, and little problem in accounting, the public official may owe us as citizens no more than a terse statement of the justification for the public decision. But in more complex cases, where the value conflicts are great and the accounting problems are substantial, I believe public officials should provide a more thorough value analysis as one of the central justifications of public decision. Indeed, this is how I would define responsibility in bureaucratic decisionmaking. Without such an accounting, citizens can never know how and why their officials decided to act as they did. Without that knowledge, it is hard to see how the idea of democratic control of administration can be anything more than a dangerous fiction.

One public official who has made an attempt to perform explicit value analysis is former Secretary of Transportation William Coleman at the time of his decision on whether Concorde could land at Kennedy airport. In his written decision, Coleman performed a careful cost-benefit analysis that involved an explicit concern for legal, environmental, and political values. In short, Coleman sought to give the interested parties and the public a full accounting of his thought processes and of his own weighing of relevant values. As he wrote in his decision,

> This decision involves environmental, technological, and international considerations that are as complex as they are controversial, and do not lend themselves to easy or graceful evaluation, let alone comparison. I shall nonetheless attempt in some detail to explain my evaluation of the most significant issues—those raised in the EIS, by the proponents and opponents of the Concorde at the January 5 public hearing, and in the submissions to the docket—and the reasons I have decided

> as I have. For I firmly believe that public servants have the
> duty to express in writing their reasons for taking major ac-
> tions, so that the public can judge the fairness and objectivity
> of such action. Moreover, explaining our reasons in writing
> may help us avoid unreasonable actions. A decision that "can-
> not be explained" is very likely to be an árbitrary decision.[1]

The strength of Coleman's analysis is that his concern to spell
out value considerations both enabled citizens to better understand the Concorde problem and, equally important, gave the
citizen an opportunity to see what kind of person, with what kind
of concerns and values, was making decisions in the office of the
Secretary of Transportation.

Another fundamental reason the value-choosing role of bureaucrats is a critical aspect of policymaking in the American
democratic system is that we increasingly lack any clear or coherent justification (or set of justifications) for government intervention in our society. There have, of course, been such doctrines in
the past which at least appeared to be well understood if not
always perfectly clear. In a much simpler world, those who advocated the view that the "government which governs least governs
best" did at least have a decision rule that provided a guide to
action. When in doubt, don't intervene. Keep government out.
More recently, the New Deal faith in government as a potent
instrument for solving critical social and economic problems also
provided a kind of decision rule. The test was to identify "critical" problems and then explain why they deserved this definition.
Of course, given an enthusiastic and adventurous government,
the New Deal test for public intervention and action did not
provide a clear or particularly stringent decision rule.

The most rigorous criteria for justifying public intervention are
probably those of economic theory, but even here we have considerable difficulty sustaining any persuasive tests of appropriate
government intervention. Modern economic theory contemplates
a market mechanism that should be allowed to function unless
certain market failures or other special conditions arise. Concepts
of market failure, externalities, merit goods, and public goods are
offered as exceptions to a general rule that the market should be
allowed to operate "freely"—or at least within constraints imposed by antitrust policy, truthful advertising, and the like. Curi-

ously, however, the exceptions to the market "ideal" have, in my view as a noneconomist, become the exceptions that very often disprove the rule. Put another way, in a complicated, intertwined economy, with a large public sector to begin with, it is easy for an alert economist to find market failures, externalities, and public goods in many different places.

If we cannot find justification for public action in a firmly rooted public philosophy, like "the government which governs least," or an economic theory, in earlier incarnations, what restraints or normative principles exist at all to suggest that government should *not* act on a particular policy problem? My answer is that in our present governmental climate, there are almost no such restraints or systematic principles. This means that a kind of "open season" exists for government, and indeed we have by now become used to a familiar pattern: if government finds a new problem like drug addiction or energy conservation or environmental protection, it will create a bureaucracy and throw a new program at it.

If this analysis is anywhere near correct, it strongly reinforces my central argument that bureaucratic policymakers are often deciding when, why, and how to act and are making substantial value choices for specific policy arenas, and in addition, are implicitly fashioning new rationales and precedents for government intervention. If this is true, it only reinforces my argument that bureaucratic policymakers owe citizens in a democracy a careful accounting of the reasons why they have decided to act, what public purposes they are pursuing, and what values they have emphasized as against reasonable alternatives. In addition, this accounting should both bolster the legitimacy of governmental action in given choice situations and strengthen the citizen's ability to comprehend the general role of government.

Administrative Process Values

Traditionally, the debate about bureaucratic power has not led to demands that administrative policymakers should justify their actions publicly and in substantive terms. We have tended to focus instead on "administrative process" values and, as such, to demand that bureaucracies be accessible, accountable, participative, responsive, and responsible. In the course of observing these process values, public officials may have to give reasons or substantive justifications, but that is not the central purpose of these administrative values. They involve at root certain tests of appropriate government procedure, and the measure of the tests is whether government is open to citizen claims and complaints and provides processes for participation, hearings, review, appeal, and remedy where an administrative error has been found to exist. These procedural values are at the heart of administrative law, and indeed, if we believed that these values and procedures were sufficiently powerful, we might pay far less heed to the substantive value dilemmas I have referred to [previously]. More precisely, if we were confident that citizens possessed strong and well-established processes for discussing administrative issues and disputes, we might not be so interested in knowing *what* exactly citizens and bureaucrats are arguing about.

I am not satisfied that these administrative process values do the job and therefore provide substantial reassurance for those worried about democratic process in an increasingly bureaucratic state. My main worry is that there is considerable analytical confusion in our ordinary use of terms like accessibility, responsiveness, accountability, and participation. To take two examples: Does responsiveness mean being available to hear the complaints of a citizen or consumer, or does it mean recognizing those complaints and satisfying them? Does accountability mean simply that a government official can give a reason for an action or explanation of a policy, or does it mean giving reasons that are satisfactory to the citizen or consumer on the grounds that accountability entails substantive obligations on the part of the official and rights (if not authority) on the part of the citizen?

Or take participation. Does it mean that citizens are "heard," or heard and listened to, or heard, listened to, and, as a result, get their way? Put simply, does the test of successful participation lie in improved procedures for decisionmaking or improved decision results? Is it possible to have improved decision procedures without improved decision results? Further, who is to participate? How widespread must participation be? How many issues or decisions must be governed by participatory procedures for participation to be considered real? What of the nature of the participatory decisions? Is it enough that most minor decisions are participated in, or must citizen participation extend to some major issues, or to all major issues? Who decides what issues are minor or major?

We could, at the risk of considerable boredom, cut and slice into all of the administrative process values in the same way and show that, under careful examination, each apparently simple idea unpacks into a great many difficult questions and vaguely understood dimensions. Is responsiveness a procedural or a substantive notion? Is accountability? And so forth.

Aside from revealing considerable complexity, this exercise reveals two important general themes. First, for each administrative value, there is both a procedural and a substantive understanding. In the procedural sense, these administrative values entail greater communication and interaction between citizens and public officials. Thus, citizens would attend meetings and speak their minds: "participation." Government would establish new mechanisms so that the citizens could more easily approach officials: "accessibility." Government might establish new decentralized techniques that would bring officials closer to the problems that they must deal with: "responsiveness." Bureaucracies might make organizational changes designed to establish what bureaucrat is in charge of what program and who is to answer for breakdowns and failures: "accountability." The substantive construction of each value concerns the question of what kinds of decisions are made. The test of the value in this case is whether the recipients of the decision feel that the "right" decision was made. It is thus hard to avoid substance even when we are discussing process values.

Second, this analysis suggests that there is, in addition to the substantive and procedural distinction, a distinction between strong and weak constructions of the process values. The values are weak when they provide only mild forms of redress for citizens and strong when they go a long way toward changing the nature of proceedings or the resulting policy. Take, for example, the value of responsiveness. Let us look at how it may be defined in both substantive and procedural senses and in strong and weak senses in each case. In the procedural sense, responsiveness may be weakly defined to mean that bureaucrats will merely listen to an angry citizen who tries to press claims. In a stronger sense of procedural change, responsiveness may require that bureaucrats

ETHICS, HARD CHOICES, AND PUBLIC POLICY

restructure their method of administration so that they can more quickly act on citizen complaints. In the substantive sense, responsiveness may mean, weakly again, that public officials will listen to what a citizen has to say and try to find answers that reflect the content of the citizen's concerns. In the stronger substantive sense, however, public officials might be required to do precisely what the citizen wishes—to respond directly, decisively, and quickly to the complaint that is being made.

So we see that our administrative process values have both strong and weak, substantive and procedural meaning and that the mere mention of the values which everyone is for—responsiveness, participation, accountability—tells us very little about what precisely is being asked for and therefore what government should provide.

This kind of confusion and conflict is only the beginning, for these administrative values are completely empty until one specifies what individuals, interest groups, or other government agencies want an official to be responsive or accountable. There is no simple or logical way to settle this issue. A black neighborhood that supports busing may ask city bureaucrats to be responsive to its claim and so may a white ethnic neighborhood that opposes busing. The Chamber of Commerce, the state government, and the federal government may ask administrators to be responsible, to uphold their "duty" to support local economic interests, state policies, or court orders. Being responsive or accountable per se provides no decisive way of settling value conflicts or making the usual hard choices between competing political interests.

In addition, the different bureaucratic values—responsiveness, accountability, and so forth—are often in direct conflict with one another. The greater the number of people participating in a decision, the less any individual can be held accountable for that decision.

There are many other practical conflicts among administrative process values. Providing for participation and accessibility and accountability takes time and administrative energy. Participatory mechanisms involving citizens and public officials are notoriously time-consuming because they are designed to nurture extensive discussion and debate. But if this is so, the value of participation conflicts directly with the value of responsiveness, which often requires or means that the government should act quickly without extreme deliberation. In addition, the point of participation, accessibility, and responsiveness is often to get particular exceptions or adjustments made for particular individuals or groups. But these exceptions will often conflict with the values of responsibility and accountability, which require that officials follow rules and laws and be able to give simple, clear, and therefore presumably general reasons for their decisions. Accounting for why X number of exceptions were made to a policy in the interests of responsiveness may not be impossible, but it is surely difficult to do if one is concerned to create an appearance of general, clear accountability.

So far I fear my analysis of "hard choices" has created more than its fair share of burdens and dilemmas for public officials. The first argument, that substantive value conflicts are both highly significant and pervasive, leads me to ask for a detailed account of a bureaucrat's value-accounting. The second part of my analysis, the examination of administrative process values, adds to the basic difficulty for bureaucratic officials by suggesting that these values are not a sufficient answer to the request for value-accounting and are themselves subject to very different interpretations and indeed may be in fundamental conflict with one another.

Having attempted to lay bare the critical role of the bureaucrat in value-choosing, I do not wish to wind up designing an impossible task for a public official or even one of Plato's guardians. Public officials cannot analyze the value dimensions and implications of every policy decision they face. Indeed, public officials not only face a variety of important new policy issues, but also administer hundreds of programs whose history may be traced back twenty, thirty, or forty years.

So which policies and problems should bureaucrats focus on if they accept the general moral obligation to exercise and illuminate significant value conflicts? One helpful answer to this question is provided by C. E. Lindblom in his development of the concept of incrementalism.[2] If Lindblom is right, there are many policy decisions that have evolved over a long period of time and are characterized by at least two important features of decision-making. First, in the course of a long evolution, such policies have been bargained over and adjusted so as to take into account a wide variety of different values and preferences. In institutions

ETHICS, HARD CHOICES, AND PUBLIC POLICY

these are policies on which the president, Congress, the bureaucracies, and interest groups have been instructing and reviewing, appropriating and authorizing, administering and revising, to a greater or lesser degree. Under these conditions we can reasonably expect that the value issues contained in a policy have been wrestled over by many political actors and for a long period of time. Any attempt to seek fresh value clarification in such policy arenas would seem to me to discount the real virtures of incrementalism and the democratic processes it contains and reflects. The second feature of this kind of long-evolving policy is that ends and means, values and policies often become greatly intertwined and hard to separate.[3] Indeed, it may be a heroic feat to sort out the discrete value trade-offs from the substantive policy adjuncts, and it may well be wise not to try.

Another way to answer the initial question is to attempt to distinguish different kinds of policy problems—be they very old or new—and then decide which kinds are most significant and suitable for value analysis.

At one end of the spectrum of public policy issues are those that involve highly technical or scientific issues. On matters concerning the Food and Drug Administration, the National Science Foundation, the National Institutes of Health, and to a lesser extent, the Atomic Energy Commission and weapons procurement in the Defense Department, the average person in a democracy is unlikely to be informed and enlightened in his or her value- and choicemaking role as a citizen by lengthy public argument about technical issues. Here the administrative process value of accountability may do the required work if in fact government officials explain (account for) their decisions to scientific peers and open the decisionmaking record to specialists interested in their highly sophisticated issues.

At the other end of the spectrum of public policy issues are those that involve fairly simple distributions to specified populations. Here one thinks of the great range of entitlements programs—allocations for food stamps, [M]edicaid, welfare, veterans' programs, compensatory education programs, and programs for the elderly or the handicapped. In these cases, where X person with Y characteristic is said to have entitlement to a government benefit, one or another administrative process value may well suffice to insure that a bureaucracy is meeting its statutory and normative obligations. I refer to the process values of accessibility and responsiveness; and we should notice in this regard that congressional staffers spend a great deal of their time seeking to insure in precisely this way that administrative officials are responsive to constituents whom they believe to be eligible for a particular program.

Of course, there is a great deal of space on the policy continuum between highly technical issues, where accountability may seem to be the appropriate government response, and highly distributive programs, often involving entitlements, where accessibility and responsiveness to individual claims may seem to fulfill the moral obligation of public officials to their clients. I cannot precisely define all the possible issues that occupy this middle ground and would not want to spend the time required to do so. Rather, I would argue that for issues that are not highly technical or distributive, the test of whether they deserve a careful value analysis depends on whether they (a) cut close to certain main public values and (b) have substantial policy implications. The test is of the depth of value conflict and the scope of policy impact. Applying this simple test, certain "new" policies clearly warrant careful attention: for example, busing, health insurance, abortion, affirmative action, environmental protection, open housing, and school financing. These are "potent" issues for value analysis, in my view, because one only needs to mention words like liberty, equality, community, and property rights to see immediately that these issues contain a great deal of value content. . . .

Toward a New Public Philosophy

In sum, I believe that our government is increasingly a "bureaucratic democracy"—in which policy decisions are increasingly located within bureaucratic settings, and bureaucrats, at the stages of both policy formulation and implementation, play a highly significant role in decisionmaking and value-choosing. If this is so, we cannot have a viable discourse about our public philosophy if bureaucrats do not express and clarify major policy choices. One other Lindblom argument cuts deeply on this point. In a recent writing, he expresses the fear that there may be a trouble-

316
ETHICS, HARD CHOICES, AND PUBLIC POLICY

some circularity in our democratic process if public (and private) leaders are the major source of guidance to others who then feed back preferences to government based importantly on this guidance.[4] This is a perfectly fair claim, but it seems to me that citizens are in a worse position as democratic actors if bureaucratic officials do not articulate and clarify policy choices at all or hardly at all. Being subject to influence, guidance, or even indoctrination by public officials is one kind of danger for us. Being oblivious to the character and consequences of policy decision strikes me as potentially even more insidious. For while the possibility certainly exists with the first danger that our preferences will be engineered, there is also the possibility that we, as citizens, will retain some perspective or critical distance in appraising what government tells us we want. But where we do not even know what the debate is about because we cannot see into government and government is not "talking," the possibility of healthy skepticism or even independent judgment is greatly diminished.

Thus, I believe that the best hope for creating a more lively and cogent public philosophy is for bureaucratic policymakers to take the lead in opening up the debate. I do not know what substantive public philosophy is likely to emerge as a result, but I do believe an opening up of bureaucratic thinking and value-choosing is a procedural precondition of useful substantive argument—whatever its form or consequence.

NOTES

1. Department of Transportation, the Secretary's Decision on Concorde Supersonic Transport, Washington, DC, February 4, 1976, p. 7.
2. For a further elaboration and analysis see C. E. Lindblom, *The Intelligence of Democracy* (New York: The Free Press, 1965), and Lindblom, "The Science of Muddling Through," *Public Administration Review,* 19 (Spring 1959).
3. C. E. Lindblom, "Strategies for Decision Making," *University of Illinois Bulletin* (1971), p. 13.
4. C. E. Lindblom, *Politics and Markets* (New York: Basic Books, 1977), chap. 15.

Why Policy Analysis and Ethics Are Incompatible
Douglas J. Amy

According to many public policy analysts, ethics really has no role to play in the policy formulation process. Douglas J. Amy's article, "Why Policy Analysis and Ethics Are Incompatible," examines this position. Within it are the claims that ethical analysis is impossible, impractical, unnecessary, or that it is not even an analytic technique. Amy examines each of these points, finds their flaws, and makes appropriate recommendations. For him, ethics is excluded in public policy formulation for reasons that have nothing to do with ethical analysis but with the fact that policy analysts, administrators, legislators, and bureaucrats are threatened by the challenges of moral evaluation. Ethics and policy analysis *are* closely compatible, but due to the "politics of ethics," Amy says, the two have been held strictly apart.

An increasing number of scholars and practitioners of policy analysis have argued that ethics—the systematic investigation of the normative dimensions of policy issues—should have an important place in the practice of policy evaluation.[1] One commentator has called for the adoption of a "value critical" approach to analysis in which "values themselves become the object of analysis."[2] Similarly, another observer has argued that "the missing ingredient in current policy analysis" is the ability to address moral questions directly.[3]

Compelling arguments have been offered for the integration of ethics into policy analysis. One of the most persuasive is the simple fact that normative issues lie at the very heart of policy decisions; "social policy is, above all, concerned with choice among competing values."[4] Thus, a policy analysis that avoids examining the inevitable clashes between such values as equality,

Douglas J. Amy, "Why Policy Analysis and Ethics Are Incompatible," *Journal of Policy Analysis and Management*, vol. 3, no. 4 (1984), pp. 573–591. Copyright © 1984 by the Association for Public Policy Analysis and Management. Reprinted by permission of John Wiley & Sons, Inc.

efficiency, justice, property, and freedom runs the risk of being largely irrelevant to contemporary policy choices. Furthermore, as one writer has observed, an explicit examination of normative issues is particularly necessary in our current society, one "which is, for a variety of reasons, no longer confident about the priorities among its values, and which is becoming increasingly aware of the inherent difficulty of choosing among values in conflict."[5]

In addition, ethicists are fond of pointing out that policy analysis already *is* a normative activity—that any analysis which seeks to recommend a "good" policy or the "best" policy necessarily involves moral and ethical judgments. The attempt to engage in "value-free" analysis cannot eliminate the normative dimensions but can only obscure them. The result is that normative assumptions are surreptitiously and arbitrarily introduced into studies (imbedded in the definition of the problem being studied, in the models used in the analysis, in the choice of alternatives to be investigated, etc.) and are beyond the range of public scrutiny.[6] Wouldn't it be more useful and desirable if the normative assumptions underlying policy decisions were made explicit and subjected to critical analysis?

But the fact is that most practicing policy analysts still largely ignore ethics despite the strong arguments for their inclusion in policy analysis and despite the availability of methods for including normative evaluations in policy studies.[7] Furthermore, there is little indication that analysts are moving in the direction of more systematic analysis of ethical issues in their policy reports. To be sure, one often finds in reports a reference to some of the ethical implications of a policy proposal—such as its equity impact. But such issues are typically only mentioned in passing and are not the subject of any kind of rigorous analysis. The only form of ethical analysis routinely used by analysts is utilitarianism, in the form of cost-benefit analysis; and, as many critics have pointed out, this can be a limited and even misleading form of ethical thinking.[8] Rarely are other ethical perspectives or the work of leading ethical thinkers invoked. And in those few cases which do include systematic ethical debate—such as the work done on biomedical policy issues—the discussions have been initiated almost exclusively by ethicists, not policy analysts.[9]

This neglect of ethical analysis extends to graduate schools, where the atmosphere of scholarly investigation would seem most conducive to the inclusion of moral concerns. Even in graduate programs where faculty claim to be sensitive to the ethical dimensions of policy issues, relatively little classroom time is spent on them. Courses in Ethics and Public Policy tend to focus on only the most narrow definition of ethical problems—the personal dilemmas of the individual analyst or policymaker, such as conflict of interest or whistle-blowing. Rarely do such courses address the more common and substantive normative issues in policy choices—controversies involving issues of justice, morality, equality, and so on.[10]

But why do analysts shun ethical debate? There are a number of possible explanations. Common arguments maintain that normative analysis is either unnecessary, impossible, impractical, or undesirable. These rationalizations do not seem persuasive or sufficient. Yet their general acceptance among policy analysts requires that they be examined with some care.

Probably the most common argument used to exclude ethics from policy analysis is the contention that moral and value judgments are completely subjective and therefore not amenable to rational analysis.[11] This position—known generally as value relativism—is rooted in positivism, the philosophical approach that continues to dominate policy analysis and other areas of social science. The assumption is that social scientists must draw a sharp distinction between facts and values, and since facts alone can be evaluated empirically, they are the only fit subject for scientific investigation. Thus, the argument continues, while policy analysts can legitimately analyze factual questions, such as the probable impact of a certain policy, values questions concerning whether a policy is good or just or equitable are beyond the bounds of rational analysis.[12]

Ironically, while policy analysts continue to cling to value relativism, most moral philosophers abandoned it over 30 years ago. They now widely agree that moral and value claims can be subject to some degree of rational analysis.[13] The arguments supporting this claim are, of course, lengthy and complex, and this is not the place to recapitulate them in their entirety. It is useful, however, to sketch out the main contours of the argument.

The main point made by moral philosophers is that moral and value judgments are more than mere preferences. Preferences do not require reasons or justifications, but moral stands do.[14] A preference for strawberry ice cream doesn't require justification. But when someone makes a moral claim—that capital punishment is good, for example—one expects such a position to be supported by reasons. Indeed, as one philosopher and political theorist has pointed out, if someone asserts that capital punishment is good but claims to have absolutely no rationale for this view, others will probably assume the individual is not serious or is very neurotic.[15] In other words, in everyday life it is normally expected that moral and value judgments are decisions based on reasons and rational justification. And these reasons and justifications form the basis for the rational analysis of ethical positions. It is believed that arguments proffered for a particular position can be evaluated. In fact, one main school of rational moral analysis is called the "good reasons" school, and is based on the assertion that we can distinguish between good and bad reasons for adopting a moral position.[16]

It is important to note that while moral philosophers argue that we can inject *some* rationality into the consideration of moral questions, they are not claiming that moral positions can be established empirically, as in scientific proofs. Rather they maintain that moral discourse has its own unique kind of rationality and its own style of validation—that moral justifications should be evaluated, not as true or false, but as powerful or weak, convincing or unpersuasive. Frank Fischer makes this important distinction in his book *Politics, Values, and Public Policy,* when he points out that "science refers to the 'proof' of the law of gravity but political philosophy refers not to Mill's 'proof' of liberty but rather to his 'magnificent defense' of it."[17] In its essence, then, rational ethical analysis consists of evaluating the adequacy of the arguments offered up in defense of a moral position.

What would this rational ethical analysis look like in practice? Let us consider as a brief example the distribution of health care. Gene Outka, a leading ethicist, has observed that there are a number of competing notions of social justice that could be invoked to justify various policy approaches to distributing health care.[18] For example, one notion of justice that could be invoked is "To each according to his merit or desert." This is a common conception of justice and one that is quite persuasive and powerful when used to justify the distribution of grades on exams or the distribution of salaries in a company. But as Outka argues, the argument is ill-suited to the area of health care. Illnesses often have little to do with merit because "they occur so often for reasons beyond our control or power to predict. They freqently fall without discrimination on the just and unjust, i.e., the virtuous and the wicked, the industrious and the slothful alike. . . . [Thus] it seems unfair as well as unkind to discriminate among those who suffer health care crises on the basis of their personal deserts."[19]

After analyzing a number of theories of justice, Outka finally concludes that the strongest and most appropriate notion of justice that should govern the distribution of health care is "To each according to his need." He maintains that ill health is the most proper and most fair basis for the distribution of care, and he marshals arguments and evidence to support his position. This ethical judgment leads him in turn to favor certain health care policies over others.

This example is a simple one, but it demonstrates the main contention of many moral philosophers, that one can in fact begin to establish which moral arguments are most appropriate and powerful in justifying a certain ethical position. In other words, rational ethical analysis is possible. Moreover, several policy analysts have already devised methods for integrating rational ethical analysis into policy studies.[20] Thus, policy analysts can no longer rely on the tenets of positivism or value relativism to justify the neglect of normative issues.

Another common argument against the inclusion of ethics in policy analysis is the assertion that moral inquiry is simply unnecessary. This argument comes in two versions—one weak and the other stronger. The weak version assumes that analysts needn't be concerned with ethics because "in a democratic society value differences are resolved by the political process."[21] Value decisions, in this view, are best left up to policymakers, and need not or should not be the subject of policy analysis. Such a position is accurate in the sense that all policy questions are eventually resolved politically, but it disregards the fact that ethical analysis can help make those decisions better ones. Analysis of ethical questions is not intended to take the place of the political process, but to improve it. The whole purpose of engaging in ethical analysis is to enhance the level of ethical argument and the quality of ethical decisions that take place in the policymaking process. Technically speaking, ethical analysis is not necessary in a democratic society, but then neither is policy analysis in general. The point, however, is that both can certainly be useful additions to the policymaking process.

A stronger version of the argument that ethics is unnecessary centers around the assertion that the profession already has an adequate technique for evaluating normative questions—cost-benefit analysis. Proponents consider the technique sufficient for most policymaking purposes.[22] However, as many critics have pointed out, cost-benefit analysis is not only fraught with a number of methodological problems,[23] it is also severely limited in its scope of evaluation. Cost-benefit analysis only seeks to maximize one value—efficiency—but frequently other values compete and conflict with efficiency in policy decisions. Even economists, the main champions of cost-benefit analysis, will admit that at least one other value, equity, ought to be considered in policy choices.[24] In fact, however, there are a number of other ethical concerns besides equity—such as justice, liberty, democracy, the environment—that also merit consideration in policy decisions.

The main problem is that cost-benefit analysis is not equipped to handle the multiplicity of value concerns that are inevitably present in policy choices. And the attempt to reduce all ethical concerns to cost-benefit terms is likely to be futile and even misleading. Many of the ethical problems faced by policymakers "can undoubtedly be translated into the language of [cost-benefit] analysis, but it seems . . . that the translation will more likely obscure than clarify the important moral dimensions of the choices decisionmakers face. Nor does this perspective provide any independent basis for critical thinking about the principle of efficiency itself, or about the adequacy of the social decision process."[25] Thus, if ethical analysis is to be done correctly, it must be more comprehensive and more complete. And analysts who wish to do justice to the investigation of the normative dimensions of policy decisions must be trained, not only in cost-benefit analysis, but also in the full range of ethical traditions and analytic techniques. They must, for example, not only acknowledge that equity issues are important, but also take the next step and become familiar with various theories of equity and distributive justice that can be applied to policy decisions.

*   *   *

Some analysts may avoid normative analysis because they fear injecting their own biases into the inquiry.[26] Concern about the influence of one's own moral views is, of course, legitimate and undoubtedly accounts for the emphasis on "value-free" analysis. There are, however, two possible responses to this rationale for avoiding ethics. First, it is a mistake for analysts to confuse preventing personal values from entering the analysis on the one hand, and preventing the *subject* of values from entering into the analysis on the other.[27] Many ethicists believe that it is clearly possible to investigate the subject of ethics while at the same time maintaining one's objectivity.[28] Indeed, one of the imperatives of ethical analysis is to critically examine all sides of an ethical debate—both the arguments and counterarguments involved—before drawing any conclusions. It is thought that this process of balanced and systematic analysis of ethical issues helps to ensure that the ethical recommendations of the analyst are not a mere product of his or her particular biases, but the result of rational and objective analysis that can be justified to others.

But even if one rejects the feasibility of achieving "objectivity" in normative matters, there is still another strong argument for engaging in ethical analysis. This argument suggests that an explicitly normative approach to policy analysis is in fact the best protection against the possibility of the analyst's personal values creeping undetected into policy deliberations. In a value-critical approach all of the normative considerations are out in the open for everyone to see. Normative arguments and assumptions are labeled as such—and thus policymakers are alerted to their presence. In contrast, the normative decisions present in so-called "value-free" analysis tend to be hidden deep in the assumptions of the analysis—for example, in the choice of the options chosen to be analyzed—and in that form they are more likely to enter unnoticed into the policy debate. Thus, if it is true, as ethicists have argued, that all phases of policy research inevitably involve a number of normative assumptions, then it would be better to make these premises explicit and subject them to analysis, rather than pretend that they are not there.[29]

It makes little sense, then, for analysts to avoid ethics out of a fear of injecting their own biases into policy studies. Indeed, the more that analysts engage in normative analysis, the more they will become sensitive to the ethical dimensions of their work, and this itself may be one of the best safeguards against the unintended introduction of their own normative biases into policy considerations.

A final objection to the inclusion of ethical investigations in policy analysis is the contention that while inclusion may be possible and desirable, it is simply too impractical. One form of this argument maintains that ethical analysis is too abstract and philosophical to provide practical guidance for specific policy choices. And anyone familiar with modern moral philosophy would sympathize with this assertion. Indeed, ethicists have generally concentrated on conceptual and methodological questions, rather than on the concrete applications of moral arguments. Even proponents of ethics admit that ethical thought often tends to focus on hypothetical cases, rather than on the moral situations faced by policymakers in their daily experience.[30]

Yet during the last decade, moral philosophers have turned increasingly to the practical, real-life implications of their work.[31] And in those instances in which ethical thought has been systematically applied to specific policy issues, the results have been promising. Undoubtedly the best example of this is the case of biomedical ethics, where the work of ethicists has influenced policymaking directly. Much of the work in this area has been sponsored by the Hastings Center, a leading institution in the application of ethics to medicine, health policy, and public policy. In the 1970s, researchers there initiated a project focusing on the difficult question of how to define death. They began by looking at the broader philosophical dimensions of this problem, but eventually concentrated on fashioning a specific legal definition utilizing the notion of "brain death." Their work was eventually used in its entirety by the Michigan state legislature, and forms the basis for the definition of death in 20 other states. As one commentator observed, "the 'impractical' theorizing of the ethicists had enormous practical impact."[32] Of course, not all ethical analyses would be this influential in shaping public policy; but the point is that ethical analysis can certainly have a direct bearing on common policy decisions.

In addition, ethical analysis is sometimes considered impractical because of the time required to complete a thorough inquiry. It is suggested that analysts rarely have time to complete an adequate cost-benefit analysis, let alone embark on an analysis which incorporates other forms of ethical evaluation. For example, in a recent review of a book on ethics and policy evaluation, one scholar complained that if policy analysts tried to address all the normative dimensions of policy issues, "that analysis would land on the decisionmaker's desk far too late to be of any use in all but the least complex policy decisions."[33]

Again, one can easily sympathize with this concern. While ethicists at the Hastings Center had several years to develop a new legal definition of death, an analyst working in a government bureaucracy might have to produce an ethical analysis in a matter of days. Undoubtedly, it would be difficult for practicing analysts to provide fully complete an intellectually rigorous ethical analysis in so short a time. But even if analysis cannot be accomplished under ideal conditions, the process need not be excluded from policy studies. Analysts have always had to cope with time and resource constraints that prevent them from doing the kind of complete analyses they would prefer.[34] For example, they rarely are able to model all the possible results of all the various policy options. Yet time pressures do not prompt the analyst to abandon modeling or other complex analytic techniques; instead shortcuts are devised to complete the analysis. One would expect the investigator of ethical questions to develop similar kinds of shortcuts.

In brief, there is little reason to believe that ethical analysis is inherently more complex or impractical than other techniques used by policy analysts. Therefore, suggestions that it be excluded on these grounds are ultimately unjustifiable.

Obviously many of the common arguments against the inclusion of ethics in policy analysis are quite weak. Why then do these contentions persist when they are largely unsupported? And more importantly, what are the real reasons why ethics is neglected in policy analysis? To answer these questions, one must consider the politics of ethics—in particular, how ethical analysis poses a threat to the professional interests of both policy analysts and policymakers. While ethical analysis may be intellectually sound, it is an endeavor that conflicts with the practical politics of the institutions that engage in policy analysis.

*   *   *

Let us first consider the professional and political problems that ethical analysis poses to analysts. To begin with, the pursuit of ethical analysis can easily undermine the all-important relationship that exists between client and analyst. Most analysts work for clients who have a strong commitment to a set of goals or programs and who would not be pleased by a report that raised questions about the basic desirability or worth of those programs. And yet there is a tendency in ethical analysis to raise just those kinds of annoying questions.

The potential difficulties for analysts are most obvious in the bureaucratic setting in which much of public policy analysis takes place. Bureaucratics are inherently and strongly hierarchical institutions which put an emphasis on consensus and following orders.[35] They are not debating societies, and they are not designed to encourage frank discussion and dissent. Given these institutional realities, there is little incentive for analysts to raise basic ethical questions. In fact, as one researcher discovered, analysts who try to raise serious questions about basic agency policy are very quickly perceived as threats to their superiors. "[T]he bureaucratic situation encourages analytical work within the consensus of ongoing programs and approved policies. Therefore, the policy analyst who departs from the bureaucratic consensus is bound to run the risk of being attacked, discredited, ignored, or even fired."[36] The seriousness of the risks involved in violating bureaucratic consensus is amply illustrated by the fate of whistle-blowers, who have frequently been harassed, investigated, demoted, transferred, and pressured to quit. Analysts pressing for ethical investigations and debates may not be as threatening as whistle-blowers who expose corruption and waste in federal agencies, but both are exposed to the same pressure to avoid asking potentially embarrassing questions. As one recent whistle-blower complained, most analysts are "conditioned" not to buck the system. "It's not blatant. It's just a steady environment of not making waves."[37] It is not surprising, then, that most policy analysts prefer to play it safe and simply accept their client's normative perspective as given.[38]

To be clear, the problem here is not that clients of analysis are amoral or wish to ignore values entirely. This is obviously not the case. Many administrators, for instance, have a strong commitment to the values embodied in their programs. But this very commitment makes them wary of ethical analysis. Since ethical analysis necessarily involves the examination of clashing norma-tive perspectives, it almost inevitably raises arguments critical of reigning policy and threatens the smooth pursuit of the dominant values of the organization, whatever they may be.[39] Thus, a serious investigation of organizational values and priorities would not have been welcome either in the proenvironmental Interior Department under Carter or in the prodevelopmental Interior Department under Reagan. There is nothing particularly new in this observation—political scientists like Charles Lindblom estab-lished several decades ago that bureaucrats have little inclination to seriously reconsider basic policy orientations.[40]

Beyond the analyst-client tensions that ethical analysis can engender, normative investigations may also tend to undermine the foundations of policy analysis as a profession. All professions cultivate a certain image that serves to promote and legitimize the work of its practitioners. In the case of policy analysis, this professional image is of analysts as purely technical advisors whose work is value free and apolitical. This image is deeply rooted in the history of the profession. When policy analysts were first gaining influence in the federal government in the early 1960s, it was fashionable to believe that policy questions no longer revolved around "passionate" ideological issues, but were primarily technical in nature.[41] In President Kennedy's words, "The fact of the matter is that most of the problems, or at least many of them that we now face, are technical problems, are administrative problems."[42] The profession of policy analysis rode into government on this wave of technocratic optimism.

Positivism provided the intellectual underpinnings for the technocratic role of the analyst in government.[43] Trained in posi-tivist social science, analysts could draw a sharp distinction be-tween normative questions and factual questions. In practice, this meant that analysts could focus on questions of means, while leaving questions of ends to policymakers. It was thought that politicians would set social goals, and analysts would give them technical advice on how these goals could best be achieved.[44] This view helped to legitimize the role of the analyst in the political system. Thus, while analysts were unelected, their par-ticipation in policymaking was politically acceptable because they were never involved in setting policy goals. As scholars of policy analysis have noted, positivism, with its fact-value dichotomy, played an important role in justifying and furthering the profession of policy analysis.

A broadly positivistic conception of the nature of social science dovetailed quite nicely with the notion of policy-making as technical problem solving and with the normatively passive role of the [policy analyst] *vis-à-vis* the policymaker. Indeed, on this conception, social scientists could hardly play any role but this if their activities were to be intellectually honest and politically legitimate. . . . Thus, the belief that policy questions were technical questions and the positivist belief that the social sciences could provide expert factual and instrumental knowledge needed for the solution of these problems converged to create a powerful intellectual rationale for the rapid rise of [policy analysis].[45]

Given the professional importance of positivism to policy analysts, it should not be surprising that they have not rushed to embrace ethics. Ethical analysis would require abandoning many of the central tenets of positivism; and this in turn would undermine the carefully tended technocratic image of the analyst and the comfortable role that the profession has carved out for itself in the policymaking system. An intimate connection exists between the intellectual distinctions made in positivism (the fact-value dichotomy, the means-ends dichotomy) and the important distinctions made between the professional roles of analysts and policymakers. As ethics begins to blur the intellectual distinctions, it also begins to blur the professional distinctions. This can only make everyone uncomfortable. It is for this reason that analysts continue to cling to questionable positivist notions like value relativism. The positivist approach to values may be intellectually weak, but nevertheless it provides a number of professional advantages.

The fact that ethics is antitechnocratic not only helps to explain the reluctance of analysts to supply ethical analysis, but also points to why administrators in particular fail to demand it. Administrators are reluctant to encourage ethical investigations both because the inquiry itself might raise questions concerning cherished program goals and because the style of analysis conflicts with the technocratic ethos which dominates bureaucratic politics. Like analysts, administrators prefer to maintain a technocratic image. As policymakers, they constantly face political risks for their decisions. And since they are unelected policymakers, bureaucrats are particularly vulnerable to accusations that they have exceeded their legislative mandates and actually engaged in policymaking. In order to protect themselves and minimize these risks, bureaucrats often take refuge in a technocratic defense of their decisions, asserting that they are not making value decisions but merely designing the most efficient program. Of course, the notion that bureaucratic decision-making is nonpolitical is an illusion, but it is an illusion that suits the political and professional needs of adminstrators.[46]

What ethical analysis does is to undermine this valuable illusion. It emphasizes that administrators are in fact engaged in value-laden policymaking. When confronted with a group of inquisitive reporters, irate citizens, or hostile congressmen, it would make little political sense for bureaucrats to follow the advice of some scholars and begin discussing the various ethical deliberations involved in their decisions.[47] It is much safer to fall back on conventional technocratic justifications.

Again, clearly administrators are not wholly insensitive to the ethical implications of their decisions. In fact, these implications may often be the subject of informal discussions. But the point is that such ethical deliberations are *ad hoc,* and they are unlikely to be made public or to be the subject of careful and systematic investigation in formal agency studies and reports. Instead, the dominant style of public justification for administrative decisions is technocratic, because it increases the appearance of political legitimacy and presents the fewest political risks.[48] To investigate publicly the ethical difficulties surrounding agency policies would only invite unwelcome public scrutiny. It would amount to painting a target on one's chest. The unfortunate case of Rita Lavelle in the Reagan EPA aptly illustrates the political dangers involved in making public what should be kept private. She lost her job and much more when it became public that she had used political considerations in deciding when and how to fund the cleanup of hazardous waste sites. Like political considerations, moral and ethical considerations are often best left behind closed doors, and kept out of public policy studies.

*   *   *

The technocratic ethos permeates not only the bureaucracy but the entire political system. Consider Congress, for example. On the surface, this legislative body seems very different in political style from the bureaucracy. It is relatively egalitarian instead of hierarchical; and it thrives on debate, not enforced consensus. One might expect that ethical inquiry and debate could flourish here. And while this is true to some extent, politicians also evince a distinct preference for technocratic styles of policy analysis and justification. They, like administrators, find this approach to be politically useful. The role of policy analysis in the 1978–1979 congressional debate over the deregulation of natural gas is illustrative. One researcher found that much of the discussion centered around "an incredible number of econometric studies."[49] The disagreements between advocates and foes of deregulations were fought out primarily in terms of the adequacy or inadequacy of the empirical models used to predict price changes, elasticity of supply, and so on. The researcher concludes that this focus on the technical and quantitative issues actually served to obscure the real issues at the heart of this policy disagreement—issues that concerned one's political assumptions about such questions as the value of the free market, the redistribution of income, and the validity of antitrust measures. These assumptions were the real determinants of a legislator's attitude toward deregulation. However, "the massive staff effort behind these studies [did little] to clarify these real issues."

Why then did the representatives and senators use the studies as heavily as they did? First, some members hid behind the studies: even though they may have made their decisions on other grounds, they felt more comfortable knowing that if something should go wrong, they would be able to say they simply went along with the experts. The second reason is evident from something Representative Stockman said. Asked why he and other members preferred debating the quantitative conclusions of opposed econometric studies to debating the basic assumptions that went into them, Stockman answered: "Nobody wants to say it's all based on a basic value. My position is that the free market does work, but that is a pretty thin fig leaf for something as important as this." A fig leaf! Members of Congress are ashamed to discuss public issues without hiding behind the numbers provided by economists. In a post-Weberian world, where "facts" and "values" are thought to have distinct cognitive foundations, politicians are embarrassed about basing political choices on principles of justice or "basic values." Or, they are ashamed to acknowledge it when they debate issues in public.[50]

The relationship between politicians and ethics is more complex, however, than this statement makes it appear. For example, not all politicians are "ashamed" to publicly embrace ethical principles. There are clearly some politicians who relish taking moral stands and explaining their policy stands in terms of some deep commitment to a set of ethical principles. But the ethical declarations that are made publicly by most members of Congress tend to be of the "mom and apple-pie" sort. They tend to be commitments to such vague and noncontroversial values as freedom, peace, family, and democracy. Politicians usually shy away from intense ethical debates, or controversial ethical issues that might be politically damaging. They prefer to take refuge in a more technocratic form of analysis. Politicians, like bureaucrats, often find it safest to justify controversial decisions on technical grounds ("It was the only feasible option." "It's the most cost-effective approach."), and thus conveniently avoid the riskier and trickier task of justifying those choices on moral or political grounds. Likewise, analysts have slight incentive to pursue the moral dimensions of policy questions since the studies most in demand are quantitative and nonethical.

Strong professional and institutional pressures account for the politicians' reluctance to get involved in ethical controversies. As congressional scholars have frequently noted, members of Congress are typically obsessed with re-election, and tend to avoid political controversies that might alienate important segments of their constituency.[51] They are also motivated by career ambitions within Congress.[52] Through a constant process of bargaining, log-rolling, and compromise they seek to enhance their influence among legislative colleagues. These kinds of accommodating behaviors obviously inhibit a vigorous attention to potentially difficult and devisive ethical issues. The legislator who demonstrates a reluctance to compromise risks being labeled obstructionist by colleagues. Yet questions of right and wrong, justice and injustice, are rarely amenable to compromise.

Again, there are some exceptions. Those members of Congress who come from particularly safe districts, or who see themselves primarily as mavericks or ideologues, will often not hesitate to get directly involved in controversial ethical issues. But these are exceptions; in general, the realities of everyday institutional and career pressures in Congress encourage members to downplay ethical controversies and ethical policy analysis.

Besides career and institutional pressures, there is another reason why policymakers do not demand more ethical analysis of policy issues: their reluctance to question the basic tenets of American ideology. Ethical investigations have an uncomfortable way of exposing the ideological implications that often lie buried under the "practical" façade that politicians like to put on policy decisions. As we have seen, ethical analysis tends to focus attention on the moral underpinnings of policy issues; but these moral controversies are often linked with larger ideological controversies— controversies that politicians are even more hesitant to address. As a number of political observers have noted, American politicians have always seemed reluctant to question the basic tenets of liberal capitalist ideology.[53] Instead of seeing politics as involving the debate over the basic characteristic of our political, economic, and social system, American politicians have always preferred to portray politics more as a matter of practical problem-solving. The assumption is that current economic and political arrangements are basically justified and that policy need only involve minor adjustments—"tinkering with the machine." Some have suggested that this technocratic tendency is not simply an attribute of our politicians, but a deeply ingrained part of American political culture as well.[54]

One might argue that this tendency to avoid ideological debate is quite natural and occurs in most societies. Indeed some researchers have concluded just that. Yet others would argue that Americans have taken this tendency to an extreme, that American politicians seem allergic to ideological debates when compared with officials of the other Western democracies, where, for example, the debate between capitalism and socialism is alive and well.[55]

In Western European democracies some citizens and major political leaders alike consider a broader range of alternatives on the grand issues than do Americans. Some leaders of the British Labour Party are reviving, and probably radicalizing to a degree, an earlier Labour radicalism that the party muffled over the years as it rose to and exercised governmental authority. More than Americans, Europeans debate central planning, major income and wealth redistribution, and private property in production. They debate a wider range of restrictions on corporate discretion.[56]

Some observers conclude that there is in fact an unusual amount of ideological hegemony in the United States. More to the point, it seems that standard approaches to policy analysis do little to encourage critical analysis of reigning ideology and in fact tend to take basic ideological tenets for granted. As one eminent politicial scientist and policy scholar has observed, when ideological tenets do appear in policy studies, they are usually "introduced into analysis as though settled facts."[57]

Ethical analysis has a disconcerting tendency to force policy-makers to confront these previously unexamined political and economic assumptions. This is because it is often difficult to fully analyze ethical questions without touching upon the political and economic theories with which they are intimately connected. Ethical questions have a tendency to begin a chain of analysis that all too often leads into the heart of some ideological controversy. First, ethics makes clear that all policy decisions, even those which appear to be purely "practical" or to be purely a matter of "efficiency," are actually based on certain normative assumptions. Then, upon examination, these normative assumptions are often found to be part of a larger set of ideological assumptions. As political theorists point out, ideologies are in fact made up of interwoven sets of mutually supporting values and theories.[58] It is quite difficult, for example, to separate notions of freedom from theories of capitalist economics or to separate the value of equality from theories of socialist economics. Thus, when one starts investigating ethical issues, it is all too easy to eventually get involved in the larger ideological issues to which they are connected.[59]

Consider, for example, David Stockman's statements regarding his rationale for natural gas deregulation. Recall that when asked why he preferred discussing statistics rather than the basic assumptions involved in economic policy, he replied, "Nobody wants to say that it's all based on a basic value. My position is that the free market does work, but that is a pretty thin fig leaf for something as important as this." Note the implied connection between values and economic ideology and his reluctance to investigate either. Consider also the discussion of justice in medical care that was mentioned earlier. A debate about justice and health care delivery immediately raises the issue of distributing health care on the basis of need. This in turn raises the issue of socialized medicine—and we are again forced to question the virtues of the free market, the hallmark of American economic thought.

It seems likely, then, that ethical analysis is avoided not only because of career and institutional pressures, but also because it leads to difficult questions about the basic tenets of the American way of life—questions that are not always easily answered. Given our traditional reluctance to get involved in basic ideological debates, it is hardly surprising that ethical analysis is not particularly popular in American politics. Indeed, for those comfortable with current political, social, and economic arrangements, ethical analysis threatens to open the door on an ideological Pandora's box.

But if there are so many professional and political obstacles to ethical investigations, why the obvious popularity of cost-benefit analysis, which is admittedly a form of ethical evaluation? Policy studies prepared by bureaus and agencies are often full of tables demonstrating the costs and benefits of various program options. Doesn't the popularity of cost-benefit analysis demonstrate that ethics and policy analysis are not incompatible?

In fact, cost-benefit analysis is popular in policy analysis because it gives the appearance of ethical analysis without involving the risks. It purges moral analysis of all of its difficult—and essential—characteristics. In cost-benefit analysis, ethical decisions do not involve difficult choices between competing values and moral principles. Instead, the analysis only seeks to maximize one value—efficiency—and effectively ignores other values such as justice and liberty. Ethicists consider this a serious deficiency in cost-benefit analysis, and they claim that it tends to "obscure rather than clarify the important moral dimensions of the choices facing policy-makers."[60] But what is a flaw to ethicists is an advantage to analysts and policymakers. For them, it is politically useful to have a normative method which obscures the difficult moral dimensions of decisions; for that is the only kind of ethical approach compatible with technocratic rationalizations of policy.

In cost-benefit analysis, ethical inquiry is conveniently reduced to a process of calculation. Instead of a difficult philosophical procedure that examines clashing moral arguments, the analysis becomes a technical activity largely concerned with price determinations. It is this objective, empirical appearance, that has made cost-benefit analysis one of the favored decision-making tools of analysts and administrators. Ironically, then, cost-benefit analysis is popular not in spite of its ethical and intellectual shortcomings, but *because* of them, for it is these very shortcomings that make the technique politically and professionally acceptable. Analysts can recommend the "best" program option without getting bogged down in potentially messy and embarrassing ethical issues. As an example, when David Stockman opposed the EPA's plan to reduce acid rain in the Northeast, he did not try to confront the many normative and environmental issues involved, he simply informed President Reagan that the plan would cost too much.

Thus, the success of cost-benefit analysis does little to undermine the notion that ethics and policy analysis do not mix. Indeed, properly understood, its success demonstrates not how much policy analysts wish to confront difficult normative questions, but how much they tend to avoid them.

To sum up, the standard arguments against the integration of ethics and public policy analysis are clearly weak. Professional, political, and institutional factors provide a much more plausible explanation for the neglect of ethics. Ethical analysis is shunned because it frequently threatens the professional and political interests of both analysts and policymakers. The administrator, the legislator, the bureaucrat, and the policy analyst all shy away from the risks involved in ethical inquiry.

All this is not to say that ethical analysis can never find its way into policy considerations. Indeed, there are several reasons to believe that connections between ethics and policy issues will continue to be made. First, there are some policy issues that are so explicitly moral in nature—such as abortion—that analysts and clients simply cannot avoid dealing with the moral arguments involved. In such cases, it becomes difficult to ignore the inherent connections between analysis and ethics. Second, ethicists have in fact begun to apply ethical analysis to many policy questions. This trend will undoubtedly continue even if policy analysts do not take up this task. And finally, a more explicitly normative style of policy analysis is clearly an option for those relatively independent policy analysts who work in academia or in private policy study organizations. These analysts are often not subject to the same kinds of career and institutional pressures that exist in governmental institutions, and thus may be more free to address normative issues in a more open and systematic way.

The fact remains, however, that ethics and policy analysis are professionally and politically incompatible. And, without a significant shift away from the current technocratic style of policy analysis or an increased emphasis placed on ethical and ideological issues in American politics, ethical inquiry is unlikely to become an integral part of policy analysis.

NOTES

1. Some of the principal works on this subject include: Martin Rein, *Social Science and Public Policy* (New York: Penguin Books, 1976); Lawrence Tribe, ed., *When Values Conflict* (Cambridge, MA: Ballinger, 1976); Duncan MacRae, *The Social Function of Social Science* (New Haven, CT: Yale University Press, 1976); and Frank Fischer, *Politics, Values, and Public Policy: The Problem of Methodology* (Boulder, CO: Westview Press, 1980).

2. Rein, p. 13.

3. Robert Dorfman, "An Afterword: Humane Values and Environmental Decisions," in Tribe, p. 162.

4. Rein, p. 140.

5. Tribe, p. xii.

6. Peter Brown, "Ethics and Policy Research," *Policy Analysis,* 2 (Spring 1976).

7. For examples of how ethics could be incorporated into policy studies, see the works of MacRae and Fischer.

8. For an interesting discussion of some of the problems of using utilitarian moral approaches in modern politics, see Stuart Hampshire, "Morality and Pessimism," *The New York Review of Books,* January 25, 1973.

9. See, for example, Tom L. Beauchamp and James F. Childress, *Principles of Biomedical Ethics* (New York: Oxford University Press, 1979); and K. E. Goodpaster and K. M. Sayer, eds., *Ethics and Problems of the 21st Century* (Notre Dame, IN: University of Notre Dame Press, 1979).

10. Peter Steinfels, *The Place of Ethics in Schools of Public Policy* (Hastings-on-Hudson, NY: The Hastings Center, 1977), p. 3.

11. For an early version of this argument against ethics, see Herbert Simon, *Administrative Behavior* (New York: Macmillan, 1947), pp. 45–60.

12. For a more detailed description of positivist reasoning, see "Contemporary Noncognitivism," *The Encyclopedia of Philosophy* (New York: Macmillan, 1967), vol. 3, pp. 106–109.

13. Fischer, pp. 65–100.

14. This argument can be found in Charles Taylor, "Neutrality in Political Science,"

Philosophy, Politics, and Society, 3rd series, Peter Laslett and W. C. Runciman, eds. (London: Basil Blackwell, 1978).

15. Taylor, p. 43.

16. For a detailed explanation of the good reasons approach and other related approaches, see Fischer, pp. 65–100.

17. Fischer, p. 90.

18. Gene Outka, "Social Justice and Equal Access to Health Care," *Journal of Religious Ethics,* 2 (Spring 1974), pp. 11–32.

19. Outka, p. 14.

20. See Fischer and MacRae for examples of methods of integrating normative analysis into policy analysis.

21. Steinfels, p. 5.

22. Joel L. Fleishman and Bruce L. Payne, *Ethical Dilemmas and the Education of Policymakers* (Hastings-on-Hudson, NY: The Hastings Center, 1980), p. 5.

23. For a description of some of the internal problems of cost-benefit analysis see B. Guy Peters, *American Public Policy* (New York: Franklin Watts, 1982), pp. 291–306.

24. Edith Stokey and Richard Zeckhauser, *Primer for Policy Analysis* (New York: Norton, 1978), pp. 277–286.

25. Fleishman and Payne, p. 5.

26. Brown.

27. Brown, p. 338.

28. Brown; Rein also makes this point, though in a somewhat different way. He argues that analysts usually mistakenly assume that there are only two ways to approach values in analysis: the "value-neutral" approach that ignores values, or the "value-committed" approach in which personal values are promoted. He suggests a third alternative: a "value-critical" approach which neither ignores values nor takes them for granted, but makes them the subject of systematic analysis. Rein, pp. 78–79.

29. Brown, p. 334.

30. Goodpaster and Sayer, p. viii.

31. For one example of "applied ethics," see Beauchamp and Childress.

32. Douglas Colligan, "Rent-a-Conscience," *Omni,* May 1981, p. 116.

33. Fred Kramer, review of Frank Fischer's *Politics, Values, and Public Policy* (Boulder, CO: Westview Press, 1980), in *American Political Science Review,* 76(1) (March 1982), pp. 120–121.

34. For a discussion of why policy analysis techniques cannot be as rigorous as those used by social scientists, see Mark H. Moore, "Social Science and Policy Analysis: Some Fundamental Differences," in Daniel Callahan and Bruce Jennings, *Ethics, The Social Sciences, and Policy Analysis* (New York: Plenum, 1983).

35. For more on the hierarchical nature of bureaucracies and its inhibiting effects, see Guy Benveniste, "The Serious Game of Survival Inside Bureaucracy," *Bureaucracy,* 2nd ed. (San Francisco: Boyd and Fraser, 1983), chap. 4.

36. Arnold Meltsner, *Policy Analysts in the Bureaucracy* (Berkeley: University of California Press, 1979), p. 292.

37. Peter Earley, "Why Blow the Whistle?" *The Washington Post* (national weekly edition), January 2, 1984, p. 32.

38. Brown, p. 338.

39. For more on this point, see Anthony Downs on the development of "bureaucratic ideologies" to further efficiency in bureaucratic organizations, *Inside Bureaucracy* (Boston: Little, Brown, 1967), chap. XIX.

40. Charles Lindblom, "The Science of Muddling Through," *Public Administration Review,* 1959.

41. For one version of this "end of ideology" thesis, see Daniel Bell, *The End of Ideology* (Glencoe, IL: Free Press, 1960).

42. Callahan and Jennings, p. xv.

43. Since "technocratic" is a term I will be using frequently in this piece, let me define it more precisely. A technocratic approach to policy and policy analysis is one that largely ignores the basic normative and political dimensions of policy decisions and assumes instead

that using information, modeling, technical analysis, etc., is the key to making good policy decisions. For a more detailed discussion of this approach to policymaking, see Jeffrey Straussman, *The Limits of Technocratic Politics* (New Brunswick, NJ: Transaction Books, 1978).

44. For a description of the centrality of this means-end dichotomy to policy analysis and an insightful discussion of its political implications, see Brian Fay, *Social Theory and Political Practice* (London: George Allen and Unwin, 1975).

45. Callahan and Jennings, p. xvii.

46. For a recent example of the assertion that administrative decisions are intensely normative, see Douglas Yates, "Hard Choices: Justifying Bureaucratic Decisions," in *Public Duties: The Moral Obligations of Government Officials,* Joel Fleishman et al., eds. (Cambridge, MA: Harvard University Press, 1981).

47. For more on why some think administrators should reveal their value deliberations, see Yates.

48. For an interesting discussion of the political symbolism of information and analysis, and how policymakers use it for legitimation purposes, see Martha S. Feldman and James G. March, "Information in Organizations as Sign and Symbol," *Administrative Science Quarterly,* 26 (1981).

49. Michael J. Malbin, *Unelected Representatives* (New York: Basic Books, 1980), chap. 9.

50. Malbin, pp. 233–234.

51. David Mayhew, *Congress: The Electoral Connection* (New Haven, CT: Yale University Press, 1974).

52. Richard F. Fenno, *Congressmen in Committees* (Boston: Little, Brown, 1973), p. 1.

53. One of the first to make this observation was Louis Hartz, *The Liberal Tradition in America* (New York: Harcourt, Brace, 1955); a more recent assertion can be found in Charles Lindblom, *Politics and Markets* (New York: Basic Books, 1977), chaps. 15 and 16.

54. For example, Kenneth Keniston once argued in *The Uncommitted* (New York: Harcourt, Brace, and Jovanovich, 1965) that Americans seem obsessed with "how-to" questions, to the neglect of more basic questions of "what-to-do" and "why" (chap. 9).

55. Lindblom, *Politics and Markets,* chap. 15.

56. Lindblom, *Politics and Markets,* p. 212.

57. Charles Lindblom, *The Policy-Making Process* (Englewood Cliffs, NJ: Prentice-Hall, 1980), p. 39. I am clearly implying here that policy analysis and policymaking would in fact benefit from a more explicit and systematic investigation of the ideological assumptions underlying U.S. policy decisions. One could, of course, disagree with this assertion. This, however, is not the place to get into a lengthy debate over this issue. It should be noted, though, that my position—that there is an inherent value in questioning basic policy assumptions—is one that I share with Frank Fischer, Martin Rein, and most others writing in the area of ethics and public policy.

58. For a brief discussion of the interrelationship between values and ideology, see Kenneth Dolbeare and Patricia Dolbeare, *American Ideologies,* 3rd ed. (Chicago: Rand McNally, 1976), pp. 5–7.

59. It should be mentioned that these kinds of interconnections between ethics and political and economic theories have often been explicitly recognized by those promoting ethical policy analysis. They have argued that what is needed is not simply to add on ethics as a separate part of policy analysis, but to create a more comprehensive and integrated approach to policy analysis that incorporates the normative, theoretical, and empirical elements of analysis. For examples of what this kind of approach would look like, see Fischer, and also Martin Rein, "Value-Critical Policy Analysts," in Callahan and Jennings.

60. Fleishman and Payne, p. 5.

CHAPTER 6

ETHICS IN STATE AND LOCAL GOVERNMENT

Introduction

A book on the essential problems of ethics in government would be incomplete without a section that deals with issues that arise at the state and local levels. While it is true that many of the same problems can be readily found at all levels of government, there are enough distinctions that can be made in the ethics area between the federal government, and the states and their local subdivisions to warrant a specific examination. Indeed, distinctions can be easily drawn between these levels with respect to the different kinds of tasks that are performed and responsibilities held by the different governmental units.

The federal government has responsibilities that are broader in scope than those of state and local governments. For example, military and foreign policy are issues with which the executive and legislative branches of the federal government must contend. States and their subdivisions, though, are primarily and more directly responsible for such areas as voting, education, health, community planning, zoning, and so on. While the federal government certainly has influence in a number of these tasks, state and local governments provide their services much more directly. For this reason they are the governments that are closest to the people. Given these differences, it should not be surprising that there are different ways in which the ethics crisis in government manifests itself. What is surprising, however, is the dimension of the problem, manifested by the rate of growth in corruption that has invaded the nation's Statehouses and city halls.

In the last twenty years, the number of state and local officials who have been convicted of various improprieties by the federal courts has grown tenfold. Moreover, the states have found it necessary to implement new ethics laws, step up enforcement of existing law, and establish ethics commissions as a response to this growth in corruption. This explosion of mischief-making drives home the point that there truly is an ethics crisis in government and that it knows no boundaries within governmental entities. The first selection in this chapter, Elder Witt's "Is Government Full of Crooks or Are We Just Better at Finding Them?" provides an excellent survey of mischief-making at the state and local levels.

And while the widespread growth of corruption remains unchecked, state and local officials must also contend with the many moral mazes that are peculiar to their environments. One of the most difficult choices that these officials must wrestle with goes by the name of the "NIMBY" phenomenon. "Not in My Backyard" is a phrase that contains a host of problems for these officials. It refers to the problem of deciding how to provide certain necessary but controversial services in a community in which there is great public opposition to the providing of those services. Among the controversies that give rise to the NIMBY phenomenon are managing hazardous-waste disposal, opening or expanding landfills, placing a halfway house in communities that will serve to rehabilitate convicted felons, placing group homes for the mentally retarded in residential areas, and allowing zoning variances for almost any reason, which almost consistently causes adverse public reaction.

Another ethics issue that continuously haunts state and local governmental entities is that of patronage—the practice of elected and appointed officials making appointments and awards based upon favoritism and partisan politics. Its philosophical underpinnings are imbedded in the phrase "To the victor belong the spoils." The patronage system is one in which political power is wielded unabashedly by a victorious political party to dole out rewards to the party faithful. Patronage has been criticized by many as making a mockery out of the concept that merit should form the basis of civil service; it usually results in inefficiency and higher than necessary costs to the taxpayer. Yet, there are others who defend the modern spoils system. The issue of patronage is examined by J. Christine Altenburger in "Patronage: Ethics Gone Amok."

Although there are several differences between the federal,

state, and local governments, there are nonetheless many commonalities that give rise to some of the same problems in the ethics arena. Among some of these universal issues are political campaign financing and the mudslinging factor in political campaigns, conflicts of interest, accepting gifts, entertainment, and travel from those who do business or who seek to do business with a governmental entity, and using the "revolving door" between government and industry. These problems occur at all levels of government, in addition to many illegalities and corrupt practices such as bribery and kickbacks, fraud, and many other questionable activities.

In response to a seemingly ever-growing list of improprieties, many states have taken a protective stand and instituted a number of measures to combat the ethics crisis at their level and within their subdivisions. New laws, the strengthening of current statutes, beefed-up enforcement, the establishment of ethics regulatory agencies and commissions, and stiffer penalties for violations and infractions are recent examples of steps that a number of states have taken to address the ethics crisis. As a primary example of this effort by the states, two selections in this chapter are devoted to the ethics reform movement in New York State. In the first, Governor Mario Cuomo relates the measures inaugurated by his office and the New York Assembly. This selection is followed by a terse report of the New York State Commission on Government Integrity to Governor Cuomo, which addresses many of the ethics challenges facing New York State, and the recommendations of the commission on steps to take as it attempts to achieve ethics reform.

The selections of this chapter allow for two concluding observations about the ethics crisis in government as it has developed at the state and local government level. First, while there are ethics concerns common to the federal, state, and local governments, there are also ethical issues, problems, and dilemmas that arise solely within the states and its subdivisions. Second, the reform movement at the levels of government closest to the people appears to be more active than that at the federal level. The efforts reported here about New York State's reform are but a sample of much more work being done throughout the nation by states, cities, counties, and other entities.

The increased activity in the ethics arena by state and local governments may be due to political considerations in which state and local government officials feel the need to enact reform measures as a kind of public relations effort. Another possibility is that institutional size may play a role. Since the states and their subdivisions are smaller, they are better positioned to make substantial changes in their operations than is the behemoth we know as the federal government. It is at this subnational level that one professional association has been especially useful. The International City Management Association (ICMA) is composed of appointed administrators who serve in cities, counties, regional councils, and other local governmental units. Its "Code of Ethics with Guidelines," adopted in 1990 and reprinted here, is instructive for its breadth and depth in treating many responsibilities of appointed local officials.

It may well be that state and local officials are responding to a new public concern with ethics in government. Perhaps their reform movement is a genuine response to the public mistrust of government that has resulted as the crisis in government ethics has grown. In short, it may be that the ethics reform movement that we are witnessing is a grass roots phenomenon in the initial stages of its development. It may be the expression of a people who have seen the threats to the democratic process that corrupt government represents and who have decided that these threats are intolerable. The ethics reform movement just now beginning within many state governments, then, could be the first step toward the creation of a government free from the effects of an ethics crisis. One major manifestation of this movement is the effort to limit the terms of elected officials. The rationale here is that less time in office will enhance overall ethical behavior. Harvey L. White in "Ethics, Accountability and Term Limitation" examines the pros and cons of this trend. Time will tell if such a movement will have this desirable outcome.

343

Is Government Full of Crooks or Are We Just Better at Finding Them?

Is Government Full of Crooks
or Are We Just Better at Finding Them?
Elder Witt

In this article, Elder Witt explores the extent of corruption in state and local government and its steady rise over the past two decades. As Witt points out, ten times as many public officials in state and local government are convicted on federal corruption charges today as were twenty years ago. This startling statistic leads Witt to raise the question found in the title of his work: "Is Government Full of Crooks or Are We Just Better at Finding Them?" The answer seems to be a combination of factors: more corrupt officials, more opportunities for them to be corrupt, more sophisticated evidence-gathering technology, and a public willingness to prosecute state and local wrongdoings. The article provides a compendium of corrupt activities that have plagued state, city, and county governments throughout the nation.

The figures are startling. Ten times as many state, city, county and other local officials are convicted on federal corruption charges today as were 20 years ago. For all the reforms over those two decades, the government that is supposed to be closest to the people seems more corrupt than ever.

"Our democratic system is in crisis," declared New York's Commission on Government Integrity, ranking New York City's recent scandals the worst since the ones that shattered the empire of Tammany Hall more than half a century ago.

In 1970, 10 state and 26 local officials faced federal indictment. By 1987, that annual number had climbed to 102 state and 246 local officials. That does not even include prosecutions under state and local law; no reliable figures exist for them. But no one who has studied the issue disputes the trend: more public officials

Elder Witt, "Is Government Full of Crooks or Are We Just Better at Finding Them?" *Governing* (September 1989), pp. 33–38. Reprinted with permission. Copyright 1989, *Governing* magazine.

ETHICS IN STATE AND LOCAL GOVERNMENT

facing trial and jail than anyone in politics would have dreamed possible two decades ago.

Every locality has it own story. Pennsylvania state Treasurer R. Budd Dwyer shot himself to death in front of rolling television cameras after being convicted of bribery. Former Syracuse, New York, Mayor Lee Alexander, onetime head of the U.S. Conference of Mayors, [faced, in 1989] 10 years in prison for extorting over $1.2 million from city contractors. More than 150 county commissioners in Oklahoma have gone to jail for defrauding taxpayers of millions of dollars through an intricate kickback scheme. Sixty of Mississippi's county supervisors have been convicted of similar crimes. An elaborate FBI sting operation probing illegal campaign contributions has ensnared several key members of the California legislature.

One lawyer in Chicago, asked how many traffic court judges he had bribed over a 10-year period, had this to say: "I didn't count them. I just bribed them. It was kind of like brushing your teeth. I did it every day."

It sounds like an epidemic. But is it? Some of those who have studied the issue longest don't think so. "Almost certainly, we are less corrupt than we were," says Suzanne Garment, a resident scholar at the American Enterprise Institute. She is at work on a book about corruption. "Read any of the histories of states and cities of 75 years ago," she says, "and you see a system that is very different. Less gets stolen from the public now."

Are we electing rascals to office in record numbers, or are we simply finding and punishing actions that used to be routinely ignored? Is it massive corruptions, or just massive exposure? The question is simple enough, but the answers are many and complex.

For one thing, there are a lot more laws for public officials to break than there used to be. New laws are the standard legislative response to scandal. "We're proscribing a lot today that we accepted as perfectly normal activities performed in the course of public service 15 or 20 years ago," says Ed Feigenbaum, who is directing a study of public corruption for the Hudson Institute.

"Revolving door" statutes are an example. They scarcely existed 20 years ago. The law showed little interest in what a public official did when he left office. Today, there are all sorts of restrictions. In Connecticut, to cite one example, any former executive-branch official is forbidden for life to represent anyone but the state on any matter he previously handled and in which

345

Is Government Full of Crooks or Are We Just Better at Finding Them?

the state has an interest. A state regulatory official risks going to jail if, during his first year out of office, he goes to work in the industry he once regulated.

In Massachusetts in the 1960s, the average state legislator would have thought nothing of hiring members of his immediate family to work in his legislative office. Today, he could be slapped with a $2,000 fine if he did that. Nepotism is a clear violation of the state conflict-of-interest law enforced by the state ethics commission.

The catalyst for much of this was Watergate. That national political scandal involved federal officials, but it set off an explosion of new laws in the states. In 1973, only a handful of states had ethics agencies. By 1978, half had set them up. Today, all states have designated some office to fulfill this function, and 38 of them have independent agencies. Cities and communities are also busy setting up such boards; Maryland's Ethics Commission reports that there are nearly 100 local ethics agencies in that state alone.

What has emerged from the past 20 years, however, is not a clear system of rules, but an inconsistent and confusing patchwork. It is not always easy for either public officials or those doing business with them to be sure of what they can and cannot do. In some states, says Page Bigelow of the Institute of Public Administration, "there's one county where you can take someone in government to lunch, and in the one next door you can't and you're breaking the law by even asking."

A fair number of state and local officials indicted in the 1980s have thus run afoul of laws that did not exist in the 1960s. But a larger number have fallen victim to increasingly sophisticated federal prosecution. The federal presence in state and local corruption cases has grown steadily in the past two decades, and it has involved the use of weapons that local law enforcement generally does not possess.

Some of this is a simple matter of technology. Twenty years ago, for example, it was very hard to tape the conversation of a public official under suspicion unless he conducted it in a room already wired for sound or over a tapped telephone line. Today, the use of "body wires"—difficult-to-detect recording equipment placed on the person of a government informer—allows a prosecutor to tape the suspect anywhere: in a parking lot, on a side-walk, even in the middle of an open field.

"Audio tapes are crucial," says John R. Hailman, the assistant U.S. attorney who has overseen the Mississippi corruption cases for the northern half of the state. Once a public official on trial sees or hears himself in the actual process of making a question-able transaction on tape, he can usually expect to receive the full wrath of a jury. "You just can't answer a tape," says Hailman.

Not all state courts accept evidence procured with body wires. But federal courts do, and federal prosecutors can use it to try state and local officials in federal court for a variety of federal offenses. Without such wires, many of the public corruption cases prosecuted in the past decade would never even have been brought, and the total number of officials convicted would be much lower.

The same is true of elaborate undercover operations in which law enforcement agents set up fictitious criminal schemes or entire business enterprises to catch corrupt public officials. Be-fore the 1980s, this was not often done; such "stings" were used mainly to pursue drug suspects or identify and convict profes-sional thieves. But the FBI's Abscam operation of 1980, in which agents posed as Arab sheiks and offered congressmen bribes to introduce immigration bills, changed the situation in a dramatic way.

In the years following, Abscam came under considerable attack by critics who considered it entrapment, but it stood up to U.S. Supreme Court scrutiny and has been copied, in one variation or another, all over the country. Undercover enterprises snared local judges in Chicago and, most massively, the county commis-sioners in Mississippi and Oklahoma.

In Operation Pretense in Mississippi, three FBI agents went to work for a construction equipment company whose owner was outraged at the dishonesty he found in dealing with county gov-ernment. The undercover agents, in the words of John Hailman, one of the federal prosecutors in charge, "had the appropriate accents and 'good ole boy' demeanors to be accepted as crooked local salesmen. They wore caps saying Mid-State Pipe and chewed liberal amounts of tobacco." They used body wires to tape their conversations with the county supervisors who received kickbacks.

In both the Mississippi and Oklahoma cases, state officials actually took the first steps toward gathering evidence. The Mis-sissippi auditor's office discovered that counties had not only paid far too much for heavy equipment, but sometimes couldn't find it

347

Is Government Full of Crooks or Are We Just Better at Finding Them?

when asked about it. Oklahoma's auditor noticed that one county reported purchasing enough lumber to rebuild every bridge in the area four times—and yet none of the bridges had been repaired.

Strong political ties and weak state laws hamstrung local district and county attorneys when they tried to pursue these clues. In Mississippi, state law requires that a person be tried in his home county. The county supervisors, who were the target of the investigations, were also the employers of the sheriff and the county attorney. In Oklahoma, there was an additional problem: The kickback scheme involved suppliers and officials in almost every county in the state. The power of the county attorney stopped at the border of his county.

And in both states, as in most of the country, the attorney general had relatively limited law enforcement authority. He could not convene a grand jury with authority to subpoena witnesses. So it was the federal government that prosecuted the county supervisors, who were convicted of extortion and mail fraud.

The prosecutors who went after these supervisors say that it was not a matter of finding new forms of corruption. They are convinced that bribery has existed in county government in their states throughout the century. What happened was the arrival of modern evidence-gathering technology and a federal will to act in these particular states.

"The contest against political corruption in America," journalist Walter Lippmann once wrote, "is very much like the competition among designers of naval armaments. At one time the reformers have a gun which can pierce any armor plate; then a defense against that gun is developed." Over the past 20 years, the anti-corruption forces have had the technology. Whether a defense against it will be developed remains to be seen.

But the massive increase in corruption cases is not entirely a matter of new laws or new technology. It also in part reflects the higher monetary stakes involved in state and local government decisions.

"Corruption follows money," says Diana Henriques, author of *The Machinery of Greed,* a study of abuse of public power. "The larger the budget, the greater the allure." The amount of money spent by state and local government has increased nearly eight-fold over the past 20 years, to more than $900 billion a year, an enormous increase even in constant dollars.

It is one downside of the devolution of federal power to other levels of government. As state and local governments expand in size and power, they become more attractive targets of corruption.

Increasingly, governments are setting up special districts, commissions and government "authorities" to handle their expanded responsibilities in a more "business-like" fashion. This is a governmental frontier that many of the public access and disclosure requirements that affect more traditional agencies do not penetrate.

In some cases, the officials who run these new entities are corrupt; in others, they are simply corruptible. "When you give people the authority to make 'red light, green light' decisions that are very valuable to people, you've created a situation that's vulnerable to abuse," says Henriques. "Unless you vaccinate that situation somehow, you are placing enormous temptation on the frailties of human nature."

Corruption in a special government authority usually has a modest and relatively innocent beginning, Henriques found. "No one worries that a few contracts out of so many are being steered in a certain direction. But no one knows when to stop, and so it proceeds until the authority is so riddled with abuse that the program can't be saved."

In the end, a much-needed and very well-intentioned program may be scrapped, and the people it was supposed to serve are the ultimate victims. "The political fixers and influence peddlers move on to some other program, wherever the money is," she says.

A local government horror story in Bergen County, New Jersey, came to light . . . as a result of investigative reporting by a local newspaper, the *Record*. The paper spent months looking into the work of the Bergen County Utilities Authority and found "an agency out of control." The authority was $600 million in debt, having awarded multimillion-dollar bond underwriting contracts on a no-bid basis to investment banking firms that had made large campaign contributions to county officials.

The *Record* portrayed Wall Street as the instigator of "pay for play," the strategic use of campaign contributions by bond underwriters to ensure that they would win bond business. When Bergen County had its first election for county executive in 1986, the Wall Street investment firm of Bear, Stearns, through individual and corporate donations, was the biggest campaign contributor. In the two years preceding the election, Bear, Stearns

had earned millions for underwriting bond issues for the Bergen
County Utilities Authority.

The New Jersey Senate has asked the State Commission on
Investigation to determine whether any laws were broken in the
relationship between the securities industry and the public authority.

"You can't fault the bond dealers for playing by rules, written
and unwritten, which confront them," says Henriques. "They'll
play the game any way the public officials demand. If the officials
want competitive bidding, they'll give competitive bids. If they
want tickets to the Giants game, they'll get tickets to the Giants
game."

The corruption of the Bergen County Utilities Authority could
not have taken place on anything resembling the same scale 20
years ago. The authority existed in those days, but it did not
build sophisticated facilities and therefore did not need to raise
huge sums of money. It was a small-scale sewer commission. Wall
Street had no reason to be interested in it.

In this case, corruption was more than anything else a function
of growth and development. The fast-growing county's need for
waste treatment facilities, and government institutions that could
provide them, far outpaced its ability to keep those institutions
under control. And the utilities authority, as a modern special-
purpose unit of government rather than an old-fashioned unit, lay
outside the traditional mechanisms of accountability.

Special units of government are not inevitable centers of corruption. The numerous state lotteries created in recent years
illustrate how government can protect itself against corruption by
acknowledging its vulnerability, selecting leaders who will guard
against even the appearance of impropriety (the first lottery
directors in many states were former FBI agents) and providing
adequate oversight for the operation. The key to avoiding trouble
in most of the lotteries was the recognition in virtually every state
that a gambling operation was inherently corruptible and required special controls. Where the threat is less obvious, the
safeguards tend to be less thorough. These are the kind of situations, Henriques warns, in which "the temptation is enormous
and the perception of risk minuscule."

The same warning applies to another common state and local
innovation of recent years—the creation of partnerships between
government and private institutions. Those moves are made to
save money and improve services, and sometimes they do. But

they represent one more step away from accountability, and from clarity as well. As the line between public and private blurs, the night-and-day world of extortion and bribery fades into a twilight zone of ambiguous shades and shifting standards.

Earlier this year [1989], Milwaukee County Zoo Director Gilbert Boese experienced firsthand the difficulties of operating in this situation. He resigned as zoo director after the county ethics board began investigating charges that he had failed to disclose benefits provided him by the Zoological Society of Milwaukee County, the zoo's private "partner." The benefits included a yearly 10 percent addition to his county-paid salary as well as travel expenses, including an African safari. Boese's wife was, at the time, the executive director of the Zoological Society. After leaving his public post, Boese become the society's president and his wife moved to another organization.

There was no crime involved here, and it could be argued that no serious ethical violation even took place. Nonetheless, these events became a major news story in the Milwaukee papers and ended up tainting not only Boese but also his superior, Milwaukee County Executive Dave Schultz. The publicity that surrounds issues such as these creates a heightened ethical sensitivity in the public, a greater willingness by prosecutors to investigate corruption charges and, ultimately, more indictments and more convictions.

And when it comes to explaining the "epidemic" of corruption cases, the point about public values may be the most important point of all. They have changed for a variety of reasons in the past 20 years, but they have changed. Public values determine what level of corruption a democracy will tolerate, and what acts it will prosecute.

Or so argues one of America's leading scholars of corruption, Brooklyn College history Professor Abraham S. Eisenstadt. To call public officials corrupt, in Eisenstadt's opinion, is to say two things: "It is to blame them for subverting the moral standards governing the way they conduct their office; but no less importantly, it is to speak of the moral rules by which the community operates."

For a blunt-spoken comment on the dramatic changes that have taken place in those rules, one can do no better than Lou Farina. The former Chicago alderman spent more than a year in prison after being convicted of extorting $7,000 from a building contractor.

"Anyone who goes into politics today is nuts," Farina says. "If a restaurant owner donates $500 to your campaign and then gets in trouble with a health inspector, he'll bring the citation to you and ask if you can help. Years ago, if you were an alderman, you'd say, 'Give it to me, I'll do the best I can.' You'd call the judge up, say, 'This is a good man, can you help him out?' Today you go to jail for that!"

Patronage: Ethics Gone Amok
J. Christine Altenburger

Among the more prevalent ethics problems to emerge at the state and local levels of government is that of abusive patronage, in which public officials use the power of their office to make appointments and award contracts to members of their political party. In "Patronage: Ethics Gone Amok," J. Christine Altenburger describes the historical and legal foundations of the practice of patronage as she exposes the many inherent negative ethical ramifications of it. Given the fact that patronage is essentially a form of favoritism, the politics of patronage subverts any merit system that might form the basis of a civil service. As a kind of "spoils system," Altenburger claims that patronage conflicts with several basic ethical tenets, such as the principles of "do no harm," respecting individual rights, and following the canons of justice. With a number of concrete examples and illustrations that demonstrate the prevalence of this practice and its harmful effects, Altenburger concludes that the patronage system stands in need of immediate reform. Of course, it has stood in need of immediate reform ever since the Colonial period in American history.

Patronage Quiz

Test your "patronage position." Do you agree or disagree with the statements below, or do you consider the point debatable?

J. Christine Altenburger, "Patronage: Ethics Gone Amok." Previously unpublished article. Printed with permission of the author.

1. When politicians are contending for victory, if successful, they claim, as a matter of right, that "to the victor belong the spoils of the enemy."

   Agree____Disagree____Debatable____

2. The cost of the practice of patronage is the restraint it places on the freedoms of belief and association. It breeds inefficiency, corruption, and ineffective administration.

   Agree____Disagree____Debatable____

3. On balance, the contribution to our political processes made by patronage hiring practices outweighs the relatively modest intrusion on First Amendment rights. Patronage stabilizes political parties.

   Agree____Disagree____Debatable____

4. Patronage cannot be justified on the basis of a need for a loyal work force and the need to strengthen political parties. This does not mean that it is necessarily inappropriate when filling high-level policy positions.

   Agree____Disagree____Debatable____

Response to the Patronage Quiz

Does one's "patronage position" depend upon where one sits? Probably. Elected officials, in general, might be expected to agree with statements 1 and 3, and somewhat disagree with 2 and 4. Conversely, nonelected administrators/managers and "reformers" would be inclined to support 2 and 4; not 1 and 3. It is understandable that a Justice of the United States Supreme Court could spend hours debating the issues of "freedom of belief and association," with the Court deeply divided on the practice of patronage. It is precisely this lack of agreement, with important arguments advanced by all sides, which renders the topic appropriate for ethical analysis. Put another way, the practice of patronage has most often been viewed as a political or legal issue. If the discussion is raised to the higher level of considering its attributes in the light of ethical behavior, guided by ethical principles, can the haze that clouds this practice begin to lift? This is the overarching question considered in this presentation.

Running throughout the following discussion is a well-established ethical precept: ethical public officials must distinguish between what they have a right to do, and the right thing to do. This distinction becomes a critical point, because public officials continue to be afforded broad opportunities to "play the patronage game," legally bringing onto the public payroll individuals not qualified for their positions—with all of its implications. The public official bent on power-wielding will tend not to worry about the consequences. The ethical official *will* worry, and will exercise power, governed by moral principles—the basis of leadership.

Introduction

Patronage Defined

Jay M. Shafritz, in *The Dorsey Dictionary of American Government and Politics,* defines patronage as "the power of elected and appointed officials to make partisan appointments to office or to confer contracts, honors, and other benefits on their political supporters." Nepotism is noted as "any practice by which office-holders award positions to members of their immediate family."[1] For the purpose of this article, patronage will include nepotism. It will imply appointments without regard to qualifications.

A Note from History

The first statement of the Patronage Quiz is drawn from the Clay-Marcy debates of 1832, with Senator Marcy vigorously defending the practice of rotation in office (patronage). The practice is about as old as the Republic; it has been an issue for about as long. Those wishing a review of the historical highlights should read Loverd and Pavlak, "The Historical Development of the American Civil Service."[2] It is significant that this is the lead article in a book on public personnel management. After all, while the subject of patronage is most frequently viewed in a political context, its end results have to do with the competency, talent, and integrity of those who constitute the civil service of the country—national, state, and local. It was the end results of patronage—widespread corruption and inefficiency—throughout much of the nineteenth century that rallied reformers and the business/industrial community to a "stamp out patronage" campaign.

Very often a cause is advanced by an event that dramatically lends meaning to its preachment. Such was the assassination of President Garfield by a disgruntled job seeker. Note his claim to a job (from a letter in the files of the U.S. Office of Personnel Management) in return for party loyalty:

March 26, 1881

General Garfield:

I Understand from Co. Hooker of the Nat'l committee that I am to have a consulship. I hope it is the consulship at Paris, as that is the only one I care to take . . . Mr. Walker, the present consul, has no claim on you for the office, I think as the men that did the business last fall are the ones to be remembered.

Very respectfully,

Charles Guiteau

Guiteau did not get the job. Shortly thereafter, he assassinated Garfield. So much for the argument that the practice (or denial) of patronage does not sometimes hurt. Frederick C. Mosher, commenting on the state of the nineteenth-century civil service, laid it on the line: "Few reform movements in American History could draw so clear a distinction between right and wrong, between the 'good guys' and the bad guys.' It was a campaign to stamp out evils that were clear and obnoxious."[3]

It is not the purpose here to dwell on this country's reform of its civil service. Suffice it to say that the Pendleton Act of 1883 put in place for the federal government a merit system that sought to establish the neutrality of the federal civil service: open and competitive examinations for selection, promotion, and protection from arbitrary dismissal or other disciplinary actions. The Hatch Act of 1939 rounded out the concept of merit by restricting the political activity of federal officials/employees. The whole system was managed by an independent Civil Service Commission. The Civil Service Reform Act of 1978 made significant changes, including restoration of the system as an executive function, and removal of some 7,000 top-level civil servants from the protection of the system. Basically, however, the system continues to be grounded on the principles of merit established in 1883. The number of federal employees covered has grown over the years until today some 90 percent fall under the protection of civil service. Many of the states and some local governments have followed the federal lead and have merit systems in place.

Has, then, the "stamp out patronage" campaign succeeded? There can be no question of its positive impact. The civil service/merit systems that now cross the country have removed from politicians, at least in terms of the law, thousands of government jobs. But to conclude that patronage has been stamped out overstates reality. In a different vein, to conclude that all patronage should be eliminated may not be correct or desirable, either. Hear the United States Supreme Court.

The Constitutional Issues

It is significant that the cases that have reached the United States Supreme Court on the subject of patronage are of recent vintage—1976, 1980, and 1990. Thus, regardless of the spread of merit systems, the practice of patronage remains an issue. The Court's decisions are instructive not only as to Constitutional rights; the decisions also argue the impact of patronage on the American political process and on the management of the public's business—with little agreement.

Elrod v. *Burns* (1976): Richard Elrod, a Democrat, was elected Sheriff of Cook County, Illinois, in 1970, succeeding a Republican. Consistent with past practice, he dismissed a number of incumbent (Republican) employees, because they lacked Democratic affiliation and were unable to secure Democratic sponsorship. In a close decision, the Court held the dismissals to be unconstitutional. Statement 2 of the Patronage Quiz is drawn from the majority opinion. It noted the infringement on the freedom of belief and association but found that the practice of patronage breeds inefficiency, corruption, and ineffective administration. In a stirring dissent, Justice Powell countered by observing that the history and long-prevailing practice across the country support the view that patronage hiring practices make a sufficiently substantial contribution to the practical functioning of our democratic system to support their relatively modest intrusion of First Amendment interests. (Statement 3 of the Quiz.) The majority opinion sanctioned the continuation of patronage hirings for policy-level and "confidential" positions.

Branti v. *Finkel* (1980): The Court, in this case, expanded and strengthened its holding in *Elrod,* saying that the ultimate inquiry is not whether the label "policy maker" or "confidential" fits a particular position. Rather, the question is whether the hiring authority can demonstrate that party affiliation is an appropriate requirement. The case involved two assistant public defenders from Rockland County, New York, both Republicans. When a Democrat was appointed as their boss, he tried to replace them with members of his own party. The Court found party affiliation not to be a job-related requirement.

Rutan v. *Republican Party of Illinois* (1990): This case involved state employees. In addition to patronage hiring decisions, the Court was asked to decide the constitutionality of several related political patronage practices—whether promotions, transfers, and recalls may be constitutionally based on party affiliation and support. The Court, in a five to four decision, ruled that such practices could not—that they are an impermissible infringement on First Amendment rights. Statement 4 of the Patronage Quiz is drawn from the majority opinion, written by Justice Brennan. Justice Scalia, in a dissent, said that "It [patronage] is a political arrangement that may sometimes be a reasonable choice, and should therefore be left to the judgment of the people's elected representatives."

The closeness of the decisions in the above cases would seem to indicate that the Court has not had its final say on the subject of patronage. It is also fairly safe to conclude that the Court's decisions have dampened the environment for the practice of patronage. But the total impact is not yet clear. What is obvious, however, is that a politician determined to have his way in hiring and other personnel practices will most often not only find it possible to do so but will be upheld by the law. To restate the theme noted earlier, this point moves the practice of patronage to the ethical playing field—what public officials legally have the power to do, and want to do, versus what best serves the public interest.

Some Problems of Patronage

Game-Playing and the Merit System

There are lots of ways to "get around" a merit system. This section provides a few illustrations. It begins with an example taken from the *Federal Political Personnel Manual*. This publication was prepared under the tutelage of Fred Malek, who was chief of the White House personnel office under President Nixon. Here's his "example of the rape of the merit system."

Let us assume that you have a career opening in your Department's personnel office for a Staff Recruitment Officer. Sitting in front of you is your college roommate from Stanford University in California who was born and raised in San Francisco. He received his law degree from . . . the University of California. While studying for the bar he worked at an advertising agency handling newspaper accounts. He also worked as a reporter on the college newspaper. Your personnel experts judge that he could receive an eligibility rating for a GS-11.

The first thing you do is tear up the old job description that goes with the job. You then have a new one written, to be classified as GS-11, describing the duties of that specific Staff Recruitment Officer as directed toward the recruitment of recent law graduates for entry level attorney positions, entry level public information officers for the creative arts and college news liaison sections of your public information shop, and to be responsible for general recruiting for entry level candidates on the West Coast. You follow that by listing your selective criteria as follows: Education: BA and LLB, stating that the candidate should have extensive experience and knowledge by reason of employment or residence on the West Coast. Candidates should have attended or be familiar with law schools and institutions of higher education, preferably on the West Coast. The candidate should also possess some knowledge by reasons of education or experience of the fields of college journalism, advertising, and law.

You then trot this candidate's Application for Federal Employment over to the Civil Service Commission, and shortly there-

> after he receives an eligibility rating for a GS-11. Your personnel office then sends over the job description (GS-11) along with selective criteria . . . When the moment arrives for the panel to "spin the register" you insure that your personnel office sends over two "friendly" bureaucrats. The register is then spun and your candidate will certainly be among the only three who even meet the selective criteria, much less be rated as among the "highest qualified" that meet the selective criteria. . . .[4]

Tinkering with job descriptions and selective criteria is one way to get around the requirements. It is possible, too, to manage examination outcomes. For example, where there is a Civil Service Commission charged with administering the personnel system, typically that commission promulgates the rules governing the selection process. Also, typically, those rules assign weight to an oral examination as part of the process, along the lines of the following illustrations:

1. (Entrance level) The written examination shall be weighted at 70 percent; the oral examination at 30 percent.
2. (Promotion) The written portion of the examination shall be weighted at 30 percent. The oral examination shall be equal to 35 percent. The (personnel) record evaluation shall be equal to 35 percent.

Civil Service Commissions, for the most part, are political appointments (Mayor and/or council). In principle, once appointed, these commissions are to function independently. A politician, determined to influence hirings, promotions, and disciplinary actions, however, can attempt, through appointments, to have commission members who will be sensitive to political "requests." With 30 points, or 65, to allocate on the basis of an oral "examination" and/or record evaluation—both subjective processes—it is not all that difficult to have the final eligibility that comes out in the proper "political order."

There are other ways, too, for politicians to get their people on the public payroll. The use of temporary or part-time hirings (some of which eventually become permanent) offer a convenient opportunity for patronage. Generally, such positions lie outside the requirements of a merit system.

As part of the typical merit system there is a cut in the hierarchy of positions that determines where the classified positions end and the nonclassified/exempt positions begin. Depending on where the cut is made, there is usually still a sizable playing field left for patronage. The use of noncompetitive examinations, and unassembled examinations enlarges the maneuvering room for appointments and promotions.

In fairness, more than one observer has noted that the bureaucratic morass that surrounds some merit systems, particularly at the federal and state levels, invites temptations to circumvent the system. It can even be argued that opportunities for such maneuvering serve the best interests of government. Thus again the point: in deciding how to use their discretion/power, ethical public officials will agonize over options and implications in search of the right thing to do. They will guard against some of the unethical temptations that usually come into play:

- Rationalization. "The job's not all that important. Joe [unqualified] can't do a lot of damage."
- Self-deception: "Everyone fudges the system. It's politics."
- Self-indulgence: "My nephew's out of work; got a wife and kids to support. Why shouldn't I use my position to help?"

How Widespread Is Patronage?

Gaining a handle on the practice of patronage in this country is a formidable task and beyond the scope of this paper. As we learn in civics and Political Science 101, our federal system of government grants to the states all powers not delegated to the federal government, including the power of each state to put in place its own system of local government. Thus, we have fifty different systems of local government in the country, each with its own language with respect to personnel systems. Some local governments are required to have merit/civil service systems; others are not. Some limit merit/civil service coverage to selected public employees, often policemen and firemen. The complexity does not end here.

Table 1 makes three important points. First, in terms of opportunities for patronage, the numbers lie clearly with governments

ETHICS IN STATE AND LOCAL GOVERNMENT

Table 1

Number of Governments in the United States, 1967–1987

Type of Government	1987	1967
TOTAL	83,237	81,299
U.S. Government	1	1
State Governments	50	50
Local Governments	83,186	81,248
Counties	3,042	3,049
Municipalities	19,200	18,048
Townships	16,691	17,105
School Districts	14,721	21,782
Special Districts	29,532	21,264

Source: U.S. Census of Governments, as reported in the "Introduction" to the *Yearbook* of the International City Management Association, Washington, DC, 1979 and 1990.

at the local level. In 1985 the Census Bureau reported that 60 percent of the public work force—some 10 million people—are employed at the local level. Second, the table forces a recognition of the fact that school districts and special districts (and public authorities) are part of the local government system—a very neglected part of the system. Third, with some 83,000 units, it is possible to make only generalized assumptions about the degree of patronage and its impact.

One assumption argued here is that there are still bountiful opportunities to practice patronage. The following observations, based on the *Yearbook* previously cited, are offered to support this argument, with some particular reference to the state of Pennsylvania:

Some of the nation's 3,000 counties, approximately 600, are now professionally managed, i.e., they have a chief administrative officer or chief executive, either elected or appointed. Many of the 600 might be expected to have merit personnel systems in place. One might speculate that most of the others continue to have an open door to patronage.

In Pennsylvania there are 67 counties. The state law governing them provides for merit selection and promotion only for police and fire personnel, and then only for the state's two largest counties. Other than these very limited categories, personnel practices are under the control of county Boards of Commissioners. These boards may provide for merit personnel systems. It is a fairly safe conclusion that most do not. Add to this the category of county "row officer"—independently elected positions such as treasurers, controllers, recorders of deeds, clerks of court—controlling hundreds of jobs. Conclusion: county officials wishing to find jobs for friends, relatives, and political supporters should not have much of a problem.

What little attention has been paid to patronage has often focused on large cities, frequently after it has reached the scandal stage and caught the attention of the national media. Taken as a whole, not much is known about the prevalence of patronage in the 83,000 plus units constituting the government system. Approximately 4,000 local governments are recognized by the International City Management Association as meeting that association's standards for professional management. It is within this group that one might expect to find personnel practices in the hands of a professional manager, operating on a nonpartisan basis. It is a safe guess that merit personnel systems are not observed in a majority of the other local government units. Take Pennsylvania again. There are 2,574 general local governments: 54 cities, 970 boroughs, 91 townships of the first class, and 1,459 townships of the second class. Some of these jurisdictions are professionally managed and operate under sound merit personnel systems. In most, however, the elected governing bodies are free to control personnel practices, except for full-time police and fire personnel. The state does place the hiring, promotion, and disciplining of these personnel within the jurisdiction of a civil service commission appointed by the governing body—except for the 1,459 townships of the second class. For them there are no civil service requirements. While it might be argued that most are small and patronage does not matter, the population range is from 29 to 52,000. But more important, is it appropriate to argue that public jobs in small communities do not count—that they are so simple that anyone can do them? Therefore, why not my brother-in-law? This argument fails both ethically and logically. All public jobs are important. They may be even more so in a small jurisdiction with limited resources, where the few employees must function as jacks-of-all-trades, and where every dollar counts.

Before leaving Pennsylvania, there is another provision in state law governing the 1,459 second-class townships that should cause an ethical eye to blink twice. Members of the Board of Township Supervisors (the township governing body) may employ *themselves* as roadmaster, laborer, township secretary, or treasurer.

How much is known about patronage practices in the nation's school districts, and in the thousands of special districts and authorities? Not much. But surely it is not unfair to speculate that there is ample opportunity to award public jobs other than on the basis of merit. Taken together, there are thousands of public jobs, and substantial funds, involved. Their functions are critical, whether they involve the education of children or managing a city water supply. They have long basked in the glow of efficiency and operate on a nonpartisan basis. Every now and then, however, we get a glimmer into their operations that calls such a conclusion into question. Two of the cases that follow provide more than a glimmer.

Patronage: Is It Ethics Gone Amok?

The morality of the spoils system was seen by some as the primary issue of debate when the practice was in full bloom in the nineteenth century. R. Fulton Cutting put it this way:

> The real crime committed against society by the spoils system is moral . . . it poisons our institutions at the fountainhead, corrupting the electorate and creating a political conscience antagonistic to morals.[5]

It may be overly dramatic to conclude that what is at stake in weighing the impact of patronage is our institution of government. But, on the other hand, to shrug off patronage as inconsequential in terms of its influence is unworthy of those who profess to care about the image of government and its efficiency and effectiveness. The cases that follow attempt to support this conclusion.

A simple paradigm, in the form of three ethical principles, is offered as a means of evaluating the practices revealed in the cases. These principles are easily recognizable by those familiar with the literature on ethical traditions and reasoning.

- Do no harm. Optimize the public good. Self-interest must yield to the public interest.
- Respect the rights, dignity, and freedom of individuals.
- Observe the canons of justice. Both benefits and burdens should be fairly distributed by government.

Illustration 1

The Power of Patronage

Federal indictments, in addition to listing extortion and bribery counts, charged that a city official and a former official used their ability to place people in city jobs as a tool to turn a city agency into a money-making machine. These officials controlled the City Parking Violations Bureau from the outside, because they used the power of political patronage to put their associates into key jobs . . . They turned the P.V.B. into their own private property, and it doesn't belong to them.

The New York Times
March 27, 1986

Conclusion: Ethics gone amok.

Illustration 2

The Case of the Undercover School Superintendent

A segment of "60 Minutes," February 25, 1990, dramatized not only the harmful affects of patronage, but also the distorted sense of public duty held by those who thrive on its practice. The Superintendent of Schools in Queens, New York, Coleman Glenn, recorded twenty-one undercover tapes, over a period of eight months, to gather information on corruption and unethical conduct on the part of School Board members. Among the revelations caught on tape:

- The main job of a political leader is to get jobs for friends, relatives and supporters, whether or not they are needed, and whether or not they are qualified.
- Make-work jobs were costing the School District around a million dollars a year.
- Teachers lacked books to support the curriculum. The library

was in disarray. Chairs were lacking. Only $250 was available for laboratory equipment. And more.
- Highly qualified, experienced individuals were passed over for positions such as Principal in favor of political supporters who were lacking in qualifications.
- The Superintendent was threatened with losing his job if he did not cooperate and hire the people wanted by a particular School Board member.

A member of the School Board who was not implicated in the scandal was asked by Harry Reasoner of "60 Minutes" why School Board members engaged in patronage. The reply: "Egos . . . That's the type of thing that makes them feel great and feeds off their egos . . . A lot of people would owe them because of their work . . . later on those favors are returned."[6]

Conclusion: Ethics gone amok.

Illustration 3

One Big Happy Family:
The Allegheny County Sanitary Authority (ALCOSAN)

It was noted earlier that not much is known about the political versus professional operation of public authorities and special districts. For the most part, it takes a scandal to capture the community interest and bring reform. The case of the Allegheny County Sanitary Authority brings to light what can occur when no one is "watching the store" and patronage brings together, particularly at the top levels, a group of friends, relatives, and other politically well-connected individuals. The Authority serves much of the greater Pittsburgh, Pennsylvania, area.

ALCOSAN is a joint city-county Authority. At the time of this story—1981–1987—the city appointed three members of the five-member board; the county, two. There were no restrictions on appointments, and typically appointments had gone to members of the City Council. The Authority Board appoints the Executive Director of the Authority, who is then accountable to the Board. At the time the scandal broke, the Executive Director was James Creehan. Mr. Creehan resigned in 1987 after the County Controller alleged a "pattern of abuse" at the Authority. The facts and commentary that follow come from the two major newspapers that cover the Pittsburgh metropolitan area: the *Pittsburgh Press* and the *Pittsburgh Post-Gazette*.

A Scan of Creehan's Political Connections

- Active in campaigns of Pennsylvania Governor Robert Casey. This includes a loan of $20,000 to one of Casey's campaigns. Creehan is also alleged to have loaned money to a county judge to help cover his campaign debts.
- Active in local Democratic politics. Served as a council member in a local borough; was a tax assessor for Allegheny County. Friends with members of the City Council. Sponsored by a council member for ALCOSAN Executive Director.
- Engaged in a business venture with the (then) city finance director, who is quoted as saying that Creehan is a "very, very capable manager . . . He's taken care of people, some very prominent people, when they were really down and out."

A Scan of Personnel Practices

Among the full-time ALCOSAN employees were:

- 10 current and past Democratic Party Committee members.
- Son-in-law of Creehan.
- Son of real estate partner of Creehan.
- Son and son-in-law of ALCOSAN Board member/city council member. Cousin of another Board member/council member. Aide to another city council member. Wife of another city council member.
- Brother of another ALCOSAN Board member who was also Chairman of the County Democratic Party Committee.
- Father of the City Controller.

Summer Jobs Program

The audit by the County Controller revealed that ALCOSAN spent nearly $1.6 million on a summer jobs program from 1981 to 1986. As many as 482 temporary employees were on the payroll at one time, far exceeding the Authority's 312 regular employees. Reportedly, only a few worked for the Authority. Most were said to have been assigned to other agencies or, possibly, did not work at all. Hiring was done by the Authority Board. The payroll was dotted with children, grandchildren, other relatives, and other politically connected persons.

And More . . .
- A Democratic Party ward chairman acknowledged that he helped fugitive Donald McCune to get a job with ALCOSAN as a field investigator. McCune was later indicted on four counts of extortion. He was also convicted of car theft while employed by ALCOSAN. He listed as references an ALCOSAN Board member and the county judge referred to earlier.
- An ALCOSAN Board member accepted money in return for the promise of a job.
- A former neighbor of an Authority Board member posed as an electrical engineer and gained more than $101,000 in no-bid contracts. It was later revealed that he was not a licensed engineer as claimed on his résumé.
- More than two-thirds of the legal fees paid by ALCOSAN between 1981 and 1986 went to the Philadelphia law firm where the Governor was associated.
- The lion's share of ALCOSAN insurance was purchased from an agency owned by a friend of both Creehan and an ALCOSAN Board member/council member.

Conclusion: Ethics gone amok.

Summary Observations, Illustrations 1–3

Do no harm. Respect individual rights. Be fair. All three ethical commands are violated by the practice of patronage as illustrated in the three cases. Public jobs belong to the public, not to public officials. There should be fair and open competition for (most of) these positions, resulting in competency for the job to be filled. There should not be discrimination in hiring or promotions.

Perhaps the greatest harm that comes from the practice of patronage is the damage that it does to the reputation of government, and the erosion of public trust that follows. It conjures up an image of self-serving, self-indulgent public officials, padding the public payrolls with incompetent people. But, the rain falls on the just as well as the unjust; there also exist public officials who serve nobly in pursuit of the public good, highly qualified, dedicated public employees—who, unfortunately, because they come under the broad umbrella of civil servants, are tainted by the same scratchy brush of patronage.

The principles of the ethical paradigm are broad. There are, however, some subsets that link patronage and ethics with core principles or commands of good public administration.

Be accountable. All three cases would seem to violate this command. Take ALCOSAN, for example. Patronage is only the tip of the iceberg. Aided and abetted by the "right" appointments, other questionable practices can follow. The newspaper accounts of the ALCOSAN scandal discussed extravagant and undocumented travel expenses—more than $141,000 between 1981 and 1986. Specific exposures demonstrated a total and blatant disregard for public accountability. Take the Board member who submitted an expense account for a trip to Kansas City that he never made. (He was in Atlantic City.) There were trips to various cities in Europe to highly technical conferences for which Board members had no background. The County Controller's audit revealed other questionable practices, such as breaking contracts into smaller parts (piecemealing) to avoid competitive bidding.

The points to be made are these: first, such practices would not easily go unchallenged if the right people (friends, relatives, political supporters) were not in the right place. The ALCOSAN case, and also the Parking Violations Bureau case, are clear examples of how an organization can be "taken over" to satisfy personal interests over the public interest. Second, where there is a lack of public accountability, can corruption be far behind? There were indictments in the Parking Violations Bureau scandal. In the Queens case, a (former) head of the School Board pleaded guilty to charges of coercion and fraud in connection with hiring practices. Some of the ALCOSAN revelations demonstrate corrupt, as well as unethical, conduct.

Provide supervision for all employees. Patronage can cast this command into disarray. When an employee is politically well-connected, with a political patron, a supervisor attempting to hold such an employee to performance standards, or to take disciplinary action may himself be the subject of recrimination.

Maintain high morale. High morale and productivity go hand in hand. Patronage is often viewed as bringing into the organization individuals who did not have to prove themselves for their appointments. It can result in employees with political patrons being treated differently: doing little work, showing up late or not showing up at all, not being required to meet the same standards, not being supervised. Promotions may go to patronage appointments ahead of more qualified candidates in the organization (the Queens school district case). High morale and the motivation to work are linked. Only motivated personnel are directed toward achieving an organization's goals.

Be attentive to cost and efficiency factors. Patronage can have severe consequences on both the cost and efficiency of government. Payroll padding was only one of the evils demonstrated in the cases. When patronage means finding a job or appointment for someone who is not qualified, one of two things happens. Either another qualified individual must be hired who can do the job, or the unqualified individual attempts work beyond his capability, resulting in inefficiency or, worse, jeopardy to the public health, safety, or welfare, depending on the nature of the work.

Patronage and Ethics: Not Always Clear-Cut

Illustration 4

Not all ethical questions with respect to patronage lend themselves to easy or conclusive answers. Another quiz will illustrate this dilemma:

You are a member of a city council. There are two vacancies in your police department, and the city proceeds to hire two new officers. Under civil service the positions are publicly advertised, there is a competitive examination, and the top three names are certified to council. Your son has taken the test and achieves the top score. He is hired by a unanimous vote of council.

Yes____No____Should there be a rule prohibiting relatives of elected officials from competing for city jobs?

Yes___No___Should you have discouraged your son from applying for the police job in the first place?

Yes___No___Should you have voted on his appointment?

When this case was presented to elected officials for their consideration, most had no trouble in answering No to the third question. One official, however, argued that it was not a conflict of interest to vote when his son had fairly competed, and it was his right to vote. There was a lively debate with respect to the other questions, centering largely on the issues of individual rights and fairness. These factors were seen as outweighing possible "harm," which might result from the public perception of hiring the son of a council member, or possible problems of supervision or morale within the police department. Where lies "right"?

Concluding Observations

1. There needs to be more communication, more debate, about ethics, more discussion of dilemmas and solutions. It would be naïve to conclude that talk will change the conduct of public officials determined to indulge themselves in the prerogatives of public office. But if there is enough publicity about the ethical dimensions and impact of a practice like patronage, it may result in a consciousness that was not there before. Real progress in strengthening our institution of government can come only if ethical conduct is internalized in the hearts and minds of those who bear the burdens and privileges of public office.

2. In the meantime, Codes of Ethics should provide prohibitons against patronage and nepotism. States, in addition to addressing their own problems with respect to patronage, should insist on personnel practices at the local level, including school districts, special districts and authorities, which can help to close the door to patronage abuse.

3. Public officials in leadership positions must understand that all good leaders are also teachers.

Patronage is government's setting a bad example, and teaching a wrong lesson.

NOTES

1. Jay M. Shafritz, *The Dorsey Dictionary of American Government and Politics* (Chicago: The Dorsey Press, 1988), pp. 375, 398–399.
2. Jack Rabin et al., eds., *Handbook on Public Personnel Administration and Labor Relations* (New York: Marcel Dekker, 1983).
3. Frederick C. Mosher, *Democracy and the Public Service* (New York: Oxford University Press, 1968), p. 65.
4. As in Jay M. Shafritz, Albert C. Hyde, and David H. Rosenbloom, *Personnel Management in Government* (New York: Marcel Dekker, 1986), pp. 57–58.
5. Dwight Waldo, *The Administrative State* (New York: The Ronald Press), 1948, p. 28.
6. CBS News, "60 Minutes," vol. XXII, no. 23, February 25, 1990, transcript, pp. 10–15.

New York's Ethics Reform: Restoring Trust in Government
Governor Mario M. Cuomo

In this article, Governor Mario Cuomo relates the drive toward ethics reform that has recently occurred in New York State. He reports on the contents of two recent state laws: the Ethics in Government Act and the Accountability, Audit and Internal Control Act. These measures have had the effect of bolstering New York State's conflict of interest prohibition, strengthening the regulations against the "revolving door" between government and industry, requiring comprehensive financial disclosure from public officials in the state, and providing a concerted effort in the area of internal control and accounting for all state governmental entities. The Ethics in Government Act also established a State Ethics Commission and a Legislative Ethics Committee, with broad powers to monitor compliance with the new ethics provisions. Cuomo contends that these efforts have, to a degree, restored public confidence in New York State government.

In New York and in the nation, government is built on a constitutional foundation. We look to government to make real the rule of law. The miracle that it has worked so well for so long is a result of the solemn compact that requires everyone who

Mario M. Cuomo, "New York's Ethics Reform: Restoring Trust in Government," *Journal of State Government* 62 (September/October 1989), pp. 176–179. © 1989 The Council of State Governments. Reprinted with permission from *Journal of State Government*.

seeks the benefits of this democracy to live by the laws that created it—everyone, including public officials who are given the privilege and responsibility of governing.

Everyone who is part of the machinery of government in an appointed or elected capacity has an overarching duty of trust, honesty and responsibility to the public. Being in such a delicate and powerful position, government officials are not as free as ordinary citizens might be to conduct their public or private lives. They have a new life, a new sworn obligation to be scrupulously forthright and truthful in all of their dealings. It is a mantle they don freely, and because they choose it, they are bound to live by those new, more stringent rules.

This is not to say that our insistence on significant ethical standards is limited to those who serve in the public sector. Technological advances and the increasing sophistication of our society give rise to new opportunities and require new rules and standards to govern our conduct. For example, a wide range of ethical issues confronts the medical profession in such areas as AIDS, organ transplants, genetic engineering and life-support systems. In journalism, we have observed debate about the ethics of inquiring into the personal lives of presidential candidates and other political leaders at all levels of government. In the business world, revelations of insider trading have focused attention on the need for stricter standards of conduct and for internal controls.

But, while the ethics debate is not restricted to government, it has a particularly critical role in assuring the integrity and accountability of our governmental institutions which, in turn, are a measure of the strength of our democracy. Without an effective code of conduct that applies to those who govern, government will not have the trust and confidence of the people.

No part of a public official's life really goes unscrutinized. Any action, public or private, is open to positive or negative interpretation. As such, the laws addressed to regulate the ethics of those who govern must deal not only with bald impropriety, but also with the *appearance* of impropriety.

Because such laws deal with appearances as well as direct actions, they are much more than simple regulatory mechanisms. They must impose on government and the people who make up the governmental structure a set of standards of ethics and accountability that truly fits the expectations of the people—because it is the people of the state and the nation whose ultimate consent is the foundation of government.

At the same time, in all fairness to our public officials, the rules that govern their ethics and their spending must articulate standards with precise clarity. The rules must be working guidelines rather than abstract descriptions. They must be instruments that effectively apply the principle as well as properly declare it. Otherwise, there will be a chilling effect on government's interest in carrying out its ordinary workings, let alone risking forays into new, untested areas on behalf of the public interest.

In 1987, I signed into law two measures consistent with these principles that have brought New York from a position far behind other states to the forefront on ethics in government. They are the Ethics in Government Act and the Accountability, Audit and Internal Control Act of 1987, separate pieces of legislation linking, for the first time in this state, working mechanisms for governmental ethics reform and government entity accountability. Never before in the 212-year history of New York State's government has the Legislature done so much to regulate the private interests of public officials.

While this legislation is not the final word on the ethics and accountability of government and government officials, these acts can mark the beginning of a new era of reform. They show the direction in which the state intends to move, toward an enduring assurance of sound, honest government that can be trusted to advance the common good economically, reasonably and intelligently.

What types of situations create a potential for unethical conduct in government? Some examples quickly come to mind. A state employee charged with awarding a no-bid contract may have a substantial financial interest in a company seeking to obtain the contract. Legislators who are also attorneys may have more than one problem. They may seek to represent their clients before an agency whose matters they vote upon regularly, or they may represent clients on matters that may pass through their committee. Further, employees of a state agency may leave government service for a position in the private sector and then represent clients before their former agency. At the very least, each of these situations creates an appearance of impropriety and an opportunity for undue influence and favoritism—or worse.

The Ethics in Government Act addresses situations such as these. First, it strengthens and adds new conflict-of-interest prohibition to govern the conduct of public officers and employees as well as certain political party officers. The prior code of ethics was striking in its weakness; it failed to address many critical issues that could have given rise to improprieties. The Ethics in Government Act amended this code to add important restrictions for statewide elected officials, legislators and state and legislative employees who hold policy-making positions or receive compensation above a specified grade level (currently, approximately $50,000) and for political party officials in counties with a population of 300,000 or more or who earn more than $30,000 for their party position. Under the new law, these individuals are barred from appearing before state agencies and from communicating with state agency personnel with respect to matters being handled by private firms of which they are a member. In addition, these public officers and employees are barred from doing business with the state in the absence of competitive bidding.

The conflict-of-interest prohibitions are further strengthened by new provisions addressing the so-called revolving door, which arises when a government employee leaves public service for a private-sector position that might involve dealing with the state. Under the new legislation, former state officers or employees are barred for two years from appearing or practicing before the agency that previously employed them. In addition, such individuals are barred forever from appearing or practicing before any state agency in relation to any case, proceeding, application or transaction with respect to which they were directly concerned and in which they personally participated or which was under their active consideration.

A second major focus of the new ethics code is a comprehensive financial disclosure requirement. All elected officials, as well as all employees or unpaid appointees who hold policy-making positions or employees who earn more than $50,000 in government salaries are required to make full and complete disclosure of their financial interests. This provision allows public review and scrutiny of the private holdings of public servants to assure that these holdings do not pose a conflict with respect to the officials' public responsibilities.

A third facet of the ethics legislation concerns the creation of strong ethics commissions with subpoena power to monitor compliance with the new provisions, investigate violations and impose penalties for wrongful conduct. This enforcement mechanism is a critical component of the new legislation. Under the prior law, enforcement of the ethics provisions was the responsibility of district attorneys. However, ethics rules are based on the "appearance" standard rather than the outright venality with which prosecutors are more used to dealing. This, coupled with the usual heavy load of more "traditional" criminal cases on the prosecutor's docket, resulted in insufficient enforcement for violations of the appearance-based standards of an ethics code. A body whose primary mandate is to receive and review financial disclosure statements and monitor compliance with conflict-of-interest prohibitions provides a constant oversight mechanism and can be expected to bring vigor, including the use of criminal sanctions, to the enforcement of ethics rules.

The Audit Act provides an important complement to the new Ethics Act, but the Audit Act had a different genesis: Unlike the Ethics Act, neither the public nor the press called for its enactment. The executive and legislative branches acted together on their own initiative to create it.

Specifically, the Audit Act provides for three distinct protections. The first is internal administrative and accounting control systems for all state governmental entities. This protection consists of rules and checks designed to safeguard assets, confirm the accuracy and reliability of accounting data, deter and detect fraud, waste, abuse and error, and assure that personnel actually perform the services for which they are being paid. The second protection is a mandatory internal compliance review to enable state officers to know whether the system of rules and checks is being followed.

Finally, and most important, the Audit Act requires external audits by independent accounting firms at least once every two years of the Office of the Governor, the Division of the Budget, the Department of Law, the Department of Audit and Control and the Legislature. These independent accounting firms will pore over the actual books and records, reviewing and commenting publicly on the effectiveness of the measures and procedures that these governmental entities have adopted in order to ensure the integrity of their operations.

*   *   *

Since I signed the Ethics and Audit Acts into law in 1987, we have gotten off to a good start with implementing this legislation. An agreement reached with the Legislature in 1988 permitted early formation of the State Ethics Commission, which has the power to enforce the Ethics Act for executive branch officers and employees, and the Legislative Ethics Committee, the parallel body for the legislative branch. I am grateful for the willingness to serve of the individuals I appointed to the State Ethics Commission [in 1988]. The chairman is Elizabeth D. Moore, the director of the State Office of Employee Relations. The other members are Joseph J. Buderwitz Jr., an attorney and former chairman of the Board of Public Disclosure, Angelo A. Costanza, a western New York businessman and civic leader, Dr. Norman Lamm, the president of Yeshiva University, and Robert B. McKay, the distinguished law professor and former dean of New York University Law School. The commission immediately began to educate the covered employees and officers concerning the new Ethics Act, to issue important advisory opinions and to set up the process for collecting and reviewing the thousands of financial disclosure forms that were filed [in 1989].

There are, however, further legislative steps that I would like to see taken. Upon the recommendation of the Ethics Commission and the Commission on Government Integrity, chaired by Dean John Feerick of Fordham University Law School, I proposed legislation . . . to strengthen the ethics law further by permitting the Ethics Commission or the Legislative Ethics Committee and criminal prosecutors to conduct parallel civil and criminal prosecutions; current law permits a criminal prosecution only upon referral by the Ethics Commission or the Legislative Ethics Committee. In addition, I proposed legislation that was recommended by the Commission on Government Integrity to address reforms in local government ethics. After extensive state-wide meetings and a hearing, the Commission on Government Integrity proposed a bill that contains a minimum standard of ethical conduct applicable to all local government, regardless of size, and contains workable annual and transactional disclosure requirements.

Such state and local government ethics legislation discussed will again be part of my reform agenda [in 1990]. And there will be another item on that agenda that directly impacts government integrity: campaign finance reform.

This is an urgently needed reform I have advocated throughout my tenure in public office. Like weak ethics laws, poor campaign finance laws plainly undermine public confidence in government. It is essential that we eliminate the evils of the enormous contributions and vast expenditures. The current system forces candidates to raise and spend huge amounts of money to stay competitive. I have had experience trying to raise money for political campaigns, both when it was extremely difficult against wealthy opponents and when fund-raising has been easier. I do not like the current process either way, and I do not know many politicians who do.

The Assembly under the leadership of Speaker Mel Miller has passed my proposed campaign finance bill for state executive and legislative offices in the last two years. The Senate so far has not said yes but neither have they said no. New York City has enacted sound campaign finance legislation. I hope that we at the state level can build on this next year, and I will push hard for statewide campaign finance reform.

Another important area for reform relates to the pension rights of a public official who has been convicted of an official corruption crime. In 1987, I asked the Commission on Government Integrity to examine the adequacy of laws, regulations and procedures relating to ensuring public servants are duly accountable for the faithful discharge of their public trust. In response, the commission, after considering the need, concluded that government integrity would be promoted by the prompt passage of pension forfeiture legislation.

Based in part on the commission's findings and upon a proposal made by State Comptroller Edward Regan in 1988, I submitted, as part of my 1989 legislative program, a bill providing that the public retirement pension rights and benefits of persons convicted of certain felonies relating to their public employment shall be subject to possible forfeiture. Some progress has been made in discussions of this proposal with the Legislature. I am convinced that pension forfeiture is an effective means of deterring the commission of work-related felonies and will continue to press this proposal.

I also believe that a serious interest in ethics in government requires a strong commitment to open government. Some things need to be secret, but they are far fewer than government officials are inclined to believe. A greater open-door policy with greater access to government officials and information is necessary. Events again and again confirm the wisdom of the late U.S. Supreme Court Associate Justice Louis D. Brandeleis' observation that "sunlight is the best disinfectant."

New York's strong open meetings, whistle-blower protection and freedom of information laws could all be improved. To that end, I am urging legislation to extend the open meetings law to political caucuses in single party dominated localities, to extend the freedom of information law's presumption of disclosure to the Legislature and to insure whistle-blower protection to those who take good faith allegations of misconduct to the media.

The work of improving integrity in government can never be considered finished. I am proud to have already accomplished significant reform, but I am also eager to do more.

Our goal is to build the strongest possible relationship of trust and confidence between the people and government. Because special powers are wielded by those in government, because government should set an example, because government spends other people's money and because history teaches the potential for abuse and favoritism, the public has a right to hold government officials to an especially high standard of ethical conduct.

When we enact laws that set this high standard in a clear way, we do a service to all concerned. By strengthening the credibility of government and the standing of public service, we create an environment in which the important task of advancing the common good through vigorous government can better continue.

Integrity and Ethical Standards in New York State Government
A Report of the New York State Commission on Government Integrity

The following selection contains excerpts from a letter that reports to the Governor of New York the findings of the New York State Commission on Government Integrity. It is one example of the ethics reform measures undertaken by many states. The Commission was formed by Governor Mario Cuomo and served under the leadership of John D. Feerick. After working for forty months, the popularly named Feerick Commission issued its final report that included some very strong language about the problems of ethics in New York State. The Commission's report to Cuomo concludes that there is much work that needs to be done and recommends several creative ways for New York State to enter an age of ethics reform. Moreover, the Commission seems to contradict the more optimistic tone of Cuomo's evaluation of New York State's ethics reform that is expressed in the previous selection.

September 18, 1990

The Honorable Mario M. Cuomo
Governor, State of New York
State Capitol, Executive Chamber
Albany, New York 12224

Dear Governor Cuomo:

This letter constitutes the final report of the Commission on Government Integrity.

The Commission was created by Executive Order 88.1 and directed to examine a wide variety of subjects concerning government integrity in New York State. Since its inception, the Commission

Integrity and Ethical Standards in New York State Government, A Report of the New York State Commission on Government Integrity [author's title], September 18, 1990, State of New York, Commission on Government Integrity, New York, NY.

has submitted 20 reports containing specific recommendations for reform of New York laws, regulations and procedures. Some of these recommendations can be implemented by executive order; others require action by the New York State Legislature. Most of the recommendations would impose no additional cost on the taxpayer. . . .

We would be remiss if we did not acknowledge the extraordinary dedication of the Commission's staff . . . throughout our tenure. Their service to the citizens of this State was exemplary.

The Commission has had an active existence. It met frequently, conducted 25 days of public hearings, . . . questioned more than 1000 individuals privately or publicly, and examined many thousands of government records and documents. In all, the Commission exercised its subpoena power 213 times. As part of its investigative work, the Commission uncovered evidence of possible violations of law which it has transmitted to the appropriate law enforcement authorities as directed by the Executive Order. The Commission also has conducted investigations that did not result in reports or hearings, testified in support of its recommendations before committees of the New York State Legislature, and addressed numerous citizen and government groups throughout the State of New York.

The Commission has engaged in extensive litigation in state and federal courts to enforce its subpoenas and respond to efforts designed to hinder its investigative work. The results of the litigation were uniformly favorable to the Commission's authority, in some instances establishing new legal precedents. . . .

Based on the Commission's work over the past 40 months, it has found that the laws, regulations and procedures of New York State fall woefully short in guarding against political abuses in an alarming number of areas. We have thoroughly exposed these weaknesses repeatedly in our hearings and reports. Despite significant steps taken in New York City and a few other local governments and a tentative beginning by the State in 1987 with the passage of the Ethics Act and the creation of this Commission, we are of the unanimous view that New York State has not yet demonstrated a real commitment to ethical reform in government.

Our State trails the pack in the area of government ethics legislation, a field in which we should play a leadership role. The campaign finance law of the State is a disgrace and embarrassment; incumbents are favored unfairly by the State Election Law; the laws governing access to the primary ballot are completely at odds with the democratic principle of open elections; judges are elected in a manner that weakens the independence of the judiciary; personnel practices are tainted with politics; municipal officials are given little guidance in handling conflicts of interest; and untold millions of taxpayer dollars are wasted as a result of flawed contracting procedures.

As we have repeatedly emphasized, the area that cries out most urgently for immediate legislative action is campaign finance. The Commission recognized early in its work that there was no more important source of erosion of confidence in government. Continued investigations reinforced that belief. Indeed, New York State may have the most primitive system in the United States. Consider the following deficiencies:

First, there are no meaningful limits on the size of campaign contributions. They are so high that to call them "limits" is a mockery. Moreover, the $5000 annual limitation on corporations is easily evaded by using subsidiary and related corporations to make contributions.

Second, the State Board of Elections lacks the wherewithal to enforce existing limits on campaign contributions. It does not have the resources; it does not have the required degree of independence from those it must police; and its makeup of two members from each major political party inevitably results in either logrolling or frequent deadlocks.

Third, New York State's current disclosure rules do not produce disclosure. The statements filed by candidates do not have to be typed or even be legible, and many are not. Moreover, candidates do not have to reveal their contributors' employers; political advertisements do not have to state their sponsors; and the Board of Elections is not required to publicize widely the information it receives. The effect of the current disclosure requirements is to allow candidates to hide their sources of support. It appears that government in New York does not want the public to know who pays the cost of bringing their leaders to office. The State's failure to address the issue of disclosure emphasizes the lack of commitment to government ethics reform in New York.

Fourth, we found at both the State and the local level a

widespread and corrosive practice of public officials soliciting campaign contributions or support from public employees and from those entities doing business with government. This practice inevitably leads to at least a strong potential for abuse.

In order to perform its investigative work, the Commission was required to launch a massive project to computerize for the first time in the history of the State the Financial Disclosure Records of the Board of Elections. The Commission disseminated the information yielded by this project throughout the State and provided the Board with the results of our work. This is merely a start. It remains for the political leaders of the State to take the steps necessary to remedy the alarming weakness in the area of campaign finance disclosure and enforcement.

You cogently testified before our Commission: "I believe that a continued improvement by our legislature, a persistent, undeviating emphasis on reform by the executive—together with your help—can make this the beginning of the most exciting reform era in this State's history." Overall, we have found that the unwillingness of New York's political leaders to embrace major ethics reforms in the many areas referred to erodes government integrity. We have given careful consideration to the urgent need for ethical government in New York State and have made many important recommendations. In our view, the leaders of both major parties have failed the citizens of New York by not insisting upon much needed ethics reforms.

Regrettably, there has been no serious public debate of ethics issues in the halls of government in Albany since 1987—debate which would have served to inform the people of the State. Instead partisan, personal and vested interests have been allowed to come before larger public interests. At a time when people around the globe are looking at democracy as a model, we are not proud of New York's failure to take a strong leadership role in areas of ethics reform.

We believe that you, along with Senate Majority Leader Marino and Assembly Speaker Miller, can play a major role in creating the political will and giving the citizens of New York a period of ethics reform of which they can be proud. We urge that this be done.

The work of our Commission in laying out an agenda for restoring the public trust in New York is at an end. However, we as private citizens will continue to press for government ethics reform. The Commission has presented you with a strong set of recommendations for reform pursuant to the broad mandate of your Executive Order. We continue to hope that you and other New York leaders will give government ethics reforms the emphasis which they deserve and make this an era of reform rather than one of shame and squandered opportunity.

Respectfully submitted,

John D. Feerik, *Chairman*
Richard D. Emery
Patricia M. Hynes
James L. Magavern
Bernard S. Meyer
Bishop Emerson J. Moore
Cyrus R. Vance

ICMA Code of Ethics with Guidelines

The International City Management Association (ICMA) is the professional association of appointed administrators who serve in cities, counties, regional councils, and other local government units. The following selection is a reprint of the "ICMA Code of Ethics with Guidelines" that was adopted by the ICMA Executive Board in May of 1990. The Code is instructive for its breadth and depth in treating many responsibilities of appointed local officials. It contains provisions and guidelines for acting in such general areas as the obligations of appointed officials to the public, to their locally elected officials, and to each other. More specific issues also raised in the document include confidentiality on the job, political activities, gifts, investments and other conflicts of interest, endorsements, and outside employment. Taken as a working document, the ICMA Code provides assistance to local officials as they attempt to meet the many responsibilities of their jobs and resolve the various moral mazes that they inevitably will encounter.

"ICMA Code of Ethics with Guidelines," as adopted by the ICMA Executive Board, in *Who's Who in Local Government Management*, 1990–1991. Reprinted with permission from the International City Management Association.

The purpose of the International City Management Association is to increase the proficiency of city managers, county managers, and other municipal administrators and to strengthen the quality of urban government through professional management. To further these objectives, certain ethical principles shall govern the conduct of every member of the International City Management Association, who shall:

1. Be dedicated to the concepts of effective and democratic local government by responsible elected officials and believe that professional general management is essential to the achievement of this objective.
2. Affirm the dignity and worth of the services rendered by government and maintain a constructive, creative, and practical attitude toward urban affairs and a deep sense of social responsibility as a trusted public servant.

Guideline

[Advise] officials of other municipalities. When members advise and respond to inquiries from elected or appointed officials of other municipalities, they should inform the administrators of those communities.

3. Be dedicated to the highest ideals of honor and integrity in all public and personal relationships in order that the member may merit the respect and confidence of the elected officials, of other officials and employees, and of the public.

Guidelines

Public confidence. Members should conduct themselves so as to maintain public confidence in their profession, their local government, and in their performance of the public trust.
Impression of influence. Members should conduct their official and personal affairs in such a manner as to give the clear impression that they cannot be improperly influenced in the performance of their official duties.
Appointment commitment. Members who accept an appoint-

ment to a position should not fail to report for that position. This does not preclude the possibility of a member considering several offers or seeking several positions at the same time, but once a *bona fide* offer of a position has been accepted, that commitment should be honored. Oral acceptance of an employment offer is considered binding unless the employer makes fundamental changes in terms of employment.

Credentials. An application for employment should be complete and accurate as to all pertinent details of education, experience, and personal history. Members should recognize that both omissions and inaccuracies must be avoided.

Professional respect. Members seeking a management position should show professional respect for persons formerly holding the position or for others who might be applying for the same position. Professional respect does not preclude honest differences of opinion; it does preclude attacking a person's motives or integrity in order to be appointed to a position.

Confidentiality. Members should not discuss or divulge information with anyone about pending or completed ethics cases, except as specifically authorized by the Rules of Procedure for Enforcement of the Code of Ethics.

Seeking employment. Members should not seek employment in a community having an incumbent administrator who has not resigned or been officially informed that his or her services are to be terminated.

4. Recognize that the chief function of local government at all times is to serve the best interests of all of the people.

Guideline

Length of service. A minimum of two years generally is considered necessary in order to tender a professional service to the municipality. A short tenure should be the exception rather than a recurring experience. However, under special circumstances it may be in the best interests of the municipality and the member to separate in a shorter time. Examples of such circumstances would include refusal of the appointing authority to honor commitments concerning conditions of employment, a vote of no confidence in the member, or severe personal problems. It is the responsibility of an applicant for a position to ascertain conditions of employment. Inadequately determining terms of employment prior to arrival does not justify premature termination.

5. Submit policy proposals to elected officials; provide them with facts and advice on matters of policy as a basis for making decisions and setting community goals; and uphold and implement municipal policies adopted by elected officials.

Guideline

Conflicting roles. Members who serve multiple roles—working as both city attorney and city manager for the same community, for example—should avoid participating in matters that create the appearance of a conflict of interest. They should disclose the potential conflict to the governing body so that other opinions may be solicited.

6. Recognize that elected representatives of the people are entitled to the credit for the establishment of municipal policies; responsibility for policy execution rests with the members.

7. Refrain from participation in the election of the members of the employing legislative body, and from all partisan political activities which would impair performance as a professional administrator.

Guidelines

Elections of the governing body. Members should maintain a reputation for serving equally and impartially all members of the governing body of the muncipality they serve, regardless of party. To this end, they should not engage in active participation in the election campaign on behalf of or in opposition to candidates for the governing body.

Elections of elected executives. Members should not engage in the election campaign of any candidate for mayor or elected county executive.

Other elections. Members share with their fellow citizens the right and responsibility to exercise their franchise and voice their opinion on public issues. However, in order not to impair their effectiveness on behalf of the municipalities they serve, they should not participate in election campaigns for representatives from their area to county, school, state, and federal offices.

Elections on the Council-Manager Plan. Members may assist in preparing and presenting materials that explain the council-manager form of government to the public prior to an election on the use of the plan. If assistance is required by another community, members may respond. All activities regarding ballot issues should be conducted within local regulations and in a professional manner.

Presentation of issues. Members may assist the governing body in presenting issues involved in referenda such as bond issues, annexations, and similar matters.

8. Make it a duty continually to improve the member's professional ability and to develop the competence of associates in the use of management techniques.

9. Keep the community informed on municipal affairs; encourage communication between the citizens and all municipal officers; emphasize friendly and courteous service to the public; and seek to improve the quality and image of public service.

10. Resist any encroachment on professional responsibilities, believing the member should be free to carry out official policies without interference, and handle each problem without discrimination on the basis of principle and justice.

Guideline

Information sharing. The member should openly share information with the governing body while diligently carrying out the member's responsibilities as set forth in the charter or enabling legislation.

11. Handle all matters of personnel on the basis of merit so that fairness and impartiality govern a member's decisions, pertaining to appointments, pay adjustments, promotions, and discipline.

Guideline

Equal opportunity. Members should develop a positive program that will ensure meaningful employment opportunities for all segments of the community. All programs, practices, and operations should (1) provide equality of opportunity in employment for all persons; (2) prohibit discrimination because of race, color, religion, sex, national origin, political affiliation, physical handicaps, age, or marital status; and (3) promote continuing programs of affirmative action at every level within the organization.

It should be the members' personal and professional responsibility to actively recruit and hire minorities and women to serve on professional staffs throughout their organization.

12. Seek no favor; believe that personal aggrandizement or profit secured by confidential information or by misuse of public time is dishonest.

Guidelines

Gifts. Members should not directly or indirectly solicit any gift or accept or receive any gift—whether it be money, services, loan, travel, entertainment, hospitality, promise, or any other form—under the following circumstances: (1) it could be reasonably inferred or expected that the gift was intended to influence them in the performance of their official duties; or (2) the gift was intended to serve as a reward for any official action on their part.

It is important that the prohibition of unsolicited gifts be limited to circumstances related to improper influence. In *de minimus* situations such as tobacco and meal checks for example, some modest maximum dollar value should be determined by the member as a guideline. The guideline is not intended to isolate members from normal social practices where gifts among friends, associates, and relatives are appropriate for certain occasions.

Investments in conflict with official duties. Members should not invest or hold any investment, directly or indirectly, in any financial business, commercial, or other private transaction that creates a conflict with their official duties.

In the case of real estate, the potential use of confidential information and knowledge to further a member's personal interest requires special consideration. This guideline recognizes that members' official actions and decisions can be influenced if there is a conflict with personal investments. Purchases and sales which might be interpreted as speculation for quick profit ought to be avoided (see the guideline on "Confidential Information").

Because personal investments may prejudice or may appear to influence official actions and decisions, members may, in concert with their governing body, provide for disclosure of such investments prior to accepting their position as municipal administrator or prior to any official action by the governing body that may affect such investments.

Personal relationships. Members should disclose any personal relationship to the governing body in any instance where there could be the appearance of a conflict of interest. For example, if the manager's spouse works for a developer doing business with the local government, that fact should be disclosed.

Confidential information. Members should not disclose to others, or use to further their personal interest, confidential information acquired by them in the course of their official duties.

Private employment. Members should not engage in, solicit, negotiate for, or promise to accept private employment nor should they render services for private interests or conduct a private business when such employment, service, or business creates a conflict with or impairs the proper discharge of their official duties.

Teaching, lecturing, writing, or consulting are typical activities that may not involve conflict of interest or impair the proper discharge of their official duties. Prior notification of the appointing authority is appropriate in all cases of outside employment.

Representation. Members should not represent any outside interest before any agency, whether public or private, except with the authorization of or at the direction of the appointing authority they serve.

Endorsements. Members should not endorse commercial products by agreeing to use their photograph, endorsement, or quotation in paid or other commercial advertisements, whether or not for compensation. Members may, however, agree to endorse the following, provided they do not receive any compensation: (1) books or other publications; (2) professional development or educational services provided by nonprofit membership organizations or recognized educational institutions; (3) products and/or services in which the local government has a direct economic interest.

Members' observations, opinions, and analyses of commercial products used or tested by their municipalities are appropriate and useful to the profession when included as part of professional articles and reports.

Ethics, Accountability, and Term Limitation
Harvey L. White

Term limitation has recently become a fierce source of debate in government ethics. Proponents feel that limiting the number of terms that a member of a legislature can serve will enhance the overall ethical character of these institutions at all levels of government. Harvey White, of the University of Pittsburgh, reviews the pros and cons of the term limitation movement.

A recent effort to assure the ethical behavior of public officials and to improve the overall accountability of government has been expressed through the concept of "term limitation." Simply put, term limitation is merely a limit placed on the number of terms that legislators and elected executives are allowed to serve. Because this restriction has extensive political, financial, and Constitutional implications, however, the term limitation movement is embroiled in political debate.

For a "new idea," term limitation is not really very recent at all. It has been an issue since the First Continental Congress, when members were precluded from serving more than three years in any six-year period. In 1951, the United States Constitution was amended to limit the number of times a person can be elected to the office of President. Thirty states have imposed some kind of limit on officials elected statewide. Many cities have limits on the number of terms a person can serve as mayor. Measures in Kansas City, Missouri, and San Jose, California, have also placed limits on the terms of city council members.

The current movement for term limitation stems from suggestions that legislative bodies would be more responsive to the needs of constituents if the terms of office of members were restrained. It is argued that entrenched legislators tend to come under the control of special interest groups, and to have a "gridlock" type of attitude on critical issues such as crime, trans-

Harvey L. White, "Ethics, Accountability and Term Limitation." Previously unpublished article. Printed with permission of the author.

portation, taxes, public debt, and the environment. It is further argued that this entrenchment makes it almost impossible for women, minorities, "citizen legislators," and others who would be closer to their constituencies to get elected. Term limitation, as proponents view it, would make legislative institutions more representative, more accountable, and thus more ethical.

Accountability and Term Limitation

The issue of legislative accountability is steeped in political debate. Elected public officials are theoretically accountable to the political sovereignty of the voters. Competitive elections are supposed to make politicians accountable to the voters. However, incumbents at all levels of government are routinely reelected to office with little competition from challengers. Thus, advocates of term limitation contend that there has been a virtual disappearance of competitive elections in recent years.

More than 95 percent of incumbents in the U.S. House of Representatives seeking reelection in 1988 won, and most by margins that could not be termed "competitive." The winners either were unopposed or beat their opponents by at least forty percentage points in 242 of 435 districts; the margin was twenty to forty points in 128 districts. Only six incumbents seeking reelection, in 1988, lost, and five of them had received negative media involving their personal (nonlegislative-related) affairs. Term limitation advocates point out that the routine reelection of House members has turned the national legislature into a permanent government, insulated from its constituents.[1]

Critics of legislatures have also pointed to resource inequities between incumbents and their challengers as another justification for term limitation. Of particular note is legislative staff support and campaign contributions. For example, the House of Representatives has nearly tripled its staff during the last two decades. House members have put a large portion of this staff to work in district offices. Augmented Congressional staff in district offices is equivalent to year-round campaign personnel, who keep incumbents before voters in a way virtually no challenger can rival.[2]

Campaign contributions are also resources that contribute to the noncompetitive nature of Congressional races. Organized interest groups have heavily backed incumbents. Of $50 million contributed to Congressional candidates in 1989 by political action committees, more than 90 percent went to incumbents. Advocates of term limitation argue that "Congress has become a house of lords, a ruling elite insulated from accountability to all but the interests who spend lavishly to win attention."[3] Time, term limitation proponents insist, has made members of American legislatures at all levels both corrupt and ethically bankrupt.

Ethics and Term Limitation

Power, prestige, and other amenities, which accrue with tenure in office, are said to have allowed legislative members to place themselves above the set of morals, principles, and values that is applied to others in our society. As opposed to models of political honesty and responsibility, they frequently pursue their own self-aggrandizement. Tenure is also thought to facilitate the development of interpersonal relationships and institutional commitments that encourage legislators to tolerate unethical behavior by their colleagues. In contrast to this tolerance, legislatures have consistently demanded higher ethical standards of behavior from executive branch officials, who stay in office for shorter periods of time. Such double standards have led some critics to conclude that ethical reform is beyond the scope of most legislatures without term limitation.

As columnist Michael Kramer sees it, the premise of term limitation is the only option left for the public: "If there must be life after Congress, then maybe finally, its members will consider the national interest before their own reelection."[4] Others see term limitation as an infringement on the Constitutional rights of voters to select their representatives.

Constitutional Issues and Term Limitation

Opponents of term limitation argue that it is unconstitutional because it deprives people of the right to choose their own representatives. Because the Supreme Court has never considered a challenge to legislative term limits, no one can speak with certainty about their constitutionality at this time. Still, challenges are being raised. A 1990 case was filed in Kansas City, Missouri, by council members about to lose their seats because of a local term limitation measure. These council members insist that electoral districts should be entitled to keep any representative they choose. Similarly, officials in California have indicated their intent to challenge the term limitation measure passed there.

One school of thought even questions voters' authority to limit terms for members of Congress. The Constitution of the United States does not directly address the issue of term limitation for members of Congress. The Constitution does indicate in Article 1, Section 4, however, that "the times, places, and manner of holding elections for Senators and Representatives shall be prescribed in each state by the Legislature thereof; but the Congress may at any time by law make or alter such regulations." Opponents of term limitation believe that they will prevail in the courts, because determining legislators' terms of office is a Congressional prerogative. Yet, in the long run, they are determined to convince voters that it is simply a bad idea that would significantly reduce the quality of government.

Term Limitation—A Symptom or a Cure?

Opponents of term limitation argue that long tenure in elected office has many positive aspects. Longevity enables lawmakers to discern the nation's real needs; to find out where the levers of powers are and to use them to advantage, in order to get votes that benefit their districts. Besides, they point out, the longevity of legislators is overstated: state legislators' tenure in office is, on the average, between eight and nine years. Also contrary to the detractors' case is the fact that there has been a two-thirds turnover in Congress in the past twelve years. Term limitation is viewed, therefore, as reform gone amok and would only diminish legislators' ability to serve their constituents. They insist that it would serve only to discourage the most qualified from seeking office and would deprive the legislative branch of government of its most experienced people. This outcome would, in turn, lead to a deterioration in the quality of legislation. Opponents, therefore, conclude that "the public will suffer if term limitation is instituted."[5]

Opponents of term limitation also insist that it will upset the balance of power prescribed by the Constitution. They believe that the executive branch would be strengthened and the role of the bureaucracy enhanced. Further, it would make legislators more dependent on lobbyists and special interest groups, for policy advice. In essence, it is argued that term limitation is an illusory, short-term solution for symptoms rather than a cure for major problems.

Efforts to enact term limitation measures, according to Thomas Cronin, only divert attention away from democracy's more basic problems: decaying parties, corrupt campaign finance arrangements, gerrymandered (uncompetitive) legislative districts, and immoderate incumbency advantages.[6] Though strong arguments exist against term limitation, a movement is developing to push for its implementation.

A Term Limitation Movement?

A 1990 *New York Times*/CBS poll revealed that close to three-quarters of the American population favor term limitation for members of Congress, their state legislatures, or both.[7] Limitation measures have been enacted in Colorado, Oklahoma, and California. Supporters are predicting that as many as twenty states will have term limitation proposals on their ballots by 1992. The plan is to use the initiative process to place the issue directly before the voters.[8] While these initiatives are likely to affect only state offices, the overriding goal, according to the Americans for Term Limitation, a national lobby for term limitation, is to force Congress to adopt a Constitutional amendment limiting Congressional terms.

NOTES

1. Everett Carll Ladd, "Congress and Its Reputation: The Issue of Congressional Performance," *Current* (December 1990), pp. 16–17.
2. Ibid.
3. Michael Kramer, "Congress: Twelve Is Enough," *Time* (May 7, 1990), p. 34.
4. Ibid.
5. *The New York Times*, November 11, 1990.
6. Thomas E. Cronin, "Term Limits: A Symptom, Not a Cure," *The New York Times*, December 23, 1990.
7. Survey by the *New York Times*/CBS poll of March 30–April 2, 1990.
8. *Washington Post*, January 21, 1991.

394

ETHICS IN STATE AND LOCAL GOVERNMENT

ADDITIONAL REFERENCES

Ladd, Everett C. "Congress and Its Reputation: The Issue of Congressional Performance." *Current*, no. 328 (December 1990).

Mydans, Seth. "California Politicians Reel After a Vote Limiting Terms." *The New York Times*, November 11, 1990.

Peirce, Neal. "Term Limitation Movement Spreading Like Wildfire." *Washington Post*, January 21, 1991.

Rowan, Carl. "Constitutional Term Limitation Is a Foolish and Dangerous Idea." *Washington Post*, January 21, 1991.

"Send That Congressman Home." *National Review* (November 19, 1990).

Taylor, Paul. "Voters' Display of Anger Puts Incumbents on Notice: More Term-Limitation Measures Expected." *Washington Post*, September 20, 1990.

"Term Limits: Voter, Heal Thyself." *The Economist* (September 29, 1990).

"Term Wake." *Wall Street Journal*, February 8, 1991.

CHAPTER 7

THE PROBLEMS OF INSTITUTIONALIZING ETHICS IN GOVERNMENT

Introduction

This book has surveyed and examined various ethical issues, problems, and dilemmas that constitute the current ethics crisis in government. It has shown that there are two major manifestations of this crisis: the occurrence of mischief-making on the part of public officials and the need to resolve numerous moral mazes that public officials face. This last chapter will raise the possibility that ethics may be incorporated into the operations of government by means of reform. Thus, we will describe a number of reform measures that seek to institutionalize ethics in government and to examine the problems that typically accompany ethics reform.

There is nothing new about the idea of ethics reform. Nevertheless, as the previous chapter on ethics in state and local government has shown, there is something of a grass-roots movement in ethics reform presently underway in the United States. At the federal level as well, various measures have been adopted to effect changes in executive and legislative branch ethics. Perhaps the most dramatic instance of federal reform was the creation of the U.S. Office of Government Ethics (OGE).

The OGE was established by the Ethics in Government Act of 1978 and reauthorized by Congress in 1988 for an additional six-year period. Originally OGE was part of the Office of Personnel Management. It became a separate federal agency on October 1, 1989. OGE's general mission is to provide direction on policies within the executive branch to prevent conflicts of interest. OGE pursues its goal through regulatory activities, the overseeing of financial disclosure requirements, education and training, issuance of advisory opinions, and the enforcement and evaluation of conflict of interest laws throughout all agencies of the executive branch.

Originally conceived as the preeminent federal watchdog agency, critics have contended that OGE's attempt at ethics reform is in actuality little more than window dressing. First of all, OGE's scope of concern is limited to the executive branch. In fact, the bulk of federal ethics laws regulates the behavior of only executive branch individuals. Congress retains the monitoring of its members (and their staffs) through the operations of the House or Senate ethics committee. Thus, OGE's mission is decidedly circumscribed by law and limited in its scope.

Second and more important, OGE is woefully understaffed and underfunded to carry out its designated mission. Evidence for this charge can be found in the first selection of this chapter, which is composed of excerpts from OGE's *First Biennial Report to Congress,* submitted in March, 1990. OGE reports that the full-time equivalent number of employees on its staff had originally been twenty-nine. It grew to thirty-five in the fiscal year 1989 and was projected to be fifty-three in 1990. Also, it was authorized an appropriation of not more than $2 million when it became an independent agency and now receives an authorization for $3.5 million.

Since the mandate of OGE is to monitor all federal agencies, to be responsible for overseeing the financial disclosure process for executive branch appointees, and to provide training and education on issues including ethics, it is difficult to see how OGE will ever accomplish its set goals with its budgeted level of resources. Critics contend that OGE lacks any real muscle to accomplish its watchdog role. They conclude that OGE is not much more than a public relations ploy by the federal government, established merely to give the public the impression that ethics is taken seriously.

The criticism of OGE brings the first major obstacle to genuine ethics reform into relief. Unless there is a real commitment on the part of politicians to institutionalize ethics, then, at best, piecemeal work will be the result. Patchwork attempts, public relations efforts, and quick fixes are poor alternatives when it comes to resolving the fundamental and profound ethical problems that continue to plague government. Unless resources are allocated to address the crisis of ethics in government, it will not abate and

probably will deepen. Institutionalizing ethics in government simply cannot be accomplished without a significant commitment of
time and money.

Another problem that serves as an obstacle to genuine ethics
reform is that of adequate ethics laws. For many, pertinent legislation is the best vehicle for reform. Prohibitions against mischief-
making that carry stiff penalties for violations can serve as a
strong deterrent, according to this line of thinking. What the
federal government needs to do is to take stock of existing
legislation and enact and strictly enforce measures that will alle-
viate the crisis in ethics. Ethics legislation and enforcement, then,
is also a key to ethics reform.

There are, of course, many detractors from this view that
consider legislation as a panacea for government's woes. Arguing
that morality cannot be legislated, the detractors will point to the
already long list of ethics laws on the federal books. Even with
the many statutes that deal with all kinds of ethics infractions, it
seems that ethics violations have increased. The idea that resolu-
tions in some form serve as a deterrent, therefore, must be mistaken. In addition, these critics argue that current law in this area
is itself in need of much reform, since it is confusing, misleading,
and not much help to federal employees as a guide for their
conduct. Concurrence with this view implies, then, that ethics
reform must involve legislative action.

Such was the original thinking of the President's Commission
on Federal Ethics Law Reform. Created by President George
Bush with his first Executive Order, the Commission pored over
the many unconnected pieces of federal ethics law and made
twenty-seven recommendations for change. As the excerpt from
the Commission's report to the President, reprinted here, demonstrates, the Commission felt uneasy about ethics legislation, in
general, but found it possible to recommend many new legislative
initiatives, in addition to suggesting many changes in current law.
Others also have called for ethics law reform on the basis of the
conviction that existing law is a mass of confusion and mayhem.
"Gray Areas of Federal Ethics Law" by Rosslyn Kleeman, which
follows, is representative of this view.

In addition to the lack of commitment to ethical behavior, a
shortage of funds, and poor laws that tend to confuse rather than
enlighten, another obstacle to ethics reform occurs on the indi-

vidual level, in the form of personal attitude. Since the concept of professionalism in government seems to be in jeopardy, it is the central focus of discussion in the remaining two entries. This approach argues that the main reason why there is widespread fraud, waste, and mismanagement in government is that there is little sense of professionalism and pride in public service today. People in public administration simply do not hold their work in very high esteem; nor does the public. Public service is consistently found low on the list of employment choices for recent college graduates. Retaining quality career public administrators is an increasingly difficult task, with great turnover rates now the norm. And as the public is treated to scandal after scandal by the media, their impressions and perceptions of government as a body of trustworthy individuals who have the public interest at heart are considerably weakened.

Low perceptions of public service, both inside and outside of government, lead to poor morale and lagging productivity. Both John A. Rohr, in "The Problem of Professional Ethics," and the "Summary and Main Conclusions" of the report of the National Commission on the Public Service (also called the Volcker Commission after its chairman, former Federal Reserve Bank Chairman Paul Volcker) speak to this concern by calling for both increased professionalism and productivity in public administration. Rohr links professionalism and ethics by an examination of autonomy in public service, while the Volcker Commission takes a long look at the practical problems of professionalism in the federal government.

Ethics reform may also be achieved via organizational development efforts. In this context, the question is whether the introduction of certain organizational mechanisms might be a useful way of institutionalizing ethics in the workplace. Many private sector organizations have implemented programs that seek to integrate a concern for ethics into the daily practices of managers and executives. The public sector could learn from these private sector development strategies. Among the kinds of mechanisms that have been used are ethics training, formally implemented statements of values and beliefs, internal ethics audits, appointment of an ethics ombudsman, and so on. These organizational changes in the private sector have had the effect of making a clear statement to employees that ethics matter and that they can expect internal support when they are confronted by the moral mazes that are so commonly found in the contemporary workplace.

We may conclude that the major obstacles to ethics reform include the lack of resources in the form of money and time, an already confusing set of ethics laws, the problems of lack of professionalism and pride in the public workplace, and the absence of organizational mechanisms that can institutionalize ethics in government. No doubt, these obstacles will pose some delays in the ethics reform movement. But there is little doubt that reforms are necessary, given the dimensions of the continuing ethics crisis in government and the public's sense that this crisis must be alleviated if its threats to the public's trust and to the democratic process are to be removed.

First Biennial Report to Congress
U.S. Office of Government Ethics

Established by the Ethics in Government Act of 1978, the U.S. Office of Government Ethics (OGE) is the ethics watchdog agency of the executive branch. The following excerpt from OGE's *First Biennial Report to Congress* provides a glimpse of the many authorized responsibilities of OGE. OGE engages in supervisory activities, issues advisory opinions, provides education and training, and assists in the enforcement of conflict of interest statutes that regulate all executive branch agencies. Perhaps the most difficult task the OGE has is the monitoring and reviewing of executive branch public financial disclosure statements. The report highlights the results of OGE's annual survey that is designed to show the status of ethics at each of the federal agencies. Critics have alleged that the enormous amount of work mandated to OGE cannot be adequately done given the budget levels that Congress has authorized for it.

First Biennial Report to Congress, U.S. Office of Government Ethics, March, 1990.

Scope of Report

Public Law 100-598 of November 3, 1988, reauthorized the Office of Government Ethics (OGE) for a period of six years. As amended thereby, the Ethics in Government Act of 1978 (Act) now requires, at 5 U.S.C. app., § 408, that the Director "shall, no later than March 31 of each year in which the second session of a Congress begins, submit to the Congress a report containing— (1) a summary of the actions taken by the Director during a 2-year period ending on December 31 of the preceding year in order to carry out the Director's functions and responsibilities under this title; and (2) such other information as the Director may consider appropriate.

This report, the first submitted under the new requirement, covers only that portion of the calendar year remaining after passage of Public Law 100-598 (November 3, 1988), plus the entire 1989 calendar year. Future reports will encompass the full two-year period specified in the Act.

This report includes data and information collected from staff members of the Office, as well as from each executive branch agency. Agency data, reported to this Office annually under § 402 of the Act, has been synthesized so as to evaluate the strengths and accomplishments of agency ethics programs generally.

Mission

The Office of Government Ethics was established by the Act to provide "overall direction of executive branch policies related to preventing conflicts of interest on the part of officers and employees of any executive agency." Specific responsibilities, as outlined in the Act (5 U.S.C. app., § 402) fall into six general areas:

- *Regulatory authority*—develop, recommend and review rules and regulations pertaining to conflicts of interest, post-employment restrictions, standards of conduct, and public and confidential disclosure in the executive branch.
- *Financial disclosure*—review executive branch public financial disclosure statements to determine possible violations of

applicable laws or regulations and recommend appropriate corrective action; administer executive branch and blind trusts.

- *Education and training*—implement statutory responsibility to "provide information on and promote understanding of ethical standards in executive agencies."
- *Guidance and interpretation*—prepare formal advisory opinions, informal letter opinions and policy memoranda on how to interpret and comply with requirements on conflict of interest, post-employment, standards of conduct, and financial disclosure in the executive branch; consult with agency ethics officials in individual cases.
- *Enforcement*—monitor agency ethics programs and review compliance, including financial disclosure systems; refer possible violations of conflict of interest laws to the Department of Justice, and advise them on prosecutions and appeals; investigate possible ethics violations and order corrective action or recommend disciplinary action.
- *Evaluation*—evaluate the effectiveness of conflict of interest laws and recommend appropriate amendments.

History

OGE was created as part of the Office of Personnel Management, where it operated until becoming a separate agency on October 1, 1989, pursuant to Public Law 100-598. Congress initially authorized OGE to receive an annual appropriation not exceeding $2 million. As a result of reauthorization by Public Law 100-598, OGE's authorized ceiling was raised to $2.5 million for FY-89 and to $3.5 million for each subsequent year through FY-94, in order to accommodate its expanding role and the need for a larger staff. The full-time equivalent (FTE) level of employees increased concomitantly from 29 at the close of FY-88 to 35 at the close of FY-89, with a projected 53 full-time equivalent employees by the end of the current fiscal year. . . .

Expansion of OGE Responsibilities

The Office's responsibilities and workload have expanded significantly during the period of the report. Under Public Law 100-598 the Office was tasked with instituting procedures whereby it would:

- require annual reports from each agency, describing and evaluating its ethics programs;
- distill that information and report biennially to Congress, summarizing all OGE actions taken to accomplish its responsibilities;
- monitor all agency referrals to the Attorney General of possible violations under the conflict of interest statutes;
- insure that each agency has written procedures on both public and confidential financial disclosure collection and review, which conform to laws and regulations;
- establish due process procedures for ordering and monitoring corrective action by executive branch employees and for recommending investigations of and/or disciplinary action for employees, to insure individual compliance with ethics laws and regulations;
- conduct hearings as needed for executive branch employees under the procedures established above, to determine whether corrective orders or disciplinary action are indicated;
- establish procedures for ordering and monitoring corrective action by agency officials with regard to their agency ethics programs;
- operate as a separate agency, with responsibility for all personnel/administrative matters.

A new order on executive branch ethics, issued April 12, 1989 (Executive Order 12674), requires that OGE:

- promulgate regulations establishing a single, comprehensive and clear set of executive branch standards of conduct;
- develop, disseminate and update an ethics reference manual for executive branch employees, describing the relevant statutes, regulations, decisions, and policies;
- promulgate regulations interpreting the general conflict of interest statute (18 U.S.C. § 208);
- promulgate regulations interpreting the statute prohibiting the supplementation of salaries (18 U.S.C. § 209);

- promulgate regulations establishing a revised system of confidential financial disclosure for executive branch employees, to complement the public disclosure system;
- review all implementing regulations issued by agencies in furtherance of the above-described OGE regulations, to insure consistency;
- coordinate the development of annual agency ethics training plans and require mandatory annual briefings for certain executive branch employees;
- serve in a consulting capacity for all agencies in the granting of exemptions from the conflict of interest statute, pursuant to 18 U.S.C. § 208(b)(1).

The Ethics Reform Act of 1989, which was enacted into law on November 30, 1989, will necessitate that OGE:

- issue new regulations implementing revised post-employment restrictions at 18 U.S.C. § 207;
- promulgate new regulations implementing the revised public financial disclosure requirements;
- issue regulations implementing 5 U.S.C. § 7351 on gifts to supervisors and review regulations to implement 5 U.S.C. § 7353 on gifts to employees from outside sources;
- consult with the General Services Administration on regulations to implement new 31 U.S.C. § 1352 on agency acceptance of travel reimbursement;
- collect semi-annual agency reports of travel payments exceeding $250 accepted under 31 U.S.C. § 1352, and make them available to the public;
- issue regulations under 18 U.S.C. § 208(b), to define financial interests generally exempt from the § 208(a) conflict provisions as being too remote or inconsequential to affect the integrity of services, and to provide guidance to agencies for issuance of individual § 208(b) waivers;
- collect copies of all agency waivers under 18 U.S.C. § 208(b)(1) or (b)(3) and make them available to the public;
- issue regulations regarding tax relief for certain OGE-certified asset divestitures, and review all requests for divestiture certificates;
- issue regulations implementing new statutory provisions on outside earned income, honoraria, and outside employment.

Efforts were undertaken during the period of this report to begin implementing each of these responsibilities, though many of them will require a long-term commitment. The ensuing report details those efforts, as part of the Office's actions taken during the period covered.

Analysis of Annual Agency Ethics Reports

Introduction

This section of the narrative summarizes the reports of the agencies by Designated Agency Ethics Officials (DAEO) for 1989. This is pursuant to the 1988 OGE Reauthorization Act which imposes a new requirement for submission of annual agency reports and, at a minimum, the statute requires the agency to furnish a description and evaluation of its ethics program (5 U.S.C. app. 5, § 402(e)). An additional section of the statute requires that OGE submit a report to Congress by March 31 of each year in which the second session of Congress begins. Therefore, a critical part of this biennial report is this narrative on the state of agency ethics programs. In order to do this effectively, efficiently, and uniformly, OGE issued an annual survey which agencies were sent in October 1989 and were required to return by February 1, 1990.

OGE used a survey format which was as complete and inclusive as possible. It was expected that information retrieval systems would not be in place for some of the information requested and, accordingly, as it was so late in the year, some information simply would not be retrievable. In these cases agencies were required to make the best estimate possible, where actual data was not available, and to note it on the relevant section of the survey. No attempt has been made to independently verify this data. It should be noted that providing this survey late in 1989 enabled agencies to address any deficiencies in the system they will use for retrieving data for the next survey due February 1, 1991.

The purpose of this summary is to provide a government-wide

picture of the state of ethics programs in 1989. In order to achieve this goal the survey was composed of open-ended, multiple choice and yes/no questions, or a combination thereof. . . . Analysis was done to provide benchmarks representing the general issues, character, and make-up of the ethics programs conducted by the DAEO's. What follows is a descriptive analysis of ethics programs without trying to highlight any one agency or program. . . .

Organization

Questions 1 through 10 of the survey address the organization of the agency. The total number of full-time agency employees covered by the survey was 4,941,479[1] with a median average of 667 per agency. It should be noted that three military service departments accounted for approximately 64 percent of that total.

Question 3 asks for the organizational unit to which the DAEO is assigned. Slightly more than 75 percent of the DAEO's are in a legal office. . . . more alternate DAEO's than DAEO's hold positions in a legal office.

. . . Although the total number for full-time employees who work on ethics is 125, the median average is less than 1. The total for part-time employees is 6,139 with a median average of 4. Comparing the full-time total (125) to that of part-time (6,139), it is clear that most of ethics officials in the executive branch have more than one major responsibility.

Executive Order 12674 states that, when practical, an agency should have a separate budget line item for ethics. Of the 100 surveys returned, only one agency had a separate line item in its budget.

Evaluation

Questions 11 through 15 addressed the agency's effectiveness in meeting the goals of its ethics program. Goals of the agency in carrying out ethics were covered in question 11. The range of responses included: employee awareness of ethics, understanding standards of conduct, advising departing employees on post-employment issues, oversight of the financial disclosure process, and developing improved standards of conduct. Understanding standards of conduct was the dominant goal; in contrast, the goal least alluded to by agencies was developing improved standards of conduct. . . .

When agencies were asked how effective they had been at implementing these goals, 88 percent reported that they had been very effective, and nine percent felt that they were minimally effective. It should be noted that two agencies did not respond to this question because they were presently drafting goals, or they followed another agency's ethics program.

If an agency reported that it was not fully effective, it was asked to explain how it was going to become more effective. Their answers were categorized by OGE as: larger budget, increased ethics staff, greater authority from agency head, authority given to someone in higher position, independent budget authority, and other. None of the agencies felt that greater authority from the agency head or independent budget authority would increase its effectiveness. Increased ethics staff and "other" were the dominant categories. Some of the choices for "other" were providing better training, improving new personnel briefings, and updating procedures regarding the entry of new employees.

Only 34 of the agencies surveyed stated that the Inspector General (IG) or other internal review authority periodically evaluated their ethics program. Of the 34, only 23 said that reports were issued and recommendations made. Thirty-two of the 34 reported that the IG or other authority followed up on their recommendations, whether or not a formal report was issued.

Formal reviews of ethics programs done by the DAEO or someone designated by the DAEO were even less frequent. At the 26 agencies where such reviews were done, reports were issued or recommendations made at 14 agencies. Twenty-five of the 26 agencies had the DAEO or designee follow up on the recommendations whether or not these were formally reported.

Agency Authority

Questions 16 through 21 addressed the agency's ethics regulations or restrictions. Written approval/notification prior to outside employment or other activities was required by 64 agencies. Only 35 had promulgated any waivers under 18 U.S.C. § 208(b)(2), which for most of the reporting period states that such waivers may be granted, ". . . if, by general rule or regulation published in the Federal Register, the financial interest has been exempted from requirements of clause (1) hereof as being too remote or too inconsequential to affect the integrity of Government officers' or employees' services."

When questioned about the organic act limitations, 23 agencies did have such limitations. Moreover, 60 agencies have a statutory gift acceptance authority.

Enforcement of Criminal and Civil Statutes

This section of the report concerns financial disclosure and potential violations. Question 22 addresses whether there was one office within the agency that coordinates all referrals of potential violations of 18 U.S.C. §§ 202-209 to the Department of Justice. Seventy-six agencies stated that they have one office that does the coordination. Of these 76 agencies, 32 agencies use the general counsel's office, 18 agencies use the DAEO's office, 17 agencies use the IG's [Inspector General's] office, 5 agencies use the agency head's office, and 4 agencies use an office other than the three specified above. . . . Question 22 also asks, if there is not one office within your organization that coordinates all referrals, what office(s) refer such matters directly to the Department of Justice. Twenty-three agencies use the IG's office as the referring office, 18 agencies use the general counsel's office, 13 agencies use the DAEO's office, 9 agencies use some other referring office, and 3 agencies use the agency head's office. . . . The final part of the question asks, if an office(s) other than the DAEO's office coordinates all referrals to the Department of Justice or refers such matters directly, does that office(s) notify the DAEO of all such referrals made. In 36 instances agencies said such offices notify the DAEO.

In answer to the question concerning whether there is one office within your agency that coordinates all referrals to the Department of Justice of allegations of failure to file or filing a false public financial disclosure report (SF 278) [pursuant] to 5

U.S.C. app. 4 § 204, or false filing of a public report [pursuant] to 18 U.S.C. § 1001, 85 agencies said yes. Although there appears to be a broad systematic agreement on handling these issues as noted in question 23 above, only one such case occurred in the executive branch in 1989.

Question 24 asks for statistics related to the referrals from the agencies to the Department of Justice. The number of referrals to the Department of potential violations of 18 U.S.C. §§ 202-209 was 106 with 72 declinations. The total number of declinations resulting in administrative actions was 20. There was one referral under 18 U.S.C. § 1001 for filing a false public report, and no referrals for failure to file a public report.

Education and Training

Questions 25 through 38 address education and training. These questions focus on what information is available to employees and what type of training is provided. Copies of standards of conduct were distributed at 89 of the agencies surveyed, while 77 agencies briefed new employees on these standards.

Agencies were given six categories to choose from as to what kind of training materials they used, and were instructed to indicate more than one if it was appropriate. Eighty-six agencies used copies of agency regulations, 71 used lectures and 64 used videos/films. Slides were used by 28 agencies and only 5 agencies used computer-based training. Fifty-five agencies used some other types of materials to train their employees. Some of the more common choices the agencies specified for "other" were using a newsletter, summaries of the laws, memoranda, handouts, personal briefings, case studies, and using OGE's pamphlet "How to Keep Out of Trouble." . . .

For question 36, asking agencies to identify who is authorized to provide written advice on standards of conduct and the conflict of interest statutes, answers were assigned to seven different categories. The first category, the DAEO, was used at 65 agencies. Forty-five agencies used a legal office for written advice. At

41 agencies another person was authorized to provide written advice. At 22 agencies the deputy DAEO/deputy standards of conduct counselors (officials or officers) were authorized to provide written advice. The director of personnel was used at two agencies, additionally IG's at two agencies were authorized to provide written advice, while at none of the agencies was the agency head to provide such advice. . . .

The next question in the survey asks where the written opinions are maintained. The dominant choice was a legal office within 47 agencies. The second choice was the DAEO's office which 37 agencies used to maintain their written opinions. Only 15 agencies maintained their opinions in agency files, and five agencies maintained their opinions in some other area. The personnel office is where three agencies kept their opinions. Only one agency used the Inspector General's office to keep written opinions. . . . In response to question 38, 87 agencies reported that written opinions were made available to employees seeking ethics guidance.

Enforcement of Standards of Conduct

The enforcement of the standards of conduct is addressed in question 39. It asks for the total number of adverse actions taken in 1989 based wholly or in part upon violations of the standards of conduct.[2] By far the option with the most actions was "other" with a total of 2,047 and a median average of slightly less than 1. It should be noted that one agency accounted for 52.2 percent of the actions categorized as "other." Had four more agencies been added the five would have accounted for 87.4 percent of the total. Of the 2,047 actions 1,069 were for abuse of overtime and general misconduct, 295 were for improper attitudes at work, 150 were for abuse of rank, 149 were for violations of standards of conduct, and 126 were for insubordination.

The total number of actions for misuse of other government property is 499 with a median average of slightly less than 1. The total number of actions taken because of misuse of government vehicles is 279 with a mean average of 3 and a median average slightly below 1. The total number of actions taken against conflicting outside interests is 80 with a mean average of 1 and a median average of slightly less than 1. Conflicting financial interests had a total of 48 with a mean and median of approximately one. There were 47 actions taken for acceptance of gifts with a mean and median average of slightly less than 1. . . .

Public Financial Disclosure

Question 40 addresses the total number of public financial disclosure reports (SF 278's) required to be filed in 1989 by permanent full-time employees, as opposed to special Government employees [SGE's], and the total number of reports actually filed. The total number of new entrant reports required to be filed was 2,983, while the total number filed was 2,754. The total number of annual reports required was 14,102 with 14,029 actually being filed. The required amount for termination was 1,732 while the amount filed was 1,528. The total amount for combined annual/termination reports was 2,694 with the amount filed being 2,658. . . .

Question 41 concerns the total number of specific actions taken in regard to public financial disclosure reports required to be filed by permanent full-time, non-PAS [Presidential Appointee Schedule] filers in 1989. The total number of actions for Career SES [Senior Executive Service] filers was 694, while the total number for other filers was 797. . . . It should be noted that "other" accounts for 67 percent, or 846 actions in the graph; of that number 5 agencies account for 95.2 percent of the "other" category. The "other" type of actions include 551 letters of caution, 180 § 208 warnings, and 75 notices of applicability of waivers.

Sixty-nine agencies stated that there are no written procedures other than those published by OGE (excluding those in the Code of Federal Regulations) for the collection, review, evaluation, and public inspection of public financial disclosure reports.

Question 43 asked for the total number of requests received to inspect public financial disclosure reports and the total number of reports inspected during 1989. The total number for PAS was

234, the total number for Career SES was 148, and the total number for "other" was 209. . . .

Confidential Financial Disclosure

Questions 44 through 46 address the issues of confidential financial disclosure. Question 44 asks the total number of confidential financial disclosure reports required to be filed in 1989 by permanent full-time employees, as opposed to special Government employees, and the total number of reports actually filed. The total number of civilians required to file a confidential financial disclosure report was 186,497 with a median average of 60. The total number of civilians who actually filed confidential financial disclosure reports was 172,305 with a median average of 50. The total number of military who are required to file a confidential financial disclosure report was 18,762, and the total number actually filed was 17,716. . . .

Fourteen agencies do not require complete reports to be filed annually, of which 6 agencies require negative reports.

Question 46 asked for the total number of specific actions taken in regard to confidential financial disclosure reports required to be filed by permanent full-time employees in 1989. The total number of divestitures was 204. The total number of resignations from outside positions was 38. The total number of written disqualifications was 3,797. The total number of waivers was 251. The total number of reassignments was 72. The total number of "other" was 1,752. It should be noted that five agencies accounted for 88.1 percent of the total of "other."

Special Government Employees

The final part of the survey was about special Government employees. Question 47 addresses the total number of special Government employees (SGE's) who serve as advisory committee members or as experts/consultants, and were required to file financial disclosure reports in 1989; along with the total number who actually filed. Advisory committee members were required to file 6,339 confidential reports, while the actual number of reports filed was 1,318. Experts/consultants were required to file 1,475 confidential reports, while they only filed 1,241 reports. It should be noted that one agency accounted for 5,000 of the advisory committee member-required reports that apparently were never filed, and for 186 expert/consultant reports that were apparently never filed. Advisory committee members were required to file 51 public reports, although they filed 50 reports. Experts/consultants were required to file 124 public reports, while the number actually filed was 125. It should also be noted that another agency, which reported 34 confidential reports and 1 public report filed by SGE's, did not indicate how many reports were required to be filed. . . .

Seventeen of the agencies surveyed stated that SGE's were *not* required to file a financial disclosure report in 1989. Of the 17 the total number of advisory committee members *not* required to file a report was 7,514, while the total number of experts/consultants who were *not* required to submit a report was 19,687.

Eleven of the agencies surveyed granted a total of 326, section 208(b)(1) waivers to SGE's in 1989 consisting of 293 waivers granted to advisory committee members and 33 to experts/consultants.

Conclusion

This chapter summarizes the first statutorily required annual report from the DAEO's to OGE. The analysis is descriptive, as it was meant to be, and is designed to provide a preliminary benchmark of how the average agency ethics program carries out its responsibilities.

There are areas of analysis which have not been pursued. For example, all 99 agencies are represented equally, even though the 13 major departments [constitute] more than 90% of all of the executive branch employees covered. Since slightly more than half of the agencies represented have fewer than 1,000 employees, a more accurate picture might come from focusing on the larger agencies or just the major departments. Qualitatively, it reasonably could be argued that regulatory agencies, because of their different mission, ought to be analyzed separately from other agencies. And, arguably, many Department of Defense components should be compared with each other.

Accordingly, the analysis presented here is not meant to be exhaustive, but is simply a beginning for OGE to understand the dynamics of agency ethics programs through their annual reports. The staff at OGE will continue to analyze data and look for control variables (e.g., major departments, regulatory agencies, etc.) which will help to explain why ethics programs are effective. By OGE's 1992 Report to Congress, OGE will have had three agency surveys generating three annual reports. These surveys will facilitate the establishment of more definitive benchmarks for the 1992 report. It is hoped that such analyses will reveal both successful strategies and ineffective program elements, thus enabling OGE to provide better overall guidance to agencies as well as realistic standards for the agency head and the DAEO.

NOTES

1. According to Office Personnel Management there were, as of September 1989, 3,010,010 civilian employees, 2,176,821 uniformed personnel for a total of 5,236,831 executive branch employees. The difference between the summary statistics in the survey and these figures is accounted for by rounding, 17 agencies not responding, and the differences in time (i.e., September 1989 versus December 31, 1989).

2. For this purpose, an adverse action is any action covered by Chapter 75 of title 5 of the U.S. Code and includes suspensions of 14 days or less; however, it does not include actions based on time and attendance violations.

From *To Serve with Honor*
Report of the President's Commission on Federal Ethics Law Reform

With his first Executive Order, President George Bush created the President's Commission on Federal Ethics Law Reform. In March, 1989, the Commission submitted its recommendations to the President in a report, which is excerpted here. All of the Commission's twenty-seven recommendations deal in some way with ethics legislation at the federal level. In some instances changes have been suggested in presently existing statutes; in others, new legislation is urged to plug perceived gaps in federal law. Among the more controversial recommendations are those that would have federal ethics laws do more regulating

To Serve with Honor, Report of the President's Commission on Federal Ethics Law Reform, March, 1989.

of members of Congress, as well as their staffs. The Commission's investigation and pressures from the Bush Administration prompted some of the ethics reform measures enacted by the Congress in 1990, one of which involved the House's banning the acceptance of speechmaking honoraria for its members in exchange for a pay raise. The Senate reduced the amount of honoraria that its members could accept for outside speaking engagements but did not ban this source of personal income entirely.

Introduction

We have approached the President's request to evaluate existing ethics rules with twin objectives: to obtain the best public servants, and to obtain the best from our public servants.

Ethical government means much more than laws. It is a spirit, an imbued code of conduct, an ethos. It is a climate in which, from the highest to the lowest ranks of policy and decision-making officials, some conduct is instinctively sensed as correct and other conduct as being beyond acceptance.

Laws and rules can never be fully descriptive of what an ethical person should do. They can simply establish minimal standards of conduct. Possible variations in conduct are infinite, virtually impossible to describe and proscribe by statute. Compulsion by law is the most expensive way to make people behave.

The futility of relying solely or principally on compulsion to produce virtue becomes even more apparent when one considers that there is an obligation in a public official to be sure his[1] actions appear ethical as well as be ethical. The duty is to conduct one's office not only with honor but with perceived honor.

We must start with a *will* at the top to set, follow, and enforce ethical standards. President Bush has given this Commission his first Executive Order, by which he has set initially the ethical tone he expects to pervade his Administration.

That order and this report are but a beginning. Each cabinet officer, head of an agency, subordinate official with supervisory authority—each must lead by example, by training and educating coworkers, by fair, just and persistent enforcement of the laws.

This necessity of leadership applies with equal force to the legislature. What the Framers rightly considered the most powerful branch bids fair to be the least accountable branch. That is a dangerous combination, recognized by thoughtful Members themselves. We do not exclude the judiciary, although more rigorous and easily understood standards have obviated many problems there.

We believe that public officials want to follow ethical rules, and that they will do so if the laws are clearly delineated, equitable, uniform across the board, and justly administered. As Napoleon said: "There is no such thing as a bad soldier; there are only poor officers."

Ethical rules and statutes rest on moral standards. They are supposed to carry a certain moral authority, as are most laws. When the lawmakers prescribe laws for others but not for themselves, in the eyes of the public the essential moral authority is diminished. This is why it is essential to create ethical rules for the legislative branch as closely similar to those of the judiciary and the executive as is possible, given their differing functions. Instead of statutes applying to only one branch or two, standards should be applicable to all. No part of the Federal Government should be satisfied with a standard of less than absolute honesty in the conduct of public officials.

While our analysis is based on certain fundamental functions which conflict of interest restrictions are intended to serve, our analysis also incorporates the four key principles noted by the President when he signed Executive Order 12668 creating this Commission. One, ethical standards for public servants must be exacting enough to ensure that the officials act with the utmost integrity and live up to the public's confidence in them. Two, standards must be fair, they must be objective and consistent with common sense. Three, the standards must be equitable all across the three branches of the Federal Government. Finally, we cannot afford to have unreasonably restrictive requirements that discourage able citizens from entering public service. . . .

We begin by recommending that the conflicts of interest statute forbidding decision by an executive branch official on a "particular matter" in which he has a financial interest be extended to non-Member officers and employees of Congress and the judiciary, thus striving to achieve (at least in part) the level playing

THE PROBLEMS OF INSTITUTIONALIZING ETHICS IN GOVERNMENT

field desired in the ethics laws. Judges are already covered by very strict statutory standards, but there are difficult problems in applying a statutory standard to Members of Congress.

We favor centralizing the issuance of interpretive regulations for the executive branch in the Office of Government Ethics, and we suggest the creation of a similar centralized ethics authority within the legislative branch.

As the newcomer prepares to enter Government service, he or she must fill out various forms disclosing assets and income. This frequently leads to the realization that the prospective official has assets and sources of income which, if retained, would create a recurring conflict of interest with governmental duties. While this conflict can be accommodated by refusal from decision-making or a waiver where the interest appears so small as to have no influence on the official's conduct, yet our strong recommendation is that the prospective official be encouraged to divest these troublesome assets at the very outset. If the official could do that by postponing the tax liabilities by a rollover of the troublesome assets into neutral holdings such as Treasury bills, municipal bonds, or bank certificates of deposit, then many more officials would do so. A divestiture of troublesome assets and reinvestment in neutral holdings is the single most important device we have encountered to eliminate completely or at least to mitigate greatly subsequent conflicts of interest. Many of the problems we discuss would never be problems at all, if such a change of holdings had occurred at the outset of the official's public service.

Since not all conflict problems can be erased by divestiture, we recommend that the Office of Government Ethics exercise a rulemaking authority to deal with *de minimis* issues, pension plans, mutual funds, the investments of charitable organizations, and the industrywide effects of some rulings on individual companies. With executive branchwide standardized positions promulgated by the Office of Government Ethics, the compliance of individual public servants with the rules will be much simpler and easier, and the general public as a whole will have a vastly better understanding of exactly what holdings are permissible, and the nature of those retained by public officials filing annual disclosure reports.

This whole process should encourage seeking advice. One principle which helps to avoid a conflict of interest, and even an appearance of such conflict, is the age-old principle which should permeate the whole governmental ethical compliance system, *i.e.*: "No one shall be a judge in his own case." The possibility of a conflict of interest can be put to rest by submission to an impartial ethics authority, and following the advice received.

We have made specific and uniform recommendations in regard to the thorny problems of augmentation of Government income by private sources, a cap (with the exact percentage yet to be determined) on outside earned income of senior officials of all three branches, a ban on honoraria, and on outside boards and directorships. We believe there must be some cap on most types of outside income earned by the public servant, otherwise many public servants would slowly edge into private activity as a disproportionate source of income, to the detriment of their expected public service. This danger is enhanced every year that governmental salaries lag further and further behind those which can be obtained by the same individuals in private enterprise. We would propose, however, that the President be authorized to exempt from the cap any category of income he determines to be generated by a type of activity which did not pose ethical issues or detract from full performance of official duties.

The disgracefully low compensation for public service affects also the increasingly notorious problem of honoraria. Executive branch rules now prohibit executive branch officials from receiving honoraria for any speeches, writings, or other actions undertaken in their official capacity. In stark contrast, in the legislative branch honoraria for speeches, writings, public appearances at industry meetings, or even at breakfast with a small group, have become a staple and relied-upon source of income up to, in some cases, the limit of thirty or forty percent of the Member's salary. Some Members earn several times their governmental salary by honoraria, and give the excess to charities of their choice. This practice, which some Members of the legislative branch defend as both inevitable and proper in an era of recognized meager and unfair compensation, obviously produces several evils: first, the Member is diverted with increasing frequency from the performance of official duties; and second, the honoraria all too frequently come from those private interests desirous of obtaining some special influence with the Member. While we believe that no position of a Member of the legislative branch could be

THE PROBLEMS OF INSTITUTIONALIZING ETHICS IN GOVERNMENT

changed by a $2,000 honorarium, the honorarium is often perceived to guarantee or imply special access to the particular Member by the granting organization.

In the judicial branch, the apparent evil is simply the diversion of time from judicial duties. The groups before whom judges appear are usually professional groups who are genuinely interested in the judge's views on legal problems, and whose members have no expectation whatsoever of any special influence with a court. Individual lawyers or members of the public do not feel free to pick up the phone and talk to them; contact between bench and bar is in the decorum of a public courtroom.

Outside boards and directorships represent another diversion of a public official's time and energy. Sometimes they produce actual conflicts of interest, many times they create an appearance of a conflict of interest. Our recommendation is that senior public officials not serve on the boards of commercial enterprises, and that participation by such individuals in the management responsibilities of charitable organizations be carefully guarded, particularly if there is a danger of abuse of the public official's name for fundraising purposes.

Gifts, travel, entertainment, and simple meals have caused ethical problems for years. We encountered the most amazing diversity of interpretation within the executive branch and a stark disparity between the three branches. Our recommendation is a uniform and, we hope, reasonable policy in all branches as to what may be accepted without creating an appearance of impropriety.

Negotiation for future employment while the public official is still serving has always created a disruptive effect on the work of the agency involved, and frequently real problems of a conflict of interest. Our recommendation is designed to make clearer and brighter the lines of what may be done and not done, and to minimize any disruptive effect.

Post-employment restrictions center on the question of the period of time during which former employees should be barred from contacting certain parts of the Federal Government with which they were previously associated. At the present time there is no statutory bar in the legislative and judicial branches, but there are four separate bars in the executive branch. Our recommendations attempt to equalize and simplify these post-employment restrictions. We recommend the extension of the one-year cooling-off period now applicable to senior employees of the executive branch to comparable positions in the legislative and judicial branches. Separate inconsistent and duplicative post-employment restrictions should be considered for repeal. The existing lifetime bar in the executive branch regarding representation on particular matters handled personally and substantially by the former employee should be extended to the judiciary. To thwart the former employee who wants to "switch sides," there should be a two-year ban on using or transmitting certain types of carefully defined non-public information.

We think compartmentalization in each branch in applying these restrictions has its place, but it should not be abused. We recognize compartmentalization in limiting the ban for the legislative branch to one House only, and for the judicial to the specific court with which the former employee was affiliated. In the executive, we make no recommendation changing the responsibility of the Office of Government Ethics to prescribe compartmentalization in large departments, where a person working in one of numerous large sub-agencies would have little contact or influence with other agencies, but we do recommend that compartmentalization within the Executive Office of the President be abolished, as not consonant with the standards and objectives of this device.

We have carefully studied the question of whether the validity of the actions of the former employee, in making representations on behalf of others to the part of the branch with which he was previously affiliated, should depend on whether the employee receives compensation for such representational activity. We find that the injection of the element of compensation would vitiate the worthwhile objectives of the prohibition itself, and that there is no logical or constitutional justification for it. As a practical matter, requiring the element of compensation to make the representation improper would create a large loophole, which would inevitably be exploited to the Government's detriment. If representation of another person is improper, it is improper whether compensation is involved or not. We believe, however, that there should be no restriction whatsoever on a former employee's right to present his views on policy issues in any form—testimony, press articles, speeches, interviews—and indeed personally to present his own interests anywhere.

Financial disclosure has been variously described as the linchpin of the ethical enforcement system, as the disinfectant sunlight which makes possible the cleaning up of abusive practices. We have made three basic recommendations on financial disclosure, two to strengthen it, the other to simplify it. To strengthen financial disclosure, to make it more meaningful, we would raise the highest limit describing assets to "$1,000,000 and over," and the highest limit describing income "$250,000 or over." We believe the present intermediate bands of assets and income are so close together as to be somewhat meaningless, and would leave to the Office of Government Ethics the responsibility of recommending the number and size of the categories between the $1,000 and $1,000,000 or $1,000 and $250,000 marks. To strengthen disclosure for political appointees we would eliminate the home mortgage and family debt exceptions, because in our view the existence of heavy obligations, no matter what the laudable purpose of assuming those obligations may be, is something about which the public should be informed. We are also recommending a simplification and increased uniformity to the extent possible of the disclosure forms required by the Senate committees, the White House, and the FBI, and propose that a coordinating committee with representatives from all three branches be convened to address this task.

We now turn to the structure of federal ethics regulation. In the executive branch we recommend the strengthening of the Office of Government Ethics for its advice, consultation, and rulemaking function. We would continue the principal investigative, enforcement and compliance responsibility in the individual departments and agencies for several reasons. We think there should be one overall set of government regulations interpreting the ethics statutes, promulgated by the Office of Government Ethics. Variations from these uniform regulations should be permitted only on a showing by the individual department or agency that such is necessary for its particular mission, and on the approval of the Office of Government Ethics. Likewise, the final authoritative interpretation of the regulation should rest with that office, to prevent the divergent standards and interpretations now current. The Office of Government Ethics should promote uniformity by an enlarged and strengthened training mission for the ethics officers in the individual agencies, and for an annual review of their plans and programs.

In contrast to the rulemaking centered in the Office of Government Ethics, we recommend that the investigative enforcement and compliance function retain principally the responsibility of the individual departments and agencies. The Cabinet secretary or the head of an independent agency is the person whom the President should hold responsible for ethical standards in his agency. He must therefore have the responsibility for investigation, enforcement, and producing compliance with the overall executive branch standards within his department. Furthermore, the agency inspectors general and ethics officers are closer to the facts of any violation, and would probably do a better job of investigation. Likewise, training and education within the department or agency are the responsibility of that agency, although assisted, reviewed, and checked by the Office of Government Ethics.

In the legislative branch we recommend the establishment of a joint ethics officer with an adequate investigative staff to investigate alleged offenses and bring the results of the investigation and recommendation for enforcement to the appropriate Congressional ethics committee.

The Commission recommends additional enforcement mechanisms. In this area we are especially indebted to the work already done by the Congress and embodied in the legislation introduced in the last Congress and in current proposed legislation. These new enforcement measures were singled out for praise by President Reagan in his message vetoing the legislation for other reasons. We believe that in addition to continuing the felony level penalties, there should also be misdemeanor penalties to give some flexibility in enforcement. Likewise, there should be civil penalties, which can be in some instances more persuasive and better tailored to the offense than criminal penalties. The Attorney General should have authority to seek injunctions to restrain conduct violative of ethical standards. We pass no judgment on the wisdom of the independent counsel device for investigating and prosecuting ethical violations, but we do urge that if the independent counsel device is retained, it apply to both the executive and legislative branches. If the device is retained, we also urge that it be strictly limited to the very highest officials in each branch, as this is the only area in which there may be justification for it.

In closing, we would emphasize that in addition to serving specific functions, our recommendations are also offered to stimulate the continuing development of the ethics system within the government. We believe that the implementation of these recommendations will serve both the public interest in protecting the integrity of the government, and the federal employee's interest in preserving an individual sense of pride and honor in serving the public good. . . .

NOTE

1. Masculine or feminine pronouns appearing in this report refer to both genders unless the context indicates another use.

Gray Areas of Federal Ethics Law
Rosslyn Kleeman

One of the more overwhelming aspects of work in the federal government is the sheer number of rules, regulations, and laws that pertain to the federal workplace. The Public Law, the United States Code, Executive Orders, agency guidelines, policies, and regulations—all of these statutes and rules come together and create a morass of confusion for the typical federal government employee. Rosslyn Kleeman examines this problem in her article "Gray Areas of Federal Ethics Law." Kleeman uses the issue of the "revolving door" between the federal government and business as a case example of how confusing the situation can be. The "revolving door" is a term used to depict the questionable activity of a federal employee's taking a job with a business with which that employee has had substantial dealings while on the federal payroll. Kleeman shows how regulations on the prohibitions against this activity are contradictory, confusing, and misleading in both intent and language. Her message is that work clarification in these gray areas is desperately needed so that well-intentioned federal employees do not unintentionally find themselves in trouble.

Rosslyn Kleeman, "Gray Areas of Federal Ethics Law," *The Bureaucrat* (Spring 1989), pp. 7–10. Reprinted by permission.

As you sit in your office reading the newspaper articles about the ethical problems of Michael Deaver, Lyn Nofziger, Edwin Meese III, and others, you are interested because they were public employees, albeit perhaps at a higher level than you. But do their problems bear any relationship to predicaments you have to be concerned about? Very likely. In fact, although you may not always realize it, you are probably confronted by ethical concerns daily when making what you believe to be routine decisions.

Both the professional associations you belong to and your government agency have ethical standards which you are expected to use to guide those actions. But not all ethical standards are simply advisory in nature. In the federal sector, on which this article will focus, the government has a set of criminal laws (18 U.S.C. 203–209) passed by the Congress and standards of conduct based on Executive Order 11222 which set the legal boundaries of ethical behavior for most federal employees. Violate one of these laws and you can end up with a hefty fine, a jail term, or both. Violate the standards and you can lose your job.

Contractor-Related Problems

Nowhere is the potential for ethical problems greater than for current and former employees of the Department of Defense (DOD) or the Department of Energy through which billions of dollars of federal contracting dollars flow and where headlines frequently proclaim infractions. In a study of former DOD personnel who went to work for contractors (GAO/NSIAD-86-180BR, July 23, 1986) the General Accounting Office found that about three-fourths of the 5,000 people surveyed had some degree of responsibility while they were with DOD which they said affected defense contractors.

Almost half of those surveyed viewed their responsibilities as substantial. For over 25 percent of them, their responsibilities as federal employees applied to the defense contractors for whom they subsequently worked. Many people worked on the same DOD project or program as federal employees and as contractor employees. Most continued work-related discussions with DOD officials, often with people with whom they had previously worked.

These and similar situations present a real opportunity to take a spin through the legendary revolving door, using expertise and contacts to gain entry to a former employer's lucrative contracts and coffers. Without an intimate knowledge of federal conflict of interest statutes, that trip through the revolving door could result in running into criminal charges.

Gray Areas

Are there always clean, clear lines of demarcation between what is permissible and not permissable, between the ethical and unethical, in the federal laws and standards? Unfortunately not. We have many gray areas where there is an enormous potential for conflict of interest both while on the job and after leaving the public service.

There are many causes for both lack of knowledge and confusion over these statutes and ethical standards. While there are training courses given by designated agency ethics officials, these vary in both quantity and quality from agency to agency. The Office of Government Ethics (OGE) has published a pamphlet called "How to Stay Out of Trouble," but some have questioned whether its focus is appropriate.

There are also no government-wide regulations with examples which spell out all of the conflict of interest statutes' provisions. In fact, there are only regulations for one of the five key statutes—18 U.S.C. 207, the post-employment conflict of interest law.

Compartmentalization

Confusion is also caused both by actions permitted by certain portions of the laws and by the wording of those laws. As to the permissible actions, one specific provision in 18 U.S.C. 207, for example, prohibits former senior employees from lobbying officials in their former agency for one year after they leave the government. The law, however, contains a proviso that if the OGE director determines that the functions of a subagency or bureau are separate and distinct from the remaining functions of the department or agency, he may designate separate subagencies or bureaus within a department or agency so that the scope of the one-year no-contract restriction is limited.

Thus, Michael Deaver was able to contact officials of the Office of Management and Budget after he left the White House because the Executive Office of the President had been "compartmentalized." Although it might have appeared to raise ethical questions, the law permitted such contact.

Similarly, this compartmentalization provision may have been applicable in some of the previously mentioned cases of DOD officials dealing with their former fellow employees. Within DOD, the Army, Navy, Air Force, and Defense Mapping Agency are considered separate "statutory" agencies, and the Defense Communication Agency, Defense Intelligence Agency, Defense Nuclear Agency, National Security Agency, and Defense Logistics Agency are considered separate "nonstatutory" agencies. Senior officials generally may leave any of those units and contact any of the other units within DOD. Many members of Congress have vowed to end this compartmentalization of agencies, closing what they believe to be a loophole in federal ethics law.

Permissible Action

Another example of a gray area in the ethics law concerns permissible action by a former employee. Like compartmentalization, this issue will undoubtedly be examined for change in the next session of the Congress. One section of the postemployment conflict-of-interest law (18 U.S.C. 207[a]) prohibits a former employee from representing someone else to the government on any "particular matter involving specific party or parties" in which he or she "participated personally and substantially."

Suppose, while a federal employee, you were "personally and substantially" involved in what is generally considered to be a "particular matter involving a specific party or parties" in your agency. This might be a contract investigation involving the government and a private employer. You leave the government in the middle of the case and go to work for the same employer you were investigating. You work on the same case, now on the other side, and tell one of the private company representatives who in your former department he should contact and what to say. You disclose a great deal of information about what the government knows and doesn't know about the case.

You can do that, under the law, as long as you don't contact involved current federal employees directly, either by appearing before them or by oral or written communication. Assistance in representation is permitted by the Ethics in Government Act, as amended. While this action might appear to raise unethical questions, it is not illegal.

Personal and Substantial

The problem with certain words in the ethics laws, like "particular matter," "negotiating for employment," "specific parties," and "knowingly," to name a few, is that they might be interpreted in several different ways. As noted above, 18 U.S.C. 207(a) prohibits all former federal employees from representing someone else before the government on matters in which they were "personally and substantially" involved. What, you might ask, is "personal and substantial" involvement?

Suppose a colleague consults you about an issue that has come up in your office. You quickly reply saying how you think the matter should be resolved. You are only one of several people to comment in this manner. Is your role in this issue "substantial participation"?

The safe answer is yes. Previous rulings by the Department of Justice and the Office of Government Ethics indicate that a person's part in the resolution of an issue may be considered "substantial" even though many other people participated in the discussion, the particular issues the person addressed were procedural in nature, and the amount of effort expended was minimal. Thus, something you believe would not be considered "substantial participation" might be viewed that way in an investigation or in a court of law. This is just one example where compliance or noncompliance with federal ethics laws can hinge on how certain key words and phrases are interpreted.

Particular Matter Involving Specific Parties

Another source of possible confusion concerns the phrase "particular matter involving a specific party or parties." What do those words mean? Let's assume you were personally and substantially involved in setting the policy objectives of a program in your agency. After the program begins to operate, you leave the government, go to work for a private employer, and contact your former colleagues about that same program in order to get grant money for your new employer. You are contacting some of the same people you worked with before you left the government and eventually your new employer gets a large grant from your old office. Is that prohibited?

Although this might appear to raise ethical questions, it probably would not be a violation of the law because setting policy objectives is generally not considered a "particular matter involving a specific party or parties." According to OGE regulations, such a matter typically involved a "specific proceeding" or "isolatable transaction" between "identifiable parties," not just involvement in general policy matters.

The situation, however, is different if you are a current employee involved in policy matters which you know will affect you or your family's financial interest. According to OGE and the Department of Justice, because the law for current employees (18 U.S.C. 208) says only "particular matter" while the postemployment law speaks to a "particular matter involving a specific party or parties," the scope of the matters in which a current employee may not participate is different from that for former employees.

This difference may be hard to discover on your own, because there are currently no regulations covering the conflict of interest law for current employees. Using the definition of "particular matter involving a specific party or parties" in the regulations covering former employees could lead to a violation of the law.

Negotiating for Employment

Here's another ethics quandary, one in which there has been a related recent actual case. While you are in your office tending to business you are approached by a representative of a large corporation whose services are connected to work your office does. The representative asks if you might be interested in working for his company. He mentioned a salary double what you are now receiving, a company profit-sharing plan, and an unlimited expense account. All travel would be first class. The job is in your home city, Washington, DC, so you would not have to move.

As you sit with him in your tiny office, with a thin film of asbestos over your furniture and a burnt-out fluorescent bulb overhead, you realize that the offer sounds good, but you don't want to say yes until you have had a chance to think it over. If this offer is generous, another might be in the offing that is even better. You decide to weigh your options, so you tell him you may be interested and you agree to talk again in the future. He leaves your office and your mind is racing.

One place it should be racing is to the ethics laws, particularly 18 U.S.C. 208, because at that point you are probably "negotiating for employment," and the statute forbids you from further participation in any decisions which you know would affect—in any way—the financial interest of anyone with whom you are negotiating for employment. The penalty for violating this statute is up to a $10,000 fine, two years in jail, or both.

Rules of Behavior

In reviewing even the few examples cited here, it is easy to see how well-meaning federal employees could run afoul of the law while unscrupulous individuals could use some of the available loopholes. Although the statutes are not easily understood and may be disagreed upon, even by ethics experts, it is important that detailed understandable guidance and adequate training in the law are readily available.

More generally, though, how does one determine whether something is an "ethical concern" even though it may not be a violation of the law? A good general rule is that if you think something is an ethical concern, chances are it is. The more difficult question is, in considering those concerns, how do you know which decision is the right one?

A good answer to that question is be conservative. If there is a chance for error, err on the side of too little rather than too much. For example, if someone offers you a gift and you have to wonder if you should accept it, don't. You'll never get in trouble that way.

There are other rules of thumb. How would you feel if the acceptance of the gift were disclosed to the press? Might some people consider it proper? Would it make you uncomfortable? And although the acceptance of the gift may be within the technical limits of the law, in some cases the appearence of a conflict may violate your organization's standard of conduct. Might it not be wise, if there is any question, to avoid embarrassing yourself and your office by just saying no?

Leaders' Examples

What criteria do most employees actually use to guide their behavior? Although laws and standards of conduct are useful guideposts, employees often learn organizational rules and behavior patterns by example. The most visible examples of appropriate (and inappropriate) behavior are the actions of organizational leaders.

Equally important are the actions (or lack thereof) meted out to those who fail to comply with organizational rules. If an organization's standards of conduct indicate that a particular action is unethical or even illegal, yet top managers regularly violate that standard, what credence is that standard likely to have with employees? Likewise, if a standard of conduct is violated and, upon detection, no effective enforcement action is taken, the standard will be rendered meaningless.

Financial Disclosure

Consider the situation where a high-ranking agency official has filed improper financial disclosure reports for almost every year he has been in office. He forgets to disclose sizable interest-free loans to himself and his wife. He fails to list the assets held in his investment partnership on the basis that the partnership is "blind." On each occasion he ultimately corrects the disclosure form, but only after public controversy. How seriously are his employees and other employees covered by the same statute likely to take the disclosure requirements?

Regulatory Action

Another top executive in a budget-approval position calls a person in another agency over whom he has budget authority and discusses a proposed regulatory action against a company in which the official owns a quarter of a million dollars of stock. Action against the company is delayed for several months. When the events become public, the official says he did nothing wrong. After further press accounts, he is sent what may be regarded as a "congratulatory reprimand" by his supervisor. The official is told not to take such action again, but the letter primarily congratulates him on what a fine job he has done for the agency. What message does this send to others?

Hiring Practices

Or what if a top official improperly influences his agency to hire former clients of his law firm? The incident is investigated, found to be true, but the official is allowed to "retire" some two years after the investigation has been completed. Meanwhile lower-level officials who have created the appearance of impartiality are suspended, demoted, or dismissed immediately. Doesn't this corroborate the impression of a "dual" ethical standard—one for the top level and and one for the bottom?

Most federal employees are probably unaware of specific details of federal conflict of interest laws and regulations. They have never been told of their importance and where to find them, nor do they know what is in them. Yet most employees are aware of incidents similar to those cited above and they incorporate them into their perceptions of their organization's informal code of ethical behavior. If top officials are allowed to act in such a manner, they wonder, why shouldn't they do so also?

Conclusion

Is there a dual system of ethics within most organizations—one which is policy and one which is unspoken and generally covers the gray areas mentioned earlier? It is hoped that a willful, egregious violation of the stated rules of ethical behavior will be dealt with through formal sanctions. Actions which fall outside those narrow walls will undoubtedly be judged according to the informal rules of ethical behavior.

How, then, can a more positive informal ethical standard be achieved? The answer is obvious. If we want not just to meet the exact requirements of the law but to have ethical organizations and employees with ethical internal values, let us be sure that those who are in positions of authority and visibility are ethical in their actions and are held responsible for their actions. Actions speak louder than statutes.

The Problem of Professional Ethics
John A. Rohr

In "The Problem of Professional Ethics," John A. Rohr examines the relationship between the universal principles of ethics and traditional professional practices. With true professionals exceptions to universal principle are the rule; this inconsistency constitutes a major problem with professionalism. For if professional practice requires exception to ethical principle, does it not become morally suspect automatically? Rohr suggests that this seeming contradiction in professional ethics, where exceptions to universal principles of ethics are turned into the ethical principles of a professional code of conduct, is justified by the overriding value of the professions to society. Rohr then compares public administration to other professions and finds that they all have the idea of autonomy as a central feature. For Rohr, autonomy in the profession of public administration is an absolute necessity. Those who dedicate their lives to public service need to be free from manipulation, so that they can best serve the public interest. This is an overriding value of public administration, and it thereby justifies as a bona fide profession.

John A. Rohr, "The Problem of Professional Ethics," *The Bureaucrat* (Summer 1982), pp. 47–50. Reprinted by permission.

Professional codes and statements of ethics often engender cynicism and derision. This is because these statements, couched in terms of broad and generous public spirit, frequently harbor self-serving sentiments which, when exposed, embarrass the professions and delight their critics.

The purpose of this article is to explain why professional statements tend to be self-serving and to examine the ethics of public administration in light of this explanation. In so doing, I hope to illuminate an aspect of professionalism that should be of particular interest to the public administration community.

Universal and Particular

Popular discussion of ethical issues tends to be framed in the language of universals—do not steal, do not lie, love your neighbor, etc. This sort of language immediately creates problems for the discussion of professional life. That is, professional life deals with a particular aspect or role in one's life; it does not exhaust one's humanity. The limited (or particularistic) character of role morality immediately challenges the universal quality of most moral propositions. When we say one should not lie or steal or that one should love one's neighbor, we are usually thinking about human beings as such rather than physicians, journalists, public servants, *et al.*

Principles vs. Exigencies

Universal principles come under considerable pressure when they confront the exigencies of professional life. Familiar examples abound: may a physician lie to his or her patient if there is good reason to believe that the truth would considerably retard the patient's recovery? May an investigative reporter lie to "Deep Throat" to get information that will expose wrongdoing in Richard Nixon's White House? May a "double agent" lie to protect national security?

Clearly, these are not the sorts of examples we have in mind when we announce as public doctrine the straightforward, moral principle that lying is wrong. Professional life demands exceptions from these universal moral principles and therefore becomes morally suspect. We fear that the exceptions may soon swallow up the rules and that the chaste simplicity of the moral principle—don't lie—will be fatally compromised by the "what ifs" of the professions' casuistry.

Role Morality

To be sure, it is not only the professions that put pressure on universal moral principles. In a certain sense, all moral acts in the concrete are examples of "role morality"—I act as spouse, parent, citizen, believer, consumer, voter, TV-viewer, neighbor, taxpayer, welfare recipient, etc. Circumstances may arise in each of these roles that call for an exception to a well-established moral rule—e.g., the familiar example of the parent who steals bread to feed a starving child.

The problem of professional ethics is particularly acute, however, for two reasons. First, there is the elite nature of professional life. Only the few can be physicians, attorneys, and engineers, but all of us are or can be spouses, parents, citizens, or consumers. As a democratic people, we are more comfortable with an exception that, given the proper circumstances, is open to all of us opposed to an exception that is available only to the few. Better to trigger exceptions by circumstance than by status.

Just This Once

Secondly, the foundation of the professional's exception differs from the foundation of the exceptions demanded by ordinary persons in ordinary activities. The latter usually rely on a "just this once" argument. The father steals bread today, but tomorrow he will have a job, or sell his wares, or visit the welfare office, or receive money from a rich uncle, or beg for the wherewithal to support the family. Quite literally, he practices *situation* ethics. A unique set of circumstances has conspired to override the rule that bids us respect the property of others; but the rule is overridden "just this once." If he were to institutionalize his behavior, we would say he had taken up a "life of crime"; that he was no longer a concerned parent but a thief. The point here is that moral character is usually determined by one's habits (virtues or vices) rather than by isolated actions.

Professionals, on the other hand, *do* institutionalize the exceptions they seek. The exceptions are hailed as ethical principles of the profession. A successful defense attorney owes no apologies for making a clever argument that diverts the jury's attention from incriminating evidence and contributes to the erroneous verdict that a guilty defendant is innocent. Psychologists do not blush about the statement in their *Ethical Standards* that the use of deception in research is permissible if the knowledge cannot be generated in any other way. The spy who lies successfully to the enemy stands quite ready to do it again. Attorneys, psychologists, and spies do not appeal to a unique set of circumstances to justify their behavior. On the contrary, their behavior is based on a *principled* demand for exceptions from the rules by which the rest of us are supposed to live.[1]

Public Interest and Self-Interest

The tension between universal principles and particularistic demands is crucial for understanding why professional codes, despite their public service language, are frequently in fact self-serving. The reason is that the justification for the exceptions the professions demand from universal moral rules is grounded in an implicit, utilitarian assumption that the profession itself can produce sufficient benefits to society to outweigh whatever harm is caused by its departure from customary morality.

To clarify this point, let us take several examples from the profession of law.[2]

1. The client is the prosperous president of a savings and loan association. In leaner days he had borrowed almost $5,000 from a man working for him as a carpenter. He now wishes to avoid repaying the debt by running the statute of limitations. He is sued by the carpenter and calls his lawyer. [*Zabella* v. *Pakel*, 242 F. 2d 452 (1957)]
2. The client has raped a woman, been found not guilty by reason of insanity, and institutionalized. He wishes to appeal the decision by asserting a technical defense, namely, that he was denied the right to a speedy trial. [*Langworthy* v. *State*, 39 Md. App. 559 (1978), rev'd, 284 Md. 588 (1979)]

3. A youth, badly injured in an automobile wreck, sues the driver responsible for the injury. The driver's defense lawyer has his own doctor examine the youth; the doctor discovers an aortic aneurism, apparently caused by the accident, that the boy's doctor had not found. The aneurism is life-threatening unless operated on. But the defense lawyer realizes that if the youth learns of the aneurism he will demand a much higher settlement. [*Spaulding* v. *Zimmerman*, 116 N.W. 2d 704 (1962)]

In each of these cases, professional ethics would counsel counter-intuitive judgments in favor of the banker, the rapist, and the driver. The reason for this, of course, is that the attorney's moral commitment to the client overrides broader principles of what our common sense tells us is right in each of the examples.[3] Such a commitment can itself be normally justified only on the grounds that (1) the integrity of the legal system demands it, and (2) the legal system itself is so valuable to society that, on balance, we do well to tolerate occasional injustices because of the rich benefits the system provides.

Ethics and Self-Interest

Such an argument may well be challenged on empirical grounds, but for the purposes of this article it is the *structure* of the argument rather than its validity that is of interest. The justification for professional conduct that defies common-sense notions of right is necessarily grounded in an affirmation of the overriding importance of the profession itself. It is the necessity for making this kind of argument that forges the link between professional ethics and self-interest. Because of the tension between the particularistic demands of the professions and the universal character of moral discourse, the professions must argue that they are worthy of the moral exception they demand. In effect, they must argue that what is good for the profession is good for society, America, humanity, or whatever.

Needless to say, such an argument is freighted with peril. To invite attention to the close connection between the interests of one's profession and broader public interests can lead to keen embarrassment. Indeed, at times it can expose professional self-adulation as ludicrous and absurd.[4]

Overriding Value

I am not interested in the preposterous aspects of professional ethics. Suffice it to say that all professionals, poor sinners like the rest of us, suffer the thousand natural shocks that flesh is heir to. It is the *argument* for professional ethics, an argument rooted in the nature of professional life, that is instructive for our purposes. No matter how upright and decent the members of a profession might be, they will at times demand exceptions from ordinary rules of morality and, when they do, they must justify their demand in terms of the overriding value of their profession for the society whose rules they would transcend. Such an argument quite properly invites close scrutiny and not a little skepticism.

Public Administration As Profession

Codes of ethics for government employees labor under the suspicion of being self-serving statements. This suspicion can arise from several aspects of government service, but, for the purpose of this article, I shall narrow my focus to the ethical concerns over political manipulation of the career civil service. Such interference is, of course, anathema to our sense of professionalism.

Value-laded Word

I have deliberately used the value-laded word "manipulation" to signal the improper nature of the political activity to which we object. We are, of course, to be "accountable" and "responsive" to the political leadership, but we should not be subjected to "political interference," "meddling," or "partisan pressure"—in a word, "manipulation." Language of this sort goes to the heart of the merit system and is thematic in public service codes of ethics.[5] A recent reaffirmation of this position came from the first director of the Office of Personnel Management, Alan K. Campbell. In response to the charge that the creation of the Senior Executive Service (SES) would lead to the "politicization" of the civil service, Campbell replied that the SES will provide "appropriate responsiveness to the government's political leadership, while resisting improper political influence."[6]

One might be tempted to dismiss Campbell's delphic utterance as question-begging verbiage, but this would be a mistake—at least for our purposes. In scoring "improper political influence," Campbell proclaimed the ancient faith of civil service reform. Professional orthodoxy commits us to the belief in resistance to such influence as a cardinal principle of professional ethics. This is all quite obvious. What we tend to ignore, however, is the self-interest character of this principle.

Sphere of Autonomy

In saying that we as government officers or employees should resist improper political influence, we carve out for ourselves a sphere of autonomy within the governmental process. Such autonomy is crucial for any group that aspires to professional status. The client does not tell the attorney how to cross-examine a hostile witness; the hospital administrator does not tell the physician what medicine to prescribe; the traveller does not tell the engineer when the bridge is safe; indeed, the baseball owner does not tell the manager when to change pitchers—unless the owner is George Steinbrenner.

In each of these examples, there is a sphere of professional autonomy that attorneys, physicians, engineers, and baseball managers guard jealously. It is in their interest to do so, but it is also in the interest of their client, patient, team, etc. So also with public administrators. It is in their interest to protect their administrative "turf" and, in so doing, they make government more efficient and effective and thereby promote the public interest.

So the argument goes and it's not a bad argument. To put a finer point on it, however, my position, reductively, is that in exercising certain aspects of governmental authority we must be exempt from the democratic principle of subordination to political leadership and this in the name of democracy itself. To put the argument this way recalls the attractiveness of the old politics-administration dichotomy. Here was a conceptual tool that finessed the potential embarrassment in our claim to a sphere of autonomy from the elected leadership. Indeed, it defined the problem out of existence. The discretionary character of contem-

438

THE PROBLEMS OF INSTITUTIONALIZING ETHICS IN GOVERNMENT

porary public administration has discredited the dichotomy and
forced administrators to assert their autonomy in a more forthright manner.

The Law Is Supreme

A remarkable example of this forthrightness appears in the
"Principles for the American Society for Public Administration"
adopted by ASPA's National Council on July 12, 1981. The third
of ten principles reads as follows: *The law is supreme. Where laws
or regulations are ambiguous, leave discretion, or require change,
we will seek to define and promote the public interest.*

To be sure, the law is supreme but it is no secret that the
hallmarks of contemporary public law are its ambiguity and its
conferral of broad discretion on administrative agencies. Reduced to its simplest terms, the above statement is an announcement of our intention to share in governing the Republic; for he
who defines the public interest surely governs. The announcement is not a bureaucratic power play; it is a candid (perhaps too
candid?) statement of what conscientious administrators have
been trying to do for a long time. Given the fact of administrative
discretion, what criterion other than the public interest is suitable
for its exercise?

Not Uncommon

We should not be surprised to find such a statement in a code
of ethics. As we saw earlier in this article, it is not uncommon for
professional ethics to demand an exemption from ordinary societal standards. This is precisely what we are doing when we claim
a sphere of autonomy from political leadership. The ASPA statement is simply a positive formulation of the more familiar negative proposition that the political leadership should not manipulate
us in the exercise of our administrative discretion.

This is an example of a particularistic demand against the
universal, democratic principle that all governmental activities
should be accountable to the electorate. This self-interested claim is
grounded in the long-term benefits the sound exercise of administrative discretion can bring to a democratic regime. Like other
professional groups, we can make claims that are either plausible

or outrageous. In this untidy world, they are usually a little bit of both.

Conclusion

If public administration resembles other professions in cherishing a sphere of autonomy, it also differs from them in some important ways. The precise grounds on which we base our claim for autonomy may be less clear for us than it is in other professions. The "learned" professions of law, medicine, and religion can point to a lengthy period of formal training that is followed by a certification process prior to ordination, admittance to the bar, etc. The profession of engineering is more relaxed than law, medicine, and some churches in determining who belongs to the profession, but, like the learned professions, engineering also bases its professional status on technical knowledge.

The profession of journalism relies less on formal training than the professions mentioned above. The journalists' claim for exceptional ethical standards rests on the vital role they play in rendering operative the public's "right to know."

Our profession lacks these advantages. In the days of the politics-administration dichotomy, we could ground our profession in the administrative skills which, by definition, were distinct from politics. The discretionary character of contemporary public administration has taken this argument from us. We know Carl Friedrich was right when he said (in his *Public Policy and Administrative Responsibility*) that to execute public policy is to make it. Our problem is that we are really claiming an expertise in governing—a claim that is not likely to fall on sympathetic ears in a democratic society. It is for this reason that I believe the question of professionalism in public administration will always be somewhat controversial in the United States.

A Glimmer of Hope

There is one line of argument that might possibly legitimate our claim to share in governing the Republic. In the famous 1803 case, *Marbury* v. *Madison,* Chief Justice Marshall developed an argument in support of the power of the federal courts to declare acts of Congress unconstitutional. The argument rested in part on the oath taken by judges to uphold the Constitution of the United States. Marshall's point was that it would be immoral for judges to enforce legislative enactments contrary to the Constitution they are sworn to uphold.

Marshall ignored the fact that not only federal judges but presidents, senators, representatives, state legislators, and "all executive and judicial Officers, both of the United States and of the Several States" are required to take an oath to uphold the Constitution. The significance of Marshall's argument is that it suggests a link between the oath of office and the legitimacy of exercising an otherwise questionable power—like that of judicial review of acts of Congress. Perhaps the statutory mandate that requires from public administrators an oath to uphold the Constitution could provide a glimmer of hope for legitimating a principled defense of professional autonomy.

NOTES

1. For a thorough discussion of the problems of lies, see Sissela Bok, *Lying: Moral Choice in Public and Private Life* (New York: Vintage Books, 1978).

2. These cases are taken from the *Report from the Center for Philosophy and Public Policy*, Volume 1 (Summer 1981), p. 6. They are discussed more fully in David Luban, "Calming the Hearse Horse: A Philosophical Research Program for Legal Ethics," *Maryland Law Review* 40 (1981).

3. A good contemporary discussion on legal ethics can be found in Geoffrey Hazard, *Ethics in the Practice of Law* (New Haven: Yale University Press, 1978). Hazard discusses in considerable detail the ethical problems that flow from the commitment to the client.

4. See *Virginia State Board of Pharmacy* v. *Virginia Citizens Consumer Council, Inc.*, 425 U.S. 748 (1976); *Bates* v. *State Bar of Arizona*, 433 U.S. 350 (1977); *Ohralik* v. *Ohio State Bar Association*, 436 U.S. 447 (1978).

5. See the six editions of the codes of ethics adopted by the International City Management Association since 1924.

6. *Public Administration Times*, August 1, 1979, p. 1.

Rebuilding the Public Service
Summary and Main Conclusions of the Report of the National Commission on the Public Service

This excerpt from the *Report of the National Commission on the Public Service*—commonly known as the Volcker Commission after its chairman, Paul Volcker—provides an overview of the major problems that stand as obstacles to productivity in the federal workplace. Beginning with a survey of the "erosion in the quality of America's public service," the report goes on to make several recommendations that could enhance public service and attract talented people to it. The report highlights the trend of recent years in which the federal government has been unable to fill key posts and retain specialists because of factors such as low pay and high stress on the job. The trend is ominous, because it tends to result in mediocrity and inefficiency throughout government, especially in agencies in which specialized skill is a necessity. Interlaced throughout these recommendations is the theme of public trust and the need for the federal government to address the problems of ethics and integrity in both the executive and legislative branches.

The central message of this report of the Commission on the Public Service is both simple and profound, both urgent and timeless. In essence, we call for a renewed sense of commitment by all Americans to the highest traditions of the public service—to a public service responsive to the political will of the people and also protective of our constitutional values; to a public service able to cope with complexity and conflict and also able to maintain the highest ethical standards; to a public service attractive to the young and talented from all parts of our society and also capable of earning the respect of all our citizens.

A great nation must demand no less. The multiple challenges

"Rebuilding the Public Service," Summary and Main Conclusions of the Report of the National Commission on the Public Service, pp. 1–9 (Washington, DC: Volcker Commission, 1989).

thrust upon the Government of the United States as we approach the 21st century can only reinforce the point. Yet, there is evidence on all sides of an erosion of performance and morale across government in America. Too many of our most talented public servants—those with the skills and dedication that are the hallmarks of an effective career service—are ready to leave. Too few of our brightest young people—those with the imagination and energy that are essential for the future—are willing to join.

Meanwhile, the need for a strong public service is growing, not lessening. Americans have always expected their national government to guarantee their basic freedoms and provide for the common defense. We continue to expect our government to keep the peace with other nations, resolve differences among our own people, pay the bills for needed services, and honor the people's trust by providing the highest levels of integrity and performance.

At the same time, Americans now live in a stronger, more populous nation, a nation with unprecedented opportunity. But they also live in a world of enormous complexity and awesome risks. Our economy is infinitely more open to international competition, our currency floats in a worldwide market, and we live with complex technologies beyond the understanding of any single human mind. Our diplomacy is much more complicated, and the wise use of our unparalleled military power more difficult. And for all our scientific achievements, we are assaulted daily by new social, environmental, and health issues almost incomprehensible in scope and impact—issues like drugs, AIDS, and global warming.

Faced with these challenges, the simple idea that Americans must draw upon talented and dedicated individuals to serve us in government is uncontestable. America must have a public service that can both value the lessons of experience and appreciate the requirements for change; a public service that both responds to political leadership and respects the law; a public service with the professional skills and the ethical sensitivity America deserves.

Surely, there can be no doubt that moral challenge and personal excitement are inherent in the great enterprise of democratic government. There is work to be done of enormous importance. Individuals can make a difference.

But unfortunately there is growing evidence that these basic truths have been clouded by a sense of frustration inside government and a lack of public trust outside. The resulting erosion in the quality of America's public service is difficult to measure; there are still many examples of excellence among those who carry out the nation's business at home and abroad. Nevertheless, it is evident that public service is neither as attractive as it once was nor as effective in meeting perceived needs. No doubt, opposition to specific policies of government has contributed to a lack of respect for the public servants who struggle to make the policies work. This drives away much of our best talent which can only make the situation worse.

One need not search far to see grounds for concern. Crippled nuclear weapons plants, defense procurement scandals, leaking hazardous waste dumps, near-misses in air traffic control, and the costly collapse of so many savings and loans have multiple causes. But each such story carries some similar refrains about government's inability to recruit and retain a talented work force: the Department of Defense is losing its top procurement specialists to contractors who can pay much more; the Federal Aviation Administration is unable to hold skilled traffic controllers because of stress and working conditions; the Environmental Protection Agency is unable to fill key engineering jobs because the brightest students simply are not interested; the Federal Savings and Loan Insurance Corporation (FSLIC) simply cannot hire and pay able executives.

The erosion has been gradual, almost imperceptible, year by year. But it has occurred nonetheless. Consider the following evidence compiled by the Commission's five task forces on the growing recruitment problem:

- Only 13 percent of the senior executives recently interviewed by the General Accounting Office would recommend that young people start their careers in government, while several recent surveys show that less than half the senior career civil servants would recommend a job in government to their own children.
- Of the 610 engineering students who received bachelors, masters, and doctoral degrees at the Massachusetts Institute of Technology and Stanford University in 1986, and the 600 who graduated from Rensselaer Polytechnic Institute in 1987, only 29 took jobs in government at any level.

- Half the respondents to a recent survey of federal personnel officers said recruitment of quality personnel had become more difficult over the past five years.
- Three-quarters of the respondents to the Commission's survey of recent Presidential Management Interns—a prestigious program for recruiting the top graduates of America's schools of public affairs—said they would leave government within 10 years.

If these trends continue, America will soon be left with a government of the mediocre, locked into careers of last resort or waiting for a chance to move on to other jobs.

But this need not and should not be. By the choices we make today, we can enter the 21st century with a public service fully equipped to met the challenges of intense competition abroad and growing complexity at home. The strongest wish of the Commission is that this report can be a step in that process, pointing toward necessary changes, while serving as a catalyst for national debate and further efforts at all levels of government.

America should and can act now to restore the leadership, talent, and performance essential to the strong public service the future demands. To those ends, the Commission believes:

- First, the President and Congress must provide the essential environment for effective leadership and public support.
- Second, educational institutions and the agencies of government must work to enlarge the base of talent available for, and committed to, public service.
- Third, the American people should demand first-class performance and the highest ethical standards, and, by the same token, must be willing to provide what is necessary to attract and retain needed talent.

These three themes—*leadership, talent,* and *performance*—shape this report. They are both wide-ranging and interrelated. They also provide a framework for a concrete agenda for action, directed toward a series of basic goals discussed in further detail in the report that follows. Specifically, to strengthen executive *leadership,* we call upon the President and Congress to:

- Take action now by word and deed to rebuild public trust in government;
- Clear away obstacles to the ability of the President to attract talented appointees from all parts of society;
- Make more room at senior levels of departments and agencies for career executives;
- Provide a framework within which those federal departments and agencies can exercise greater flexibility in managing programs and personnel; and
- Encourage a stronger partnership between presidential appointees and career executives.

To broaden the government's *talent base,* we call upon educational institutions and government to:

- Develop more student awareness of, and educational training for, the challenges of government and public service;
- Develop new channels for spreading the word about government jobs and the rewards of public service;
- Enhance the efforts to recruit top college graduates and those with specific professional skills for government jobs;
- Simplify the hiring process; and
- Increase the representation of minorities in public careers.

To place a greater emphasis on quality and *performance* throughout government, we ask for the public and its leaders to:

- Build a pay system that is both fair and competitive;
- Rebuild the government's chief personnel agency to give it the strength and mandate it needs;
- Set higher goals for government performance and productivity;
- Provide more effective training and executive development; and
- Improve government working conditions.

To further these basic goals, the Commission makes a series of specific recommendations throughout the report. . . . Twelve key proposals deserve mention here:

First, Presidents, their chief lieutenants, and Congress must articulate early and often the necessary and honorable role that public servants play in the democratic process, at the same time making clear they will demand the highest standards of ethics and performance possible from those who hold the public trust. Members of Congress and their staffs should be covered by similar standards. Codes of conduct to convey such standards should be simple and straightforward, and should focus on the affirmative values that must guide public servants in the exercise of their responsibilities.

Second, within program guidelines from the President, cabinet officers and agency heads should be given greater flexibility to administer their organizations, including greater freedom to hire and fire personnel, provided there are appropriate review procedures within the Administration and oversight from Congress.

Third, the President should highlight the important role of the Office of Personnel Management (OPM) by establishing and maintaining contact with its Director and by ensuring participation by the Director in cabinet level discussion on human resource management issues. The Commission further recommends decentralization of a portion of OPM's operating responsibilities to maximize its role of personnel policy guidance to federal departments and agencies.

Fourth, the growth in recent years in the number of presidential appointees, whether those subject to Senate confirmation, noncareer senior executives, or personal and confidential assistants, should be curtailed. Although a reduction in the total number of presidential appointees must be based on a position-by-position assessment, the Commission is confident that a substantial cut is possible, and believes a cut from the current 3,000 to no more than 2,000 is a reasonable target. Every President must have politically and philosophically compatible officials to implement his Administration's program. At the same time, however, experience suggests that excessive numbers of political appointees serving relatively brief periods may undermine the President's ability to govern, insulating the Administration from needed dispassionate advice and institutional memory. The mere size of the political turnover almost guarantees management gaps and discontinuities, while the best of the career professionals will leave government if they do not have challenging opportunities at the sub-cabinet level.

Fifth, the President and Congress must ensure that federal managers receive the added training they will need to perform effectively. The education of public servants must not end upon appointment to the civil service. Government must invest more in its executive development programs and develop stronger partnerships with America's colleges and universities.

Sixth, the nation should recognize the importance of civil education as a part of social studies and history in the nation's primary and secondary school curricula. Starting with a comprehensive review of current programs, the nation's educators and parents should work toward new curricula and livelier textbooks designed to enhance student understanding of America's civil institutions, relate formal learning about those institutions to the problems students care about, and link classroom learning to extracurricular practice.

Seventh, America should take advantage of the natural idealism of its youth by expanding and encouraging national volunteer service, whether through existing programs like ACTION, the Peace Corps, and VISTA, or experiments with initiatives like President Bush's Youth Engaged in Service (YES), and some of the ideas contained in the Democratic Leadership Council's citizen corps proposal.

Eighth, the President and Congress should establish a Presidential Public Service Scholarship Program targeted to 1,000 college or college-bound students each year, with careful attention to the recruitment of minority students. Admission to the program might be modeled on appointment to the military service academies—that is, through nomination by members of Congress—and should include tuition and other costs, in return for a commitment to a determined number of years of government service.

Ninth, the President should work with Congress to give high priority to restoring the depleted purchasing power of executive, judicial, and legislative salaries by the beginning of a new Congress in 1991, starting with an immediate increase of 25 percent. At the same time, the Commission recommends that Congress enact legislation eliminating speaking honoraria and other income related to their public responsibilities.

Tenth, if Congress is unable to act on its own salaries, the Commission recommends that the President make separate recommendations for judges and top level executives and that the Congress promptly act upon them. Needed pay raises for presidential appointees, senior career executives, and judges should no longer be dependent on the ability of Congress to raise its own pay.

Eleventh, the President and Congress should give a higher budget priority to civil service pay in the General Schedule pay system. In determining the appropriate increase, the Commission concludes that the current goal of national compatibility between public and private pay is simplistic and unworkable, and is neither fair to the civil service nor to the public it serves. The Commission therefore recommends a new civil service pay-setting process that recognizes the objective fact that pay differs by occupation and by localities characterized by widely different living costs and labor market pressures.

Twelfth, the President and Congress should establish a permanent independent advisory council, composed of members from the public and private sector, both to monitor the ongoing state of the public service and to make such recommendations for improvements as they think desirable. The Commission applauds President Bush's pledge of leadership of the public service. Indeed, his recent statements reflect the spirit and concerns that led to the creation of the Commission. However, the problems that make up this "quiet crisis" are many and complex and have been long in the making. Corrective action will not only require presidential leadership and congressional support, but must be part of a coherent and sustained long-term strategy. The proposed independent advisory council is designed to ensure that the state of the public service remains high on the national agenda.

This report speaks directly to a number of audiences: to the *American people* about the importance to their civic institutions of talented men and women; to *young people* about the challenges and satisfactions they can find in serving their government; to *candidates for elective office* about the long-term costs of "bureaucrat bashing"; to the *media* about the need not only to hold public servants to high standards but also to recognize those who serve successfully; to *university schools of public affairs* about developing curricula for training of a new generation of government managers; and to *business leaders* about the importance of quality government support to the private sector.

Finally, the report speaks to the *civil service* about its obligation to the highest standards of performance. The Commission fully supports the need for better pay and working conditions in much of government. But the Commission also recognizes that public support for those improvements is dependent on a commitment by the civil servants themselves to efficiency, responsiveness, and integrity.

INDEX

464

INDEX

468

INDEX